# Chaos me!

## THE UNBELIEVABLE FUNNY & SMART STORY OF HOW RANDOMNESS IMPROVES YOUR BRAIN

*This book is dedicated to you and to the improvement of your effectiveness*

**Chaos me!**
*The unbelievable funny and smart story of how randomness improves your brain*
Yaron Ilan MD

Copy Editing: Allyn Fisher-Ilan
Cover and cartoons: Studio Clean Line, Betty Sasson

Contact: Ilan@hadassah.org.il
ISBN 9781792628870

YARON ILAN, MD

# Chaos me!

*THE UNBELIEVABLE*
*FUNNY & SMART STORY*
*OF HOW RANDOMNESS*
*IMPROVES YOUR BRAIN*

---

*The scientist who swapped the routine*
*for a random road to success*

# Contents

# ABOUT THE BOOK

The loss of his wife to a terminal illness jolts Dan into making an odd career shift. He abandons the sense of orderliness he once embraced, replacing it with a more random approach to life. In his search for greater meaning he begins to explore a whole range of topics from history, art to science, computers, and cyberspace. Dan's quest reflects upon our brains' uncanny ability to adapt to change. His journey illustrates how the engine that runs our bodies is a lot more capricious than we realize, and that we can apply this realization to getting past obstacles on the road to self-improvement.

Our brains adapt so readily to training regimens, that such routines lose their benefits over time. This book explores ways to get past these obstacles by setting aside order and routine and seeking what many of us tend to think of as anathema to normal living – chaos. The chaos achieved by mixing up your brain in a figurative blender can improve its neuron connections and by so doing, help you develop greater creativity and open up new ways to enhance your life.

# ABOUT THE AUTHOR

Dr. Yaron Ilan is Director of the Department of Medicine at the Hebrew University-Hadassah Medical Center, Jerusalem, Israel and a former vice dean of its medical school. He had post-graduate training at Yeshiva University's Albert Einstein College of Medicine and Mount Sinai Medical Center in New York and was a visiting professor at Harvard University. His main area of research is development of immunomodulatory drugs for fatty liver disease, diabetes, inflammatory bowel disease and liver cancer. An owner of dozens of patents, Dr. Ilan has had more than 260 articles published by medical journals. He has invented a number of drugs and medical devices being developed by pharmaceutical firms, and has founded several biotech companies. One of these, Oberon Sciences, advances the use of randomness to improve life efficacy.

Jerusalem, Kefar Tavor, Israel, 2018; Boston, US, 2019

# INTRODUCTION

This is not a philosophical book, even if it does quote some philosophers.

It is not a self-help book, even though it may help you, nor a super-smart book about physics, even if it contains some wisdom from that field.

It is also not a how-to-succeed-in-life book. There have been too many of those.

What this book will do, is share some stories and recent scientific findings. None of them will claim to be the ultimate truth.

There will be no conclusions. Recipes for success may exist, but I'll make the claim that they are not universal.

In this book I want to open a conversation and read aloud things that I think might be of interest to you. They will come from various sources: books, Wikipedia, research articles, blogs, commentaries and so on. I did my best to be true to the original sources, so that you can also interpret them by yourself. I do add some in-depth discussion from my own perspective.

I present you with questions to ponder—the source materials will not provide all the answers.

Our brain controls every organ in our body and continuously adapts to put itself in order. It does this so that the changes which occur in our lives and our environment don't affect the orderly manner in which our other organs do their work.

We all want improvement. We want to improve our manner, our financial status, our love life, our professional life and our ability to learn. We are always told that we need to study and practice and the more we study and practice, the better off we'll be. This is true and many studies have shown that the more we practice, the better we get.

However, it is just as well known, that while practice does lead to improvement, we tend to reach a plateau from where it becomes harder to make progress. No matter how much they practice, the fastest runners cannot run much faster.

Our brain uses sophisticated mechanisms to adapt itself to any training regimen and this adaptation process reduces the benefits of further training.

This book is about finding a way to get around that obstacle by seeking improvement through chaos. Chaos improves how neurons connect in the brain, improves creativity by allowing it to focus on the bigger picture rather than the details, opening a whole new landscape of ways in which we can improve our lives.

This is intended to be an interesting (and funny) book that tells you stories. When you start reading, I ask that you put your brain in a blender. What comes out of the blender in the end really depends on me... Sorry, no, it depends on you.

This is not a real introduction to the book. The real introduction will be at the end of Chapter 1. The second Chapter 1. This book has two first chapters.

Please climb into a small spaceship and sit in a comfortable chair. Take a cup of coffee, or a beer, or just a glass of water, relax and watch. Once we take off, and reach a high enough altitude, we will enter a story based on the internet browsing I've done for you. One association after the other. Not too much will be required from you. Just enjoy.

# CHAPTER 1
## The iPod shuffle—enjoying uncertainty?

Tuesday, January 11th, 2005 was a cloudy day in San Francisco, with a little rain. Steve Jobs, CEO of Apple, walked onto the stage at the Macworld Conference & Expo in his black shirt and blue jeans to give the opening keynote address. It was another one of his excellent performances. For the first hour and a half, he reviewed the iMac and various other developments, before saying: "I would like to move on to iPod, the world's best music digital player." He was silent for a few seconds and then said the famous sentence that everyone was waiting for: "But there is one more thing" [1].

The audience laughed.

"We want to make something that is great, and that is even easier to use than the existing iPod," he said, "iPod users discovered a whole new way of listening to their music, and what is that: shuffle. With shuffle we do not have to find our music, it shuffles it out for you. So today we are introducing the iPod shuffle… 240 songs, a million different ways".

For the first time, people could listen to their songs in random order.

The iPod Shuffle was the smallest model in Apple's iPod family and was the first iPod to use flash memory. It was designed to be quickly loaded with a selection of songs, which it would then play in random order. Apple believed that owners of existing iPods often set their devices to "shuffle," and the new iPod Shuffle was a much more cost-effective device for listening to music in this way [2]. The idea for the iPod Shuffle came from the "autofill" feature of the iTunes software, which randomly selected songs from a user's music library. A year or so later Steve Jobs announced that Apple had sold 10 million first-generation iPod Shuffles.

What did Apple think when designing the Shuffle? Why was it so successful? Was is because we like "controlled surprises"? Here, the surprises were controlled because users knew what songs they had uploaded, even though the playing order was random. In advertisements for the Shuffle, Apple used phrases such as "life is random, so am I," "give a chance a chance," and "enjoy uncertainty" [3].

Do we like randomness in these controlled surprises? Do we enjoy uncertainty in general? Don't let your brain answer now—wait a while.

Whether Steve Jobs or anyone else in Apple understood the deeper meaning of their "shuffling," we will never know. Sometimes great artists, innovators and companies create much greater products that they understand at the time of creation, and the full meaning only becomes clear later. The Shuffle may be an example of this kind of phenomenon.

In May 2015, Dan Knight wrote in the Low Mac journal that "Shuffle in iTunes and iPods are not as random as we would think" [4]. He claimed that once you use the Shuffle setting in iTunes a few times, you "come to realize that it is anything but random. Some tracks keep coming up while others are ignored." He suggested that selecting the shuffle setting creates a more-or-less random playlist and then keeps on using the same playlist going forward. "Randomness means that one cannot predict what will come next or find a repeatable pattern. Randomness is not entropy and doesn't mean a pattern may not repeat, only that any repetition is part of even larger randomness." He also claimed that making a pattern impossible to repeat eliminates randomness, "just as if we rolled a 6-sided die and rejected any value that had a show in the previous five rolls" [4].

At around the time that the iPod Shuffle was being marketed, a man named Dan was sitting in his backyard in Long Island, New York. He was 72 and had lost his wife to cancer five years previously. He liked to read about successful people and watching all the "Steve Jobs" shows on YouTube—his keynote address from his time as Apple CEO. In his retirement, Dan was a physicist. Well, not a real one. He had studied physics and he liked it, but life had taken him to other places. He had other hobbies too—computers and artificial intelligence.

Sitting in his backyard, he was disappointed at seeing so many buildings around him. When he and his wife had moved there, almost 40 years ago, they were young and enthusiastic, eager to start their lives. At that time, the area was half empty, mainly trees, and the closest store was half a mile away. Now the closest store was a shopping mall and many of the smaller stores were gone. He had heard on the radio that the popularity of online shopping had killed off small businesses.

Dan was pondering what Steve Jobs had in mind when he came up with the iPod Shuffle. He knew that it was hard to get a computer to generate proper random numbers [5]. A computer follows its instructions blindly and therefore tends to produce output that is entirely predictable.

He had once listened to a lecture explaining two of the most common methods for generating random numbers by computer. The first were called Pseudo-Random Number Generators (PRNGs), which used pre-calculated tables to produce sequences of numbers that appeared to be random. And the second were True Random Number Generators (TRNGs), which worked by coaxing the computer into actually rolling a die, or equivalently, using some physical phenomena that was easier to interface with a computer than an actual die [5]. He hadn't given these much thought since, but really, what did pseudo-random mean? Generating randomness was not a straightforward thing.

PRNGs are computationally efficient and can be used to generate many numbers in a short time. However, the numbers they generate come in periodic sequences that will eventually repeat and so cannot be used in applications where numbers must be unpredictable as well as random.

In contrast, TRNGs extract randomness from physical phenomena external to the logic of the computer. One of the most effective such phenomena is radioactive decay. The time it takes for a radioactive source to decay is entirely unpredictable and relatively easy to identify and feed into a computer. TRNGs are inefficient compared to PRNGs because the speed at which they generate numbers is tied to the underlying physical phenomena. However, they have the important property of being non-deterministic, so that the sequence of numbers can never be predicted and never repeat, except by random chance. TRNGs are non-periodic [5].

Dan remembered one of his professors discussing such things but hadn't given it any further thought until now, as he read about the lack of "true randomness" in the iPod Shuffle. He began to think about the contrast between pseudo- and true randomness. He Googled the subject to learn more.

Very quickly, he discovered that computers generate pseudo-random numbers according to particular rules seeded by hardware parameters such as the system clock, component temperatures or how long the system has been running since last rebooted. He found that they can make even more random sequences by combining together two or more different random number generators. He picked up the iPod Shuffle on his desk. The way it was designed, the easiest way to properly randomize the playlist was to uncheck the shuffle function and then enable it again to generate a new random playlist [4].

Did Steve Jobs realize that shuffling is much more than "enjoying uncertainty", as Apple referred to it in its ads? Dan asked himself whether this genius had thought about the place of this "pleasant randomness" in other areas of life. Was Jobs the kind of mastermind who understood that the randomness that he'd created to generate happiness might be much more than just fun?

Everyone told Dan that 70 was the new 50. He was retired, pretty healthy and not sure what to do with his life. He had always thought that simple order and keeping to a schedule were the best ways to achieve a peaceful life. His wife had often repeated this sentence. He wondered whether the randomness that Jobs talked about was only good for listening to music and that perhaps order and routine were better for the bigger things in life. Having thought that, he wasn't really sure what these "bigger things" were. But thinking about his children, and their different perspectives on various areas of life, he realized that their "big things" were his "small things." He didn't know how they perceived his big questions about careers, life and so forth.

Dan liked studies which showed that people became happier as they got older even if most of these studies found that the happiness arose from decreasing expectations [6]. We are happier when the difference between our expectations and our lives is small. At 72, he had no intention of lowering his expectations, but did that mean he was not going to be as happy as he could be? But if 70 is the new 50, then maybe it wasn't wrong to keep some big dreams. The iPod Shuffle story made him think about happiness and about his late wife. Order or randomness?

He was not sure about randomness and chaos. He felt that it was critical for him to understand whether or not chaos was dangerous. Jenny had always told him that it was. But could it be beneficial? Dan had grown up in the 1970s and asked himself whether Jobs was trying to move everyone back to those "hippy" years? If he was a real genius, as Dan believed, this couldn't be so.

The aim of this book is to take you one step forward towards using your brain better through a unique type of "ordered chaos." This type of chaos may underlie better creativity, performance and satisfaction.

But does it exist?

This kind of mental state feels somewhat hard to understand and we have to ask whether we can generate it for ourselves. In fact, it is not so difficult to understand or difficult to generate. In the next few chapters, I will share some stories and examples that show how to do it.

# ONE MORE CHAPTER 1
## (FOR THE SAME PRICE)

## Catch a Fish

There are hundreds of versions of this story and I am not sure which the original was.

During a lunch break at a "top-CEO meeting" at a New Orleans convention center, one of the "top CEOs" was walking on the beach. He saw a fisherman in a nice T-shirt and asked him "how old are you?"

The fisherman was surprised and replied, "I am 52."

"What do you do?"

"I fish," was the answer.

"No, my question was *what do you do*?" the CEO asked, thinking that the fisherman was joking.

"I fish," was the answer.

"Did you ever think of buying a small boat and using a net rather than a fishing rod?" the CEO said, becoming serious.

"Why?" asked the fisherman, also becoming serious.

"So that you can catch much more fish," answered the CEO, smiling.

"Why do I need to catch more fish?" asked the fisherman, smiling back.

"Well, that is easy—you'll make more money by selling more fish and then be able to buy a bigger boat, go further out to sea and catch even more fish." explained the CEO.

"Why would I want to do that?" asked the fisherman.

"Easy—you'll make much more money and be able to build a business exporting fish."

"And then what?" asked the fisherman.

"Well, you'll become the CEO of a big fish company," answered the CEO.

"And then what? Why would I want to have all this money and be a CEO of a fish company?" asked the fisherman.

The CEO paused for a second, and then said, "Well, you'd be able to buy the freedom to do whatever you like. What do you like to do?"

"I like fishing, and that's what I'm doing now," the fisherman said, smiling. "I don't need to go through that whole process just to reach the place where I am now."

Dan had often heard this story in the office, in many different versions. What it meant to him, was that he should stick to his routine and be happy. He shouldn't try to jump too high, as it might hurt him, and even if he succeeded, at the end of the day, it would only leave him in the same place he was now.

Several times, Dan wondered whether he would prefer to be the CEO of the computer services company he worked for or the "fisherman." He always thought that most people, if not all, would prefer to be the CEO. His mother always wanted him to be a CEO. It would have improved his image in the eyes of his neighbors and also the type of car he parked in his garage.

He once read a fascinating book: "Triggers: Creating Behavior That Lasts—Becoming the Person We Want to Be." This book supported the concept that not only does the environment affect us, but we also very much care about what other people say to us and do to us[7].

We can be a CEO and carry on doing the same thing for years, or we can go fishing. But can a CEO go fishing?

Dan wondered whether it would make him less creative if he decided to fish for fun? Or could fishing for fun increase his creativity? Was he less creative than a CEO? Perhaps his subconscious might generate better, more powerful and more random ideas just by giving it some more fun-fishing time?

Dan remembered his first days in college. His teachers told him that in science, many discoveries start with an idea and hypothesis which is then examined using a controlled study. The results of this process were what scientists call "evidence-based." However, the problems with such results often come when we try to apply them to everyday life. If we experiment on mice in a lab, can we apply the results to humans? If we do experiments on 50 university students, can we apply the results to the average person? Even if we do a controlled experiment on "ordinary people" under "ordinary life conditions," it is not possible to control all the confounding parameters, so that the conclusions may still not be widely applicable. Dan realized this, but still, his teachers taught him that science can only progress in an evidence-based way.

This book will present you with some concepts and ideas. Some you will find interesting. Some of them will be evidence-based, others not. For some of the topics, you will find yourself wanting to know more. You can use Wikipedia. I did it and Dan did, too. All of the websites and references I used are quoted and marked in the text. This is the best I can do to keep the concepts presented as clear as possible. I found most of the summaries I quoted to be insightful and some of them to be really good.

So what to do with this book? My suggestion is just enjoy reading it.

Listen to the stories and think about some of the ideas. I only ask you to stand up and fish with our rod, nothing more. Some of the ideas may sound unrealistic and I also had similar feelings as I wrote them. Some will make you think. Some will be applicable to your life, while others will not. These you might find useful in a year or later, or not at all.

Imagine yourself standing on a beautiful beach and fishing, enjoying yourself without aspiring to turn your hobby into a business – in this case, a fish factory. On the other hand, you may actually want to build some sort of company and the ideas I present here may be useful for that endeavor, or for improving relationships, making better products, improving yourself and much more. Or you may not.

If you just read and think, you might reply. And yes, I am listening.

There are no compulsory steps you must take, nor any precise recipes to follow. Enjoy the story and if you get more out of it than that, count it as a gift.

# CHAPTER 2

## Randomness: "I am convinced God does not play dice."

If I ask you what randomness means you may think it is an easy question and that it is just a common term for the absence of order. If you look it up in the Oxford English Dictionary, you will find that "randomness is the quality or state of lacking a pattern or principle of the organization; unpredictability" [8]. Elsewhere, it is defined as "uncertainty of an outcome looking into probabilities or information entropy" [9].

However, we are not especially interested in mathematical definitions or the meaning of randomness in statistics. Taking a more historical view, in ancient times, fate was very much associated with the concepts of chance and randomness. Some ancient cultures developed ways for making predictions in an attempt to overcome randomness and fate. In her book on religions of the ancient world, Sarah Iles Johnston describes some of the old traditions of divination and prophecy. For many old religions "everything had to be arranged very carefully before a procedure began, or else the results might not be trustworthy" [10]. Chance and prophecy were viewed differently by different religions, but in most, there was a wish to avoid randomness and center ritual around orderly actions.

Dan hated fishing. He had only two hobbies—he liked to read and he liked art and music. He was the kind of boy whose classmates would laugh at. He was bothered by questions of randomness and joy and sometimes wondered whether it was loneliness that caused him to fall into such preoccupations. Reflecting on this, he dived into Wikipedia and learned that 3000 years ago, the Chinese were the first to study chance and formalize odds. In the West, it was only in the 16th century that Italian mathematicians began to formally calculate the odds associated with various games of chance [9]. Later, in 1888, John Venn wrote a chapter in his book "The Logic of Chance" called "The conception of randomness." [11]. Venn was born in Hull, in the North of England and was a lecturer in "moral sciences" at Gonville and Caius College, Cambridge. "So, I am not the first one to be bothered by chance and randomness," Dan laughed out loud. Since Jenny died and he was left alone, he often found himself talking to himself and laughing. He thought it might be interesting to Google this guy, Venn.

The first edition of Venn's book was printed in 1866, and in the preface, he wrote that "the science of probability occupies at present a somewhat anomalous position. It is impossible, I think, not to observe in it some of the marks and following disadvantages of a sectional study…But for the general body of thinking men, its principals seem to be regarded with indifference or suspicion. To many persons, the mention of probability suggests little else than a notion of a set of rules, very original and profound rules no doubt, with which mathematicians amuse themselves by setting and solving puzzles. Probability has been very much abandoned by mathematicians, who as mathematicians have generally been unwilling to treat it thoroughly." He wrote this in September 1866 in Gonville and Caius College. Dan thought to himself how little had changed since that time.

In his book "Annotated Readings in the History of Statistics", Herbert Aron David describes how Venn illustrated the "truly random character" of the digit by using it to generate a discrete random walk in two dimensions[12]. In the "random walk" model of random sequences, each element in the sequence is interpreted as a step left (if 0) or right (if 1) along the integer line. Many consider Venn's diagram to be the first description of a random walk in mathematics. This guy really liked randomness.

As a student of physics, Dan knew that in the 200 years since Venn's period, much progress had been made in devising algorithms related to randomness, and that much of this had found its way in computerized algorithms and into many other fields of science. Some of these were used by his peers in the days when he led a team of developers in a New York computer service company—he had to know about these algorithms.

Physicists believe that all material systems are governed by physical principles. However, when it comes to living things, they can have difficulty showing how physical principles explain all the complex, "purposeful" activity that can be found in living cells. The biophysicist Max Delbrück expressed the difference between biology and physics as follows: "...every biological phenomenon is essentially a historical one, one unique situation in the infinite total complex of life. Such a situation from the outset diminishes the hope of understanding anyone living thing by itself and the hope of discovering universal laws, the pride, and ambition of physicists. The curiosity remains, though, to grasp more clearly how the same matter, which in physics and chemistry displays clean and reproducible and relatively simple properties, arranges itself in the most astounding fashions as soon as it is drawn into the orbit of the living organism. The closer one looks at these performances of matter in living organisms the more impressive the show becomes. The meanest living cell becomes a magic puzzle box full of elaborate and changing molecules ..."[13].

Peter M Hoffmann, in his review paper, "How Molecular Motors Extract Order from Chaos," explains that physicists often do not understand how fundamental life processes relate to the underlying physics[14]. They consider biology to be a kind of elaborate stamp collecting, to paraphrase a quote often attributed to Rutherford. At the same time, many biologists are not familiar enough with physics to relate the biological functions back to fundamental physical concepts. Biological physics is a field that aims to bridge this gap in understanding.

Dan had never asked himself before why exactly he should care about all this. Was it really relevant to him or was randomness something that should be left to the scientists.

Dan once took a course on the history of physics and learned, that in the 19th century, scientists modeled the random motions of molecules during the development of statistical mechanics. This theory was used to explain different phenomena in thermodynamics and the properties of gases [9].

Dan has always kept away from quantum mechanics, even though his father used to encourage him to challenge himself. He always felt that quantum mechanics was too vague. He was more attracted to areas of physics that felt more connected to real things. But he knew that it was associated with randomness and wondered whether now might be the time to engage with it.

Dan knew that physicists only apply quantum mechanics to the atomic level and lower, claiming that phenomena at these scales of distance are intrinsically random—that even in experiments where all causally-relevant parameters are controlled, there is always some aspect of randomness [15-17]. Reflecting this, quantum mechanics never specifies the outcome of a process, only relative probabilities [18, 19]. A standard example is radioactive decay. If a single unstable atom is placed in a controlled setting, it cannot be predicted how long it will take for the atom to decay. One can readily calculate the probability that a particle will decay in a given time period, but not exactly when it will decay[20].

Dan wondered about how randomness at the atomic scale related to events in his life and his surroundings. He was not good at applying the concepts of physics to the real world. He once complained to a college friend, Jeremy that "people are trying to force the laws of physics into other areas of life and this is wrong". This was years ago but it was something he still thought about.

Jeremy was a physicist who went into quantum mechanics and ended up teaching it. They kept in touch for many years. He once told Dan about hidden variable theories, which claim to underlie quantum mechanics with a hidden, deterministic layer. They claim that quantum mechanics is incomplete [21]. The hidden layer means that "in the processes that appear random, properties with a certain statistical distribution are at work behind the scenes, determining the outcome in each case" [9].

So perhaps there was no inherent randomness in the world after all?

Dan liked to read about Albert Einstein. He once told Jeremy that Einstein was a strong proponent of hidden variable theories because he objected to the fundamentally probabilistic nature of quantum mechanics [22].

Dan and Jeremy were friends, but even so, there were many things they didn't like about each other. Their friendship began when they were roommates at college. From the beginning they liked to sit in the bar and discuss physics, but they very quickly learned that they couldn't live together in the same room. This was because Dan was a very orderly person, and at the time, thought this was the only way to be a physicist. Jeremy was the opposite and living proof that Dan was wrong. Jeremy could not keep a single routine in his life, but despite this, was an excellent physicist. He turned his random life into something of a religion.

Jeremy once showed Dan a private letter that Einstein wrote to Max Born, on March 1947. In it, he said: "I admit, of course, that there is a considerable amount of validity in the statistical approach which we were the first to recognize as necessary given the framework of the existing formalism. I cannot seriously believe in it because the theory cannot be reconciled with the idea that physics should represent a reality in time and space, free from spooky actions at a distance... I am quite convinced that someone will eventually come up with a theory whose objects, connected by laws, are not probabilities but considered facts, as used to be taken for granted until quite recently". Later on, he famously declared, "I am convinced God does not play dice," [21, 23].

"He was wrong," said Jeremy "and so are we."

Now sitting in his backyard, Dan wanted to talk with Jeremy again. He knew he was the right person to discuss randomness with. Jeremy now lived in Arizona but had come to his wife's funeral. Dan thought this was a nice gesture, especially since he wasn't sure he would do the same if Jeremy's wife Edna died.

Dan planned to call Jeremy and invite him to his house for the weekend. In the meantime he went back to reading about the history of randomness.

It seemed that randomness was often seen as in conflict with the deterministic ideas of some religions which posit that the universe was created by an all-knowing god who is aware of all events, past and future. Likewise, it is hard to square randomness with the idea that the universe has a purpose. This is one of the motivations for religious opposition to evolution, in which random variation plays a role. In Hinduism and Buddhist philosophies the past and future are connected via the concept of Karma, and this rules out randomness along with the idea of a "first event" [24].

However, in some religious contexts, procedures that are commonly thought of as randomizing are used for divination. For example, in cleromancy, a form of sortition, the casting of lots is believed to reveal the true will of God or other or other supernatural entities [25].

Dan was a physicist but did not work as one professionally. As such, he often wondered what relevance it had to ordinary human beings.

He remembered one dinner with Jeremy and their wives. Edna was a biologist and very interested in evolution, and in one conversation, mentioned that evolution via natural selection required random genetic mutations. She explained that random variation was required so that individuals would have different traits that would be selected for by the different survival chances associated with those variations [26, 27]. In this way, natural selection allowed feedback about the environment, and the challenges of existing within it, to be captured in the genome [26, 27]. The natural variation this process requires is commonly described as "random" [27].

However, there is plenty of evidence that while variation exists it is not completely random. In particular, it is not uniform along the genome or in time, it is not unstructured, and is neither memoryless nor independent of the environment. Edna was one of those scientist who argued that mutations could not be modeled as a properly random process, and that if it was, it would actually be inconsistent with evolutionary theory [26, 27]. Maël Longo states: "We argue that one significant aspect of biological evolution is the continual change of the appropriate phase space and the unpredictability of these changes" [28]. While this argument may not be universally accepted, it suggests that evolution and development require a very particular form of randomness related to the appearance of new behaviors.

Dan had left that dinner puzzled. He was even more puzzled now, when he started to think again about all the issues of randomness in life.

This concept of randomness implies the generation of new possibilities in place of predetermined events. If this was true in life, he was curious to know whether randomness could help him improve himself or whether he would need to wait for evolution-dependent randomness to help him. But waiting for evolution might take too long.

Edna explained to the two physicists how our characteristics emerge from the interaction of our genes with the environment, and how, while the genes were hard to change there was a random element to their interaction[29]. For example, while some people are genetically more prone to developing freckles than others, their environment and primary exposure to light are also significant factors. In addition, the locations where they develop the freckles appear to be random [30, 31].

So, if most critical issues in our lives are controlled by our genes, the environment and by randomness, and we cannot do much about the first two, can we harness the randomness to our benefit?

Dan knew that many theories about randomness had their origins in the study of probabilities in gambling. When we enter a casino, we are readily aware that the environment is governed by probability and that while some people will win, most will lose, and the house will always receive its share. All mathematical theories of probability and randomness have evolved from a wish to calculate probabilities. Statistics, which we all enjoy hearing about from time to time, is concerned with distributions of probability, for example the probability that a person will belong to a particular category.

Dan hoped to find some meaning for himself as a person but reflected that it had all been too much for one day.

Before sleeping, he remembered something else from one of his courses, from the many scientific theories relating to random sequences. The name that came to mind was Andrey Kolmogorov, who in 1963, published a theory called "Kolmogorov Randomness". The idea was that a sequence of bits could be considered random if and only if it was shorter than any computer program that could generate the sequence, meaning that random sequences were those that could not be compressed[32, 33]. The Kolmogorov complexity of an object, such as a piece of text, was correspondingly, the length of the shortest computer program that can produce the object as output. It is a widely used measure of the computational resources needed to specify an object.

Dan found out rapidly that this was far from the only way of thinking about random sequences. He encountered recursive randomness and Schnorr randomness, which are based on recursive computation [34], and that randomness occurs in numbers such as pi, whose decimal digits constitute an infinite sequence that never cyclically repeats and certain well-defined statistical properties [9]. In statistics, randomness is commonly used to generate random samples, which are important in surveys, where you want to infer general conclusions from the responses of small groups of people. This can be done by drawing names out of a hat or using large tables or random digits. In information science, irrelevant or meaningless data is referred to as noise. It is modeled as transient disturbances sampled randomly from underlying distributions [9, 35].

Dan became even more tired. But even so, it had been one of those weekend days that refreshed him. He liked it when his mind was bothered by questions, but this time especially, because the questions were interesting, and at the same time, critically important, too.

## A response to the criticisms of this book made by the New York Times Book Review

There is really no need for a response because there was no review—I only imagined it. However, these are the responses, just in case...

### CRITICISM #1:

**Response:** There are no to-do lists in this book because it is not a self-help book. It is a book that attempts to make the reader think. No more. If you think, you might arrive at an understanding that allows you to plan action. The plans will be different for different people.

### CRITICISM #2:

**Response:** No, it is not a typical science book. It is not intended to be comprehensive but rather blends together some stories, facts, ideas, scientific data and some nonscientific data. The blending takes place in the reader's brain.

## CRITICISM #3:

**Response:** This is by no means a textbook. It does not try to be a comprehensive discussion of everything in every subject, but rather, a collection of glances at many different subjects. Some of these glances may not be through the most perfect windows.

## CRITICISM #4:

**Response:** No, I did not "just cut and paste" from Wikipedia. Knowledge is not invented by one person and to add something means building on previous work. The best way to credit the work of others it builds on it. I can only hope that others will do the same with this book. I provide an extensive list of sources and do my best to communicate their ideas in the way they were originally expressed.

## CRITICISM #5:

**Response:** Why do people read at all? No one is forced to continue after the first few pages. If the reader gets something out of the book, even just marking one or two sentences or copying a paragraph into their diary, then the time was well spent. If they get nothing out of it, even this means they got something, if only a clearer idea of what they do not believe in.

## CRITICISM #6:

**Response:** You are right. Many of the chapters and sections are not in the "right order". There are many repetitions and many relevant topics are not covered, but this is a book about how randomness can be helpful and it should be somewhat random.

## CRITICISM #7:

**Response:** Sorry, you missed what the book is all about. In two words, it is about "intellectual challenge". In four words, it is a "funny experience of intellectual challenge".

# CHAPTER 3
## Applications of randomness: Is it fair?

The next morning, Dan took the Long Island Rail Road to his office in the city. Monday mornings were always busy.

Dan was always bothered by questions. It happened to him many times and his colleagues always used to tell him that it was because he was lonely at home. This time though, he felt it was different and he knew he had to talk with Jeremy. He would ask him to visit on one of the upcoming weekends.

It was strange, though. Why should he be bothered by questions of randomness? He knew that randomness in quantum mechanics applied to atoms. But what about the issues of extracting joy from the uncertainness in the iPod shuffle? Dan looked out through the window of the train at the same view he had been seeing for years and wondered whether there was anything that he might apply randomness to.

At first glance, defining the word randomness seems almost useless by definition. However, in many areas of life, people have used randomness as a method for making things fairer. This has been described in politics, society, religion and mathematics. Dan thought this lack of bias might be helpful [9]. Curious, he looked at some pages as he rode on the train to work.

Cleisthenes of Athens at around 570 BC. He was a statesman and founder of Athenian democracy. For several years he served as the chief archon, the highest magistrate of Athens [36]. In the struggle for power that followed the fall of tyranny in Greece, Cleisthenes was unable to impose his leadership and it was Isagoras, the leader of the more conservative nobles, who was elected chief archon. According to tradition, this was the point when Cleisthenes took the people into a partnership [36]. He carried out a complete reform of the system of the government which was approved by a popular assembly in the year 507 BC.

The Spartans opposed this movement and Cleisthenes and his relatives were exiled. The Spartans did not want to see a democratic Athens, but they misjudged the attitude of the people and had to withdraw. The Athenians recalled the exiles and carried out the original decision. Cleisthenes convinced people to change the basis of political organization from the family and clans to the locality. In this new picture, public rights and duties depended on membership of a group or community, which kept a register of its members and elected its own officials. Ten new tribes were formed to take the place of the old blood tribes in a somewhat random grouping that diminished the influence of some of the leading holy families.

*Isonomia*, the principle of equality of rights for all, was a significant achievement and ensured that positions on the committees that ran Athens were allocated equitably [37].

Perhaps for the first time in history, the concept that fairness, justice and quality can be approximated by randomization had been established.

Dan thought that the Greeks were right in using randomization to ensure justice. These same principles are still used in the selection of jurors and in military draft lotteries.

There are many times when we meet randomness in our daily lives. Gambling is one of them. "Random devices" including dice, roulette wheels and shuffling playing cards have been developed for games of chance. The aim of all of them is to generate randomness in a fair way. All gambling requires the ability to generate randomness in a fair way.

Dan remembered one of the old jokes his father liked to tell.

What's the difference between prayer in church and prayer in a casino? In a casino, we mean it.

We would never put a coin in a gambling machine if we did not believe that it was fair and unbiased. In most jurisdictions, the processes that generate the randomness are regulated by government and in many countries there are specific gambling control boards [38]. These boards are also responsible for circulating rules and regulations that dictate how gaming activities are conducted.

Dan came across a nice paper by Anthony Cabot and Robert C. Hannum called Gambling Regulation and Mathematics: A Marriage of Necessity [39]. In the introduction to their paper, they outlined the connection between fairness and randomness: "Probability is at the foundation of the gaming business. Every wager in a casino is designed and calibrated according to the laws of chance to exact a certain percentage of the players' money. This is how the casino makes money." In the short run, a player may win or lose, but in the long run, the gods of probability will always catch up. Mathematicians call this the "law of large numbers." For casinos, this law guarantees revenue with no risk. There is no luck when it comes to the business of casino gaming--it is all mathematics.

The *law* of large numbers is the claim that an infinite sequence of independent, identically distributed Bernoulli trials will have the property of large numbers [40, 41].

Mathematical issues arise in gaming law and regulation. A game based on flawed mathematics, in which the house advantage is misrepresented, deliberately or otherwise, may not satisfy the standards of fairness and honesty necessary for protecting the integrity of gaming.

Integrity is an important regulatory concern for two reasons. First, the government has an interest in protecting customers from being cheated by unscrupulous operators, and in most cases, only government can have access to the information required to ensure fairness and honesty. Second, the wellbeing of the industry depends on the perception that it is honest and fair.

When we hear the word randomness, it doesn't sound like it has anything to do with fairness and justice. But it does.

The chance of winning the National Lottery jackpot in the UK is 1 in 13,983,816, while there is a 1 in 2,330,636 chance of getting five numbers plus the bonus ball [42]. To gain an advantage, some people try to pick on the most commonly drawn numbers. One approach is to choose the numbers that come up most often. The most frequently drawn ball is the number 44. Since the National Lottery began in the UK in 1994, it has been drawn 253 times. The other most common numbers are:

38 – 251 times
40 – 249 times
23 – 248 times
39 – 246 times
33 – 245 times

However, the frequency of appearance is not related to how likely they are to be drawn together. In fact, the chance of these number being drawn as the winning combination is the same as any other six.

Dan found an enlightening article in the Telegraph, published in May 2017 that described several methods that people use to help them win [42]. Surprisingly, experts found that selecting numbers at random was the best approach. This was not because it increases the chances of winning, but because it increases the chances of winning larger amounts. By using a system for selecting numbers, you increase the probability that you will choose the same numbers as others. This makes it less likely that you will have to share the jackpot with others Dr. John Haigh, emeritus of mathematics at Sussex University was quoted in this article: "If we pick the least popular numbers and win, then we will probably share our jackpot with fewer people." [42].

Dan remembered a story that he had once heard about drawing straws, a selection method used by a group to choose someone to perform a task after no one has volunteered [42]. The leader takes a number of straws, one of which is shorter than the others, and holds them in his fist in a way that makes them all appear to be the same length. Each member of the group then draws a straw. At the end of the draw, the person with the shortest straw is the one who must perform the task. Drawing straws is a fair game in which your chance of drawing the short straw is exactly the same as everyone else's.

On 20 November 2015, a Mississippi state election was settled by drawing straws after both candidates received 4,589 votes. It resulted in Blaine Eaton being re-elected to the Mississippi House of Representatives [43].

Dan is not a great sports fan, but he thought about how in games such as football and soccer, it is customary to use a coin toss to randomly select the starting condition or even decide a winner in the case of tied games. The annual National Basketball Association (NBA) draft lottery determines the selection order for the first 14 picks of the NBA Draft [44].

The order is determined using ping-pong balls in a procedure that takes place in a separate room prior to the national broadcast. Select members of the media, NBA officials, representatives of the teams and an accounting firm all attend the draw. Fourteen ping-pong balls, numbered 1 through 14, are placed in a lottery machine. There are 1,001 possible combinations when four balls are drawn out of 14, without regard to their order of selection, and prior to the lottery, 1,000 of those 1,001 combinations are assigned to the 14 participating lottery teams.

The randomness needs to be fully transparent. The lottery machine used in the 2016 draw were manufactured by the Smart Play Company, a manufacturer of state lottery machines used throughout the United States. Smart Play also weighs, measures and certifies the ping-pong balls before the drawing [45].

All 14 balls are placed in the lottery machine and are mixed for 20 seconds before the first ball is removed. The remaining balls are mixed for another 10 seconds, after which the second ball is removed, and so on until four balls have been removed. The team that has been assigned the combination receives the number one pick. The same process is repeated with the same ping-pong balls for each pick. If the same teams is selected more than once or the unassigned combination is drawn, then the result is discarded. Drafts are extremely important to the teams involved and randomness is essential to the fairness of the process.

Dan's train arrives in the city. As he walks toward the staircase to his office, he knows it will be one of those days he thinks about retirement. At the age of 72, why should he continue to work? Even though his children have encouraged him to retire for years, deep in his heart he knows that sitting alone in his house might be the end of him.

# CHAPTER 4

## Can I use randomness for making better decisions?

When Dan reached his office, he went to the kitchen and made himself coffee. He did not like to get one downstairs like the young guys on his team. He was one of the few in his office that still used the old coffee maker in the kitchen.

He decided to spend his day in the office reviewing randomness. He already knew from his train ride how randomness is associated with fairness. So could randomness be a good thing? It is common knowledge that randomness is essential to ensuring proper sampling in opinion polls and in statistical sampling. But it is not obvious why or how it works.

From his days in college, he knew that mathematicians have developed many algorithms for generating random numbers.

"Monte Carlo methods" are a broad class of computational algorithms that rely on repeated random sampling to obtain numerical results. The method was first used by scientists working on the atom bomb [46]. It is named for Monte Carlo, the Monaco resort town renowned for its casinos. The method can be used to solve any problem that has a probabilistic interpretation.

Searching the web, Dan discovered that there are companies that develop software to apply this technique to problems of risk analysis and decision-making. He looked at one such company, Palisade[47].

Monte Carlo methods help people account for risk in quantitative analysis and decision making and it is widely used in such fields as finance, research and development, project management, energy, manufacturing, engineering, insurance, oil and gas, transportation and environment.

Making a decision using randomness? This concept really made Dan curious.

We all know that in almost every decision we make, we do some kind of risk analysis. This applies to simple, everyday decisions, such as what to eat or wear (not always straightforward...) and also to bigger decisions, such as who to marry, what to study, where to live, what profession to pursue, selecting a perfect workplace (which does not exist...)

In every decision, we are faced with so many factors that there is always some uncertainty or ambiguity. In some decisions, we know the possible consequences. For example, if you drink alcohol, you increase the risk of liver disease. Likewise, if you don't brush your teeth, you increase your risk of getting a toothache. However, in many decisions you do know the future consequence of your choice. It would be great if we had a machine to work all this out, but until such a machine is invented, we have to live with the uncertainty. Even though we can Google everything, it is still tough for us to predict the consequences of many of our decisions.

Monte Carlo simulation is one method that we can use to help predict the outcome of decisions and gauge the risk associated with them. For every decision, we need to provide the probabilities for each of the different outcomes. The method then provides us with the extreme probabilities corresponding to the riskiest decisions and the likely outcomes of conservative, middle-of-the-road decisions [47].

How does it do this? The simulation builds models for possible results, substituting a range of values or probability distribution for any element that is inherently uncertain. It recalculates the result of the process many times, each using a different random sampling from each probability distribution. The output of the simulation is a distribution of possible outcomes.

Dan thought that this sounded a bit complicated. However, most of us do not understand how our cellphone works even though we use it for hours every day.

Forget about mathematics. Would you like an application to help you decide who to marry by calculating the risk of divorce (such as those used in many reality television programs like Married at First Sight)? Or one that could help you with any major decision? The Monte Carlo system uses probability distributions.

Dan liked probabilities. He went back to the kitchen for more coffee then returned to his desk to surf some other sites looking for probability distributions [47], which describe the uncertainties associated with variables in risk analysis. He found several examples including the bell curve, or standard curve, which a user can specify by providing the mean, or expected value, and the standard deviation, to describe the variation around the mean. Values around the mean are most likely to occur. The distribution is symmetrical and describes many natural phenomena such as the distribution of body weight among a group of people. There is also the lognormal distribution, which is asymmetric and positively-skewed. This is used to represent quantities that cannot go below zero but have no maximum value, such as stock prices.

He also read about uniform distribution, in which all values have equal probability of occurring, and the user need only define the maximum and minimum values. In a triangle distribution, the user must specify the most-likely minimum and maximum values. Likewise, for the PERT model, where the extremes are less emphasized that in triangular distribution. Finally, there are the discrete models in which the user specifies the probability of each particular outcome. For example, in a lawsuit, there may be a 20% chance of favorable verdict, a 30% chance of adverse verdict, a 40% chance of a settlement and a 10% chance of mistrial [47].

During the simulation, values are sampled at random from the input probability distributions. Each set of samples is an iteration. The result of each iteration is recorded and the process is repeated many times to generate a probability distribution that represents all possible outcomes. With this distribution, you know the likelihood of any particular outcome.

But is it helpful? It may seem trivial to marry a partner when there is only a 20% chance of divorce instead of one where there is a 40% chance. However, Monte Carlo simulations provide many advantages over deterministic or single-point estimate analyses. Probabilistic results tell us the relative probability of different outcomes while sensitivity analyses indicate which inputs are most important for influencing the bottom line. Scenario analyses help us model which combinations of inputs leads to particular outputs. Finally, there is the correlation between inputs in Monte Carlo simulation, it is possible to model interdependent relationship between input variables. It can help you understand when some factors go up, which follow them up and which go down [47].

So randomness can help us make decisions.

It can also help physicians and pharmaceutical companies quantify the effectiveness of new drugs. These decisions are based on randomized controlled trials that use various methods to randomly select which patients receive the drug and which receive the placebo. In this way they can measure the effectiveness of the drug in the optimum way.

Dan felt hungry and went for an early lunch, safe in the knowledge that randomness can be helpful.

# CHAPTER 4 PART 2
## Random processes

After lunch, Dan returned to history. His father often told him we can learn from those who lived before us.

Question: Why aren't we doing well in history?

Answer: Because the teacher keeps on asking about things that happened before we were born!

Probability theory has its origins in games of chance, which have a long history of having been played for thousands of years [48, 49]. In 1654, the French mathematicians Pierre Fermat and Blaise Pascal shared a correspondence on probability motivated by a gambling problem [50]. An earlier mathematical work on probability in gambling games was written by Gerolamo Cardano in the 16th century[51]. Jakob Bernoulli later wrote Ars Conjectandi, which is considered a significant milestone in the history of probability theory [52].

In the 19th century, scientists developed the theory of statistical mechanics in which containers filled with gas are treated mathematically as collections of many moving particles.

Although many scientists, such as Rudolf Clausius, tried to incorporate randomness into their descriptions of gases, it was not until James Clerk Maxwell in 1859 that significant progress was made[53]. Maxwell presented a theory in which he assumed that gas particles move in random directions at random velocities[54].

In 1933, Andrei Kolmogorov published his book on the foundations of probability theory in which he used measure theory to develop an axiomatic framework. The publication of this book is generally considered to mark the birth of modern probability theory and the point at which the theories of probability and stochastic processes became parts of mainstream mathematics[54]. This was the same Kolmogorov Dan was reading about the night before.

Dan learned that in probability theory, a stochastic or random process is one in which probability distributions are assigned to variables[55]. These random variables are associated with set of numbers regarded as points in time and which help model how systems evolve randomly over time[56].

The set used to index the random variables is called the index set. It can be linearly ordered or mapped to a set in which elements represent points in space [57-60].

The mathematical space of a stochastic process is known as its state space. Each random variable in the collection takes values from the same mathematical space, the state space. It can be defined using integers, real lines, dimensional spaces, complex planes, or other higher dimensional mathematical elements[61, 62].

A stochastic process can have many outcomes, due to its randomness, and a single outcome of a stochastic process is termed a sample function or realization. A stochastic process is taken as a random element in a function space[63]. The values of the variables in a stochastic process are not always numbers and can be vectors or other mathematical objects. If the random variables are indexed by higher-dimensional methods, then the collection of random variables is called a random field [64, 65].

A sample function is a single outcome of a stochastic process, so it is formed by taking a single possible value of each random variable in the stochastic process[66]. An increment of a stochastic process is the difference between two random variables in the same process. For a stochastic process with an index set that corresponds to time, the increment is how much the stochastic process changes over a specified period[49, 65].

A stochastic process can be classified in different ways-by its state space, its index set, or the dependences among its random variables. One standard way to classify them is by the index set and the state space[62, 66]. When interpreted as time, if the index set of a stochastic process has a fixed number of elements, the set of integers, or the numbers, then the process is in discrete time. If the index set is some interval of the real line, then time is said to be continuous. These two types of stochastic processes are respectively referred to as discrete-time and continuous-time stochastic processes. If the index set is the set of integers or some subset, then the stochastic process can also be called a random sequence. If the state space is the set of integers or the set of natural numbers, then the stochastic process is called a discrete or integer-valued stochastic process. If the state space is the real line, then the stochastic process is known as a real-valued stochastic process or a one with continuous state space[49, 67-69].

Dan looked at some historical examples of how to apply probabilities[49].

The Bernoulli process, which is a simple stochastic process, can serve as a mathematical model for flipping a biased coin[70]. It describes a sequence of independent and identically distributed random variables, where each of them has either the value of one or zero. A Bernoulli process is a sequence of random variables, where each coin flip is a Bernoulli trial[71, 72].

Random walks are stochastic processes defined as sums of random variables or random vectors in Euclidean space, so they are processes that change in discrete time[72].

The Wiener process is one of the most important and most studied stochastic processes. It is comprised of stationary, independent increments distributed according to the size of the increments[73]. The index and state spaces are both continuous, the former over non-negative numbers and the latter over real numbers[60].

The Poisson point process is another important stochastic process that represents a counting process over a random number of points[74]. The number of points is in the interval from zero to a specified time. The Poisson variable depends on the specified time and a parameter.

Another such process is a stochastic process that has the Markov property. In a Markov process, each value depends only on the previous value. This means that the behavior of a system depends only on its current state and is stochastically independent on its past[75]. This process forms the basis of the Markov Chain Monte Carlo, which is used for simulating objects that can be described by probabilities distributions and is widely applied in

Bayesian statistics[76]. In contrast with Markov processes, in martingales the next value depends on all previous values[77] [78].

Lévy processes are stochastic process that can be thought of as generalizations of random walks in continuous time. Their main defining characteristic is that they are stationary and independent[79, 80].

Finally, autoregressive and moving average processes are types of stochastic process that are used to model discrete-time empirical time series data, especially in economics [48].

When Dan left his office at the end of the day, he knew about many kinds of random process. However, he was very unsure about how to apply them.

# CHAPTER 5

## Is God random? Can randomness drive improvement?

Dan had no time for religion. He had never described himself as an atheist but he did not like to overthink religious questions because he thought they didn't lead anywhere. He realized that the relationship between randomness and religion was not well-understood and questioned whether he should waste his energy on it. Obviously, religions did not intend to be random. But still, some forms of divination, such as cleromancy, try to use seemingly-random events to reveal divine will [9].

Later that evening, while drinking a glass of red wine—something he rarely did—Dan came across the Common Ground blog by Stephen Friberg. It was a blog about evolution, science and religion that discussed randomness in the context of the building blocks of nature [81]. It described how physicists think of a "building block" and use these objects to construct nature in "ladder-like features." New blocks are built on top of previous ones.

Astrophysics can explain how life ultimately arose from the Big Bang. To quote Friberg: "After its initial expansion from a singularity, the universe cooled sufficiently to allow energy to be converted into various subatomic particles, including protons, neutrons, and electrons. While protons and neutrons combined to form the first atomic nuclei only a few minutes after the big bang, it would take thousands of years for electrons to combine with them and create electrically neutral atoms. Next, planets were formed out of protoplanetary discs made from the debris of stars and galaxies, some planets emerging at the right distances from the sun to support environments favorable to abiogenesis, a process that leads to the emergence of amino acids that are the building-blocks of life, and to the emergence of RNA, DNA and cells, the building blocks of heredity and living organisms. Only then does evolution as Darwin describes it comes into play" [81]. These are all steps in a ladder and there is randomness in the transitions between the steps. And the higher we move up the ladder, the greater the randomness.

Friberg believes that randomness generates outlier phenomena. These are events with extremely low probability that nevertheless occur. An example would be a tsunami. Randomness can also act as a driving force to instigate change and increase complexity.

Dan was willing to accept the notion that the universe can be viewed as a laboratory housing billions of random experiments being conducted simultaneously in which every possible combination of parameters is tried. In this laboratory, new things are constantly being created and some of them become building blocks. Not only were self-replicating cells formed, but also the niches which those cells require to flourish. These structures are access by the combination of randomness with deterministic physical laws such as gravity, electricity and magnetism.

Dan says that randomness was more than just an accidental thing without purpose. Rather, it was the mechanism through which everything was fitted into the laws of nature. As such, there was no such thing as true randomness. Dan liked to think that randomness was part of nature.

Friberg wrote: "If something doesn't exist now, it doesn't necessarily mean that it won't happen in the future. The question is whether or not the laws of nature allow it to happen in the future or not… and whether a phenomenon is stable or not… whether once it is brought into existence, it will continue to exist. There are some things that don't exist at a certain time that potentially exist. Laws of nature allow for their possibility. Immediately after the big bang, cells were only potentially real, not actually real. What makes things real are the dynamical processes of growth and development that push potentiality into actuality. Essential to this process… is randomness" [81]. Furthermore, he thinks that if randomness is important or relevant to natural laws, then we can view it as a dynamical mechanism for "turning potentiality into actuality" [81].

Dan, while beginning to realize that randomness is an integral part of nature as well an integral part of decision making, came across the term "pseudo-randomness". A pseudorandom process is a process that appears to be random but is not [82]. A pseudorandom sequence exhibits statistical randomness while being generated by an entirely deterministic process [82]. The advantages of using pseudorandom over random processes are that they are easier to produce and can be used repeatedly to produce the same random sequence. These properties are very important in practical applications.

To generate a genuinely random process, you need to make accurate and repeatable measurements of a non-deterministic process. There are several ways to generate this kind of absolute randomness using dedicated hardware random number generators. In old times dice, cards and roulette wheels were used for generating random numbers. In 1947, the RAND Corporation generated numbers using an electronic simulation of a roulette wheel, ultimately published in 1955 in an article titled "A Million Random Digits with 100,000 Normal Deviates" [83]. In 1949, Derrick Henry Lehmer invented the linear congruential generator, which was used for a long time in most pseudorandom number generators[84]. However, nowadays, most generators are based on linear recurrence. With the spread of computers, algorithmic pseudorandom number generators have replaced random number tables. "True" random number generators, or hardware random number generators, are only used in specialized applications.

So it seems that many things we think of as random are actually pseudorandom.

# CHAPTER 6
## And what about pseudorandom

Dan discovered an article by Scott Aaronson entitled: "The Quest for Randomness," published by Scientific American a few years ago. It addressed the question of whether numbers can be truly random and what would be the implications for quantum mechanics, the stock market and data security [85].

Aaronson quotes a great joke about randomness from a Dilbert cartoon featuring a lizard-like creature billed as a "random number generator." Yet the only number it spits out is nine. Dilbert asks his guide whether he is sure that this is random. The guide replies, "that's the problem with randomness. We can never be sure."

Is it up to us to question what random really is? What does pure randomness mean at the level above physics?

The article raises the question of whether we can ever be sure that something is random. Can one ever rule out the possibility of a hidden deterministic pattern? Dan was trying to stay away from any fundamental questions that might involve religion. There must be another way.

In many areas of life, such as computer security, encryption keys are generated in an entirely random manner. The degree of randomness must be sufficient to prevent spies and thieves from breaking in. In other areas, such as in gambling and stock trading, people try to predict random quantities. Many believe that such quantities are not random or that they're decipherable enough to follow some pattern.

Dan found a book "Does God Play Dice: The New Mathematics of Chaos," written by British mathematician Ian Stewart [86]. In this book, Stewart explains why the science of chaos is forcing scientists to rethink Einstein's fundamental assumptions regarding the way the universe behaves.

Chaos theory has shown that many simple systems, even while obeying precise laws, nevertheless act in random ways. Perhaps God does play dice via an ordered cosmic game. Nothing is as it seems. Familiar shapes such as circles or ellipses give way to infinitely complex fractals; the fluttering of a butterfly's wings can change the weather; and the gravitational attraction of an animal in a far away galaxy can change the fate of the solar system.

Albert Einstein claimed that quantum mechanics was incomplete and that physicists should keep looking for a better theory. However, quantum mechanics is still going strong.

Dan knew that someday he would need to dive into quantum mechanics.

Dan already knew that to test whether a sequence is random, you need to perform a statistical analysis. If you want to check a sequence of numbers, you need to check whether the digits 0 through 9 appear with approximately equal frequency among the first million digits. If the digits are generated randomly, then you would expect to find that each digit appears roughly ten percent of the time [85].

However, this test is not enough to demonstrate pure randomness. For example, a sequence such as 012345678901234567890123456789… would satisfy the test but is obviously not random. Instead you can check whether all two-digit pairs, 00 through 99, occur roughly one percent of the time. However, if you know the test, you can always find a way around it. In the 1930s, David Champernowne invented the sequence 12345678910111213 14151617181920212223224…, which has identical two-digit frequencies, three-digit frequencies, four-digit frequencies, and so on. It passes the test but is manifestly not random [85].

Just because a sequence passes a particular test for randomness does not mean it is random. Aronson challenges us: "Indeed, let me now argue that no matter how smart we are in devising a statistical test for randomness, an adversary will always be able to find a deterministic sequence that passes our test" [85]. He continues: "If nothing else, such an adversary could say the following: Let S be the set of all sequences of one million digits that are declared to be random by our test. Presumably, S is non-empty because something had better pass our test! So for my sequence, I'll simply pick the first sequence in S, when the sequences are viewed as numbers and arranged in ascending order. By hypothesis, that sequence passes our test, yet I just specified it deterministically!" [85].

It seems that it is quite difficult to be random. Difficult but not impossible. In fact, there is a whole field of science call algorithmic information theory that provides methods for testing sequences and demonstrating whether they are random or not. Aronson asks us to consider a coin that lands on heads every time we flip it. Would we conclude the coin is biased? Most of us will say yes. On the other hand, we may accept the coin is normal if the following sequence appears: T H T H H H T H H H H H T T H H T H H H T H T H T H T H T T T H T. Nevertheless, both sequences have he same probability of occuring, which is $2^{-30}$. This is not a paradox, it is reality [85].

If we calculated the probability of getting a sequence that was just as random-looking and pattern-less as the one above, we would find a probability of close to one. How can we formalize the concept of a sequence of numbers being random-looking and pattern-less?

In the 1960's, three mathematicians, Kolmogorov, Solomonoff, and Chaitin, independently proposed a measure of the inherent randomness of a sequence. It is called Kolmogorov complexity. Even Aronson mentioned that it is not a fair name as all three discovered it.

The Kolmogorov complexity of a sequence $x$, abbreviated $K(x)$, is defined to be the number of bits in the shortest computer program whose output is $x$. It is therefore the length of the shortest computer program (in a predetermined programming language) that generates the object as output [33].

A sequence of 20 zeros can be described very simply by the instruction "print 20 zeros". By contrast, a long random sequence of 1s and 0s, will need a much longer program, typically one that is close to the length of the sequence itself. The simplest program is generally "print $x$", where $x$ is the sequence [85].

Consider the following two strings of 32 lowercase letters and digits [33].

## EXAMPLE 1:
abababababababababababababababab

EXAMPLE 2:

4c1j5b2p0cv4w1x8rx2y39umgw5q85s7

The first string can be described by the short description "ab, 16 times", which has 11 characters. The second one would likely need a description that included the sequence itself [33].

Kolmogorov complexity provides us with a tool to resolve the paradox of real randomness. When should we suspect a coin of being biased? We should do so when the sequence $x$ of flips of the coin satisfies $K(x)$ is smaller than $x$. In other words, we should suspect a coin if and only if there exists a pattern to the coin flips that can be described by a computer program using substantially fewer bits than the sequence of coin flips itself [85].

A random sequence, by the Kolmogorov measure, is therefore one that cannot be effectively compressed. This definition has been used to define the randomness of infinite sequences in terms of a finite alphabet. Such algorithmically-random sequences can be defined in several equivalent ways.

However, how do we know when we have found the shortest program? Might there be an even shorter one out there? [85, 87].

Algorithmic information theory is the area of computer science that studies Kolmogorov complexity. The concept of Kolmogorov complexity is based on a theory discovered by Ray Solomonoff, as part of his invention of algorithmic probability [88].

Solomonoff's theory states that among algorithms that decode strings from the descriptions, there exists an optimal one. This algorithm encodes strings in a way that is as short as any other algorithm up to an additive constant that depends only on the algorithm and not on the string. He used this algorithm and the corresponding code length to define the "universal probability" of the string [33].

And now for the Berry paradox.

The Berry paradox is a self-referential paradox which has its origin in the phase: "the smallest positive integer not definable in under sixty letters." It is attributed it to G. G. Berry, a junior librarian at Oxford's library [89]. In the

Berry Paradox, we ask for the first number that can't be described using less than sixty letters. However, in asking, we have described the number, and have done so using only fifty-seven letters! [85].

There are only twenty-six letters in the English alphabet and so there are finitely many phrases of under sixty letters. This means there are finitely many positive integers that can be defined by phrases under sixty letters and so there are other integers that can't be. There must likewise be a smallest positive integer that satisfies the property "not definable in under sixty letters". However, if the expression has fifty-seven letters, then it is definable. This is a paradox [89].

It is not possible in general to unambiguously define the minimal number of symbols required to describe a given string, if a specific description mechanism is already provided. Also, the expressions *string* and *number* may be used interchangeably, since a number can be represented by a string of symbols, e.g., an English word. Further, it is also possible to refer to any word with a number, e.g., by the number of its position in a given dictionary. This means that some long strings can be described using fewer symbols than those required for their full representation. The complexity of a given string is defined as the minimal length that a description requires to decidedly refer to the full representation of that string [89]. It therefore follows that a coin should be suspected of being crooked only if a pattern can be observed in the coin flips, and if it is possible for a program to describe this pattern using a substantially shorter sequence than the sequence of flips itself.

The Kolmogorov complexity is defined using formal languages or Turing machines, with which ambiguities about which string results from a given description can be avoided. However, the Kolmogorov complexity is not computable. This means that the definition of the Berry number is paradoxical because it is not possible to compute how many words are required to define a number, as such computation is not possible because of the paradox [89]. Nonetheless, even though the Kolmogorov complexity cannot be computed, it can be used to ensure the randomness of something.

So how can we produce a string of numbers with high Kolmogorov complexity? Pick a string randomly! If we choose a string of $n$ bits entirely at random, there is an overwhelming chance that it will have high Kolmogorov complexity based on the "counting argument."

Dan was laughing: this means merely that if we want something to be really random, it needs to be randomly selected...ha ha.

Aronson re-emphasizes this in his paper by stating that picking randomly is the only way to generate strings with high Kolmogorov complexity. However, even he admits that it is peculiar to state that "if something is random, then it is random." Replacing the "metaphysical" question of whether events are determined or random with the purely mathematical question of whether a description of the events has high Kolmogorov complexity does not necessarily make it easier to answer.

Aronson describes in his studies a primary model of quantum computation called a Boson Sampler. In this model, a stream of identical photons is transmitted through fiber optic cables, and a network of devices split the photon beam, following which the photons are examined to determine their position after the split. This measurement involves quantum mechanics, as where the photons land is random. If we know how the beam splitter network is set up, then, at least in principle, we can calculate the probability of any given outcome, or how many photons will end up in each location [85]. However, under widely believed hypotheses, no known efficient classical algorithm can produce the same probability distribution that a Boson Sampler does.

The goal of boson sampling is to sample according to a specific probability distribution. Therefore, it is useful to have a search problem, based on which the computer can output any string of bits with the specified properties [85]. Consider the search function "Find a string that occurs with large probability in the distribution and also has large Kolmogorov complexity." A string that satisfies both these criteria can only be obtained by sampling from the distribution. In this case, the Kolmogorov complexity allows us to replace the objective of the sampling distribution with the objective of outputting a fixed string that has specific properties [85].

So, would it ever be possible to be certain about something being random?

According to Aronson, if we make no auxiliary assumptions whatsoever, the strict answer is no [85].

At a metaphysical level, any sequence that is claimed to be random, no matter how pattern less it looks, could have been determined by God, the initial conditions of the universe, or whatever, to be precisely what it is. However, we may be able to come closer to the ideal (of a random sequence) than one might have thought possible, by saying "If these numbers are not random, then some fundamental assumption has to collapse."

Dan was now wondering about what the word "pseudorandom" actually meant.

He turned to the Encyclopedia of Psychology.

He found that some non-random sequences satisfy many of the properties of random sequences. The Champernowne sequence, for example, which consists of all the binary numerals for every non-negative integer listed consecutively (i.e., 011011100101110111...), is not random, as the initial subsequences of reasonable length are highly compressible. But it looks like it satisfies at least some of the parameters of random sequences. This sequence is an attempt at producing a *pseudorandom* sequence. It means that the sequence passes at least some statistical tests for randomness, yet can be easily produced [40].

Why do we need pseudorandom sequences?

Pseudorandom number generators are used in cryptography or statistical sampling to produce numbers that seem to be random for all practical purposes [40]. That is, they may be useful for some purposes, but not for others, where real randomness is a must.

A simple technique for generating pseudorandom sequences is a *symbol shift* algorithm [90]. Given an initial 'seed' numeral (s1, s2, ..., sns1, s2, ..., sn), the algorithm spits out the digits in order. It is useless if the seed is known or is correlated with the events to which the pseudorandom numbers are applied. In practical applications, the seed is selected in a way that carries no information about the application. For example, simple pseudorandom number generators obtain the seed from the time at which the seed is called for. With a finite seed, the sequence is repeated after a certain period of time.

Improved algorithms use the more complicated computable function of the seed to generate outcome sequences with an extended period that is much longer than the length of the seed [40].

If the seed is not fixed but is selected by chance, we can have chance without randomness. If a computer has a clock representing the external time, the time at which the algorithm is started can be used as a seed. If it is a matter of chance when the algorithm is started, the particular sequence that is produced by the pseudorandom sequence generator algorithm is also chance, but it is not random. This is because there is a program which runs the same algorithm on an explicitly given seed. Since this algorithm is efficient, the length of the sequence before the repeats were produced will be longer than the program code added to the length of the seed; this means that the produced sequence is compressible. Irrespective of whether the seed is produced by chance or represented in the algorithm, the sequence of outcomes remains the same [40].

Dan realized that the chanciness of a sequence can vary in whether or not it is random. This also applies to any algorithm that is fed with an input selected by chance and produces an outcome by chance, but for which the output is highly compressible.

Pseudorandom sequence generators are designed to produce highly compressible sequences. They provide a counterexample to the connection between chance and randomness. A given sequence is considered to be random based on whether it passes the required randomness tests. Thus, a pseudorandom sequence can look random, as long as the justification is weaker than truth. Suppose one sees a genuinely random sequence and forms the justified belief that it is random. The existence of pseudorandom sequences entails that things may appear precisely as they are, and yet, the sequence may not be random [40].

The take-home message for Dan was to be careful, as things that seem random may not always be so. But, for many purposes, this pseudorandomness may be sufficient.

Cryptography comes from the combination of the Greek words for "hidden" and "writing," and it is defined as the study of techniques for secure communication [91]. Cryptography is associated with constructing texts in a way that prevents the public from reading them. Information security, data confidentiality, data integrity, authentication, and non-repudiation are all central to modern cryptography [92, 93]. Pseudo randomness has several applications in cryptography. Random values are required in cryptographic methods, as their goal is to make a message as hard to crack as possible. However, because pseudorandom sequences are deterministic and reproducible, they can be discovered. Therefore, when random choices are not random enough, they may not serve the purpose of information security.

Dan was wondering whether randomness in nature is a true or a pseudo one, and what meaning it held for his life. He did not like to deal with questions for which the answers were dependent on the way we look at things. He always preferred more definite answers.

Three mechanisms can be used to explain random behavior in systems. Randomness can be derived from the environment, such as in the case of Brownian motion and random number-generating hardware. According to the second mechanism, randomness can be derived from the initial conditions, as observed in the chaos theory and in systems with behaviors that are highly sensitive to small variations in the initial conditions, such as dice rolling. The third mechanism is pseudo-randomness, which is a type of randomness intrinsically generated by the system and is used by pseudo-random number generators or algorithms.

Dan thought that he would dive into studying the random behavior of systems, but he decided to go forth with one primary question in mind: how can it make me better? "Improvement" had always been one of his primary goals, and it was one of the reasons why he went to work for the computer services company (where he was stuck for many years): he liked looking into systems and trying to improve them.

# CHAPTER 7

## Myths and misconceptions: Do not fall into these traps!

For the rest of the week, Dan found himself hunting for more data about randomness. It was an exciting field for him, and he felt somewhat sorry for not having discovered it earlier on. Somehow, in the midst of this excitement, he was also troubled by the thought that he may come up with discoveries that may deeply affect his life…he started thinking about whether it could have helped Jenny.

In the course of his reading, he came upon the notion that there are numerous well-known perceptions of randomness that are actually based on intuition and may therefore not be as random as perceived.

People have sometimes argued that when dealing with random systems, events that have already occurred are less likely to occur than those that did not [9]. This is a misconception, and the terms that are sometimes used to describe this misconception is "a due number" or the "coupon collector's problem." This is explained by the argument that "in a random selection of numbers, since all numbers eventually appear, those that have not come up yet are 'due,' and thus more likely to come up soon" [9]. This logic is faulty, as it can only be applied to systems in which the numbers that come up are removed and not returned. However, in a truly random system, there is no memory, and each selection of numbers, cards, or lottery is random in a way that past events do not affect future outcomes. This means that even if the number 7 keeps appearing in the winning numbers every month, our chances of winning do not increase by not selecting the number 7.

Another common myth is what is sometimes called the "blessed number" or the "cursed number." If we go back to the lottery ticket example, we may say "I kept selecting 9 every week, and for a year (hopefully, we did not 'invest' more than that…) it never showed up. My Aunt Suzy always selects 8, as she has eight grandchildren, and it has already appeared six times over the last three months. This logic is not valid for genuinely randomized systems and is only valid in biased systems.

We observe many events in our life that are so-called "random" but rarely occur with equal frequency. So it may seem to us that some events are "more blessed than others," depending on whether these events are good or bad for us. Dan found out that this misconception is explained by Benford's law, also called the first-digit law, which was proposed by the physicist Frank Benford in 1938. This law describes the frequency distribution of leading digits in many real-life sets of numerical data [94]. It claims that many events in nature occur as collections of numbers, in which the leading significant digit is likely to be small[95].

The law was tested on various parameters, including the surface area of 335 rivers, 3259 US populations, 104 physical constants, the molecular weights of 1800 elements, 5000 entries in a mathematics handbook, 308 numbers in a Reader's Digest issue, the street addresses of the first 342 people listed in American Men of Science, and the death rates of 418 populations. A total of 20,229 observations were presented in the paper. In the sets that obeyed the law, the number 1 was the most significant digit, as it made an appearance 30% of the time, and the number 9 was the least significant digit, as it appeared less than 5% of the time [96].

Interestingly, Dan found out that this law applies to many events that we may believe to be entirely random such as electricity bills, street addresses, stock prices, house prices, population numbers, death rates, and physical and mathematical constants [97]. For example, if we examine the distribution of the first digits in the population of the 237 countries of the world or the heights of the 60 tallest structures in the world, we will find that they follow this law. This law also calls attention to the "order in true randomness in nature," which is a somewhat difficult-to-grasp thought. Dan wondered how people were already aware of its existence close to 100 years ago. Also, can this law be applied to any and all phenomena? Like other general laws,

Benford's law can be used to explain many phenomena. However, there are many cases that are difficult to explain based on this law. For example, this law seems to be highly applicable to data that are distributed uniformly across several orders of magnitude. In fact, the higher the number of orders of magnitude over which the data are evenly distributed, the more accurately can Benford's law be applied [97]. So Benford's law would be applicable, for example, to a list of numbers representing the population of the UK or the values of small insurance claims. However, for small places with populations between 300 and 999 or low insurance claims between $50 and $99, the law may not be relevant [98]. Thus, for real-world distributions, such as in the case of large populations and stock market prices, which span over several orders of magnitude, Benford's law can be applied with high accuracy. In contrast, when it comes to the heights of human adults or IQ scores, which are distributed within only one order of magnitude, the law cannot be applied [99].

Many real-world applications of this law can be observed in phenomena with multiplicative fluctuations [99]. In the case of stock prices, they fluctuate daily. Over an extended period, as the distributions become more even, Benford's law can be applied with increasing accuracy. There are several mathematical rules which can be used to explain the concept of scaling up of distributions by multiplication, so that the law can be better applied.

Unlike multiplicative fluctuations, additive fluctuations may not be subjected to Benford's law, as they show normal distribution. For example, the number of heartbeats in an individual on one day can be expressed as the **sum** of several random variables, so this quantity is unlikely to follow Benford's law. By contrast, a possible stock price is the **product** of several random variables, so the price change factor for each day is likely to follow Benford's law quite well.

So in the case of IQ scores and human heights, the law does not apply because these variables follow a normal distribution that does not span several orders of magnitude. However, if one "mixes" numbers from those distributions with numbers from newspaper articles, Benford's law reappears. Dan found out that this can be proven mathematically. That is, if a probability distribution is repeatedly chosen "randomly," and then a number is chosen randomly according to that distribution, the resulting list of numbers will obey Benford's Law. A similar probabilistic explanation for the appearance of Benford's Law in everyday life numbers has been proposed by showing that it arises naturally when one considers mixtures of uniform distributions[100].

Dan discovered something very interesting about human nature. Based on the assumption that people who make up figures tend to distribute their digits reasonably uniformly, Benford's law can be used to detect possible frauds in lists of socio-economic data submitted in support of public-planning decisions; this was suggested by Hal Varian in 1972 [101]. Similarly, this law could be applied in criminal cases of accounting and others. In other words, one can use randomness for detection of misconduct [102]. This law was actually used to detect fraud in the 2009 Iranian elections[103].

Let's now get back to the our initial topic on misconceptions about randomness: another misconception that Dan discovered is called "the odds are never dynamic." For every incident, at its beginning, we calculate its probability. However, once we gain some information and experience in relation to the incident, we tend to re-calculate probabilities. This misconception can be explained in a simple way if consider the following example. If a woman has two children, one of which is a girl, what is the likelihood of the second one being a girl? If we calculate this based on the assumption that the second one is a new child, we may say that there is a 50% likelihood. However, if we come up with what is called a probability space, which considers all possible outcomes, the probability is only 33%. There are four possible gender combinations for two children: boy-boy, girl-boy, boy-girl, and girl-girl. Since we were told that the first child was a girl, the boy-boy combination can be eliminated. This leaves us with three options, boy-girl, girl-boy, girl-girl, in which only one of the scenarios allows for the possibility of the other child also being a girl, which translates to its likelihood being 33% [104]. Thus, when we have more information about a scenario and know how to use it, we can better predict the likelihood of events.

Another example is the Monty Hall problem [105], which was first introduced by Marilyn vos Savant in 1990:

A car is equally likely to be behind one of three doors. We select one of the three doors (Door #1). The host, who knows where the car is, reveals one non-selected door (Door #3) that does *not* contain the car. We can then choose whether to stick with our original choice (i.e., Door #1) or switch to the remaining door (i.e., Door #2). What is the probability of winning the car if we stick to our first choice versus if we switch? The surprising answer is that we have a probability of 1/3 of winning the car if we stick to our original choice, and a probability of 2/3 if we switch. Not convinced?

Let's start by assuming that Door #1 is the first choice. The host then reveals to us a door which does *not* contain the car, after which we switch to the remaining door. These are the possible scenarios in this situation:

i.   The car is behind Door #1. In this case, if we first pick Door #1 and then switch to the remaining door (#2 or #3) after the host opens either Door #2 or Door #3 to reveal that there is no car, we will end up LOSING.

ii.  The car is behind Door #2. In this case, if we first pick Door #1, the host will have to reveal that Door #3 is empty. This means that we will switch to Door #2, thus WINNING.

iii. The car is behind Door #3. If we pick Door #1, the host will have to reveal Door #2 to be empty. This will lead us to switch to Door #3, which will result in us WINNING.

Hence, in 2 of these 3 possibilities, we win if we switch.

Thus, Dan found out that information can alter the level of randomness, or that it is not truly random once information is provided. The lesson, therefore, is that when looking for things behind closed doors in our life, we must consider switching when we are provided with more information.

# CHAPTER 8
## Randomness is not chance

Dan asked his boss for a week off. Both his team and his boss noted that he was not in the throes of one of his usual preoccupations that tend to last for just one or two days. His mind seemed fixated on something deeper and more consuming.

Being a physicist, Dan tried to look for a solution among his "crowd." He tended to trust them more. The physicist Leonard Mlodinow of the California Institute of Technology has written a book about this called *The Drunkard's Walk* [106], in which he described it as the "Monty Hall Problem," which is also one of the many probability puzzles presented in this book. He uses these examples to show "how our lives are profoundly informed by chance and randomness and how everything from wine ratings and corporate success to school grades and political polls is less reliable than we believe." This book deals with the real nature of randomness or, of chance, by looking at both as psychological illusions that cause us to misjudge the world around us. The book aims to provide us with tools with which we can make better-informed decisions. Dan felt that Mlodinow was right about how randomness, chance, and probability affect our daily lives in almost every respect. "However," he asked himself, "if I believe that randomness, at least, on some occasions leads to a favorable event and may be a contributing factor to creativity, should I keep aiming to attain these somewhat 'illuminative states'?"

Dan was not sure about whether randomness and chance are the same thing. And what about the whole issue of probabilities? He decided to dedicate his week to this issue. This was not an easy task, as he discovered after a few hours of web surfing.

He started by delving into relevant pages of the Stanford Encyclopedia of Philosophy. Let me give them a *chance*, he thought, as he smiled to himself, without recognizing the implicit pun. The chapter was long, but it seemed to be comprehensive as it also quoted several physicists.

Randomness, as it is normally conceived, occurs in situations where certain outcomes happen haphazardly, unpredictably, or by chance. Each of these notions is distinct and has a different meaning. All of them, Dan felt, must have some close connection to probability [40]. Furthermore, probability by itself could be subjective or evidential, or it could be real chance. Both subjective and evidential probability is also associated with randomness.

Dan was somewhat confused, but felt that he was on the right track. The question on his mind now was how randomness and chance, or physical probability, are connected.

The word "random" is regularly used more or less interchangeably with "chancy." In fact, according to the Commonplace Thesis (CT), , something is considered to be random if it happens by chance [40]. This theory states that all chancy outcomes are random. Dan was trying to analyze this from the perspective of a physicist. He felt that the somewhat relaxed way in which chance and randomness were used interchangeably in ordinary and scientific communications, which is corroborated by the Commonplace Thesis, may be misleading. Randomness should be viewed as something that is different from chance.

The commonplace theory states that the process of random sampling does not necessarily require the presence of a genuine chance. In the case of random sampling, therefore, a probabilistic explanation may be valid. There are certain consequences if the commonplace thesis is disproven and if ordinary usage is found to be incorrect. For example, it is intuitively reasonable that if an event is indeed random, it cannot be explained. Therefore, it follows that if it happens for a reason, it is not truly random [40]. On the other hand, if randomness requires chance, then no statistical inferences that are made by "randomly" sampling a large population are valid, unless the experimental design involves genuine chance in the selection of subjects. However, the rationale for random sampling may not require chance sampling. When the sample is representative, such statistical inferences may be reliable. In that case, the random sampling has nothing to do with randomness [40].

Scientists use chance or randomness to mean that when physical causes can result in any of several outcomes, we cannot predict what the outcome will be in any particular case [107]. Some philosophers connect chance and randomness deliberately. They claim that the universe is inherently probabilistic and full of random happenings [108]. However, there are others who oppose this claim [40].

Dan also learned about the *"frequentist* approach" to objective probability, which claims that the chance of an outcome occurring is represented by its frequency in an appropriate series of outcomes [109]. Further, according to frequentists, the series of outcomes should be random, without pattern or order.

Another important finding was that real randomness and biased randomness are two separate entities. Dan decided to explore this later on. For now, it was enough that it was clear to him that chance and randomness are two separate entities, and that there exists true randomness as well as biased randomness.

Dan was aware that randomness is used in computing. In fact, after randomness was introduced into computing, how defects in the sources of randomness influence computation outcomes was studied. Similarly, there are many means by which sources can deviate from perfect randomness. In the majority of models, the strategy of the source is chosen from a given repertoire, using which the randomized algorithm is disrupted [110]. In the stochastic model of a randomized algorithm, biases in randomness can arise from an agent, a source, controller, or adversary [111].

This research led Dan to random and biased random walks. If we look at the long-term behavior of a random walk on a finite graph, biases can limit its behavior [110]. Based the assumption of a real, non-negative, "benefit" for each state, the controller strives to maximize the anticipated long-term benefit. In the field of network science, a time path process on a graph wherein an evolving variable jumps from its current state to one of various potential new states is considered as a biased random walk; further, probabilities of the potential new states are unequal. This is entirely different from a pure random walk[112]. Biased random walks can be used for the structural analysis of undirected graphs, as they can be used to extract the symmetries of graphs when the network is too complicated or not large enough to be analyzed by statistical methods. The concept of biased random walks on a graph can be applied to transportation and social networks, diffusion control, advertisement of products on social networks, explaining dispersal and population redistribution of animals and micro-organisms, community detections, wireless networks, and search engines[113, 114].

Dan discovered the bacteria walk as a good example of the application of biased random walks. The random movement of these small motile creatures is characterized by straight runs that are punctuated by brief periods of reversal that serve to randomize the direction of the next run [115]. There are systems which control these runs, and these systems can result in adherence to or rejection of a move in a specific direction. This system controls the probability of a reversal. If during a run, the system determines that conditions are improving, it sends a signal to the motor that suppresses reversals so that the cell keeps moving in the preferred direction. If, on the other hand, the system determines that conditions are getting worse, it sends a signal to the motor to change direction. The effect is to bias the random walk so that the cells migrate toward attractants and away from repellents [115]. This movement of bacteria uses environmental cues to modulate the probability of random changes in direction. By using this mechanism, individual cells never have to determine in which direction they want to move. Instead, they merely determine whether they want to continue along a particular course or change direction. The biased random walk strategy is essential to bacterial movement because it provides a mechanism whereby bacteria can direct their motion despite the fact that their cells are too small to have a sense of direction [115].

Symbolically, one can look at biased randomness as randomness that is biased with or without our awareness of it, in response to various environmental signals. So what seems to be random, may indeed not be so; instead, it may be biased by factors that are not under our control.

Dan summarized to himself: if I think of something as random, I may not be aware of any factors around me that may affect it. This means that it is not truly random but biased. This implies that humans are not much smarter than microscopic bacteria. We live in a world that we believe to be random, not noticing that there are many factors which affect it that we are not aware of.

Satisfied with this understanding of true randomness and biased randomness, Dan turned his attention to chance and probabilities.

He discovered that many years ago, a distinction between two types of probability was made. "Probability11" refers to an epistemic notion that is nowadays termed *evidential* probability, *credence* or degree of belief. The second type is "probability22," which refers to a non-epistemic, real probability, also known as *chance [116]*.

Chance is not a technical term, but rather an ordinary concept deployed in familiar situations: games of chance, complicated and unpredictable scenarios, large ensembles of similar events, and many others [40]. Philosophers are looking at and using chance for producing "interpretations" of probability. However, there are certain constraints to the use of chance as probability. For one, the mathematics of chance need to conform to the standard mathematics of probability. Moreover, chance should be objective: it should be mind-independent and not epistemic or evidential [117].

Dan found out that there are many theories about chance. Non-reductionists view chance as an independent fundamental feature of reality, while reductionists assume that the values of chances are determined entirely by other features of reality [40]. Further, some look at chance as something that concerns outcome; that is, they believe that it is conditional and is dependent on the degree of belief in the evidence.

It made much sense to Dan that chance is associated with possibility. If an outcome has some chance of occurring, then it is possible that the outcome occurs; this is called the Basic Chance Principle (BCP)[118]. Chance is also associated with actual frequencies to the extent of permitting frequencies to be evidence for the values of chances [119]. However, Dan learned that chance should not be identified with frequency: as a fair coin can produce any sequence of outcomes, there is no possibility of identifying chance as the observed frequency. That is, with regard to the association of frequency and chance, any frequency at all is not sufficient [40].

Even when there are very few instances of the relevant process that leads to an outcome, there is still a chance of that outcome occurring. In that case, the actual frequencies may be misleading or trivial. The relevance of frequencies in identical trials is derived from the assumption that in such similar trials, the same chances exist [40, 117].

Dan used to think of chance as a "single-case objective probability." He learned that this is misleading, as it falsely suggests that multiple cases have fewer claims to their chances. In reality, at least on some occasions, an outcome has a chance of being a consequence of an instance of a certain process, even when no other trials of the process occur [40]. Therefore, chances are relatively independent of frequencies, which in turn require single-case chance. For some single outcomes, such as the next toss of a coin that is biased ⅔ towards heads, only very few assignments of confidence are reasonable [40].

Chance can be viewed as a *process* notion, rather than being entirely determined by features of the outcome. Dan came across the following example: In the case of a coin toss, assuming that there is a single-case chance of 1212 for the coin landing heads, even if there is only one actual toss and it lands tails, then the chance cannot be fixed by properties of the outcome "lands heads," as that outcome does not exist. This implies that chance is founded in properties of the process that can result in the outcome: in the coin-tossing trial, these properties include the mass distribution of the coin and the particulars of the manner in which it is tossed, as well as the underlying conditions and laws controlling the trial [40].

Dan did not believe in chance. However, deep inside, he had always wondered about it: When Jenny died, his children talked about chance... bad luck...but he told them not to mention it in front of him, even though he had started to ponder about this.

Whether or not an incident occurs by chance is a property of the process that has produced it, and not a property of the incident itself. If a coin lands heads, it does not mean that the incident occurred by chance: consider that it was placed heads up and not tossed to land heads; here, the outcome is the same, but it has not occurred by chance. So whether an outcome occurs by chance is determined by the properties of the process that leads up to it or the causal context within which it occurs; it is not as simple as a particular event being the product of that particular process[40].

Dan was beset by the question of whether chances actually exist.

He realized that the best examples of probability functions that correspond with the principles of chance are those provided by physics. For example, the probability functions that feature in radioactive decay and quantum mechanics have some claim to being chance functions [40]. In fact, in quantum mechanics, some measurements of a system in a given state will not yield a result that represents a specific feature of that prior state [120]. The inability of results to reflect any prior condition of the system can be explained by various *no-hidden variables* theories, such as Bell's theory [121, 122].

Bell's theory states that the probabilities predicted by quantum mechanics for spin measurements of a two-particle entangled but spatially separated system are not equal to the joint probabilities of two independent one-particle systems. This means that an entangled system cannot be represented as the product of two independent localized systems with determinate prior states. Therefore, there is no local account of the probabilities of measurement outcomes, and the probabilities are essential features of the quantum mechanical systems themselves [40]. This means that the measurement process itself induces the transition or "collapse" of a system from a non-deterministic state into a determinate state with regard to a given quality. The probabilities of this transition are completely dependent on the state of the system and the process of collapse, based on which these probabilities by a stable trial principle.

Quantum mechanics permits two systems that are in the same state to evolve via collapse into any state which has a non-zero prior probability in the original state. The no-hidden variables theories suggest that there is no better information about the system that can shed credible light on any future states than chances; this is what makes probabilities apt in this context. Thus, these basic quantum probabilities governing state transitions can be termed "chances" [40]. The existence of probabilistic theories that cannot be plausibly reduced to any non-probabilistic theories is evidence of the existence of chances. Quantum probabilities have been generated from subjective uncertainty, in the absence of a first chance. This is further evidence for the existence of chances [123].

The conventional view of classical physics, including statistical mechanics, is that a primary probability does not exist, because the state transition dynamics itself is the deterministic factor. However, this contradicts the existence of chances [124].

All this information was too much for Dan. He felt that he lacked the knowledge required to understand it fully. Once again, he decided to keep this topic aside for later study.

As mentioned somewhere earlier on in this chapter, some philosophers use "random" to mean "chancy." A random process, in their view, is one governed by chance. They make statements such as "I group random with stochastic or chancy, taking a random process to be one which does not operate wholly capriciously or haphazardly but in accord with stochastic or probabilistic laws" [125]. This sounded somewhat redundant to Dan [40]. He felt that the term "random" should be reserved for more irregular looking outcomes.

Dan learned that we could distinguish between the randomness of the process generating an outcome that sums to its being a chance process and the randomness of the *product* of that random process. If we consider a typical case of randomness such as one thousand consecutive tosses of a fair coin, we can expect, with very high confidence, to toss at least one head. However, as that outcome has some chance of not occurring, it is accounted for by process randomness even when it does occur. In such a case, the process is random, while the outcome 'at least one head in 1000 tosses' is not a random product [40].

Dan realized that in the case of product randomness, "random" is used to characterize an entire collection of outcomes of a given repeated process. A random sample is random when there is an unbiased representation of the population from which it is drawn. It is a property of the entire sample, not of each member. A random sample should therefore be irregular in terms of the population variables of interest [40]. A random sample is one that is considered to be *typical* of the underlying population from which it is drawn. This means that it exhibits no order or pattern which is not exemplified in that underlying population. Many random samples are drawn using a random process, but they need not be. For example, if we set out to prove that the last digit of a person's minute of birth is not related to the income of their family, we could do so by choosing a random sample of family incomes from among individuals with birth minute ending in the number 7. However, the process here would not be random in any way. Instead, to ensure the randomness of a sample, random numbers should be used to determine whether an individual should be included in the sample. This conception of randomness is associated with collections of outcomes and is termed *product randomness* [126].

Product randomness plays a role in scientific inference. If we have a set of regular data, we may attempt to use it to derive a deterministic theory of the phenomenon that the data represent. On the other hand, if the data are irregular and entirely random, we can come up only with a stochastic theory. As we may not have knowledge of whether a phenomenon is chancy, it is essential to be able to determine whether the data are random or not [40]. We might think that this could be achieved simply by examining the data for patterns that will be apparent to the observer. However, psychological research has repeatedly shown that humans are imperfect in discerning patterns, seeing them in completely random data and failing to see them in non-random data [127-129].

Through this session of his research, Dan learned that not everything which intuitively seems to be random is indeed so. An objective account of the randomness of a sequence of outcomes is necessary for reliable scientific inference, and this also applies to any theories or assumptions we make in our lives.

The next phase of his study called for some investigation into biased randomness, which led him back to The Stanford Encyclopedia of Philosophy [40].

# CHAPTER 9
## Randomness versus biased randomness

Dan was looking up a *sequence of outcomes in* The Stanford Encyclopedia of Philosophy [40], which defined it as an ordered collection of events, finite or infinite. The set of all *infinite* binary sequences of outcomes was defined as the *Cantor space*. An example of a process that leads to formation of a Cantor space is an infinite sequence of independent tosses of a fair coin, where 1 denotes heads and 0 tails [40]. Each infinite sequence, whether it is orderly or not, is assigned a standard measure of zero over the Cantor space. Therefore, we cannot determine whether an individual sequence is random based on what fraction it constitutes of the set of all such sequences. Intuitively, however, most infinite sequences should be random and disorderly, and only a few will be orderly [130]. A *typical* infinite sequence is considered as one that does not have a pattern. But there are exceptional cases, of course, in which these sequences have a pattern. Also, if the process that is used to create the sequences is completely deterministic, a typical product resulting from that process would not be random. Nonetheless, it can be assumed that most of the sequences produced as part of an infinite sequence will be random. Classes of sequences which include only a small number of events. In the coin toss example, if heads comes up a hundred times in a row, this appears extraordinary because the almost infinite number of combinations that can arise in a hundred throws are divided into regular sequences, which are incomparably more numerous [131] [40].

Random sequences should be *unruly* and *familiar as well*. The set of *non*-random sequences should have a measure of zero and should be proportional to the set of all such sequences; correspondingly, the set of random sequences should have a measure of one [132, 133].

The *typicality* approach to randomness means that if a sequence is genuinely random in the long run, it has features that can be associated with the outputs of independent, identically distributed trials of a chancy process. The sequence should look as disorderly as if it were the expected product of genuine chance. Here, *typicality* is defined in relation to a prior probability function. What is the probability of a typical series of toss outcomes with a fair coin not being a typical series of toss outcomes with an unfair coin? [134] [40]

A typical sequence needs to satisfy the properties of stochasticity [135], such as the property of large numbers. Further, the frequency limit of a digit in a random sequence should not be biased to any particular value.

For a sequence to be considered as random, satisfying the property of large numbers alone is not sufficient. For example, if we look at the sequence 10101010...., it does not seem to be biased. However, it cannot be considered as random either, as it evolves in a regular and predictable manner. For this sequence to be random, certain constraints will need to be imposed, and it follows that these constraints should correspond to the properties of stochasticity and other properties of "unbiasedness" [40].

One such useful constraint is *Borel normality*, which can eliminate any predictable patterns in the sequence. *Borel normality* is a sequence within which each finite string of digits of equal length has an equal frequency in the sequence. Borel proved that sequences with a measure of one in Cantor space meet the requirements for Borel normality. Such lack of predictability based on previous elements is a prerequisite for true randomness [40].

Borel normality alone is not sufficient for randomness. As Dan learned, the *Champernowne* sequence (the sequence of digits with binary representations of each successive non-negative integer, that is, 0110111 00101110111...011011100101110111...) exhibits Borel normality but is entirely predictable because the elements of the sequence follow a general pattern and can therefore be predicted even though it cannot be predicted based on prior elements of the sequence [136] [40].

A sophisticated approach to defining randomness for a sequence with a single stochastic property was proposed by von Mises [137]. We are presented with a subsequence of a sequence of numbers and asked to predict the value of one of them. If the sequence was truly random, then any information about previous elements of the sequence and the position of the desired outcome would be of no use to us. If we assume otherwise, we are assuming that there is an exploitable regularity in the so-called random sequence. The proof for this lies in the failure of gambling systems to crack games of chance. Thus, this means that it is not possible to have a biased selection of members from an honestly random sequence [40]. Von Mises defines a random sequence as one in which every infinite subsequence selected by an admissible place selection retains the same relative digit frequencies as in the original sequence. Thus, it is impossible to select a biased subsequence and present it as exhibiting a particular property of stochasticity [137].

In the case of von Mises' random (vM-random) sequences, the most extensive set which contains only infinite sequences with the right frequency limit is closed under all admissible place selections. If the frequency limit of a digit is 1, for example, in the sequence 111...111..., then every permissible place selection determines a subsequence with the same frequency limit. According to von Mises, this is what a random sequence of trial outcomes with a probability of obtaining the outcome 1 looks like. However, this sequence does not fulfill the property of large numbers. vM-random sequences are thus the most extensive set of infinite sequences with a frequency limit of 1212 that is closed under all proper place selections [40].

Dan was thinking again of gambling. A gambling system should be represented mathematically, not as a function, but as a practical algorithm for the calculation of the values of a function [138]. Admissible place selections should be not arbitrary functions, but *efficiently computable* functions of the other outcomes in a sequence. We admit only those place selections which are *computable* functions. This applies to the von Mises sequences, which have arbitrary non-zero outcome frequencies for each type of outcome. Thus, to achieve random sequences, we should restrict standard binary sequences to those for which the limiting relative frequency of each outcome is 1212 [40].

The property of large numbers shows that almost all infinite binary sequences have a frequency limit of 1212 for each digit. However, it says nothing about how quickly this convergence happens or about the statistical properties of the initial segments. In the "random walk" model of random sequences, a sequence that fulfills the property of large numbers would be represented as a walk that ends up back at the origin but always stays to the right. Intuitively, such a sequence is not random [40]. In fact, such sequences violate at least one property of stochasticity.

*According to the law of symmetric oscillation,* a measure of one set of sequences will fall above the mean an infinite number of times and below the mean an infinite number of times [132]. This law can be applied to a measure of one set of sequences and is a reasonable property of randomness. Thus, von Mises' definition of place selections cannot be used to characterize random sequences precisely because it includes sequences that violate this law, and do not correspond to a truly random "random walk."

Dan started researching how others were trying to resolve the issue of selecting truly random sequences.

Von Mises and Church identified a class of sequences with frequency limits that were non-variant under recursive place selections. This class satisfied a number of the measure-one stochastic properties of sequences that are thought to be characteristic of randomness. However, the class of sequences they identified was too broad[40].

Martin-Löf realized that rather than look for another *single* property of sequences that would require the sequence to meet all the further conditions on randomness, it would be simpler to adopt the definition that a sequence is random if the sequence has all of the measure one properties of randomness that can be specified. *"Measure one" property of randomness can be specified* in a way that meets the requirement for a satisfactory procedure for testing whether a sequence violates the property [135]. Martin-Löf randomness is used to define a random sequence that cannot be efficiently determined to violate a measure one randomness property[139, 140]. Thus, "a random sequence could be defined as one that does not belong to any effective "measure-zero" set of sequences and thus belongs to every useful measure-one set of sequences" [40]. A valid "measure-zero" set of sequences will contain sequences that can efficiently be determined to have a "special hallmark," such as having a "1" at every seventh place. Von Mises' insight is that no random sequence will possess any of these conclusively determinable particular hallmarks. However, Martin-Löf noticed that all commonly used measure-one properties of stochasticity are useful to measure one. Any sequence that violates the property of large numbers, or the law of symmetric oscillations, will do so at increasingly long initial subsequences. Violation of any such property may be a mark of a non-random sequence. It may also indicate that the sequence which possesses such a property is an unusual one. Since the unusual properties of non-stochasticity are useful to measure zero, random sequences can be considered as those that are not unique in any conclusively determinable way [40].

Dan was looking for tests of randomness that could be used to determine whether something is random or not. It was clear to him that in most probability, no effectively computable sequence is random, and that no useful test might exist to check whether a given sequence is identical to some random sequence.

There is a universal test for assessing Martin-Löf (ML) randomness. Only a measure-zero set of infinite binary sequences are known to fail this test, and most that do are considered to be ML-random [40]. Although this test does define a useful "measure-one" property, this is not exactly a naturally graspable property. Martin-Löf's result establishes that there are random sequences which satisfy all the properties of stochasticity and that, in fact, almost all binary sequences are random in that sense. All ML-random sequences satisfy the law of symmetric oscillations [141]. Furthermore, they all have the right relative frequency limits since they satisfy the useful "measure-one" property of large numbers [40].

Intuitively, random sequences do not have regular patterns that any finite algorithm, no matter how sophisticated, must exploit to produce an infinite sequence [40]. Dan looked again into the Kolmogorov complexity, according to which a random sequence is defined as one for which the shortest algorithm that produces it is approximately the same length as the sequence itself, and the algorithm cannot be further compressed. Kolmogorov,

Chaitin, and Solomonov further characterize randomness as the algorithmic or informational *complexity* of a sequence [142]. Kolmogorov showed that there is an optimal decompression algorithm which is nearly superior to any other program [142, 143]. This means that a random sequence of a given length cannot be produced efficiently.

Kolmogorov randomness fits with the intuition about the disorder-liness of random sequences derived from the Martin-Löf account. It also fits with the notion that random sequences can be described by algorithms that are shorter than the sequence themselves, so there is no indication of the sequences having been produced according to a pre-determined plan. Kolmogorov randomness is also in agreement with von Mises' intuition that randomness is linked to the impossibility of gambling systems. To reiterate, there is no way of efficiently producing a given random sequence of outcomes using a set of initially given data any smaller than the sequence itself [40]. Thus, it is not possible to predict a genuinely random sequence because it is not possible to efficiently produce a random sequence. However, a predictable sequence of outcomes can be intuitively produced if it is specified how future outcomes can be predicted based on prior outcomes [40].

Efficient coding, such that no acceptable input is an initial substring of another acceptable input, is considered to be "prefix-free." It is called such because no member is a prefix of any other member. Consider the encoding of telephone numbers: the telephone exchange can, on the input of a string of digits that it recognizes, immediately connect us. Once an acceptable code from a prefix-free set has been input, no other acceptable code can follow it. There exist prefix-free random sequences, as there exist plain random sequences. Further, since a prefix-free encoding is of greater length than the sequence, the prefix-free code of an ordinary random sequence will be longer than an arbitrary code of it, and thus random, too. The label "Kolmogorov random" is generally used to refer to prefix-free Kolmogorov random sequences. Both plain and prefix-free Kolmogorov randomness provide satisfactory accounts of the randomness of finite sequences [40].

For any sufficiently long string, there will be some compressible initial segments. This dip in the complexity of an initial subsequence will occur infinitely often in even a random infinite sequence, and this phenomenon is known as "*complexity oscillation*" [144]. The best that can be done is to find upper and lower bounds that express ordinary Kolmogorov complexity between which the set of ML-random sequences fall. While the complexity of some initial segments is known to dip, it always remains more significant than the length of the prefix [40].

Different intuitive starting points have been known to generate the same set of random sequences. ML-randomness or equivalently prefix-free. Kolmogorov randomness is the intuitive notion of randomness, in much the same way as the coincidence of Turing machines, Post machines, and recursive functions was taken to be evidence for *Church's theory*, which claims that any one of these notions captures the intuitive notion of effective computability [40].

Schnorr randomness has been preferred to Martin-Löf randomness on account of its intuitive notion [145]. Further, it represents a convergence of ML-randomness and Kolmogorov randomness [146], and is also known to be compressible. ML-random sequences are believed to be a strict subset of Schnorr random sequences; it therefore follows that any problematic members of the former are also problematic members of the latter. However, there are certain Schnorr random sequences that fail some Martin-Löf statistical tests [40].

Is there a single precise notion of randomness that answers correctly to our natural conception of random sequences? Based on his reading of the topic, Dan was led to conclude that there may be "no single definition of randomness which can do the work of capturing every mathematically significant collection of typical points" [140]. The contradictory nature of this issue began to dawn on him. Nonetheless, Dan found Kolmogorov-Martin-Löf randomness to be a reasonable and representative example of the algorithmic approach to randomness that overlaps with almost all other plausible definitions of randomness. Overall, it is considered to be a useful working account of the randomness of sequences [40].

Dan was wondering again about how one could differentiate the some-what sophisticated notion of randomness from chance?

Randomness is fundamentally a product notion, which is applied to sequences of outcomes. On the other hand, a chance is a process notion, which is applied in every individual case to the process or chance setup which produces a token outcome. Chance, according to the conception of philosophers, is much closer to the common perception of chance among people [40].

Based on calculations of standard probability, any sequence of outcomes is itself an outcome. However, we are presented with a problem if we consider chancy outcomes in possible situations in which only very few events ever occur. Events which occur by chance may all be of the same type, in which case the sequence of outcomes is not considered as random. This problem resembles the "problem of the single case" for frequency views of chance. Randomness, like frequency, is described as a property of an outcome sequence [109]. Thus, problems may arise when the outcomes are too few or too orderly to accurately represent the randomness of the sequence that they are part of [40].

It is known that infinite random sequences have at least some non-random initial subsequences. A standard solution in the case of frequentism was to opt for a possible outcome sequence, which is a sequence of outcomes produced under the same conditions with a stable frequency limit [137].

An outcome happened by chance when the trial which generated that outcome was repeated often enough under the same conditions. One can obtain a random sequence including the outcome. This means that chancy outcomes would, if repeated often enough, produce an appropriately homogenous sequence of outcomes that is random. If the trial is repeated often enough, this sequence would be the actual sequence of outcomes. Kolmogorov randomness permits finite sequences to be random [40]. Thus, fair coins, when tossed often enough, can give rise to random sequences. The existence of a random sequence of outcomes is compelling evidence for the existence of chance. In the case of a finite random sequence, it could be inferred that the outcomes comprising the sequence happened by chance. However, there are some counterexamples to this, such as sequences of apparently chancy outcomes in the absence of randomness and apparent random outcomes in the absence of chanciness [40].

In the case of genuine chance, there is no evidence to indicate what the sequence of outcomes might be: "There is no telling whether the coin would have landed head up on a toss that never takes place. That is what probability is all about" [147].

Many philosophers are skeptical about the existence and tractability of the possible sequences apparently required by Commonplace Thesis (CT), which claims that something is random if it happens by chance. However, CT could fare better than hypothetical frequentism, as CT does not propose the *analysis of* the chance of possible sequences. According to the law of large numbers, chance processes could produce specific outcome frequencies, within the limit, with a probability of 1. Further, such outcome sequences may also behave in a way that proves the CT [40].

I need to go deeper into brain issues, Dan thought to himself.

# CHAPTER 10

## The neuroscience of randomness and creativity: We are human beings, not robots!

Dan was not a great fan of biology, but his quest to understand randomness inevitably led him to the human brain.

In an exciting paper published in the Scientific American called "How randomness rules our world and why we cannot see it" [148], an analogy is drawn between "the paths molecules follow as they fly through space, incessantly bumping, and being bumped by, their sister molecules" and "our lives, our paths from college to career, from single life to family life, from the first hole of golf to eighteenth." Dan did not like to impose the laws of physics or biology on psychology, and avoided this type of intuitive thinking as much as possible. This time, however, he did like the allegations. He very quickly learned that there are countless random collisions occuring that tend to cancel one another out because of the law of large numbers: "where improbable events will probably happen given enough time and opportunity, every once in a great while, when pure luck occasionally leads to an uneven majority of hits from some particular direction, a noticeable jiggle occurs" [148]. Based on this logic, Michael Shermer hypothesizes that as human beings we notice the improbable "directional jiggle" but tend to ignore the billions of meaningless and counteracting collisions. He suggests that our brains are not evolved enough for probability networks, and thus, we are unable to intuitively deal with many aspects of the modern world.

Dan was not sure about whether he agreed with the notion that most of us use intuition to deal with other people and social relationships. But he believed that these instincts can mislead us when it comes to probabilistic problems, such as gambling in a casino. However, for most of us, the "gambling" we engage in when making everyday decisions in our lives is more important. Some of these decisions are not critical, such as selecting the flavor of an ice-cream, while others are more critical, such as who to marry.

Mathematical principles can be used to explain many life events. For example, in the case of gamblers, they are seen to use both the "hot hand fallacy" and the "dueness fallacy" although they are aware that the roulette wheel has no memory. Hot hand fallacy is the phenomenon that a person who experiences a successful outcome with a random event has a greater probability of success in further attempts. Further, the "law of small numbers" explains why successful producers who are fired after a few box-office bombs go on to make subsequent blockbuster films after the firing [148]. Vice versa, athletes who appear on *Sports Illustrated's* cover are known to experience career dips: this is explained by the "regression to the mean," according to which the typical performance that landed them on the cover is itself a low-probability event that is hard to repeat.

Dan thought that indeed good and bad, wanted and unwanted astonishing events do not always require extraordinary causes. They can happen by chance if we wait long enough. Unfortunately, we all do not live long enough to win the lottery by chance.

Dan found an interview with Mlodinow, who said "We can improve our skill at decision making and tame some of the biases that lead us to make poor judgments and poor choices. We can learn to judge decisions by the spectrum of potential outcomes they might have produced rather than by the particular result that occurred" [148]. The conclusion was "Embrace the random. Find the pattern. Know the difference."

Still, if randomness has advantages, we may not necessarily want to clinch it.

In an unusual post in Neuroscience News, the subject of neuroscience and randomness has been discussed [149]: the post was called "How the brain 'plays' with predictability and randomness to choose the right time to act." It summarizes a study which reveals that the execution of an action is a combination of random and predictable components that are processed in different brain regions [150]. Deciding when to take action can be as important as deciding what action to take. Even under entirely controlled settings, such as in a laboratory, the timing of a subject's decisions is impossible to predict accurately. Timing is an essential part of a decision, and if it is random, it is expected to affect the result. The results of the study showed that the exact moment of the execution of an action is the combination of predictable and unpredictable components that are processed by different regions of the brain [150].

How does the brain manage to optimize the timing of actions to the circumstances while still retaining a good measure of unpredictability?

In an interview in Neuroscience News, the leading researchers of the study said, "Our goal was to better understand the mechanisms in the brain that determine the timing of actions. We were especially interested in understanding how action timing often shows great variability and apparent randomness, even when the conditions are held constant" [149]. To study this, they trained animals to perform a task that tested their patience. In response to a tone, the animals were required to decide whether they should move to a water dispenser. However, if the animals were patient enough to wait for a second tone, which was sounded after a random amount of time, before moving to the dispenser, they received substantially more water than if they had sought their reward before hearing the second tone. As expected, the amount of time that the animals were willing to wait for the second tone before they sought the dispenser was partly predictable. In this case, there was a random component that added a substantial dose of unpredictability. When recording the brain areas, they found the involvement of both random and predictable components of action timing: "The most surprising finding was that one part of the brain has nothing to do with action timing randomness. It does not care about the random part, and there is a separation of function between different areas of the brain. We found that two different regions of the brain play different roles in the generation of action timing. One area appears to keep track of the ideal waiting time based on experience. A second area also keeps track of the ideal timing and also shows variability that renders individual decisions unpredictable. This is indicative of the 'separation of powers' within the brain [149].

So how do these two regions interact? The data from the study indicate that the generation of the deterministic component of action timing happens first and that the random (or "stochastic") component is then added. It is assumed that the variability does not "flow backward," or both regions would show variability. The researchers say that "A similar interplay between optimization and generation of variability underlies the theory of evolution. We have begun to see how this plays out in the brain."

The selection and timing of actions are subject to determinate influences such as sensory signals, the internal state, and the expertly stochastic variability. The study shows how neural circuits in one part of the brain determine action timing when performing a waiting task. They found that there are two regions necessary for this behavior, and the results show an unexpected functional dissociation. A particular part of our brain is responsible for a waiting task, a different area encodes deterministic bias in action timing, and an additional area encodes stochastic variability in action timing. Distinct timescales of neural dynamics in the frontal cortex reflect different functions. This is indicative of distinct timescales in the two brain areas that are involved. The data support a two-stage model in which stochastic components of action timing decisions are operated by circuits downstream of those carrying deterministic bias signals.

In many situations, selecting the right time to act is crucial for a successful outcome. If we act too soon or too late, we may miss the target, miss an opportunity, and end up wasting time and energy. Dan was trying to understand the findings of this study in the context of his life, by inferring that learning from experience may assist in getting the timing right. Thus, it may be possible to adapt to a recent situation.

Would injecting "noise" in the timing of actions be counter-productive? If randomness is beneficial, it may pay to be unpredictable. If nature created the brain to be unpredictable, and we believe that nature is not against us, embracing randomness may indeed be beneficial.

In many sports, unpredictability is a way to win. In soccer, a skilled shooter can beat the goalkeeper if he can deliver the ball at an unpredictable time and location. Obviously, if the same action was performed in the same way, and at the same time, and everything was entirely predictable, we could be easily outwitted by competitors. Moreover, there would be no room for exploring better solutions, for creativity. We would all be robots with predictable actions. Nature does not want us to be robots.

In a PLoS News blog about neuroscience, there is an interesting discussion titled "As simple as random can be" by Jasmine Reggiani [151]. It starts by looking into the development of algorithms for trying to predict fluctuations in the stock market. Some economists will tell us that the market is not truly random and that "random mathematical models" can predict it. Different models, including sequences randomly drawn from log-normal distributions and chaotic systems, have been shown to have some predictive abilities. Jasmine Reggiani confesses, "I was fascinated by the idea of randomness as a model for complex systems. It seemed particularly interesting to explore this in the context of biological processes, especially when the laws of thermodynamics have described that all physical phenomena drift towards the chaotic state of maximum entropy. Could randomness be a model for circuit wiring and function in the brain?"

If we are not that fascinated by randomness in biological systems, we may be fascinated by it in our everyday life. Moreover, even if we are not that excited about it, maybe we want to know how to handle the randomness that we feel dictates some of the happenings in our lives or affects our decision-making abilities.

Larry Abbott from the Department of Neuroscience at Columbia University Medical Center gave a talk (quoted in the blog) at the Federation of European Neuroscience Societies Forum of Neuroscience [152], entitled "Random but crucial: How random brain wiring works." He described two distinct but very similar systems in which randomness may play a critical role in shaping the circuit and allow for its complexity.

Dan was thinking, "I may not like biological systems too much, but I may be able to learn something from them that could be applied not only to the way I select my ice-cream flavor but also to much more important decisions I need to make. Also, it does not mean that selecting from a restaurant menu is not essential."

In the brain, there is a specially structured network of connections between neurons, which are essential cells in our brain. These neuronal structures support particular functions. At the same time, there are other brain areas in which the brain cells appear to be completely randomly connected. There is scientific evidence in support of this: "some regions in the brain feature a high number of connections between neurons communicating back and forth and forming a 'recurrent network.' Others may have many neurons, yet fewer connections." [152] It follows that the activity of these brain areas may also be random. Dr. Abbott's studies have shown that these random connections work in surprisingly useful and sophisticated ways and that they are essential for brain function. Thus, randomness is not only evident in our everyday life, but is also part of our brain function.

Interestingly, using several models, this group of researchers found that randomness is crucial for healthy brain function. They discovered that some brain areas have a part that is wired in a completely unstructured way. However, some of these randomly wired areas can be associated with positive behaviors. Thus, the random areas in the brain also contribute to and even control its functions.

We need randomness.

Professor Abbott explained [152], "It is a challenge - how can we have a randomly wired system, and yet still use it for constructive purposes? How do we make sense of the world and produce appropriate responses by random circuitry? We have to interpret what looks like random events in our brain and associate them with things in the outside world. These circuits have mechanisms for doing that. Reality inside our heads is just a bunch of neurons firing. We constantly interpret these patterns of neural activity and can endow them with deep personal meaning. This process is mysterious. Brain circuits that allow random patterns of neural activity to gain meaning and acquire complex associations with behavior give us an opportunity to study this remarkable transformation in depth."

How does this occur? How does randomness contribute to specific functions or behaviors? Random circuits become valuable once our brain learns to interpret and associate them with stimuli in the outside world so that they make sense. For every learning system, one does not want to have a bias for a particular way of learning, and each of us has a different learning method. This means that for us to use the random systems we have in our brain, we need to apply stimuli that we absorb or incorporate parameters that we have learned and integrate them into our brain. Randomly wired circuits provide flexibility, so different people may come up with diverse or with similar solutions. Having this random highly flexible mechanism is healthy and crucial for our functions [152].

The type of brain cells studied in this research receives a surprisingly low number of inputs. These cells form three layers: an input layer that is highly organized and contains a limited number of sensory cells, an output layer that is equally organized and is linked to behavioral commands, and a middle layer with a high number of cells that at first glance appear randomly wired. This population of cells is very important for understanding randomness, as most other brain cells are connected at various locations by connectors called synapses that can be of varying strengths [151].

What does the random set of connections as described in these brain cells mean? [153] If we use the iPod shuffle analogy, it means that the connections these cells make with other brain cells are not more organized than shuffled combinations. So even if we know the input into these brain cells, we would not be able to predict which other cells these cells connect to [154]. The randomness of the connectivity patterns of these cells is believed to be critical to the body's ability to match sensory inputs to meanings and a variety of behavioral outputs. This complex wiring system enables learning by increasing dimensionality. Thus, cells in the brain can mix up inputs coming from a small number of cells, and can amplify their representation by at least one order of magnitude. This more complex and varied representation allows for a more straightforward categorization of the data at the level of behavioral output. Examining the connectivity of brain cells with random wiring showed that it is more diverse than random: the number of cells with the same combinations of inputs was below what is expected from chance. If we assume the number of synaptic inputs to be in the range of 1 to 6, a truly random system would have a higher probability of duplicated input combinations. This means that the system favors diversity over randomness.

Diversity is not randomness. It is described as a condition of having or being composed of differing elements [155]. So maybe randomness is just "a too simple model to understand the function of these so-called random functioning cells" [151].

Biological processes are all random: molecules bumping into one another, and cells in our brain such as neurons finding partners to connect with. Rules restrict or diversify these connection patterns, taking random processes and optimizing their functional potential.

What about the neuroscience behind creativity? In an article entitled "Creative Innovation: Possible Brain Mechanisms" [156], the researchers describe creativity as being associated with co-activation and communications between regions in the brain that are not intensely connected. The frontal lobe of the brain is described as being the most crucial region associated with creativity. Super creative people are known to have highly specialized knowledge, along with divergent thinking that is mediated by the frontal lobe of their brain, with an ability to control neurotransmitters such as norepinephrine in their frontal lobe. Interestingly, they also studied the possible association of creativity with sleep, mood and addiction disorders, and depression [157].

The three-factor model of creative drive suggests that it results from an interaction of the frontal lobes, the temporal lobes, and dopamine from the limbic system[158]. Any aberrations in the frontal lobe, including depression or anxiety, decrease creativity, while abnormalities in the temporal lobe often increase it. Interestingly, it was found that high activity in the temporal lobe inhibits activity in the frontal lobe, and vice versa. Further, high dopamine levels increase arousal and goal-directed behavior while reducing latent inhibition, thus increasing the drive to generate ideas.

Other studies have shown that creativity comprises the interaction between multiple neural networks, including those that support associative thinking, along with other default mode network functions [159]. The frontal lobes of the brain along with the part of the brain called the cerebellum collaborate to produce creativity[160]. The cerebellum consists of 100 billion neurons, which is more than the total number of neurons contained in the rest of the brain, and it adaptively models all bodily movement for efficiency. Its adaptive models for working memory process all of our thoughts, which are then fed back to the frontal lobe working memory control processes, where creative and innovative thoughts arise [161-163]. These concepts have been suggested to underlie innovations in sports, art, music, design of video games, technology, mathematics, and thought in general [164-166].

There is a theory which suggests that when we are confronted with a challenging new problem or situation, visual-spatial working memory and speech-related working memory are decomposed and re-composed by the cerebellum. They are blended in the cerebral cortex. When a person repeatedly attempts to solve difficult situations, the cerebro-cerebellar blending process optimizes the efficiency with which working memory deals with the situation or problem [162, 163, 167, 168]. The blending process continuously optimizes efficiencies and continually improves prototyping attempts towards creativity. Although this sounds interesting, it has also been criticized by other scientists [169].

Sleep helps creativity by assisting the formation of associative elements into new combinations. This is a result of changes in cholinergic and noradrenergic neuromodulation that occur during parts of our sleep [170]. Cognitive activity is positively affected by increases in the number of cognitive elements available for association. Increase in cognitive activity is associated with defocusing of attention and a more complex cognitive context, which increase the extent to which certain elements are treated as relevant to the problem. Increase in cognitive activity also increases cognitive flexibility, thus increasing the probability that diverse cognitive elements will, in fact, become associated [157] [171].

Studies have shown that watching a few minutes of a comedy film or receiving a small bag of candy can improve performance. Positive emotions can increase the number of cognitive elements available for association (attention scope) and the number of elements that are recognized as being relevant to the problem (cognitive scope) [172]; they may therefore be useful for our creativity.

According to one of the more stimulating theories of creativity, it is considered to be a by-product of a computational principle for assessing and optimizing learning progress [173]. There are extrinsic reward signals for achieving externally assigned goals, such as finding food when hungry. To maximize the effect, there are intrinsic rewards, which assist in creating a "wow effect." Creativity can be achieved without external goals. The wow effect is said to be generated when we create and predict actions and sensory inputs that are continually increasing and keep improving on them, via an artificial neural network or machine learning device that can exploit regularities in data to improve its performance over time. The resulting improvements can be assessed after learning. The wow effect can occur as a result of a sudden improvement in data compression or computational speed. It can be considered as an intrinsic reward signal. The objective function thus motivates the action optimizer to create action sequences that result in more wow effects [174]. Thus, according to this theory, the algorithm keeps learning and keeps improving.

Here is the problem with this theory: it claims that regularity underlines the process, while variable, random data, which may be considered to be "noise" in the system, does not result in any wow effect or learning progress, and is thus "boring" by nature, providing no reward. But is it so? Cannot the opposite be also true? Could random data create an even stronger wow effect? If so, it follows that the already known and predictable regularities are dull, and only the initially unknown, novel, regular (or maybe irregular) patterns in both actions and observations are temporarily interesting. This is eventually what motivates a person to perform continual, open-ended, active, creative exploration [157, 174, 175].

Dan started re-thinking these theories and looking at them from the point of view of a computer.

In the field of computer science, the focus is on automatically solving computational problems. Schmidhuber, who proposed the theory discussed above, aims to automatically invent or discover problems "in a way inspired by the playful behavior of humans, to train a more and more general problem solver from scratch in an unsupervised fashion"[174].

There are many types of computer-based algorithms designed for problem solving. An example is PowerPlay, which searches for possible pairs of new tasks and modifications of the current problem solver until it finds a more powerful problem solver that solves all the previously learned tasks as well as the new one, which the unmodified predecessor is incapable of solving. This type of algorithm may use the wow effect for solving new tasks, as it functions by improving the efficiency of previously learned skills is a way that needs less time and space. According to this concept, new skills may re-use previously learned skills. Isn't this what we all do? We attempt to apply our knowledge and understandings from experience into new situations and tasks that we confront. Isn't it a commonly held belief that old people are smarter because they have "life experience"?

In the case of computerized algorithms such as PowerPlay, new tasks and their corresponding task-solving skill are found and then validated.

Schmidhuber suggested that these models can explain the creativity of super creative scientists, artists, and comedians [173]. If we look at highly motivated scientists or composers, we see that they create experiments or music that have not been previously published or played. Creative composers receive an intrinsic reward for creating melodies with unexpected but regular harmonies that permit wow effects through data compression improvements. Schmidhuber claims that scientists and artists can scale up their creativity by implementing this theory [176].

Dan was smiling…we all think computers were created by humans, but sometimes, they can teach us something about ourselves.

# CHAPTER 10B

## Getting deep into the human brain

What can the computer algorithms that we have created (smart humans) tell us about our way of thinking? What is this broad learning mechanism and can we use it? Indeed, it has been indicated that these algorithms can shed light on creativity [177] [174].

A long-standing joke in Dan's team was "Which restaurant to go for lunch? Let us activate our deep learning algorithm."

Deep learning is a subfield of machine learning that is concerned with algorithms which are based on the structure and function of the brain; these algorithms are called artificial neural networks [178]. Deep learning involves large neural networks, and it requires considerable data and fast computers. Dan discovered an interesting blog, "What is Deep Learning?" where Jason Brownlee talks about Andrew Ng from Coursera and Chief Scientist at Baidu Research, which founded Google Brain. Google Brain uses deep learning technologies across a large number of Google services. The aim of using these computerized algorithms is to make them better so that we can make the most out of artificial intelligence.

Constructing large neural networks can train them to deal with large data sets. The more they are trained, the better their performance is. The idea is to prevent them from reaching a plateau in their performance: "Deep learning means scalable performance which keeps getting better as we feed them more data." "Deep" refers to the number of layers in these large networks. So the fundamental principle of deep learning is that results get better with more data, bigger models, and more computation. Deep learning can also be described as hierarchical feature learning. It involves new insights, more training, and better techniques.

Deep learning is all about supervised learning. However, Mr. Ng also made the point that "We should and will see more benefits coming from the unsupervised side of the tracks as the field matures to deal with the abundance of unlabeled data available" [178]. So even this super-ordered system, which learns from labeled data, can improve from something which sounds entirely random? Deep learning algorithms exploit unknown structures to discover useful representations, often at multiple levels, with higher-level learned features defined based on lower-level features[179]. In the deep learning hierarchy, features from higher levels are composed of features from lower levels. With the help of automatically learning features present at multiple levels, the system is capable of learning complex functions and mapping the input to the output directly based on the data[180]. In the case of hierarchical concepts, the concepts are formed on top of each other, and as a result, the computer can learn complicated concepts by creating them out of simpler ones[181].

Deep learning is based on learning data representations, as opposed to task-specific algorithms [182]. Some representations are loosely based on interpretations of information processing and communication patterns in a biological nervous system, such as neural coding, which attempts to define the relationship between various stimuli and their associated neuronal responses in the brain[183]. These methods are being applied in almost every field today including gaming, computer vision, speech recognition, natural language processing, audio recognition, social network filtering, machine translation, bioinformatics and drug design [184]. It is assumed that these algorithms can be used to obtain results that may be superior to those produced by human experts [185].

Artificial neural networks (ANNs) are computing systems inspired by the biological neural networks that constitute brains. These systems can improve their ability to perform tasks by learning from examples. For example, they learn to identify images that contain cats by analyzing example images that have been manually labeled as "cat" or "no cat." In other words, they learn from experience. These networks are based on a collection of connected units called artificial neurons, which are similar to axons in a brain. Each connection, or synapse, between neurons, can transmit signals to other neurons, which process the signal and transmit the response to downstream neurons in the network. As learning progresses, both neurons and their synapses vary, and accordingly, the strength of the signal that is transmitted downstream also varies [182]. Think of wires.

The neurons are also organized in layers. Different layers effect diverse changes in their inputs. Signals travel from the first layer to the last layer after traversing the layers multiple times. A deep neural network (DNN) is an artificial neural network with multiple hidden layers between the input and output layers [186]. The extra layers enable composition of features from lower layers, potentially modeling complex data with fewer units than a similarly performing shallow network.

What are the benefits of deep neural networks? This approach was designed to solve problems in the same way that we thought a human brain does. Later on, algorithms with abilities for backpropagation, passing information in reverse direction, and adjusting the network to reflect that information, were designed. It was thought to be a deviation from the way our brain functions [182].

Dan very quickly learned that these sophisticated systems are not without limitations. If you are one of those people who do not believe that a computer will ever be able to replace the human brain, you may agree with the words of Mr. Gary Marcus, a research psychologist, who wrote a few years ago that "Realistically, deep learning is only part of the larger challenge of building intelligent machines. Such techniques lack ways of representing causal relationships, have no obvious ways of performing logical inferences, and they are also a long way from integrating abstract knowledge, such as information about what objects are, what they are for, and how they are typically used" [187].

Dan tended to agree that deep learning algorithms were designed by humans based on some understanding of how our brain works, and that they would not be able to replace it. They can, however, help to do things humans cannot, using their ability to learn from significant data and analyze it in a way that can be of benefit.

In recent years, extensive artificial neural networks, including recurrent ones, were shown to be useful in both pattern recognition and machine learning. Traditionally, it is thought that the continually increasing range of problem-solving procedures can be misused by a parallel search for solutions to additional externally posed tasks. However, deep learning is distinguished by the depth of the credit assignment paths, which are chains of possibly learnable, causal links between actions and effects. It includes methods for deep supervised learning, unsupervised learning, reinforcement learning, and evolutionary computation [188].

No, there is no contradiction here. At the end of the day, if a computer algorithm wants to improve, it will need to be able to respond to reality, which is in many ways random. A computer could be better at responding to randomness as it learns from large data sets; this means that a computer could have the experience of millions of people, while every individual has only their own set of skills and the data they gain during their lifetime.

Dan was starting to imagine the future of these algorithmic developments. He was not a great fan of futurists, but sometimes, he did enjoy envisioning the future. He was thinking that at some point in the future, we might be able to download a free app to our cellphone that is connected to deep machine learning computers. We will only be asked to type in our problem, task, difficulty, and it will be solved, based on "world experience." This sounds quite efficient for purposes such as selecting the best car to fit our need. Some of us may also say that is may also lead to better results in selecting our spouse or friends, as the algorithm would be able to calculate genetic differences and several other parameters that we just cannot. A computer will thus win over us in many such tasks by producing better results with its better problem-solving abilities.

This app might be useful for creative problems too. In fact, some of the basic algorithms were designed for using these methods for the generation of creativity [174, 188, 189]. We may be able to use this application in situations where we need to become super creative or when dealing with tasks that are new and characterized by randomness.

We may think that our advantage over the app is that we know ourselves better. However, we must not fail to understand that the app knows things about us that we ourselves do not know. For example, it may have data on our genome, and more importantly, can analyze it and understand the implications of these genes in our life. It can also make predictions by comparing our eating or shopping habits, based on a database of billions of people.

Where does this leave us? One of our advantages over the app and it may be the only one, is the fact that our feelings are hard to predict. We may be able to think of several additional other advantages, for example, we may be able to be more creative and have better imagination than an app. In fact, our imagination is personal, and no one, not even the most robust computer, can compete with us on that.

# CHAPTER 11

## Look in the mirror and go on a brain trainer. Albert Einstein liked walking

Dan realized that randomness, creative people, and oddness are sometimes mentioned together. In fact, even mental health is increasingly being associated with creativity [157].

The psychologist J. Philippe Rushton described the correlation between creativity and both intelligence and psychoticism [190]. Creativity, as well as hypomanic personality, are more exceptional in schizotypal than in healthy or schizophrenic individuals [191]. Creativity was associated with mood disorders including manic-depressive disorder and depressive disorder. In the fascinating book, "Touched with Fire: Manic-Depressive Illness and the Artistic Temperament" [192], Kay Redfield Jamison describes mood disorders in such famous writers and artists as Ernest Hemingway, Virginia Woolf, the composer Robert Schumann, and the artist Michelangelo. However, these can be viewed as coincidental. We do not have to be, and may not want to become crazy while attempting to be more creative. A study of 300,000 persons with schizophrenia, bipolar disorder, or unipolar depression, and their relatives found that those with bipolar disorder as well as undiagnosed siblings of those with schizophrenia or bipolar disorder were overrepresented in creative professions. There was no overall overrepresentation, but overrepresentation in artistic occupations was observed among those diagnosed with schizophrenia [193].

There are many studies on the personality of creative people or the type of environments required to become one. The "Creativity Profiles" theory describes the following four traits: (i) Incubation: long-term development; (ii) Imagination: breakthrough ideas; (iii) Improvement: incremental adjustments; (iv) Investment: short-term goals. An additional four profiles was suggested by other researchers: (i) Idea Generation: fluency, originality, incubation and illumination; (ii) personality: curiosity and tolerance for ambiguity; (iii) motivation: intrinsic and extrinsic achievement; (iv) confidence: producing, sharing and implementing[194, 195].

Even if we believe we can answer yes to any of these, or all of these, we must remember that there is a big difference between a creative profile and making creativity happen. However, more importantly, there is a gap in predicting the creative profile of an individual, as characterized by the psychometric approach, and the evidence that team creativity is founded on diversity and difference[196]. Divergent production, or the ability to generate a diverse assortment, yet an appropriate amount of responses, to a given situation, is associated with creativity.

It may sound like creativity is something that hits us when lying on the beach or walking in the woods. However, many believe that creativity involves hard work. That is, hard-working people study the work of people before them, become experts in their fields, and build upon previous information in innovative and creative ways[197].

Motivation can predict creativity.

Intrinsic motivation can be described as the internal drive within a person to participate or invest in something based on their personal interest, desires, hopes, and goals. Extrinsic motivation, on the other hand, is external drive in the form of payment, rewards, fame, or approval from others. Both types of motivation can increase creativity[198]. Creative people tend to be more open to new experiences, and are more self-confident, ambitious, self-accepting, impulsive, driven, dominant, and hostile than people with less creativity [199, 200]. Throughout history, creative people have been known to have parents who were supportive but rigid and non-nurturing. Further, most had an interest in their field at an early age, as well as a highly supportive and skilled mentor in their field of interest. Most exceptionally, creative people devoted almost all of their time and energy to their craft, and after about a decade had a creative breakthrough of fame [201].

Dan was wondering, "so where is the randomness in all of this?"

He discovered that the investment theory of creativity views creativity from a unique perspective compared to other such theories. According to this theory, creativity depends, to some degree, on investing the right amount of effort in a field at the right time and in the right way [202, 203]. This means that if we have the essential characteristics of a required environment, we may see an opportunity to devote our time and energy into something that has been overlooked by others. This is similar to how good investors know when to buy while others do not. In other words, we know how to identify and make the most out of opportunities.

We may be convinced that creativity is one of the critical 21st-century skills, as it is one of the four Cs of 21st-century learning. Creative problem solving is needed almost daily to cope with the challenges that arise in our life today [204].

Dan asked himself again, "is it possible for me to become creative?"

There are so many creative techniques. And if there are so many, it means that none of them are ideal. Creativity techniques are methods that encourage creative actions. These methods cover several facets of creativity, and they include techniques for generating ideas, divergent thinking, re-framing problems, bringing about changes in the environment, etc. They can be used for problem-solving, artistic expression, or therapy. Some techniques require groups of two or more people, while other techniques can be accomplished alone. These methods include word games, written exercises and different types of improvisation, or algorithms for approaching problems [157]. Walking, which was an activity favored by Albert Einstein, has been shown to increase creativity [205]. Dan came across this list of creativity techniques [206]:

1. Establish a sense of purpose and the intention to pursue something,
2. Learn some foundational skills
3. Focus on obtaining domain-specific knowledge
4. Stimulate curiosity and exploration and reward yourself for achievements in this direction
5. Motivate yourself, especially by increasing intrinsic motivation
6. Build on confidence and be open to taking risks
7. Focus on mastering the task and engage in some healthy competition with yourself

8.  Increase your belief in creativity

9.  Give yourself opportunities to choose and discover new things

10. Develop self-management (metacognitive) skills

11. Learn about strategies for improving creative performance

12. Find the right balance

13. Learn aleatory techniques for exploiting randomness

14. Improvise

15. Sleep, relax, and meditate.

He was not sure where and if randomness fits into the picture.

Aleatoricism is the incorporation of chance or random elements into the process of creation. It is commonly found in music, art, and literature. It is a way of introducing new thoughts or ideas into the creative process [207].

Improvisation is a creative process that is used in the creation of music, theater, and other forms of art. It can be used to create spoken, written, or composed forms of art without prior preparation. It may seem random, but it does not involve a coin or a dice. Improvisation, also called extemporization, can lead to the discovery of new ways to act, new patterns of thought and practices, and new structures. Many artists also use improvisational techniques to help their creative flow[208].

Distraction has been shown in many studies to increase creativity[209]. Distraction, however, is in many cases a random and unpredictable event. Studies have shown that non-demanding distractions improve performance on creativity tests. The results support the concept that decision-related neural processes occur during moments of unconscious thought when a person engages in a non-demanding task. This means that if we are distracted, we do not maintain one thought for an unusually long time, which in turn allows different ideas to float in and out of our consciousness. It is what some will call an "associative process" that can lead to a creative solution or idea. We may look at this process as a positive incubation time/process that helps us bake the final cake [210].

At this point, Dan was sure about his intuition that randomness may be associated with creativity. It seemed difficult to translate this into practical steps.

# CHAPTER 12
## Actively creating randomness

*Creativity is the ability to introduce order into the randomness of nature.*

**Eric Hoffer**

*The world is governed by chance. Randomness stalks us every day of our lives.*

**Paul Auster**

A week at home out of work was very rare for Dan. Dan had only two days of his one-week leave left; he was thinking of going back to work. Sitting and browsing the internet while taking down notes on his laptop was exciting for him. It was something that he liked doing from time to time. However, he was not sure where this search was taking him.

Dan read about Eric Hoffer, an American moral and social philosopher (1902–1983). One of his famous books was "The True Believer: Thoughts on the Nature of Mass Movements" [211]. Hoffer was very concerned about the rise of totalitarian governments, such as those of Hitler and Stalin, and he attempted to identify the roots of these "madhouses" in human psychology [212]. He proposed the theory that radical cultural movements are born out of predictable circumstances: when large numbers of people collectively begin to believe that their individual lives are valueless, that the modern world is irreparably corrupt, and that the only hope for them is to join a larger group that demands radical changes. He noted that leaders of mass movements were frustrated intellectuals.

Hoffer wrote several books and papers about societies around the world. One great saying that is attributed to him had to do with creativity: he famously stated that "creativity is putting randomness into order." This seemed somewhat strange to Dan at first glance. As he had learned before, he was almost certain that randomness might be associated with creativity, but that the two do not necessarily contradict each other.

The concept that was evolving was that typically, we might not pay much attention to the random events in our lives. So many things are happening to us as every minute passes by. Think of all the emails, text messages, Facebook notes, phone calls...sounds familiar? It may be maddening to many of us, but the creative geniuses know that the randomness of nature is a rich source of stimulation that can provoke creativity [213].

Statistically, random events are those that have equal chances for each outcome. They happen by chance, without any conscious decision on our part. Most random events are not unusual if we think about them. One may also consider unusual or unexpected events as random. When we select something random, we try to do it without any knowledge of the choice that we are making [213].

We have seen before that randomness can boost creativity by providing peculiar, unusual, and surprising, unexpected, odd stimuli. Many, if not most, of these random stimuli may seem unrelated to our creative challenge; however, they can still help free us from the constraints, suppression, and limitations of "conventional, familiar solutions." Creative people seem to know how to use this random, somewhat distracting or bothering, and maybe irrelevant stimuli.

Dan was thinking to himself that when we receive such a stimulus, it is best not to throw it away. It is important that we pay attention to it and try our best to use it to inspire ideas for our challenge. Apparently, the primary challenge is that if my life is full of random stimuli, how would I know which of them I should keep and make use of, and which ones I should ignore. At the end of the day, most of the random/distracting events in our life actually distract us from doing what we need to do. We just cannot live in a world of distractions all day long. Some believe it has to do with faith, as reflected in the following quote found in an innovation blog of the Bangkok Post: "Have faith, and random inputs will give us the key to resolving our challenges" [213].

If we want to use randomness to stimulate our creativity, what should we do? What cognitive strategies do creative people use when turning randomness into inspired ideas? Perhaps we could turn to self-help books and recipes for success. Dan liked to read these books, but had never thought that they had any real impact on him.

We can start by focusing on the problem, task, challenge, or consideration that we are confronted with. If we believe that randomness can boost our creativity, we can look for those random events and happenings that can give us this boost. As strange as it sounds, actively looking for a source of randomness can inspire creativity. We may have our "regular" source of randomness. This source will provide us with the stimuli. The type of stimuli may be related or entirely unrelated to the task we are facing. It could be a walk, listening to background noise, music, or watching a film. The list of stimuli should be used to spark ideas for our challenge. These ideas are likely to be odd and unexpected, which is what we want. These odd ideas are often the seeds of great solutions. They are the incubator within which the cake is being baked, sometimes without our knowledge.

If randomness is accidental, or based on pure chance, how can we make it work for our creativity? There are some "tricks" that work for some people who want to create "inspiring randomness" or want to get into the oven where the cake is being baked. This is an exercise that was suggested in the innovation blog: Select a word at random that is not directly related to our task. Then, prepare a list of words related to that word, and use this list of words to generate ideas for our task. The random word should lead to associations, which need to then be connected to the solution of our task. For example, a person who wants to open a coffee shop could randomly select the word "museum," and then list words which are related to a museum, such as *art, exhibition, collection,* or *teaching.* He can then use those words to generate ideas for his coffee shop challenge, such as "Open a coffee shop in a museum," "Display paintings by wing artists in our coffee shop," "Host exhibitions of coffee-related topics in our coffee shop," and "Create a new artistic coffee mug every month for customers to collect." [213] This definitely seems like an exciting exercise to boost creativity and idea generation.

For many of us, a random picture can become a creative thought stimulator: Select a random picture, raise associations, and connect the associations with our task. The same technique can be applied to a random song: make associations with words. Go to a movie, or watch a random video. We can also use random quotations. Make associations with one of the topics, and use these associations, which at a first look may seem unrelated, to drive us towards a creative solution [214]. Finally, something that we can do all the time, every day, is to pay attention to what happens to us and around us. These are indeed random events. When we see something unusual or unexpected, try to associate it with our challenge or with one of our unfinished tasks. Something may click.

Creative people may know the secret to embracing and making use of randomness. We can start thinking about actively doing the same, as suggested above, or pay attention to random events that may lead to ideas which at first look irrelevant but could lead to the solution we were looking for. In his book "The Oracle Night," Paul Auster wrote, "The world is governed by chance. Randomness stalks us every day of our lives" [215]. This sentence is mostly interpreted as an ominous warning, but it is not necessarily so. We could look at randomness as an unavoidable event in our life. Alternatively, we could try to use it to boost our creativity.

Dan knew that chance and randomness are not the same thing, but he was wondering if these random events occur by chance. Can he control chance, or can he control randomness? He decided to spend the last two days of his week off exploring this. He believed that it would enable him to go back to work in a much better mood.

# CHAPTER 13

## The formula for real randomness. Can chance exist without randomness?

With two days left on his week off, Dan started looking into real randomness versus chance.

Once again, Dan turned to the Stanford Encyclopedia of Psychology. For some reason that he was unaware of, it seemed that unlike physicists, these psychologists were better at trying to explain it.

A fair coin has equal chances of landing heads and tails, but it is possible for it to land heads on every toss in an infinite number of tosses. The chance of an infinite sequence of heads, according to calculations of standard probability, is zero [216]. However, if it did occur, it would have been a result of chance. If we assume that each outcome happens by chance, the complex event that is composed by all of them also happens by chance. An outcome can happen by chance, and yet, the apparent sequence of outcomes is not random. While random sequences are a measure of possible outcome sequences of any process, chancy or otherwise, measure one does not mean *every* [40].

A fair coin may land only heads for every toss of an infinite number of tosses, but this outcome may not represent a suitable sequence. What would happen, if a fair coin were tossed infinitely many times, we may say: it would land heads about half the time. In other words, although the all-heads outcome is a possibility in the case of an infinite number of coin tosses, it does not actually occur at any of the nearest possibilities [119].

According to the non-reductionist view of chance, there is nothing inconsistent in a situation where the statistical properties of the sequence of outcomes and chance diverge arbitrarily far. It seems that such possibilities are as close as to those where the outcome statistics reflects the chances. [40]. On the other hand, according to the reductionist view of chance, a world where an infinite all-heads sequence does occur at some close possibility is different from ours. In such a world, the chance of heads is much closer to 1; this means that if a coin were tossed infinitely many times to always land heads, the coin is not after all fair. Thus, in any situation where the reductionist chance of heads is 0.5, suitable outcome sequences in that situation or its nearest neighbors *are* in fact *all* unbiased concerning outcome frequencies. This satisfies the law of large numbers, and it may also be in keeping with other randomness properties [40].

A fair coin tossed 1000 times has a chance of landing heads more than 700 times. However, such an outcome is compressible, as long runs of heads are familiar enough to be exploited by an efficient coding algorithm. Further, a 1000 outcomes is long enough to swamp the constants involved in defining the universal prefix-free Kolmogorov complexity. Such an outcome will not be random, even though it may occur by chance [40].

In 1876, Venn proposed the notion that every individual thing or event has an indefinite number of observable properties or attributes, and therefore, might belong to an indefinite number of different classes of things [217]. Consider a situation where we toss a coin on Tuesday. These are the properties of this event: it is a coin toss; it occurs on a Tuesday; it is being orchestrated by us; we are the causal factor of this event; and so on. Each of these properties can influence different outcome sequences, some of which may be random and others not. Each of these sequences is unified by a trial, and all of them are suitable for CT. A chance is relative to the type of trial [40].

Chances are not frequencies. A single-case chance is almost universally taken to be not only defined for a specific event but unique to that event. For a chance to play its role in the principal principle, there must be a unique chance for a given event that can guide our intellectual credibility. We have only one credence in a particular proposition stating the occurrence of that event [40]. When an event is a unique non-trivial single-case chance, and we can classify the trial which produced it as the sequence of outcomes of all trials of that kind, it is not random. For example, in the case of a coin that is tossed and lands heads, it happens by chance. It is of the type "coin toss which lands heads," and the sequence consisting of all outcomes of that type is not random [40]. One way to overcome this non-randomness is to claim that these are random sequences [218]. Another way is to "proceed by considering the narrowest class for which reliable statistics can be compiled." However, this provides no guarantee that there will be only one such class [219]. There are multiple classes which are equally "narrow" and for which reliable statistics can be performed. They add up to several sequences that are long enough to make reliable judgments about their randomness [220]. It necessitates the chance of an event being insensitive to the reference class. Some claim that there is *no* shield from the reference class problem so that this requirement cannot be met [109, 221] [40].

Dan learned that despite the disputes, there are cases of chance without randomness. Further, there are situations in which there is a biased chance process. For example, a sequence of unfair coin tosses will have an unbalanced number of heads and tails, and such a sequence cannot be random. However, such a sequence happens by chance. It is not random based on both the Martin-Löf and Kolmogorov style considerations. A biased sequence is more compressible than an unbiased sequence. If the sequence is long enough, then with efficient coding, it will be possible to exploit the fact that biased sequences have longer subsequences of consecutive digits, and are therefore not random. No sequences of the outcomes of a biased chance process are random, but these outcomes occur by chance [40].

Can there be randomness which permits the outcomes of biased chances to be random? Von Mises' characterization of randomness was constructed with this in mind. A random sequence is one for which there is no possible subsequence with a frequency that differs from the frequency of the original sequence.

The generalization of ML-randomness requires an independent computable probability measure of sequences. This is possible for cases where we antecedently know the chances. It cannot be used when the existence of chance is incidental to the existence of a random sequence of outcomes. For every sequence, there is some chance measure according to which it is random, which threatens to trivialize the inference of chance from random-ness [40]. This approach to randomness requires that the chanciness of a process producing the random sequence come before the randomness of the sequence [125].

There is some difficulty with the generalization of biased sequences. This is because biased sequences, while reflecting the probabilities in the process that produces them, are not random in the sense that they are disorderly and incompressible. Generalization is defined as a notion of disorderliness that is relative to the probabilities underlying the sequence. It is not intrinsic to the sequence itself in a way that is independent of the measure being used [40].

The concept of randomness is separate from the concept of disorder. The concept of disorder is an essential notion that takes the sequence at face value and is not concerned with its genesis; it simply considers whether the sequence lacks pattern. On the other hand, randomness is concerned with genesis: it does not consider solely the face value of the sequence, but asks the question of whether the sequence mirrors the probabilities of the process of which it is a product. Thus, although there is some connection between the concepts of randomness and disorder, it is not a closely knit one [125] [40].

Dan learned that Kolmogorov randomness is linked to disorderliness. A sequence featuring an even number of heads and tails, but produced by successive tosses of an *unfair* coin, is biased with regard to the underlying process. It is reasonable that this *unrepresentativeness* of the sequence is not associated with the disorder [132] [40].

When a bias in a chance process approaches extremal values, it is normal to reject the idea that the observed outcomes are random. If this is used to understand the psychology of human behavior, it means that people are not always predictable, and that their behavior does not obey non-probabilistic laws of psychology. It is, however, incorrect to say that they act randomly. There is a measure-independent notion of disorder or incompressibility of sequences, that biased sequences are less disorderly. A measure-dependent notion of disorder for biased sequences can be defined only by ignoring the availability of better compression techniques that compress biased sequences more than honest ones. The generalization of randomness permits highly non-random sequences to be called random as long as they reflect the chances of highly biased processes [40].

Randomness can be defined for biased sequences. However, there are difficulties in using this notion in defense of any non-trivial version of the Commonplace Thesis (CT). There is also some difficulty with the concept that biased sequences can be genuinely disorderly [40].

Randomness is indifferent to history, but chance can be said to be history dependent. The simplest way in which chance is history dependent is when conditions which produce a particular event change over time. Dan read this example: If we enter a labyrinth at 11:00 AM and plan to choose our turn whenever we come to a branch point by tossing a coin, when we enter, we have an X% chance of reaching the center by noon. However, in the first half hour we may stray into a region from which it is hard to reach the center, as a result of which our chance of reaching the center by noon has fallen. However, then we get lucky, and find that later, we are not far from the center; this increases our chance of reaching it by noon [119] [40]. In this example, the property which changes to alter our chance of reaching the center is how close we are to the center. There are cases where the property which changes is a previous outcome of an identical process. Any process in which successive outcomes of repeated trials are not *probabilistically independent* is defined by this feature [40].

Here is an example of chance without randomness: If we have an unbiased container from which balls are drawn *without* being replaced, each draw can be considered to happen by chance. However, the sequence of outcomes is not random, because the first half of the sequence carries information about the second half, and this aids compressibility.

A stochastic process in which the chances of future outcomes depend on past outcomes is another example. For instance, Markov chains produce a sequence of outcomes where the value of an outcome is dependent on the value of the immediately prior outcome and that immediately prior outcome can be screened off for the rest of history. It is reasonable that whether tomorrow is rainy depends on whether today was rainy, as a rainy day is more likely to be preceded by another rainy day. However, knowing that today was rainy arguably makes yesterday's weather irrelevant. If a Markov chain is the correct model of a process, then even when the individual trial outcomes happen by chance, the entire sequence of repeated trials is non-random. This means that we should expect a sunny day to be followed by a sunny day, and a rainy day by a rainy one. A condition of Borel normality, which all random sequences obey, requires that every finite sequence of outcomes of equal length have an equal frequency in the sequence. A Borel regular sequence, and hence a random sequence, cannot model the sequence of outcomes of a Markov chain, even though each outcome happens by chance [40].

Chance is not randomness. However, can randomness exist without chance?

# CHAPTER 14

## True randomness without a chance?

Dan decided to finish this last issue (for the time being) before going back to work. It was the last day of his week off. He decided not share it with his kids, and he did not leave the house. He even ordered takeaway food. Dan was not one of those who enjoyed fancy foods; he always liked keeping things simple. His friends used to think he was a miser, when in fact, he liked to spend money, even too much, on things that others appreciated less. Food was just something he was not too interested in.

Dan learned that there are cases where a random sequence potentially exists without a chance. Some of these examples can be found in classical physics.

We may view coin tossing as a deterministic process, entirely without chance. It can produce outcome sequences that can be used as a paradigm for random sequences [40]. An efficient prefix-free code for short sequences is not shorter than the original sequence. Prefix-free codes contain information about the length and content of a sequence. If a sequence is short, the most efficient code may be the sequence itself prefixed with its length, which is longer than the sequence.

All short sequences are Kolmogorov random. If randomness is lack of pattern or repetition, then sequences that are too short to display pattern or repetition must be random. For most processes, there is a long enough sequence of outcomes to overcome any "accidental" randomness due to shortness of the outcome sequence. For events that are rarely repeatable, even the merely possible suitable reference classes are small. However, unrepeatable events do exist; these are part of short sequences and are Kolmogorov random. It is unlikely that all these events happen by chance.

For example, there are random sequences that are short in which each outcome did not happen by chance [40]. A chance without randomness may occur if there is a single-case unrepeatable chance event. If one considers the outcomes alone, either all short sequences are random, or none of them are. There is no way to differentiate between different short sequences based on any product-based notion. It is sufficient to say that some single, unrepeatable events are chancy, while others are random [40].

A symbol shift dynamic can have a finite speed. It leads to chance without randomness. Physical situations in which symbol shift dynamics occur can be found in physical processes, such as a stretch and fold dynamics, of the type that is familiar in chaos theory [90]. The *baker's transformation* is an example in which at any time the system is characterized by a point which specifies its evolution over time. This means that there is a function governing the discrete evolution of the system. Thus, even though the product that is generated is random, as random as a genuine chance process can be, the outcomes do not happen by chance. Based on the prior system state, the subsequent evolution is not at all a matter of chance. The sequences generated however are random and without any chance outputs [125, 222]. Sampling the system at certain time points and observing its position at each time point can yield a sequence of arbitrarily repeated trials that produce a random sequence. None of these outcomes occur by chance. The sequence of outcomes is random, and probability plays no role. When probability plays no role, chance does not play a role either. No probability function that has features required of chance plays a role in the dynamics of this system. Thus, there is no chance in this system [40].

The baker's transformation provides a model of deterministic *macro-randomness*. It is a system that produces a sequence of states characterized by the Bernoulli property. For closed systems, in which energy is conserved over time, this is not possible. Closed systems cannot satisfy even weak randomness properties; this characteristic of closed systems is called *ergodicity*. A system is considered to be ergodic when within the limit, with a probability of one, the amount of time it spends in a given state is equal to the standard measure of state space of that particular state [120, 125, 223] [40].

A Bernoulli system is ergodic, but the opposite does not hold true. That is, if a system moves from state to state, it may be ergodic, but the state at a particular time point is dependent on history. Many physical systems cannot be ergodic. In most closed systems in which there are interactions between the constituent particles, there are stable sub-regions within the state space. These are considered to be regions of positive measure: if a system originates within such a region, it will always stay there. Naturally, such systems are not ergodic [223] [40].

One may claim that there are no physical systems that exhibit ergodicity, and therefore, that no physical system can exhibit randomness. The baker's transformation is not a genuine case of randomness without a chance, since systems like it are not physically possible. Indeed, there are physically probable new systems to which the baker's transformation theory does not apply.

Open systems that are not limited to a state space region of constant energy are paradigms of chaotic systems [90] [40]. This led to thoughts about chaos. Dan was not sure whether to get into it right now, as he wanted to finish investigating the issue of chance and randomness before returning to work.

Intuitively, he thought, the behavior of a chaotic system is random, despite the dependence on initial conditions. Thus, no matter how accurate our finite discrimination of the initial state of a given chaotic system is, there will exist states that are discriminable from the initial state. This means that the initial state could diverge arbitrarily far from the actual evolution of the system. No matter how well we know the initial condition, there is another state the system could be in that will evolve into a discriminably different future condition. This separation happens relatively quickly; the system states cannot be predicted [40]. The classical physical theory underlying the dynamics of chaotic systems is one in which probability does not feature. It is characterized by randomness, and the outcomes do not occur by chance [40]. However, whether or not the idea of chancy initial conditions is valid, the first outcome in the random sequence does happen by chance. The following states do not. Yet, Commonplace Thesis (CT) is committed to the existence of dynamical chances in those state transitions [40].

Dan had now started wondering about indeterminism.

He knew that classical physics is not deterministic; that is, cases of indeterminism do not undermine the applications of classical mechanics. Indeterminism is the inability to use the state of the system at a particular time to determine the state of that system in the future. The state of some system at a particular time point could be used to specify two future states that are incompatible but consistent with Newton's laws of motion and the initial state [40].

Newtonian laws of mechanics are characterized by the *time-reversal invariant* [120]. For every right trajectory through the state space, there is another right trajectory that results from the first. It occurs by mapping every next state in the first trajectory to its image state in which particles have the same positions; however, the signs of the components of momentum are reversed and the trajectory is run in reverse order. In these image states, the particles are in the same positions but move in precisely the opposite direction. For every right process, backward runs of the process are also lawful [40].

Classical indeterminism does occur.

The "Norton's dome" is an example in which determinism is violated. A ball is given an initial velocity along the surface of the dome toward the apex. Too little, and it falls short; too high, and it overshoots. If the ball is given the correct amount of velocity, however, it comes to a stop precisely at the apex and remains there [224]. Norton said about his dome that "One might think that we can assign probabilities to the various possible outcomes. Nothing in Newtonian physics requires us to assign the probabilities, but we might choose to try to add them for our conceptual comfort. This can be done as far as the direction of the natural motion is concerned. The symmetry of the surface of the apex makes it quite natural for us to add a probability distribution that assigns equal probability to all directions. The complication is that there is no comparable way for us to assign probabilities to the time of spontaneous excitation in a way that respects the physical symmetries of solutions. All solutions treat all candidate excitation times equally. A probability distribution that tries to make each candidate time equally likely cannot be proper; that is, it cannot assign a unit probability to the union of all separate outcomes. Alternatively, one that is proper can only be defined by inventing extra physical properties, which are not provided by the physical description of the dome and mass, Newton's laws and the laws of gravitation, and grafting them unnaturally onto the physical system." [224] [40]

Another system that violates determinism is "space invaders." These are particles that are at no spatial location at a time and form no part of the state at the time. They travel in "from" spatial infinity and assume a location over time [125] [40]. In this system, there exists indeterminism without chance.

Classical mechanics is indeterministic, but it is not chancy. That is, we have randomness without a chance distribution over the outcomes. Randomness requires two distinguishable possible outcomes and the possibility of producing arbitrary sequences of such outcomes. Chance requires two distinguishable outcomes, each of which has some chance. This is where chance and possibility can be differentiated.

In some cases, two possible outcomes exist for a process, neither of which has any chance at all, not even a chance of zero [40]. Consider a sizeable finite container full of black and white balls. The number of balls is significant; that is, the sequence of outcomes of draws should be long enough to be random. A random selection from this container from which balls are drawn without replacement until it is empty results in a random sequence outcome. This sequence meets all the criteria for a simple random population sample. However, the outcomes become less chancy as the number of balls decreases. In fact, in the case of the last ball, the chance of it being black is either 1 or 0. So this outcome does not occur by chance. Thus, the sequence generated is a random sequence that includes an outcome. Drawing a black ball, which did not happen by chance, is contrary to CT. However, this last outcome did happen by chance, since at the start of the drawing there was a definite chance that a white ball would be drawn last, as much as there was a definite chance that a black ball would be drawn last. This line of thinking neglects the time dependence of chances. CT maintains that a given outcome happens by chance if it is part of a random sequence [40].

The problems that arise in CT can be attributable to the split between product randomness and process chance.

Chance is hard, and some even think that it cannot be separated from randomness…that it requires randomness.

The frequency theory is a product conception of chance. An outcome type has a chance, just in case, it is part of a random sequence of outcomes in which that outcome type has a sound relative frequency limit [137]. Having a relative frequency limit of 1212 is a measure of infinite binary sequences, and all random sequences can be used to define collectives. Infinite binary sequences that do not converge on a frequency limit are considered to be non-random [109, 147] [40].

There are additional Humean views of chance [124]. Most are part of the product conception of chance. A possible world will not feature chances unless the best description of what events occur in that world involves a probability function. Two worlds cannot differ in terms of their chances without also differing somewhere in the events which occur.

According to the Humean view, simplicity is essential for randomness. In a world that contains a random sequence of outcomes, no short description of that sequence is possible. Descriptions that do not try to describe occurrences with all their particularities and that involve a probability distribution that makes the sequence a typical one in terms of that probability function, are less informative and much shorter, but they still fit well. Therefore, in a world containing a random sequence of outcomes, the most suitable theory is one that involves probabilities which are chances [40].

Dan was wondering again, "could there be a world with chances in which there was no random sequence?"

With the simplicity approach, some of the problems associated with the pure frequentism approach to chance can be avoided. A short unrepresentative outcome sequence, or a highly biased one, need not force the chances to take on the value of the actual frequencies.

Consider a world that is comprised of two intrinsic duplicate coins: one of the coins is tossed several times and lands heads about half the time, and the other coin is tossed only a few times and lands tails on every toss. In the outcome sequence of the second one, the frequency of heads is zero. In the most optimal system, the chance of heads would be 1212. Thus, in a world where one coin has the appropriate outcome frequencies, the frequencies of the other coin is fixed. To state this simply, both coins obeyed the same probabilistic laws such that the second one was an oasis of determinism. It looks like the second coin toss is not part of any random sequence of outcomes, since a few all-tails tosses are not random, but there is a chance involved here. The Humean account of chance is compatible with the existence of bias and with non-independent sequences of trials. On the other hand, CT is not [40].

Random is sometimes used in the context of process. Several philosophical approaches to randomness do not consider it to be equivalent to "chancy." A simplified approach is to connect randomness with *indeterminism* and to defend CT by claiming that indeterminism yields both chance and randomness [40].

There is also an epistemic view of randomness, according to which random processes are those whose outcomes we cannot know in advance and are *unpredictable* [225, 226]. That is, an event is random when its occurrence cannot be predicted with certainty [227]. Prediction involves some notion of *reasonableness*. Making predictions is rational. According to the physical theory, prediction makes certain posterior credence reasonable. Guessing is not reasonable, even if it is correct [225]. If a process is predictable, it will make available a winning betting strategy for the sequence of outcomes of that process[40].

Unpredictability alone is not sufficient for randomness.

A system is dependent on initial conditions if it is sensitively dependent on initial conditions. Dependence on initial conditions is possible even if sensitive dependence on initial conditions is not. A system that is not sensitively dependent on initial conditions is unpredictable. However, there exists an algorithm that, given some finite specification of the initial conditions, can result in future evolution of the system. The finite specification involves more precise data that characterize the system[225, 227]. Thus, unpredictably generated sequences may better fit the theoretical definition of randomness, and they show how randomness is unpredictability. When trials are not independent, future outcomes can happen by chance, even if knowing the past states of the system puts one in a position to better predict future outcomes [225] [40].

A theory is *deterministic* if any two sequences of states in models which share some state at some time point share every state at every time point. On the other hand, a theory is *indeterministic* if two systems can be in the same state at one time and evolve into distinct states [125]. Randomness and indeterminism are closely connected. An outcome happens by chance if it is produced by an indeterministic process. A possible sequence of outcomes is random if a repeated indeterministic process produces all of the outcomes. It follows that an outcome occurs by chance when there is a possible random sequence of outcomes, produced by the same process, that it is a part of [40].

There is a view that non-trivial chances require indeterminism. According to determinism, someone who has knowledge of the past and the applicable laws would be in a position to know with certainty every future outcome. Using probability under determinism must be purely subjective, and can even be considered as a side effect of our ignorance of the past or the governing laws [119] [40]. Some claim that chance and determinism are consistent. In our world, which is filled with entropy-increasing processes and apparently fair coin tosses, this means involving some probabilistic component, which is termed "chance" [124]. In classical statistical mechanics, a phase space measure is used to determine the behavior of Bernoulli and mixing systems; this is considered as a probability function, despite the deterministic underlying physics [228] [40].

Deterministic chance may exist [221, 225, 229, 230]. There are probability distributions over outcomes that are chancy, even according to perfectly deterministic theories. The reductionist view of chance permits the compatibility of chance and determinism. Determinism states that the entire history of the world can be interrupted at any moment; it raises the question of whether the entire history involves chances [117] [40]. Anti-reductionists views about chance, however, do not accept these notions [231, 232]. A deterministic chance requires the existence of a physically possible world that shares the same laws until a certain point, but diverges after that. If determinism is assumed to be true, such a divergence is not possible. That is, if that world matches ours at any time, it matches it at all times [117] [40].

The debate over the deterministic and reductionist views of "chance" is ongoing.

There are indeterministic theories that do not involve chance. According to these theories, indeterminism is secured by the existence of alternative future possibilities, which collectively do not permit or require a probability distribution [40]. A controversial class of cases of indeterminism without chance can be derived by rejecting the *universalism* of chance. It is claimed that the chance of truth applies to any proposition whatsoever [119]. If universalism is false, there may be indeterministic situations where the alternative outcomes are those to which chance does not apply. Von Mises rejected universalism, claiming that chance applied adequately only to "mass phenomena." In an indeterministic world where the indeterministic process occurs only once, the theory of probability does not apply. This means that the chances for processes that do not have sufficiently stable outcome patterns are rejected [229]. Contrarily, this theory is deterministic in the context of the Montague system, which produces sequences that are random in the von Mises/Church sense [233].

There is an arithmetically definable function that governs the evolution of a system over time, but this function is not adequately computable. That is, there exists no algorithm that can produce the sequence of states of a system. Computations in deterministic physics that feature equations of motion challenge the close connection between randomness and indeterminism. A chancy and indeterministic process may produce a non-random sequence of outcomes, and such a sequence may not be random [40].

While it is possible that a fair coin could land heads an infinite number of times, it would actually not do so. That is, the counterfactual statement "If I tossed the coin an infinite number of times, it would not land all heads" is apparently true. Some claim that the counterfactual statement is true [119, 234] [40].

A possible sequence of outcomes is random if it is not the case that, were an indeterministic process to be repeated infinitely, it will not produce that sequence of outcomes. This is controversial: whereas some suggest that randomness is "roughly interchangeable" with indeterminism [235], others claim that the main feature of randomness is some degree of independence from the initial conditions. Thus, if an experiment is performed twice with the same initial conditions, it may still produce two different outcomes [222] [40].

Some claim that the view that randomness is indeterminism makes it difficult to use randomness in science. This is because it implies that random sampling, random outcomes in chaotic dynamics, and random mating in population genetics, are not, in fact, random, despite the likelihood of their being so. Fundamental indeterminism is not a prerequisite for a randomized trial.

Confidence in the deliverance of the trials does not depend on the assurance that the trial design involves radioactive decay or any another indeterministic process [40]. If the open epistemic possibility is valid and quantum mechanics is deterministic, it means that nothing is random, not even the most intuitively compelling cases [40].

The confusion between unpredictability and indeterminism is what makes the theory that randomness is indeterminism so popular. Random sequences are almost always unpredictable; therefore, they are indeterministic. If predictability and determinism can be clearly differentiated between, confusion can be avoided [236-238] [40].

What outcomes can one expect from a repeated chance process?

If a process is chancy, a random sequence of outcomes can be expected. Conversely, it is unlikely that a sequence of outcomes that appears predictable, compressible, and rule-based, is produced by chance alone [235].

The link between mathematical and physical randomness is epistemic. Non-random sequences are used when explanations about undiscovered causal factors are required. Mathematical randomness cannot serve as an explanation for "ultimate physical randomness" [235]. That is, mathematical randomness is product randomness, physical randomness, processes randomness, or chanciness [40]. Relative frequencies are useful but not reliable indicators of chances. Outcome frequencies strictly between 0 and 1 are evidence that chance processes are involved in the production of those outcomes. However, frequentism is unlikely to be a reductive account of chance. Therefore, chances may be present if random sequences of outcomes are produced [40].

Dan noticed that there are many theories about randomness and chance and many counter-theories; it was more complicated than he had conceived it to be. He realized that attempts to derive connections among chance, randomness, and determinism had so far failed. He could end up without a definite answer. His conclusion was that chance and randomness, while they overlap in many cases, are separate concepts [40].

Before going to bed that night, he went back to the beautiful book "Four letters of love" [239], where Niall Williams deals with randomness in life and love: "There is no such thing as chance, in which my father was more or less certain, choosing to see the random chaos of his life as just a different sort of order, and if we believe in God we do not believe in chance, he told me." Williams takes it one step further by asking himself whether it is good or bad: "What did I hope for, something that would show me the way before, erase the randomness and clarify the sense of destiny." Alternatively, he offers the following solution: "How do we know what to do, how can we ever know?...We do not...I suppose we do not get what we want and then we choose one or the other ... anything can happen" [239].

If we want real randomness, we need to select our options randomly, unless we want to carry a quantum computer in our pocket.

# CHAPTER 15
## Enjoy randomness

Dan was back at work. He knew that all the information he had gained would affect his work from now on. He also felt that he had learned something that could impact his life, and maybe even his work. In fact, he felt sorry that he had not come across these questions before.

Dan was a practical person. He loved literature, music, and art. He loved computer sciences. However, he always attempted to understand them from a practical perspective. His major issue was being able to transform randomness into something useful.

As is usually the case under challenging situations, where even pure science could be used to provide answers to all questions but the ultimate one, he turned back to history.

Heraclitus (fl. circa 500 B.C.) was one of the most provocative and intriguing of the ancient Greek philosophers [240]. Dan found out that Heraclitus is regarded by several historians as the world's first creative thinker. His epigrams about life, nature, and the cosmos are represented in the works of Plato, Aristotle, the Stoics, Bishop Hippolytus, Plotinus, Goethe, Hegel, Marx, Nietzsche, Jung, Ernst Cassirer and many more. So I guess I can consider him as one of the smart ones, Dan thought to himself. Heraclitus said that "the most beautiful order is a heap of sweepings piled up at random." Dan was not sure that Heraclitus was the first to notice the beauty of randomness. But he was one of the first to put it in a way that makes us understand how we can use randomness.

Dan also learned about John Locke (1632–28 October 1704), an English philosopher and physician, who is regarded as one of the most influential of the Enlightenment thinkers and is known as the "Father of Liberalism"

[241]. It was John Locke who said "that which is static and repetitive is boring. That which is dynamic and random is confusing. In between lies art." Randomness is a great way to force our thinking to follow unfamiliar paths [214]. "It is necessary for the very existence of science that the same conditions always produce the same results." [242] Well, they do not, as is evident in our experiences with art, fashion, and science.

Dan was again wondering how he could apply this in his own life. He was convinced for now that randomness may be confusing, but it is positively surprising and not dull.

So can I try to enjoy, or make use of randomness?

# CHAPTER 16

## Can randomness lead to or boost creativity? A history of creativity

One issue that had haunted Dan since his college years was how creativity could be improved. He was always trying, albeit somewhat unsuccessfully, to show his children that creativity was the way to go. In fact, he wanted very much to discuss with Jeremy about how randomness is associated with creativity.

Several times Dan had heard his son David say, "Not all of us may want to be creative. Not all of us even think it that important. Why not let the creative ones keep inventing new things for us to use?" David was a lawyer. Dan did not like lawyers. It was not a personal dislike…he just did not like the profession. However, over the years, he had learned while negotiating with his company to provide services to their customers, that even lawyers can be creative. Dan used to tell David, "We are always being told that it is good to be creative. In fact, creative people fill up the list of those we are told we need to follow. The Steve Jobs of the world are our models. Was it not he who gave us the gift of the iPod shuffle?"

Dan was now seriously pondering the question of how randomness can help us become creative. The revelations from his web surfing over the last few days had already led him to believe that randomness is much more than just "being random." If it played such an important role in the course of human evolution, there must indeed be something good about it.

Creativity is a phenomenon that leads to the formation of something new and valuable [157]. The created item may be an imperceptible idea, scientific theory, a musical composition, or a joke, or even a physical object we invent or paint. "It can also be a legal contract," as Dan had once told

David. Because many of us think of creativity as essential, there are many theories which try to explain why some people are more creative than others. Many people also pay a premium to purchase self-help books or join courses or workshops so that they can become more creative. For example, many of us may have purchased this book in the hope of becoming more creative. In our quest to become more creative, we must not forget the importance of randomness in building creativity.

Many believe in the four P's theory of Mel Rhodes: process, product, person, and place [243]. As can be seen, the first P emphasizes on the cognitive processes involved in creative thinking. With the second P, there is focus on the creative product. Creativity in a person (the third P) is associated with intellectual habits, such as openness, levels of ideation, autonomy, expertise, and exploratory behavior. The third P, place, considers the circumstances within which creativity flourishes. It refers to the degree of autonomy, access to resources, and the nature of gatekeepers. Creative lifestyles are characterized by nonconforming attitudes and behaviors as well as flexibility [244].

Dan found a paper in the Harvard Business Review entitled "The weird rules of creativity" [245]. This paper had tried to define creativity in business: "The holy grail for companies has been innovation. Managers have gone after it with all the zeal their training has instilled in them, using a full complement of tried and true management techniques." The problem here is that no one has yet discovered the best techniques for creativity. In fact, Prof. Sutton makes the somewhat gloomy statement that "none of these practices, well suited for cashing in on old, proven products and business models, works very well when it comes to innovation." But he also suggests that "if the usual ordinary techniques do not work, take most of what we know about management and stand it on its head" [245]. His ideas for becoming creative involve focusing on thoughts without paying attention to their projected returns; ignoring what has worked before; stimulating people to fight; hiring people we do not like. Though many of these sound peculiar and random, the underlying idea is to let people look at problems through entirely new glasses, so that they can break their old routines and break from the past.

In most ancient cultures, including those of ancient Greece, ancient China, and ancient India, the concept of creativity seems to be missing [246]; these cultures tended to look at art as a form of discovery rather than creation. Many believe that creativity is an invention of Western culture. It might even have partly originated in Christianity, particularly in the texts about divine inspiration [247]. This does not mean, however, that creativity did not exist in the ancient world. In fact, one could say that many of our ancestors were much more creative than we are today. It is merely a question of how we choose to define it. Nowadays, creativity has taken on the form of a new religion. We all want our children to be creative; we want ourselves to be creative. David had teased Dan on so many occasions when he had tried to push creativity on his children.

Daniel J. Boorstin, a famous historian, thought that "the early Western conception of creativity was the Biblical story of creation given in the Genesis" [247]. According to Judeo-Christian beliefs, creativity was the sole authority of God, and anything new that was created by humans was believed to be an expression of God's creativity [248]. In Greek culture, too, there exists the view that inspiration for new things comes from the Gods. This is quite different from the contemporary way of looking at creativity, which reflects the way it was viewed during the Renaissance [157]. During the Renaissance period, creativity was viewed, not as a conduit for the divine, but as the ability of "great men" [247]. In other words, we look at creativity as an individual occurrence. This may be attributed to the intellectual movement of humanism, which is based on a human-centric outlook on the world, emphasizing on the intellect and achievement of the individual[249]. Nonetheless, we may still say that creativity is something that is sent from God, and this may also be entirely true. Dan was not about to argue about religion.

The Renaissance thinker and artist Leonardo da Vinci believed that humanism is reflected in one's continuous engagement with knowledge and creation [250]. The concept of linking creativity to the imagination is usually attributed to the Age of Enlightenment in the 18th century. Thomas Hobbes wrote that imagination was an essential part of human cognition [247]. William Duff defined imagination as a quality of genius [251]. Are these men responsible for injecting some egotism into the quest for creativity?

Creativity gained importance only towards the end of the 19th century, at a time when the arrival of Darwinism spurred an increase in interest in individual differences. In the late 19th and early 20th centuries, the leading mathematicians Hermann von Helmholtz and Henri Poincaré publicly discussed their creative processes [157]. In 1927, Alfred North Whitehead in his lectures (published as "Process and Reality") at the University of Edinburgh used the term "creativity" as the ultimate category of his metaphysical scheme [252].

Graham Wallas published in 1926 his study *Art of Thought*, which contains one of the first models proposed for the creative process; it is presented in five stages [253]:

a.  Preparation: This step involves deliberation about a problem in terms of all its features or aspects.

b.  Incubation: In this step, internalization of the problem into the unconscious mind occurs, and there are no external signs of the process.

c.  Intimation: The person experiences a "feeling" that the solution to the problem will arrive soon.

d.  Illumination/insight: Here, a creative idea is born from the preconscious, and it is slowly being processed into conscious awareness.

e.  Verification: The idea is processed and verified consciously, elaborated on and used.

It was James C. Kaufman and Beghetto who introduced the four C's model of creativity [254].

1.  mini-c: "transformative learning" that involves personally meaningful interpretations of experiences and insights.

2.  little-c: everyday problem solving and creative expression.

3.  Pro-C: professional or vocational creativity that is not necessarily imminent.

4.  Big-C: creativity that is considered significant in the given field.

Dan was disappointed that none of the above models of creativity mentioned randomness. So he steered his search in the direction of randomness and creativity. On December 2001, a summary was published in the New and Comments section of *Trends in Neuroscience* entitled "Randomness and creativity" [255]. It stated that "In an exquisitely orchestrated system such as the brain, an integrated randomizing mechanism could play an important role in eliciting novel ideas." The unexplained variability in brain responses was attributed to noises in the incoming stimuli.

At the Annual Meeting of the British Association for Advancement of Science, Dr. Roger Carpenter of the University of Cambridge reported on a group of cells in the brain which respond differently, and are independently and randomly integrated into the brain response to stimuli. The time taken by brain cells to register a flash of light varies widely from one flash to the next. This was attributed to the independent processing of clusters of cells. Considering that the brain can process multiple stimuli simultaneously, changes in response times eventually lead to different actions. This process thus results in creativity itself. The randomness provides a source of new variations in behaviors, ideas, and human activities. This quantitative approach to understanding how the brain makes decisions looks at the time needed to make a decision, and how it is affected by factors such as supply of information and individual expectations [256]. It led to a model of decision making which explains the observed variability in reaction times and correctly predicts the effects of altered expectations. The model predicts the urgency with which changes are made in our eye movements in response to low-visibility targets. The degree of urgency affected the threshold level at which a decision signal triggers a response.

Dan smiled to himself. So, we have cells in our brain that can practically generate creativity based on their random response. Perhaps this is the basis for the connection between randomness and creativity?

# CHAPTER 17
## Techniques for creativity

*One of the advantages of being disorderly is that one is always making exciting discoveries.*

**A.A. Milne**

Over the next few days, Dan spent most of his time locked up in his office and looking for the connection between randomness and creativity. His boss was aware that Dan sometimes went into these phases, but he also knew that Dan came out of these in better shape, most of the time.

As part of our quest for creativity, a multitude of studies on the creative process have been written in the last few decades. These studies have proposed several models and theories to explain the creative process, and Dan was screening these to decide which one best explains how randomness can be connected with creativity.

i.  **Incubation** is defined as a temporary break from creative problem solving that can result in insight [157, 257]. It was suggested as a technique to enable the "forgetting" of misleading clues [258]. In other words, rather than continuously thinking about a problem, we randomly interrupt our flow of thoughts about it; this could help us come up with a solution. In fact, it has been suggested that the absence of incubation may lead to us becoming fixated on inappropriate strategies for solving the problem [259]. Dan was thinking about how his teachers at school always insisted that everyone should focus and concentrate, or they would not be able to solve the problem. "Were they destroying my creativity?" Dan thought. In fact, the incubation theory contradicts earlier hypotheses that creative solutions to problems arise "mysteriously" from an unconscious mind while the conscious mind is occupied with other tasks [260].

ii.   J. P. Guilford distinguished between convergent and divergent thinking. Convergent thinking involves aiming for a single, correct solution to a problem, whereas divergent thinking, sometimes used as a synonym for creativity, involves creative generation of multiple answers to a set problem[261]. Some use the term "flexible thinking" or "fluid intelligence" for this type of creative process. Dan was not sure whether flexible necessarily meant random, but it was definitely not the opposite.

iii.  Finke proposed in 1992 a model called "Geneplore," which was based on the creative cognition approach. According to this model, creativity starts with a generative phase, in which we make up mental representations or original structures. This is followed by an exploratory phase, in which these structures lead to creative ideas. Dan interpreted this to mean that when we use our imagination for coming up with new ideas, those thoughts are structured in predictable ways based on the properties of existing structures[259] [39].

iv.   Weisberg claimed that creativity involves only ordinary cognitive processes that yield extraordinary results without involving too much of our imagination [262]. This led Dan to question the role of imagination in randomness. Perhaps there was no association after all.

v.    The explicit-implicit interaction theory of creativity was proposed by Helie and Sun, and it was based on the incubation concept [263]. The bases of this theory are the co-existence of explicit and implicit knowledge, simultaneous involvement of implicit and explicit processes, redundant representation of explicit and implicit knowledge, integration of the results of explicit and implicit processing, and iterative bi-directional processing. There is no mention of randomness.

vi.   Arthur Koestler described in "The Act of Creation" the concept of bisociation: creativity is a result of the intersection of two different frames of reference, or conceptual blending [264]. Blending sounded to Dan as a somewhat random process.

vii. The honing theory, developed by Liane Gabora, postulates that creativity is the product of the self-organizing of the worldview; that is, an individual improves, hones and re-hones his conceptions to produce an integrated worldview. There is an externally visible creative outcome that results from internal cognitive reorganization and correction of the worldview. In the face of a creative task, an individual's conception of the task is altered via interaction with the worldview and the worldview is also altered via interaction with the task. The process is repeated until the task is complete. At this point, both the task and the worldview are transformed. This theory is based on the notion of following the natural tendency of a worldview to attempt to resolve dissonance and seek internal consistency amongst its components, whether they are ideas, attitudes, or bits of knowledge [157, 265]. A central concept of this theory is a potentiality state, and it proposed that a creative thought proceeds not by random searching and mutation of predefined possibilities, but by drawing upon associations that exist due to overlap in spread neural cell assemblies that participate in the encoding of experiences in memory. Thus, during the course of the creative process, we make associations between the task and previous experiences, without understanding which aspects of the past experiences are relevant to the current task. The creative idea may therefore feel "half-baked." It is in a potentiality state because how it will actualize depends on the different internally or externally generated contexts it interacts with [157, 265]. Different works by the same person have a recognizable style even when expressed through different creative outlets.

This is explained by the honing theory to reflect the creator's uniquely structured worldview. What about environmental stimuli? Creativity is believed to flourish in a supportive, nurturing, trustworthy environment. Creativity is also correlated with childhood difficulties, which are known to induce the honing process. This theory doesn't seem to leave any room for randomness. Dan was thinking, "Does this theory undermine the importance of randomness?" Other theories on creativity seem to talk about of chance processes or accumulation of expertise. In the creativity process, does chance, perhaps, represent randomness?

viii. Everyday imaginative thoughts lead to creativity. In our everyday thinking, we often spontaneously imagine alternatives to reality. We frequently find ourselves thinking "if only..." This type of counterfactual thinking can be viewed as an example of a creative process [266]. Dan was able to sympathize with this concept, as he considered himself one of those people. He was not sure, however, whether spontaneous thinking is random. "It must be the result of some stimuli," he thought.

The abundance of creativity theories probably means that no one really understands this phenomenon. Each of these theories or a combination of several of them may be the ideal one. Although some of these theories pay attention to randomness, there is some ambiguity in their explications. At the end, despite his comprehensive reading of these theories, Dan was still confused about what creativity is. For now, he was willing to accept the notion that creativity means being better, and that randomness may have something to do with the creative process. Dan asked himself the next question, "does real creativity benefit from randomness?"

The Synopsis Randomness & Creativity Research suggests that creativity involves looser associations, defocused or focused attention, and a lack of fixedness. It is about being flexible and knowing, consciously and subconsciously, what is functional and when [267]. If we were rabbits escaping from a fox, we would be more likely to succeed if we were to follow an unpredictable path or a path that zigzags, unpredictably and randomly, rather than a predictable one. This is probably because an unpredictable path would confuse the fox and lead to him finally give up. Does the zigzag pattern here represent randomness?

If something is random, it is considered to be variable and different from a stereotypical thought [268]. People with certain psychopathology conditions provide answers that may seem random to us; can we call them creative answers? Not everything that is different and seems random is necessarily creative. Still, it does not mean that their answers are not creative. For most of us, and apparently for researchers, creativity means being both novel and "appropriate." However, we must not forget that many creative ideas seem crazy at the beginning. Does this meet the definition of being flexible, though? Dan thought that one might need some combination of randomness and a lack of focus, along with a bit of "staying on track" to be creative. Perhaps "crazy" is not a prerequisite.

He came across an exciting laboratory study in which participants were asked to insert random numbers on a computer keyboard (the random number generation task). Based on the input numbers, an analysis of their creativity, including their history of creative achievement, was performed. The results showed that both random and non-random processes are involved in creativity. Being random is predictive of creativity, which is translated into the generation of as many responses to a given task as possible. Randomness is also related to creative flexibility, or to the ability to switch between categories. A low level of randomness is also considered to be predictive of creative originality, actual creative achievement, as well as the number of unique responses [267]. In fact, creative people display more flexible cognitive control, and are better at adjusting their focus of attention as a function of task demands. It is advantageous to be as random as possible for the generation of ideas, but sticking with a particular response may be predictive of creative originality [269].

Confusing? Can we be both random and non-random at the same time? Maybe randomness is not associated at all with creativity? Is there a "recipe for creativity"? The answer presented in *The Synopsis Randomness & Creativity Research* is "next time our friends say that we are being random, hold our head up high and keep at it. However, don't forget to spot those brilliant ideas among the disorder, and focus."

Dan was still confused.

# CHAPTER 18

## Creativity, randomness, and intelligence: Think of King Solomon

A week passed, and the question of the association of randomness and creativity still bothered Dan. In the past, when he got preoccupied with something, it was always a matter of a few days until it passed. This time, he was puzzled and his mind was being bombarded by a million questions... How do we know we are creative? Does being creative also mean that we are intelligent? What are the implications of not being creative?

The formal psychometric measurement of creativity is considered to have begun with J. P. Guilford's 1950 address to the American Psychological Association [24]. Statistical analysis recognized creativity as an aspect of human cognition, similar to IQ-related intelligence. Guilford's work suggested that above a threshold level of IQ, the relationship between creativity and classically measured intelligence broke down [270]. Many researchers have tried to develop a creativity quotient that is akin to IQ, but most attempts have not succeeded [271]. For example, Guilford and colleagues developed tests to measure creativity. One of the tests is Plot Titles, in which participants are given a plot and asked to come up with original titles for the story. Quick Responses, another test developed by them, is a word-association test for uncommonness. In Figure Concepts, participants are given simple drawings of objects and individuals and asked to find qualities or features that are common to two or more drawings, based on which uncommonness scores are assigned. The Unusual Uses test involves finding unusual uses for ordinary everyday objects such as bricks. In the Remote Associations test, participants are asked to find a word that is common to two given words. Finally, in Remote Consequences, participants are asked to generate a list of consequences of unexpected events.

The Torrance Tests of Creative Thinking involves simple tests for divergent thinking and problem-solving skills, which are scored for Fluency (total number of interpretable, meaningful, and relevant ideas generated in response to the stimulus), Originality (statistical rarity of the responses among test subjects), and Elaboration (amount of detail in the responses) [272]. The Creativity Achievement Questionnaire is a self-reported test that measures creative achievement across ten domains [50]. Such tests, sometimes called divergent thinking tests, have received both support [51] and criticism [157, 273].

Several methods have been devised for the automated scoring of divergent thinking tests using the semantic approach. Neuro-linguistic programming is one such technique that is used to teach neuro-linguistic programming, a pseudoscience which shows that people are only able to perceive a small part of the world through their conscious awareness and that their view of the world is filtered by experience, beliefs, assumptions, and biological sensory systems. According to the concept behind neuro-linguistic programming, we act and feel based on our subjective perception of the world [273]. This technique was found to be valid for scoring originality [274]. Another one is the SparcIt Creativity Index Testing System created by James C. Kaufman and Mark A. Runco, which enables automated scoring of divergent thinking [275]. It is used for assessing creativity based on a combination of natural language processing, computational linguistics, and statistical data analysis.

Dan wondered whether such scoring systems could provide a measure of real creativity. He discovered that several researchers had taken a social-personality approach to the measurement of creativity. These researchers used personality traits such as independent judgment, self-confidence, attraction to complexity, aesthetic orientation, and risk-taking behavior as indicators of creativity [157, 276].

Gregory Feist showed that creative people are "more open to new experiences, less conventional and less conscientious, more self-confident, self-accepting, driven, ambitious, dominant, hostile, and impulsive." Openness, conscientiousness, self-acceptance, hostility, and impulsivity had the most potent effects from among the traits listed [277]. Intuitively, these sounded right to Dan. He had always thought that openness to experience is consistently related to creativity. He got to thinking about the art versus science debate, something that Jenny and he had engaged in a few years ago during a visit to Rome. Artists are typically characterized by higher levels of openness to experiences and lower levels of conscientiousness. While scientists also tend to be more open to experiences, they are also more conscientious and rank higher in the confidence-dominance aspects of extraversion than non-scientists [191]. Is "openness to experience" associated with randomness? We always tend to think of great artists, scientists, inventors, and other creative people as somewhat "chaotic people" who grow their hair out, forget to each lunch, and do extraordinary things by living chaotic lives.

Dan reversed back to the question of whether being creative necessarily meant being smarter. More than a century ago, the first few studies that attempted to associate creativity with intelligence were published, in which several theories for this type of an association were proposed. The Threshold Theory states that intelligence is a necessary, but not sufficient condition for creativity [278]. The Certification Theory specified that creativity is not intrinsically related to intelligence. People need to meet a mandatory level of intelligence to gain a certain level of education, which offers an opportunity to be creative. Dan also found the claim that displays of creativity are moderated by intelligence [279]. In fact, the Interference Theory claims that extremely high intelligence interferes with creative ability [280].

Dan found an excellent five-point summary by two prominent researchers, Sternberg and O'Hara: Creativity as a subset of intelligence; Intelligence as a subset of creativity; Creativity and intelligence as overlapping constructs; Creativity and intelligence as part of the same construct; Creativity and intelligence as distinct constructs [281] [157]. Below, each point is justified in detail:

a.  Creativity can be considered to be part of intelligence: Gardner's theory of multiple intelligences (MIT) is based on the examples of Picasso (spatial intelligence), Freud (intrapersonal), Einstein (logical-mathematical), and Gandhi (interpersonal) [282]. Sternberg's theory of successful intelligence considers creativity to be the main component of intelligence; it defines creativity as the ability to use pre-existing knowledge and skills to solve new and novel problems [281]. The Cattell-Horn-Carroll theory of cognitive abilities is comprehensive and supported by empirical evidence; it has informed a substantial body of research, including research on the development of tests for measuring IQ and other ability factors. For example, both fluency and originality in divergent thinking have been found to significantly affected by ability factors [283]. The Dual Process Theory of intelligence suggests a two-factor/type model of intelligence. Type 1 is a conscious process and concerns goal-directed thoughts. The type 2 model is presented as an unconscious process that involves spontaneous cognition, including daydreaming and implicit learning [284].

b.  Intelligence is a critical component in the development of creativity. Sternberg & Lubart's investment theory uses the example of the stock market. It shows that creative thinkers are like good investors: they buy low and sell high in the way that they think. Creative persons use unique ideas that are initially rejected by other people (similar to low-value stock), and they need to convince others of the value of the idea. By convincing others, they increase the value of the idea. The creative individual then "sells high" by passing on the idea to other people and moving on to the generation of another idea [276]. This theory states that successful creativity is composed of six distinct, but related elements: intelligence, knowledge, thinking style, personality, motivation, and environment. Thus, intelligence is considered as one of a group of six factors that can independently, or in combination with the other factors, lead to the generation of creative thoughts.

An additional model in this category is Amabile's Componential Model of Creativity. In this model, there are certain components that are considered to be necessary for creativity: domain-relevant skills, creativity-relevant processes, and task motivation [285]. An external component in the form of the surrounding social environment is also required. According to this model, creativity is considered to be the product of an individual who is intrinsically motivated, possesses a high level of domain-relevant skills and creative thinking levels, and is working in a highly creative environment. An interesting concept in this area is what is called the Amusement Park Theoretical Model. In this four-step theory of creativity, the metaphor of the amusement park is used to demonstrate that intelligence plays a vital role within each creative level [286]. To get to the amusement park, there are fundamental requirements such as transport to the park; in a similar way, intelligence is a prerequisite for but is not sufficient for creativity. Thus, if an individual does not have a basic level of intelligence, he or she will not be able to generate creative thoughts. The secondary requirements or subcomponents are more specific. It is akin to choosing the type of amusement park you want to visit, which may be considered analogous to the areas in which someone could be creative, such as art and science. The next level of specificity is much higher: for example, after deciding on the type of park (e.g., waterpark), a person chooses a specific park, similar to choosing a specific topic within the art domain. The final level is micro-domains, which refer to specific tasks within each domain, represented by individual rides at the waterpark or specific works of art.

c.  With regard to the third point (creativity and intelligence are overlapping yet distinct constructs), Renzulli's Three-Ring Conception of Giftedness suggests an overlap of high intellectual ability, creativity, and task commitment. Thus, creativity and intelligence are distinct constructs that can overlap under the correct conditions [287]. The PASS theory of intelligence suggests that planning is associated with an ability to solve problems, make decisions and take action and may overlaps with creativity[288]. However, this theory indicates that intuitive planning is not related to randomness.

d.  The Threshold Theory (TT) suggests that there exists a threshold between creativity and intelligence, and that a moderate level of intelligence is necessary for creativity. Both constructs are correlated to an IQ of ~120. Above this threshold, if there is any relationship at all between intelligence and creativity, it is small and weak [289]. In a study using data from the *Longitudinal Study of Mathematically Precocious Weth*, which includes a cohort of elite students differences in SAT scores at age 13 were found to be predictive of creative real-life outcomes 20 years later [290]. Further, a non-significant correlation between creativity and intelligence was reported in a gifted sample, and a significant correlation was reported in a non-gifted sample [291].

e.  Creativity and intelligence as coincident sets: There are no differences in the mechanisms underlying creativity in standard problem solving. At the same time, in regular problem solving, there is no need for creativity. Thus, creativity and intelligence are considered to be part of the same construct in problem solving. This is referred to as the "nothing-special" view [292].

f.  Creativity and intelligence as disjoint sets: Creativity and intelligence are entirely different, unrelated constructs. In one study, five creativity measures were administered to over 400 children from grades six to twelve, and these test findings were compared to results from previously administered IQ tests. Creativity and intelligence were shown to be distinct and unrelated. The high creativity group scored in the top 20% for the overall creativity measures, but they did not score in the top 20% for the IQ scores. The results were vice versa for the high intelligence group [293]. However, this concept was disproved by others, who showed that there was indeed a correlation between creativity and intelligence[294, 295].

According to some designers who are "bothered" on a daily basis with the need for creativity, "There's a myth that ideas just 'come to us' or that somehow creative inspiration is some product of divine intervention. "When we feel like all our creative cylinders are firing, doing great work and coming up with new ideas is a breeze. The flip side of feeling endlessly inspired, however, is having a creative block where no ideas come to us at all, or where all our ideas seem awful and not worth pursuing" [294]. This means that we need to be somewhat active, although not all the time, to become creative.

An important concept related to the creative process is lateral thinking. Lateral thinking entails solving problems through indirect methods. It applies reasoning that is not immediately apparent and involves the generation of ideas that may not be obtained with a traditional step-by-step logic[296]. Edward de Bono was one of the proponents of lateral thinking, and he played a big role in spreading the use of this term[297]. Such thinking is evident in the story of King Solomon wherein he resolves a quarrel over the parentage of a child by calling for the child to be cut in half so that each claimant would receive their fair half. He used the reaction to his order to make a judgment, based on the logic that the true parent would care more about the survival of the child than their ownership of the child.

Is this a "technique" that can be adopted in other situations?

Critical thinking is about judging the real value of statements and seeking errors, while lateral thinking considers the "movement value" of statements and ideas. One moves from a known idea to creating new ideas. Edward de Bono defines four types of thinking tools [298]:

a. Idea-generating tools: The use of these tools involves breaking regular thinking patterns. One can select an object at random or a noun from a dictionary, and associate it with the area they are thinking about. De Bono provides this example: the word "nose" could be randomly chosen and associated with an office photocopier; this might lead to the idea that the copier could emit a certain smell when it is low on paper so as to alert staff. With the Provocation Idea Generating Tool, a statement that is known to be wrong is used to create new ideas. A similar method is the use of provocation techniques, such as wishful thinking, exaggeration, reversal, escape, distortion, and arising. According to this method, the thinker creates a list of provocations and uses the most outlandish ones to move their thinking forward to new ideas. With the Challenge Idea Generating Tool, the question "Why?" in applied to situations in a non-threatening way…why does something exist…why is it done the way it is. Such questioning can lead to fresh new ideas.

b. The goal is to challenge anything at all, perhaps even the handles on coffee cups. The handle is placed there because the cup is often too hot to hold. But there are alternatives, such as insulated finger grips or separate coffee-cup holders.

c. According to the idea that the majority is always wrong, as suggested by Henrik Ibsen[6] [299]and John Kenneth Galbraith[7], for anything that is obvious and generally accepted as "goes without saying," question it, take on an opposing view of it, and try to convincingly disprove it. This is similar to de Bono's "Black Hat of Six Thinking Hats," which looks at identifying reasons for being cautious and conservative[300].

d. Focus tools: These tools try to broaden the search for new ideas by using "moving techniques." This entails moving from provocation to a new idea by extracting a principle, focusing on the difference, moment to moment, positive aspects, and special circumstances. Further, the Concept Fan Idea Generating Tool involves systematically expanding the range and number of concepts so that one ends up with an extensive range of ideas to consider.

e. Harvest tools: These ensure that more value is received from an idea-generating output.

f. Treatment tools: These tools are based on a consideration of real-world constraints, resources, and support[300].

Dan was not new to the idea of using creativity to solve problems, as it was a method that was employed by the company he worked for. But he was not sure if these creative techniques had any limitations in terms of their application. Would it not be nice if we could resolve ALL our problems with a little bit of creativity?

Many of the most significant non-technological innovations occur through improvements in everyday objects and tasks. This may happen either by accident or through learning from real-world experience. This idea also complements the concepts of randomness and lateral problem-solving skills. It means that we can often produce solutions whereby the problem appears as "obvious" on first perception [298].

Edward de Bono wrote: "By definition, a random word is not connected to any subject and so any word would work for any subject. In a passive information system, this would be total nonsense. However, in an active system, the random word provides a new entry point. As we work back from the new entry point, we increase the chances of using patterns we would never have used if we had worked outward from the subject area" [301]. That is, we don't have to connect a random word or image with the problem itself, but use it to get our brain thinking around the problem. By using an unrelated thing/object to associate with the problem, we end up opening new doors to solutions by stimulating a different pattern of thinking in our brain. We can also try the random input technique to get around creative blocks [294]. Indeed, Dan was looking into the concept of using randomness for his benefit. It seemed like a fun exercise.

Lateral thinking can be used to identify problems that we never thought we had, or it can be used to solve simple problems that have a considerable potential to affect life. The random input technique, which is a lateral thinking tool, involves picking a random word or an image and following its associations until we find new ideas that can be applied to our problem, as depicted in the following example [298]:

A new pet store wants us to design a logo for them, but they do not want to use paws or whiskers because every other pet store in town has paws and whiskers in their logo. We need a new and original idea. We can try using the random input technique to come up with a new idea. We start by opening a dictionary to a random page and picking a random word on that page. Assume that the word is "ottoman." We next apply all the words associated with ottoman that we can think to arrive at an idea. The aim is not to associate "ottoman" with the new logo, but to use "ottoman" as a stimulus to get us thinking in a new pattern about the problem. For instance, ottoman is associated with the Ottoman Empire, which was once the greatest and largest empire in the world. Kings ruled it. The king of the jungle is the lion. *How about a logo where a pet is portrayed as the king? A pet wearing a crown?* [294, 295].

An interesting blog by "a maker, tinkerer, writer, and designer" presents a recipe for kick-starting creativity [295].

*Start a Sketchbook: Fill a page with circles; Put some music on and draw to the beat; Fill a shallow bowl with paint and use it to stamp conventional materials such as a cork, straw, or fork; Draw clouds, come up with 15 different ways to draw them; Take a walk. Every time we reach a street corner, draw one thing that we see.*

*Keep a Journal: Document ideas, inspiration, and plans.*

*Collaborate with a friend: Sometimes, creating with a partner is the best way to find and nurture new ideas. We can get inspiration from other people through their unique outlook of the world and different way of doing things. Team brainstorming is a proven method for improving creativity.*

*Take a Class: Unrelated to our job. It can be any hobby we have. It can be an online course.*

*Be wrong: We can and maybe should allow ourselves to be free of perfection, and thus give ourselves the opportunity to explore new territory and thereby reach unexpected conclusions.*

Perfectionism is okay as long as it does not prevent us from trying new things and stepping outside of our comfort zone: make this the year that we celebrate mistakes! Many of the world's most successful innovators are not risk-averse, and would never have created their masterpieces or inventions without a ton of experimentation, testing, and iteration.

Give yourself time. Creativity requires time. Set our alarm clock an hour earlier than usual. Use this quiet time to journal, draw, write, or exercise. Do we frequently wake up in the middle of the night? Use that time for creative work. You can get a wide range of inspiration on how artists work and organize their time in the book "Daily Rituals: How Artists Work" [302].

Dan read about these techniques, but he wanted to climb a step higher.

Can us "Invite Randomness into Our Life?" Can we "infuse our life with little bursts of inspiration"? [295]. We can, in fact, enjoy "active randomness" for our own benefit. Get lost in your town. Make records of your journey through photos or written entries. Use a little of your money to buy trash at a second-hand store, and then try to turn it into treasure. Open up a cookbook at random. Close our eyes and pull three markers from a box. Color only with those markers for one week. There are many websites that provide us with so many ideas to boost creative thinking. Some of them may seem stupid or "too simple." But you must remember that many things in life are simple, and we tend to make them much more complicated than they are. Dan was not trying to be philosophical, but rather, practical. Randomness is not up in the sky and unattainable, and I should be able to find my own ways of making randomness an entry point for myself.

Dan was confused. Then he was not. He was trying to find all the associations between creativity, intelligence, and randomness. He liked the concept that there may be a threshold for intelligence that is required for creativity. But he also felt that the threshold needn't be too high. The practical question was, "Can I train myself to become more creative and can randomness be a method to reach this goal?"

His conclusion was that it is up to a person to decide whether or not they want to use randomness in his or her search for creativity.

# CHAPTER 19

## Looking at the world through "magic random lenses"

Diana was a widow who was working as a book reviewer. She did not live too far from Dan and was introduced to him by a friend a few months ago. Dan was not sure if she could be described as beautiful. He knew that she looked impressive though. Her husband had died more than ten years ago. They went out together a few times and met from time to time. Meeting her more than once a week felt too intense for Dan. Jenny's death was not that far behind him. Diana seemed not to care. In fact, what he liked about her was the fact that he did not feel any pressure to conform in their relationship. It seemed to be flowing in a random way.

It is not that the world is not random enough and we need to create more randomness. However, if randomness can be useful for us, and we sometimes want to create randomness, maybe we can consider wearing "magic random glasses."

Dan discovered a beautiful website with many beautiful pictures called "12 ways to add randomness and creativity to our photography" [303]. He thought of this as artificial randomness. Digital photography can use randomness for improving creativity. All kinds of effects can be achieved. Most importantly, they are fun. We can move our camera around in unexpected ways to add new and random elements. Good photography involves keeping our camera still while shooting to ensure fantastically sharp images. However, for randomness, in pictures and our life in general, sharp isn't always what we are after. One of the 12 ways is to add motion to shots by moving the camera while shooting: Rotate the camera, use long shutter speed, set the self-timer, and throw the camera into the air just before the shutter is released. We may also want to zoom in every once in a while. Zooming in and out provides us with a sense of movement in our images.

Can we look at the world around us in a similar way? A common problem in photos, and in our life, is poor focusing. We could correct this by focusing slightly in front or behind the part of the image that needs to be sharp. Dan was thinking, "do we not sometimes miss the real target by focusing on less important issues that should be in the background?" We could solve these issues with creative focusing, "where we do not get it slightly wrong. We make our shots obviously out of focus." Dan's take-home message was that real randomness might help us review our target from an entirely different angle [303].

Another photographic technique is to "shoot from our boots." We can look at the world differently by taking pictures with our camera placed on the ground so that we have a view of our subject from such a low angle. This can help introduce an entirely new and often random point of view for our shots. How about lying on the floor and looking at things around us? Observe the people around us. Find that random angle which lets us look differently at things. We may be able to see the world from a whole new perspective. We may capture extraordinary sights that we were not aware of before. On the other end of the spectrum, by attaching our camera to an extended monopod with a long shutter release cable, we can look at things in our life from a random height. Some of our most significant problems in life might look trivial. At the same time, we will be able to see things that we like, or that are of benefit for us, which we were unable to detect as long as we looked at it from the ground. So, in life, just as in photography, we can also randomly widen the angle to see more. Now all you have to do is wait for surprises that are just around the corner!

Overexposing is another popular technique. In actual photography, we end up with brightly burnt out images. In real life, random overexposure of our visions may provide us with a better look at things. It will bring our problems "out of the darkness." There is a technique in photography called *slow sync flash*. It is a technique for low-light shooting conditions where there is ambient light that we want to capture in addition to a theme that we would like to light up with a flash [303]. The bulb setting in our camera allows us to keep our shutter open for an extended period of time. If we choose random times, it can open up all kinds of possibilities for creativity in low-light situations.

Can I keep my shutter open when I need more light? Can I find the random light which can brighten up areas I did not look at before? Dan had begun to understand some things about random viewing. Being a practical person, or at least one that considered himself as such, he saw how this could be translated into everyday life.

Random multiple exposures on the same frame means that we can keep taking pictures randomly of the same object. If we have a digital camera that allows it, we may find this to be fun. In our life, we can look again, and again, and again, at the same task, the same person; unexpectedly, we may see a different picture. We create layers, and with the layers, the pictures keep changing. With a camera, we can override its settings by boosting it up to the maximum number of grains or noise. The idea is to go grainy: add random "noise" to our life. These can be translated as "random distractions." Dan was thinking that the word "distractions" could be a misnomer. But distractions need not be seen in a bad light. They could change the way you look at things and boost creativity.

White balance settings in our camera are meant to be used to help us compensate for different types of lights. Using different white balance settings can inject different color casts into our images. It can "warm up or cool down an image quite a bit and we get some lovely and creative images" [303].

So, we can randomly view the world in different ways to increase creativity, or more importantly, to help us resolve problems. At the same time, we can provoke randomness as a thinking strategy [304]. Michael Michalko is an acclaimed creativity expert. His bestselling books include *Thinkertoys*, *ThinkPak*, and *Cracking Creativity*, all of which deal with creativity from different angles [305]. He believes that Leonardi da Vinci was the first one to write about the importance of introducing random and chance events to produce variation in one's thinking patterns [306]. Leonardo da Vince devoted most of his life to understanding nature. He used experimentation and careful observation to master drawing and painting, and his aesthetic eye and creative mind to make scientific observations. His notebooks combine detailed observation with notes of his experiments [307].

Leonardi da Vinci said, "If we look upon an old wall covered with dirt, or the odd appearance of some streaked stones, we may discover several things like landscapes, battles, clouds, different attitudes, funny faces, draperies, etc. Out of this confused mass of objects, the mind will be furnished with an abundance of designs and subjects perfectly new...advise people to contemplate looking for longer periods at the walls, clouds, pavements, barks of the tree.., with the idea of looking for patterns and images to conceptually blend with thoughts" [306]. He believed that we could find inspiration for stunning ideas if we looked for random subjects to conceptually blend with our challenge. He himself was known to gaze at stains on walls or the ashes of a fire, the shape of clouds or patterns in the mud. He would imagine in them trees, battles, landscapes, and moving figures, and then abstractly blend the subjects of his imagination with the subject he was thinking about. This process can help unfold clear patterns of the images that we visualize. We can gradually move to the next phase by transferring our thoughts into our selected medium [306]. Steve Jobs was also known to emphasize on blending problems or working on several problems simultaneously.

Ever since Leonardo da Vinci urged artists to search for inspiration in the dirt on walls or the streaked patterns in stones, they have found that the accidental blot, the chance mark, or the naturally occurring stain can be a starting point for some extraordinary art [308]. The method recommended by Leonardo da Vinci was described by Malcolm Ludvigsen, an artist and mathematician, who showed that randomness and chance did indeed play a role in art [309]. An oil painting, when looked at carefully, appears to be nothing but a random collection of colored marks, but these resolve themselves into an image as we move away from the painting. It is this very randomness which sometimes gives the painting life and distinguishes it from a photograph, though the random element may not be visible to the viewer. This is achieved by starting with a random pattern and seeing the image in the chaos of the marks. It is also evident in early forms of cave art, where the artist sees an image, a horse for example, in the cracks and stains of a rock and then merely emphasized the patterns to create the actual image of a horse. Another source of randomness is when painting occurs by the so-called happy accident, wherein a slip of the brush produces a random but interesting mark.

On the "Thinkibility Thinking about Thinking, Creativity, Innovation, and Design" site [304], a summary by Michael Michalko, which can be found in his highly recommended book *Creative Thinking—Putting Our Imagination to Work* [310] is provided. He uses examples of how randomness can be applied to escape from standard thinking patterns. These are some of the things he said: "It is impossible not to make connections; Collect exciting stuff; Use pictures as random stimuli; Use your imagination; Take thought walks."

All this went against what Dan had always been told: "Focus, focus, focus." Dan was not puzzled. While he was the one that was always pressuring his team to focus, it was easy for him to accept the idea of actively creating randomness for improving creativity. Most importantly, he realized that the whole process could be fun.

TRIZ is a Russian creativity technique that uses randomness for problem-solving, analysis and forecasting. The concept was developed by the Soviet inventor and science fiction author Genrich Altshuller, and it was derived from the study of patterns of invention in the global patent literature [311] [312]. While working with the *Inventions Inspection* department of the Caspian Sea flotilla of the Soviet Navy in 1946, Altshuller realized that an inventive solution is required in cases of unresolved contradictions, for example, if improving one parameter impacts negatively on another. He later termed these "technical contradictions." This was the beginning of his journey towards developing TRIZ.

He was later arrested and sentenced to 25 years in the Vorkuta Gulag labor camps, partially on account of letters that he sent to Stalin and newspapers about individual decisions made by the Soviet government that he believed were erroneous [313]. Following his release, he published his research, which was based on a review of 40,000 patent abstracts to find out in what way innovation had evolved. He further developed his thoughts about technical contradictions and the concepts of the ideality of a system, contradiction matrix, and the 40 principles of invention [314]. He further wrote about ideas related to physical contradictions, laws on the evolution of technical systems, and observations of how talented and creative people work. He attempted to uncover patterns in their thinking, and to develop thinking tools and techniques to model this "talented thinking" [315]. In 1995, the Institute for TRIZ Studies was established in Boston, USA.

Altshuller's theory was developed based on much research and a review of many inventions across different fields that supported the perception of generalizable patterns in inventive solutions and helped establish methods for solving problems. Based on his theory, an algorithmic approach to the invention of new systems, as well as methods for the improvement of current systems were developed [316, 317].

TRIZ presents an approach for understanding and defining challenging problems, assuming that problems require an inventive solution. This method can help us come up with a range of strategies for devising innovative solutions. The underlying basis of this theory is that the aim of solving most problems is to overcome a dilemma or correct a trade-off between two contradictory elements. The TRIZ-based analysis attempts to systematically apply tools to find superior solutions that overcome the need for a compromise or trade-off between two elements. If we face a personal problem or task, rather than trying to find a solution in the traditional way, we are being asked for an abstraction of the problem. Looking into the "world's conceptual problems" may provide us with the "world's conceptual solutions," which can then trigger the solution to our problem. This approach is based on a multitude of established principles and solutions, which can be applied to any problem.

The first 40 inventive principles that formed the basis for TRIZ were said to account for virtually all of the patents that presented truly inventive solutions. A "conceptual solution" can be initiated by defining the contradiction which needs to be resolved and systematically considering which of the 40 principles may be applied to provide a specific solution that will overcome the contradiction in the problem at hand, enabling a solution that is closer to the "ultimate ideal result."

Doesn't this sound too simple? Dan wondered how one could resolve all their problems, overcome all their tasks, just by looking into these "conceptual solutions." But it could work if we were to focus on each contradiction separately and follow the process of (1) analyzing the contradiction, (2) searching for one or more principles that can be applied to the situation, and (3) using it/them to come up with a solution to the problem.

The core methodology of TRIZ is termed ARIZ. ARIZ is an algorithmic approach to finding creative solutions by identifying and resolving contradictions [318]. It includes the "system of inventive standards solutions," which replaced the 40 principles and consisted of 76 inventive standards and the SuField or Substance-Field model, which is a TRIZ analytical tool for modeling problems in relation to existing technological systems [319]. Sufield analysis provides a fast and simple way of considering different ideas drawn from the knowledge base. Other TRIZ-based computer programs were developed to assist engineers and inventors devise creative solutions for technological problems. Some of these programs may be used to apply another TRIZ method in order to reveal and forecast emergency situations and to anticipate circumstances that could have undesirable outcomes[319].

Every system is created to perform some functions. Dan learned that the desired function is the output from an object or substance, caused by another object with the help of some types of energy. Substances can be objects of any level of complexity. The action or means by which an action is performed is called a field. Although TRIZ was developed based on an analysis of technical systems, it has been used widely to understand and solve complex management problems [313]. For example, it is often used for cost savings analysis in government departments [320]. Many companies also use TRIZ to provide them with a competitive advantage. Samsung embedded TRIZ throughout the company. In 2003, TRIZ led to 50 new patents for Samsung; in 2004, one project alone, a DVD pick-up innovation, saved Samsung over $100 million [321]. Mars has documented how applying TRIZ led to a new patent for chocolate packaging [322]. The European TRIZ Association is a non-profitable association that provides an open community to unite efforts, suggest opportunities for global standardization, conduct further research, and provide mechanisms for exchange of information and knowledge on TRIZ-based innovation technologies [323].

What does all of this means to us as individuals? How can all of this be applied to my life? Most importantly, Dan wanted to find a clear association with randomness.

TRIZ is used to fight mental inertness and even dullness, on occasion [304]. The method is called "Focal Objects": You are required to take three entirely different objects, list out their properties and features, draw connections between their features and properties and the problem to be solved.

Writers use the technique of random inputs to overcome writer's block. The Creative Writer's Kit by Judy Reeves provides ice lolly sticks at random to choose, with opening sentences, plot twist ideas and end images: the exercise is to connect them in a compelling story [324]. The technique can be used with random words and images too. There are random word generators and random picture generators that we can use too. There are also other ways for building randomness: Visit a museum at random; Go to a movie theater and watch a movie based on a die toss; Go to a training center, and follow the course on the first floor, second room (pick random room and floor numbers); Buy a magazine we would never buy; Read a different newspaper than we usually read; Don't plan the next holiday, go with the flow, the weather and our spirit; Don't make reservations at hotels or camping sites; Change the usual way of commuting to work; Engage in unusual encounters; Organize a party for not-acquaintances; Engage in a conversation with an arbitrary person; If there are two alternatives, throw a dime to decide what to do; Have lunch with people other than from those from your department; Avoid standard hang-out places; Buy a book you would never otherwise buy for yourselves [304].

Dan found out that provoking randomness deliberately is about escaping routines and creating chances and opportunities beyond one's standard routines and worldviews. This may not be associated with TRIZ directly, but in our minds, we can study and apply techniques which we believe may be of help to us.

Dan liked to search the web. He also liked to play the association game. He would be reading something interesting that would lead to a question, which would take him to another page that had the answer, and so on. He could do it for hours. He called it "web dreaming."

We Google everything. Can we use it as our "randomization engine"?

The problem is that several of the commonly used search machines such as Google remember our preferences for sites, products, and topics. In so doing, the use of search engines reinforces our appetite for certain opinions and ways of thinking. We need to be careful about not losing our "personal randomness" by using these engines. We may want to use another computer or IP address, or use different search engines. We can look carefully at the results, as they may reveal different interpretations of our search and may provide us with other interpretations or clues [304].

Dan was having dinner with Diana that evening and was curious to pick her brain on the subject. He found out very quickly that Diana was one of those people that readily accepted these notions. In fact, she mentioned that it was something she had been practicing without any knowledge of the science behind it.

# CHAPTER 20

## Is randomness inheritable? Are our random thoughts genuinely random?

Dan was not a great fan of the biological process. He had never been comfortable with the whole issue of genes having so much control over us.

Dan had already looked into some of these issues in the past. He had discovered that developing educational techniques that are intended to enhance human creativity and that is supported by empirical research is a difficult task [325]. Looking into some of the techniques and theories described in the earlier chapters may lead to the realization that much of what we are all being told, or even intuitively think about creativity, can be easily contradicted.

The difficulty in associating creativity with cognitive architecture can partly explain the failure in advancing knowledge in this area. It has been suggested that the logic which underlies evolution by natural selection might underlie human cognitive architecture, and be responsible for enabling creativity. Several theories suggest that evolution happens as a result of natural selection, and that it is not merely created by humans. This could be the basis for our creativity. These theories also assume that human cognitive architecture evolves via natural selection. They emphasize on the importance of order in the development of creativity. Does it mean that these theories don't leave room for concepts associated with randomness?

Some consider that during the development of the human cognitive system, information is processed in the same manner as it was processed in the course of evolution by natural selection [326]. This means that similar process principles to evolutionary biology can be applied for understanding human cognition. Storing information is central to both evolutionary biology and human cognition. Our genes store information, and the information to be stored is determined by natural selection in the case of evolution. "Long-term memory" plays a similar role to genes in the case of human cognition. This means that each of us has a unique "signature," in much the same the way that we have a genetic signature. If this signature affects our creativity, and our imagination, then in most probability, no computer can imitate it.

In biological systems, sexual reproduction serves the purpose of evolution, as all the genomic information in an offspring is obtained from parents via a procedure that necessitates reorganization[325]. This restructuring ensures that offspring are not identical to either parent. Similarly, most of the information stored in our long-term memory is obtained from other people by imitation, by listening to what others say, or by reading what they write. Our surroundings, environment, experiences, and skills, all affect the information that is stored within us. When we try to imagine and use abstraction methods, all of these parameters also affect the results. In fact, we could also consider our genes to be involved in this process, rather than excluding them from the cognitive process. We can view our signature as a combination of our genes, which are intertwined with all of the events that have occurred and are happening to us during our life. Before data are stored, the information from which they are obtained are transformed and re-organized, and this may be affected by our genes [327].

With regard to the role of randomness, in evolutionary biology, it has been suggested that randomness is the engine of creativity. This is also reflected in the "randomness as genesis" principle [328, 329]. Variations between genomes ultimately can be sourced to random mutations which occur. It must be emphasized that the process may not be a simple random mutation, but that it may involve random generation and effectiveness testing too. This means that random mutations may play a role in the generation of creativity.

What are mutations? A mutation is defined as the permanent alteration of a gene. It is a result of errors that occur during DNA replication or other types of damage to DNA such as exposure to radiation or carcinogens, which may lead to error-prone repair or cause an error during repair [328]. Mutations may or may not produce apparent changes in the observable characteristics, which is our phenotype. Also, they play a part in both standard and abnormal biological processes of our life [329].

Mutations are random. They do not "try" to supply an organism with what it needs. There are theories that these random mutations might be beneficial, neutral, or harmful to us. The rate of mutation is affected by environmental factors, but these factors may not affect the direction of mutation. For instance, harmful chemicals can induce an increase in the mutation rate, but it is not necessary that the mutations that arise will impart resistance to the chemicals. Thus, genetic mutations appear to be random and do not seem to depend on the usefulness of potential mutations [330].

It is assumed that an appropriate information store is required for random processes to occur. Based on this notion, human creativity is dependent on random generation and effectiveness testing. As in evolutionary biology, random generation and efficiency tests are always dependent on the information store, such as the knowledge base. For example, we may reject many possible solutions because we "know" or "feel" that they may be ineffective or unsuccessful. Despite this ability to reject solutions based on our previous experience, skills, knowledge, and our genes, when faced with a new task, we are faced with a situation where we have to select between several solutions between which we are unable to distinguish. We may have no choice but to pick a solution at random and then test it for effectiveness. The solution that we eventually pick may or not work for us. The entire process of finding solutions repeats itself thousands of times per day, and is applied to both simple and less essential tasks, as well as some serious decisions that we make on a daily basis. These processes are part of the "creativity generator." Thus, random selections that we make can affect our creativity.

If a random generation is intrinsic to the creation of new information, as suggested by the "randomness as genesis" principle, it has certain structural implications [325]. For one, we require a mechanism that can narrow down the number of options we generate. Without getting too much into mathematics, if we are dealing with three options, there are 6 permutations to select from in a certain order. When dealing with ten options, there are 3,628,800 permutations. Do we have the ability to deal with so many options? We need a system that can narrow the options for us. Otherwise, our brains might explode every time we need to select a shirt in the morning (it already happens to some of us when we try to consider the implications of the color of shirt that we select to wear on a Monday morning).

The way our brain works, according to some theories, is by using a "narrowing mechanism" that limits the number of options [331]. Our working memory, which we put into action for every task in front of us, may act as an intermediary between long-term memory and the environment. It is our working memory that helps us to limit the number of options. It is an epigenetic system that plays an intermediary role between the information store and the external environment [326]. All of these assist with information processing within a given environment. We also require a method to link the environment to long-term memory by linking working memory to long-term memory. In the process, the features of working memory are altered. When our working memory is faced with new data from the environment, it is limited in terms of time and capacity. In contrast, when working memory deals with information from long-term memory, the capacity and time limits are expanded [332]. Vast amounts of information can be easily arranged from long-term memory for use by working memory to generate actions required by a large number of complex environments. So, our everyday decisions and solutions can be based on the information we have gathered through our life and the information we have inherited through our genes. If we accept this notion, it means that an information processing system can only function if it has acquired the massive amounts of information that are essential to its environment. The "borrowing and reorganizing principle" explains how most of this information is acquired. However, if we acquire so much information from the environment around us in addition to the information we have inherited from our parents, how does this leave room for creativity?

Before trying to understand creativity, we need to understand better how all the information we acquire is produced. Part of the information we gather is created by the type of process we use to organize it. Apparently, each of us has our own way of organizing, or not organizing, things. This "organizing method" is personal; it can tell other people a lot about us. It may reveal our way of consolidating our thoughts and our way of solving problems, overcoming obstacles, creating friendships, and much more. Apparently, any reorganization not only results in the creation of something new, but also involves the mixing up of information that was previously generated.

If all these processes are based on and re-organized from information that is already available (in the environment, our genes, and memory), how can they be described as being "truly random"?

Real novelty is explained by the "true randomness as genesis" principle. However, although such "true randomness" would be strictly random and ignore the wealth of information we already have in our genes and memory, it would still bear our "flavor" or "signature." This means that our randomness is much more personal than we believe it to be, and most importantly, our randomness is something that can never be produced by a computer software.

Selecting a random word from a book as a process of generating creative thinking is something that both people as well as a random computerized engine can do. Abstractions of these words can also be made by a computer, but these are likely to be very different from the abstractions we make. In fact, our abstractions are likely to be different from the ones that our neighbors, our spouse, or even our child comes up with. The associations of these abstractions to the task in front of us, which is what creativity is all about, is personal. It will be "tainted" by our flavor, or signature if you will, whether we want it or not. If we give five people the same recipe for a cake and all five follow the instructions word by word, it is still most likely that we will end up with five different cakes.

Coming back to biological evolution, we can say that natural selection leads to biological novelty. Thus, evolution is creative in the sense that it leads to novelty. This may also explain why we have become better at some tasks (not all) than our great-grandfathers and cavemen. Evolution by natural selection is often explained by the "randomness as genesis" principle, and if we apply this principle to cognition, it means that our creativity is at least partly explained by the same principle [325].

The random generation and testing method can explain some acts of human creativity (such as selecting the right shirt, which can also be considered as a creative act), but can it explain all of our creativity?

When we are deciding on a solution for a problem, we use our previous experience, skills, and knowledge for making the choice. That is, we tend to rely on the knowledge we already have to narrow down our options. However, if we face an entirely new problem, we may find ourselves in a situation in which two or more options are equally likely to lead to a solution, as none of the information in our long-term memory provides any indication of which one of the two options may be better. In such situations, we may rely on information that we "borrow" from someone else, Google, or any other source. For example, we may seek the advice of another person whom we believe may have more skills than we have with which to solve the problem. Alternatively, we may approach a random person on the street and ask them. If we are in a shop, we may want to consult with the person next to us or the salesperson. However, how about asking a random person in the street to assist us in choosing between John and Danny as our future husband? Would their random answer be better than our mother's advice or our thoughts on the matter? Also, if we just selected the first homeless person we saw on the street to answer this question, would the selection process be truly random?

Sometimes, borrowing information and advice, including random advice, is not sufficient. What should we do then? How do we proceed? In such cases, too, random generation and testing seems to be the only method that can yield satisfactory results [325]. We randomly pick an option and determine what the outcome of that selection is. Note that in the absence of appropriate knowledge, we cannot know the outcome of that decision before making it. Because the outcome cannot be known before a test of its effectiveness, the choice is random. When there is no information, or we feel that the information we have is insufficient for making the decision, we may have no alternative but to use random selection.

So how would we select say, a spouse, under such circumstances?

Humans tend to be creative when it comes to solving problems, making choices, and making decisions. Randomness is required for human creativity. Thus, the "randomness as genesis" principle may be the only available instrument for making choices, as it provides the basis for human creativity [325]. This does not mean, however, that all creativity is a result of randomness. Some of us tend to use randomness more than others. But the principle tells us that, whether we are aware of it or not, some of our choices, decisions, and moves, are random, even when we don't apply any active creativity techniques. Now, whether we can consider all of these random decisions as creative is a question of how we choose to define them. Dan felt that his thoughts on the matter were as good as that of any creativity expert.

Some researchers believe that creativity derived from randomness can be classified as a biological skill[333]. Making random decisions is also a matter of survival. Without it many humans may get stuck standing place for an entire day, not knowing which way to turn or what to do next.

If random selection is a skill, can we improve it? Is it like learning a new language? Would it still be random if it were learned? Some experts believe that it may be possible to encourage people to engage themselves in random generation and testing conditions that they may otherwise not normally do as a means of improving their random skills. Can these methods actually facilitate creativity?

Dan was wondering about the amount of data a person stores and whether this would affect their randomization processes. When we have a lot of information, we can use our extensive, sophisticated knowledge base to reduce the number of problems that require us to make random decisions. Most probably, we would still face some questions that require random answers. However, the more extensive our knowledge base, the more we can limit the choices for random selection. It may sound like a contradiction, but some experts think that the first requirement of creativity is an extensive knowledge base. It goes well with the concept that creative people invest a lot in gaining knowledge and experience in their field. When they reach a certain level, beyond the level of the uninitiated, they become creative and climb one step above. This climbing process may seem random, and it may well be. However, this type of randomness is dependent, or rather, evolves from a previous investment in that specific field. This explains why a cake baked by a cook, with their own personal "flavor" or "touch," is likely to be better than someone with less baking experience. This principle applies to other arts as well. Such randomness-based creativity, which is what we admire and is the type of creativity that can advance our world, is based on the hard work put in by people in acquiring certain skill sets.

*Outliers: The Story of Success*, a non-fiction book by Malcolm Gladwell[334] examines the factors that contribute to achieving high levels of success. To support his thesis, he examines many successful people in different fields: Microsoft co-founder Bill Gates, The Beatles, and Joseph Flom (who turned Skadden, Arps, Slate, Meagher & Flom into one of the most successful law firms in the world). Gladwell explains how cultural differences play a large role in perceived intelligence and rational decision making. He also explains how people such as Christopher Langan and J. Robert Oppenheimer, both known for their exceptional intelligence, met with such different fortunes [335]. He continuously emphasizes a "10,000-Hour Rule," which posits that we may achieve world-class expertise through hard work and practice for a total of 10,000 hours. The authors of the original study that presented the 10,000-hour rule have disputed Gladwell's interpretation [336]. This rule has been torn down by another published study, too [337], which challenged the notion that individual differences in performance in such domains as music, sports, and games might actually reflect individual differences in the amount of deliberate practice. Hard work was defined as engagement in structured activities explicitly created to improve performance in a domain. In a meta-analysis covering all major domains in which deliberate practice has been investigated, it was found that deliberate practice explained only 26% of the variance in performance for games, 21% for music, 18% for sports, 4% for education, and less than 1% for other professions. The conclusion was that deliberate practice is significant, but not as significant as is often argued.

Frans Johansson's book *The Click Moment: Seizing Opportunity in an Unpredictable World* states that deliberate practice is related to success only in domains that have a highly stable structure, such as tennis, chess, and classical music. In these fields, the rules never change, so we can work hard until we achieve the best results. However, in less structured fields such as entrepreneurship and music, rules can change or there may be no rules at all [338]. Take the example of Richard Branson, who began his career in the record business then branched out into other fields. Branson's Virgin Group has 400 companies under its belt and is even launching people into space [336].

Dan believed in hard work to some extent, and he was convinced that creativity is not just a spark that makes a random appearance. He was telling Diana that he was convinced about the importance of hard work, and that randomness may bring the inspiration that drives you to work hard. Thus, randomness may be a trigger for hard work, and possible success. Diana asked him that evening if he believed there was a way to get this random-creative spark without working at all or without using any active-random technique.

This was something to think about.

# CHAPTER 21

Brainstorming with our brain and with other brains

Now that Dan had gotten Diana involved in the project, both of them had started surfing the web together for more data. He was not sure whether she was doing it only on his behalf. He sensed that she had her own personal interest in the subject.

The main point of interest for them was the "randomness as genesis" principle of creativity. They found that some aspects of creativity are teachable. For example, mathematics instructors teach the "guess and check" method of problem solving [325]. Another method of creativity that was described over fifty years ago is brainstorming [339], which is a group creativity technique through which members of a group try to find a solution for a problem by producing ideas that are spontaneously or randomly generated by its members [340]. Although brainstorming is random in many ways, it can also be directed. Several experts believe that if we put several people in a room and ask them to brainstorm an idea, they come up with more creative thoughts if they are not led by instructors or given pre-prepared discussion guidelines. Dan had participated in several of these brainstorming groups over the years, in an attempt to provide better answers to their clients. He never got too deeply into it. Although he did believe that better solutions could be generated through team work, in most cases, his team discussions and meeting were very structured rather than random.

The brainstorming procedure was developed as a practical technique[341]. It placed emphasis on the generation of a large number of original ideas by a group rather than an individual problem-solving context [325]. The original assumption was that, if the number of ideas was increased, the quality of the best ideas would also increase. Many studies supported the concept that brainstorming can increase not only the quantity of ideas but also the number of good ideas. On the other hand, other studies have shown that group solving is not a must. We can merely ask many people to generate many ideas, and they may also come up with numerous good ideas [342, 343].

Diana suggested that if we accept the "randomness as genesis" principle as a basis for creativity, we can also use it to explain the effectiveness of brainstorming [325]. As explained in the previous chapter, according to this principle, innovation and creativity can be derived from the process of randomly generating ideas from a knowledge bank and testing them. Brainstorming requires the rapid generation of random ideas from an existing knowledge base. The more people in the room, the larger is the information base. It also broadens the ability for abstraction and associations with the task on the table. Each association made by a member can also broaden the associations made by others. Theoretically, this may improve the process of creative problem solving. Thus, if we can encourage a group of people to randomly generate a large number of solutions under conditions where there is not enough knowledge in each of their long-term memories, we may end up with creative solutions. Diana was of the opinion that "brainstorming may work because it maximizes the use of the 'randomness as genesis' principle to generate novel moves" [325, 340].

Osborn explains that the "creative efficacy" of brainstorming can be improved via two methods: *deferring of judgment* and *aiming for quantity[344]*. The idea was to set up an atmosphere without too many social inhibitions among group members, in order to stimulate idea generation and increase creativity. *Aiming for quantity* is used as a method to facilitate problem solving, under the assumption that the greater the number of ideas generated, the higher is the likelihood of producing a creative and improved solution. The next method is to withhold criticism (or *defer judgment*). All participants are required to focus on adding to the ideas and save any criticism for later stages. This way, all members feel free to generate unusual and crazier ideas. The aim is to encourage everyone to come up with as many ideas as possible that are beyond the "traditional" way of thinking and to look at tasks from a new perspective. These new ways of thinking might generate better solutions. Finally, brainstorming calls for combining and thus improving ideas in a synergistic way, as expressed in the "1 + 1 = 3" formula. Stimulation leads to better and more creative ideas via the process of group associations.

There are many ways in which a brainstorming session can be conducted. For instance, participants may be asked to write down their ideas anonymously, after which the whole group votes on the best ones. Alternatively, the group can be divided into smaller groups to discuss one aspect of the problem, after which the whole forum can reconvene to discuss the final solution of each group. Sometimes, ideas that were previously dropped are brought forward again once the group has re-evaluated them. This technique requires a trained facilitator. Incentives can augment the creative process. People are usually willing to work far longer to achieve unique results if they are given some compensation in exchange for their input [345]. Computerized programs can also be used to guide a brainstorming session. Electronic brainstorming (EBS), does enhance efficiency by eliminating traveling and turn-taking during group discussions. It also overcomes some of the psychological constraints associated with face-to-face meetings [340]. With the help of a software program, all the ideas that are being generated can be displayed in real time. This would stimulate brainstormers, as they would be able to focus their attention on the flow of ideas being generated without the potential distraction of social cues[346]. This technology can lead to the production of more ideas while assisting group members in focusing on the developing concepts. Such a method can also reduce redundancy: as the generated ideas are being constantly displayed, participants can avoid duplicating or repeating another participant's comment or idea.

Dan wondered if it was possible to brainstorm just with himself. This is when he discovered the method of *individual brainstorming*, which asks us to engage in free writing, free speaking, word association and drawing mind maps, which is a visual note-taking technique in which people diagram their own thoughts. Individual brainstorming can be superior to group brainstorming in some situations such as creative writing [347]. So while group brainstorming is useful in some situations, individual brainstorming may work better in others.

Dan found studies which showed that group brainstorming produced fewer ideas than individuals working separately[348]. This was attributed to a "blocking effect." That is, if a member hears someone else coming up with the idea that he or she just thought of, they may feel that their idea is less relevant. If brainstorming is a process in which "a participant generates ideas and stores them in short-term memory and eventually extracts them from short-term memory to express them," then such a blocking effect is more critical. It inhibits a person's sequence of thoughts in terms of generating their ideas and remembering them[349]. During group brainstorming, some members may build on the ideas of other members, thus decreasing the novelty or variety of ideas, even though the overall number of ideas might not decrease. This is called "collaborative fixation" [350]. Evaluation apprehension, or anxiety, may also affect some people under these circumstances, thus reducing their creativity[351]. Some individuals may feel that their ideas are not as valuable as the ideas generated by the group. Dan was wondering whether the best approach is to combine individual and group brainstorming.

Another technique which shares similarities with brainstorming is goal-free problem solving. In this method, a group of people are confronted with a problem to solve without a specific objective. By reducing the specificity of goals, and thus making them more random, we increase both learning and problem-solving skills, when compared to problem solvers presented with problems with specific goals[352]. Removing the specific goal is associated with much better and more variable solutions, which were achieved within a shorter period.

Both brainstorming and goal-free problem solving require the generation of as many solutions as possible. During brainstorming, participants are asked to produce as many results as possible without criticizing any of the solutions suggested by them or others. In the case of goal-free problem solving, participants are asked to provide as many answers as they can without reference to a target. In both methods, the generation of ideas, solutions, and results is done in an entirely random way. The results are thus produced according to the "randomness as genesis" principle. The efficacy of both brainstorming and of the goal-free problem-solving techniques is attributed to randomness [325]. Setting the right conditions for random generation of ideas and solutions and reducing working memory load can enhance creativity and improve the ability of participants to come up with better results.

The "Mindtools" website describes brainstorming as a relaxed, informal approach to problem solving with lateral thinking [353]. When properly conducted, it may encourage people to come up with ideas that may even seem a bit crazy. Some of these ideas can be transformed into creative solutions, while others can be used as a starting point for even more ideas. This method assists in overcoming brain blocks and getting us "unstuck." It also helps us move out of our regular or normal ways of thinking. A well-conducted brainstorming session can bring into play all the team members' diverse experiences and increase the richness of the ideas being explored. This means finding better solutions to the problems that we face.

Dan was thinking about individual brainstorming again. When we brainstorm on our own, we do not have to worry about other people's egos or opinions, and we may feel freer and more creative [353]. If a person feels uncomfortable about bringing up ideas in front of others, mostly his craziest ones, he may find it more relaxing to explore them on his own. Individual brainstorming can be more effective for finding solutions to simple problems, generating a list of ideas, or focusing on a broad issue, while group brainstorming is often more useful for solving complex problems. However, the degree of complexity is very subjective. Some of our most personal issues may seem simple to others but are far from simple to us.

The effectiveness of group brainstorming may be associated with the quality of the individuals who participate. We could assume that if we brainstorm with ten prominent Harvard professors, the group will come up with a different set of solutions than those generated by a group of more "ordinary people." However, it does not necessarily mean that one of these lists of ideas is better than the other. In fact, if we only include experts in a field for a brainstorming session, we may get better answers, but they may all think alike. So should participants be selected based on their expertise? This might work, for example, if we want to select the best ice cream flavor and we call in a group of ice cream experts. How about bigger problems such as economic crises? Would it not possible to generate better and more creative solutions by gathering together a group of people who have a variety of different thinking styles and are not necessarily all economists?

Whether alone or in a group, the aim of brainstorming is to encourage ourselves and others to develop as many ideas as possible, including what seem to be "irrelevant random ideas," and to stay away from the mainstream train of thought as much as possible. It should be a fun process, free of pressure, including the burden of the problem itself.

Following an individual or group brainstorming session, we will find ourselves with a list of ideas that need to then be analyzed. Some like to use affinity diagrams to organize ideas and find common themes. Several techniques including Decision Matrix Analysis and Paired Comparison Analysis have been designed to help us choose among different options [354]. The paired comparison analysis is designed to assist us in making choices based on our underlying priorities. It can also be used to compare options that don't seem to have much in common at all. Some of the most challenging decisions to make are the ones that have to be made when the options at hand do not seem to be related. To use this model, a table with all the options is created. We list our options out on a sheet of paper and compare each option to each other. We then score them according to difference, from 0 (no difference) to 3 or 5 (significant difference). Next, we consolidate the results by adding up the scores for each option. Once we see the options in front of us and we have the chance to weigh them head to head, we may find that making our decision is not as difficult as we initially believed it to be. This method can be used for producing order from randomness.

We must remember that these are only tools, and that the final decision is always ours. We need to think logically about what the table is telling us, as well as trust our instincts and experience, before making and implementing our choices.

Six Thinking Hats is another method that utilizes the concept of lateral thinking to evaluate ideas from different perspectives. It was designed by Edward de Bono as a tool for group discussion and individual thinking [355]. The concept underlying this technique is that people think in distinct ways that can be deliberately challenged; also, these distinct ways can be used in a structured way so as to help one another develop tactics for thinking about problems. These are the six different ways in which the brain can be challenged:

*Managing Blue*: Looking at the big picture and identifying the overall goal and subject that we need to think about

*Information White*: Looking for facts, data, and available information

*Emotions Red*: Examining the instinctive gut reactions and emotional feelings

*Discernment Black*: Being practical when looking at the logic for identifying the reasons to be cautious and conservative

*Optimistic Response Yellow*: Looking for the benefits and sunny side of situations *Creativity Green*: Looking into both provocation and investigation by thinking outside the box.

Each direction, or color, is symbolized by a different hat, which represents a different way of thinking [356]. Further, sequences always begin and end with a blue hat. Each of these directions is associated with certain aspects of the problem, but none of them individually represent an entirely natural way of thinking. They may, however, reflect the results of our thinking. This method can help better define the directions and solutions a thinker may come up with. A brainstorming group agrees together on how to think; then, they think, evaluate the outcomes of that thinking, and decide on what they should do next [357]. Some examples of sequences are as follows: initial ideas, Blue-White-Green-Blue; choosing between alternatives, Blue-White-Yellow-Black-Red-Blue; solving problems, Blue-White-Green-Red-Yellow-Black-Green-Blue. Companies, such as Speedo Researchers, are known to have tried the six thinking hats technique for the creation of swimsuits[358].

Malcolm Gladwell's theories on "blink" thinking are based on a similar concept. In his book *Blink: The Power of Thinking Without Thinking*[359], he talks about the ability to create solutions from limited information gained over a very short period of experience [360]. The notion is that spontaneous decisions maybe as good as the carefully planned and considered ones. This implies that, sometimes, having too much information can interfere with the accuracy of judgment. This theory states that experts often make better decisions with snap judgments than they do with volumes of analysis. The book argues that intuitive judgment is developed by experience, training, and knowledge. Being a physicist, Dan, on first reading, was not sure about this. He did feel, however, that this notion was in sync with the concept of randomness.

It was then that he chanced upon the book *Think! Why Crucial Decisions Cannot Be Made in the Blink of an Eye* [361] by Michael LeGault. This book argues that "Blinklike" judgments are not a substitute for critical thinking. He criticizes Gladwell's theory, saying that "Blink exploits popular new-age beliefs about the power of the subconscious, intuition, even the paranormal." Similarly, Nobel Prize winner Daniel Kahneman, author of *Thinking, Fast and Slow*, speaks about the advantages of rationality over intuition. He says that "Malcolm Gladwell's story has helped people, in a belief that they want to have, which is that intuition works magically; and that belief, is false." [362].

Gladwell's theory has also received some support from the community. In the article "Understanding Unconscious Intelligence and Intuition: Blink and Beyond," Lois Isenman agrees with Gladwell that the unconscious mind has a surprising knack for "thinking without thinking," but argues that its ability to integrate many pieces of information simultaneously provides a much more comprehensive explanation than thin-slicing. She writes, "Gladwell often speaks of the importance of holism to unconscious intelligence, meaning that it considers the situation as a whole. At the same time, he stresses that unconscious intelligence relies on finding simple underlying patterns. However, only when a situation is overwhelmingly determined by one or a few interacting factors, is holism consistent with simple underlying signatures. In many situations, holism and simple underlying signatures pull in different directions."[363]

Going back to the six hats technique, a typical project starts with an extended white hat action for collecting and analyzing the data and information. Thereafter, each hat is used for a specified period of time, except for the red hat, which is limited to a short time so that it is used to express an instinctive gut reaction, rather than a form of judgment. The key to using this technique efficiently is to focus on a particular approach, as required, to review a problem. For example, it could first be used to explore the problem; second, to develop a set of solutions; and finally, to select an appropriate solution by critical examination of the solutions[300].

In any collaborative thinking activity, there is a natural tendency for "spaghetti thinking," where one person thinks about the benefits while another considers the facts and so on. This can be avoided with the six hats technique, as everyone considers the same aspect of the problem together by using the same hat to look at the problem. These hats provide the direction in which they need to think next.

Additional techniques which assist in selecting between options as a team, mainly when the differences between options are entirely subjective, is the modified "Borda count" and "multi-voting." The Borda count is a single-winner election method in which voters rank options or candidates in order of preference. The candidates are assigned points according to rank. Once all the votes have been counted, the option or candidate with the highest points is declared as the winner. This system is consensus based rather than majoritarian [364]. In elections, where this method is now being used, each rank is assigned points according to the number of candidates contesting the election. In such a system, a candidate who is ranked first by the absolute majority of voters may not get elected because the method affords considerably more importance to voters' lower preferences. That is, it tends to favor candidates that are supported by broad consensus, rather than candidates who are the favorite of a majority. Thus, it promotes consensus and helps avoid the "tyranny of the majority" [364].

We can use these and other similar methods to help us generate the right solutions and reduce the number of mistakes we make. However, we can never completely eliminate all possible mistakes, not to mention that our lives would be quite dull if all the decisions we made turned out to be right. But it is also important to maintain a balance by not repeating mistakes too many times.

It was clear to Dan that randomness is good. It was also clear to him that under some circumstances, it is also required. "Blinking is not randomness though," he thought. At least not the type he was thinking about. He was now in pursuit of understanding controlled randomness, something akin to what a conductor would use to direct participants in a brainstorming session.

# CHAPTER 22
## Get random and create

Dan was having Sunday brunch with Diana. They used to meet from time to time for brunch at a nice restaurant next to the golf club. Neither of them really liked golf, but they liked to watch people playing from the balcony of the restaurant, especially if it was a beautiful day. Dan ordered salads for both of them. He was telling Diana about his "discoveries" about randomness, blinking, and solutions. Diana never liked reading these books, and much preferred to hear Dan's interpretations or representations of them.

The theory of evolution is not necessarily wrong. It also does not inevitably contradict the role of randomness as a contributing factor, or even as "the origin of creativity" [365]. By looking at creative advances in almost every field of technology, art, science or society, which has made a major change to humanity, we realize that they are all "quantum jumps." Each innovation comes out of what we already know and takes us one step, and even a few steps, forward. Many of the developments are the result of out-of-the-box thinking, while others are a result of fundamental deviations from mainstream thinking. But even the small inventions, decisions, and problem-solving tasks we engage in every day may require us to take such leaps.

Dan was reading to Diana from an inspiring blog called "Randomness as the origin of creativity." It is an investigation into random fractals as a method of producing random shapes. The author describes coming up with resemblances of shapes we see in nature. They were both looking at some of the shapes. The term "fractal" is a geometric concept related to, but not synonymous with, chaos [366]. A fractal is an object composed of subunits and sub-subunits that resemble the more massive-scale structure, a property known as self-similarity. Fractals are thus irregular objects with fractional non-integer dimensions, which display self-similarities[367]. The estimation of a fractal dimension of an object gives an ideal approximation of its real-time dimensions. A fractal structure demonstrates power-law scaling. The smaller the measuring device, the larger the length of a fractal object. Fractal analysis is a mathematical technique for quantifying complex shapes [368].

Some of the random forms they were looking at were not similar to anything they had known or seen before, and they were beautiful.

The author of the blog said, "In fact, I couldn't create such forms myself because their aesthetic value wouldn't occur to me until *after* their creation." They could not agree more. Diana was not sure how to correlate the beautiful shapes and the beautiful salads with physics.

"If this concept is true, and can be applied to another field of our life, it does not only mean that we can come up with totally new ideas using randomness, but that these can be much more attractive," Dan was telling her.

Based on this notion, the author suggests that indeed combining random experimentation with our ability to recognize a valuable solution may set up a pathway to creativity. The suggestion is to "keep messing around until we find it." We may not like this, as no one really wants to "mess around" endlessly when looking for a solution.

Our ways of thinking are typically linear and associative: Every thought that we have leads to the next thought and so on. In order for us to come up with an innovation or a breakthrough thought, we need to be able to think in a way that is different from our habitual ways, which also links us to other people's thoughts. It involves breaking our patterns of associative and linear thinking by generating unconnected random thoughts [365].

Diana told Dan that some people believe that creativity comes from our subconscious and therefore requires meditation [369]. Based on this theory, a creative need is communicated to our subconscious mind, which has a generative capacity that exceeds that of our conscious brain. When the subconscious mind finds a creative solution, it passes it back to the conscious brain, and we can use it. The "random fractals" described above imply that creativity is about identifying unique solutions among those we haven't seen as yet. It also implies that we can randomly generate these innovative and unnoticed solutions by "closing our eyes" [365]. Dan did not appreciate the sudden entry of the unconscious mind, but he was willing to accept that it may somehow be involved in the generation of randomness. It is only a matter of how different areas in our brain that we do not know too much about are defined.

It is unclear whether something that comes out of our unconscious is random, although it seems so. This "unconscious randomness" may, in fact, not be so random. It is in most likelihood derived from our personal experiences, knowledge, and many other sources. "Just because we do not fully understand it, it does not mean it is not random," Diana agreed.

The concept of random fractals suggests the existence of a "genetic code" for the generation of random images. This code theoretically drives the forms and features of these genetic fractals. "So, all I have to do is change the genetic code randomly, and the genetic fractals will take on any form. If I wait long enough, they will create a bunny rabbit." If we accept the existence of this type of a "genetic code" that underlies randomness, we may accept the hypothesis that it can be applied to all fields. If we create a genetic code that underlies mathematics and randomly alters it, we can detect a unique mathematical formula. We can do this for music, mechanical engineering, and even cooking recipes [365].

Now, what if the code, our unconsciousness, or any other generator of creativity, came up with many solutions? How would we know which one of them is the right one? In the case of art or music, we can look at or listen to many random images or songs, and pick the one WE believe is the right one, in case our brain has not already made the selection for us. However, it would more difficult for non-mathematicians or non-engineers to select the best formula in math or engineering. The question being asked is, "Can we be creative outside our areas of expertise?" Can we be a creative painter, without being an artist?

If we create something that we are not able to appreciate due to nonexistent skills, it is possible that somebody will. This points to the need to surround ourselves with people who are smarter, more creative. In this way, we can make the most out of our creativity.

Dan was telling Diana as they were walking out, "If we are very creative we can invent something which is far beyond the cognition of any person, something which no one thought about before. It may even be something people do not appreciate the creativity behind at this point in time. An inability to spot innovative solutions happens all the time to all of us. We miss opportunities because we do not realize them as such. But these could still be super creative solutions."

How often do we hear about an entrepreneur with an invention to which everyone, including ourselves, would say, "it is so simple, how come no one thought of it before?" or "I once had this thought, too bad I did not realize it is a golden egg." How many golden eggs are running through our head that we view just as ordinary eggs? How often do we say "I could easily have done that myself, but I did not"? We might have, but we didn't and couldn't recognize the opportunity when it was staring at us in the face. Diana responded in the words of Louis Pasteur (who discovered antibiotics by chance), "chance favors only the prepared mind." [370].

We could view the above quote by Louis Pasteur as being "anti-random." This is not true. In fact, it tells us that randomness may be somewhat directed…that we can control our chances. This cannot be applied in the context of winning the lottery, of course, but perhaps it can be applied in the context of coming up with innovative ideas. History is filled with stories of great discoveries that are a result of serendipity or chance. As Douglas Osheroff, a physicist who received the Nobel Prize in 1996, was quoted in his talk about how scientific discoveries are made, "most advances require both insight and good fortune" [371]. Pasteur pointed out that the opportunities granted by chance are only harvested by a prepared mind. Years of training, dedication, and even failure are necessary to prepare the mind for random innovative ideas that may come up. Similarly, Oliver Smithies, who was awarded the 2007 Nobel Prize for his work in physiology, dedicated an entire speech to chance, opportunity, and planning. He emphasized the importance of enjoying the process of getting there. Nobel laureates seem to always point to the important role of failure in success and how it generally precedes success. Most of them have used their failures as teaching points that have finally led to their success [371].

Alexander George Ogston, a biochemist, puts it nicely in his 1970 talk about discoveries in science: "Finally, in closing, I emphasize the importance of choosing a branch of science that makes our everyday work enjoyable, as mine has been. When it was not, I changed it! I also emphasize the importance for a scientist to have other interests for diversion. Mine is still flying. When science is being fickle, a happy relationship, mine is with my wife Nobuyo Maeda, can also be a source of comfort at such times and can provide a captive audience with whom to share science's much less frequent times of bliss. Scientific happiness is about sharing ideas and the daily excitement of new results with students, colleagues and other scientists. My adviser, Sandy Ogston, had it right when he summarized his view of our discipline. His words are the theme of my visit to Sweden. They capture better than I can what it means to spend a life doing science. For science is more than the search for truth, more than a challenging game, more than a profession. It is a life that a diversity of people leads together, in the closest proximity, a school for a social living. We are members one of another" [372].

There is so much wisdom in his speech that can be applied to almost every field.

Intriguingly, modern research into failure and success has shown that those who succeed approach failure differently from those who never try again and fail. Those who consider themselves as successful often over-attribute their success to their own work, and claim that they have worked hard to become ready and to become more permissive to the next random idea, opportunity, or chance. On the contrary, those who fail often assign blame to external forces that are outside their control [371]. Nobel laureates want to get this message across to current and future generations: "we must learn from failure and be prepared for chances when they arrive. Life, viewed as a series of random coincidences, is one magnificent opportunity." This means that if we have many random opportunities in front of us, even if we make the wrong decisions from time to time, and we all do, the trick is really to know how to realize as quickly as possible and with as little harm to ourselves as possible, that we have made the wrong decision, and to prepare ourselves for the next random event.

Dan was telling Diana on the drive back, "Yet, much of humanity functions in an 'anti-deBonian fashion.' Most of us are looking for the next best idea based on something we just read about. We are looking under the light." "Forget it. It won't work. Get random and create" [365]. Our innovation will randomly shine out in the dark. But we need to make the right preparations in order to be able to receive such innovations.

# CHAPTER 23
## Clustering, a sign of true randomness

*So much of life, it seems to me, is determined by pure randomness.*

**Sidney Poitier**

Dan went back home and started browsing around for more randomness. It did not seem that Diana was interested, but she seemed to be looking at it from a different angle.

There is an exciting story about randomness from the Second World War called "What does randomness look like?" The remarkable incident it describes happened in June 1944, a week after the Allied Forces' invasion of Normandy[373]. On June 13, a loud buzzing sound was heard over battle-worn London. The source of the sound was a newly developed German instrument of war, the V-1 self-propelled flying bomb, guided using gyroscopes. Their high-frequency pulsing gave the bombs their characteristic sound, earning them the nickname "buzz bombs." Within four months, the Germans had launched over 9000 such bombs from the coasts of France and the Netherlands, of which over 2000 reached their target in London. The British were worried about their accuracy. The central question was "are the bombs hitting their intended targets or do they just hit randomly?" Had the Germans worked out how to make an accurately targeting self-guided bomb? By following the places and times of almost every bomb that was dropped, British intelligence conducted a statistical analysis in order to find out whether the bombs were falling randomly over London, or whether they were specifically targeted. The British had a map on which the points at which the bombs had been dropped were marked, and they were trying to figure out if the pattern was random. Was it actually possible to determine whether the pattern was random or not?

*The Better Angels of Our Nature: Why Violence Has Declined* is a book by Steven Pinker [374], in which he argues that violence in the world has declined both in the long run and in the short run. Pinker highlights the role of nation-state monopolies on force and commerce, which makes "other people become more valuable alive than dead." He also mentions an increase in empathy as a result of increased literacy and communication, as well as a rise in a rational problem-solving orientation as possible causes of this decline in violence [375]. What does this have to do with the bombs in London? The book provides us with two patterns: the first is randomly generated and the second imitates a pattern from nature. We can take any piece of paper with random dots, and compare it to a piece taken from what nature does.

Dan was looking at beautiful pictures of glowworms on the ceiling of the Waitomo caves in New Zealand[376]. The glowworms aren't sitting around at random, but competing for food, bumping themselves away from each other. They have a vested interest in clumping together. So we can observe a pattern that seems random yet is not being generated in a random way, but rather by intention. If we uniformly sprinkle sand on a surface, it might look like this natural pattern was created by the glowworms, as we're instinctively avoiding places where we've already dropped sand. On the other hand, random processes have no prejudices and are not biased. In the sand example, the grains of sand would merely fall where they may, and may form clumps. It would look more like the pattern that would form if we sprinkled the sand with our eyes closed. The critical difference is that randomness does not equal uniformity. True randomness can have clusters[373]. Another commonly used example is that of flipping coins. If we are asked to flip a coin 100 times, the first option is to actually flip the coin and write down the results. Our data in this case will have clusters. This could mean long runs of up to eight tails in a row. While this seems surprising, it is typical for random coin tosses. On the other hand, if we are lazy and decide to make up fake coin toss results instead of actually flipping the coin, the data is expected to lack clusters. In a hundred coin tosses, not getting a single run of four or more heads or tails in a row has a 0.1% chance of ever happening.

So, differentiating "true randomness" from "fake randomness" may be easier than it seems. It seems that it is hard to fake randomness. It thus follows that deciding whether a pattern of numbers is truly random may not be so difficult.

Let us go back to London during the Second World War. The distribution of bombs that were dropped over the city in that conflict shows indeed that several areas were more heavily attacked or that the distribution among different areas of the city was not uniform. The bombs tended to be grouped in clusters. The British applied a statistical test to discover whether any support could be found for the claim that the Germans were targeting specific areas with smart bombs. A 12 km × 12 km heavily bombed region of South London was divided into 576 squares, each about the size of 25 city blocks. The number of squares with 0 bombs dropped, 1 bomb dropped, 2 bombs dropped, and so on was analyzed. In all, 537 bombs had fallen over these 576 squares. That's a little under one bomb per square, on average. Using Poisson's formula, they calculated how much clustering we would expect to see by chance. A simple random clustering pattern was revealed [377].

If one compares the maps of where the bombs actually fell and look at the map showing real random distribution, we can see how incredibly close the random prediction is to reality. It was observed that the bombs hadn't targeted a large area of the city. Instead, they had rained down at random in a devastating, city-wide game of Russian roulette. British intelligence, based on the rules of randomness, were able to conclude that the "wise bombs" were genuinely random.

Dan's next topic of research was Poisson's formula.

He learned that this concept was proposed at the beginning of the 19th century, when France had begun to collect statistical data on criminal trials due to a rise in crime. Adolphe Quetelet was a Belgian mathematician who attempted to apply probability theories used in astronomy to understand the rules that govern human behaviors. In a famous 1835 essay [378], Quetelet introduced the concept of the *homme moyen* ("average man"), by combining the social and physical characteristics of populations. These patterns, he argued, can be explained by "the general causes for which society exists and maintains itself." He believed that the "science of man" should investigate the "social body" and not the "particularities distinguishing the individuals composing it." [379] Ouellet described a similar regularity in crime statistics as found in astronomical observations. According to his theory, just as a star had an actual location, regardless of the alteration in the location measurements, there existed an actual level of criminality. Based on this concept, the average man had a statistically constant "penchant for crime," which when calculated over a course of time could reveal certain simple rules that could be used to predict future crimes[380]. Importantly, Quetelet observed that the conviction rate had been gradually decreasing with time, and assumed that this reflected a downward trend in the "penchant for crime" of French citizens[381].

Siméon-Denis Poisson, a French scientist, argued that Quetelet was missing a model for his data. One of his points of criticism was that Quetelet had not accounted for how jurors actually came to their decisions. The concept was published in 1837, in "Research on the Probability of Judgments in Criminal and Civil Matters." He introduced a formula that is today called the Poisson distribution. This method depicts the odds of a large number of infrequent events resulting in a specific outcome: What is the likelihood of the majority of French jurors reaching the wrong verdict? This formula expresses the odds of seeing unusual events, just as a result of chance. Poisson distribution predicts the pattern in which random events of very low probability occur in the course of a substantial number of trials [382]. The Poisson probability method is relevant wherever rare events of known overall probability happen randomly over a broad set of time or space divisions, and where variation in one direction is more likely than variation in the other. Such circumstances are not rare; in fact, it turns out that they are very common [382]. There are many applications and examples of this concept, which better explain how we can make use of randomness.

If, on average, 45 people are hit by lightning in a year, then based on Poisson's formula and the population size, it can be predicted that only 10 or 100 people are likely to be struck in a year [383]. The assumption is that lightning strikes are independent, rare events that are likely to occur at any given time. In another example, Ladislaus Bortkiewicz, a Russian statistician, explored why in some years a large number of soldiers in the Prussian army were dying due to horse kicks. A single incidence of death by horse kick is rare. By using Poisson's formula, he was trying to predict how many deaths were expected to compare it to the real data. The sporadic clusters of horse-related deaths that were revealed are just what we would expect if horse-kicking was a purely random process. The deaths were therefore found to be purely random. There was no mysterious magic at work in those years in which more deaths occurred [377]. Similarly, the incidence of sharks attacking people in South Africa was evaluated. The numbers are low, with an average of 3.75 per year. However, 2008 had 0 cases, 2009 had 6, and 2010 had 7 attacks. Using Poisson's distribution, it was found that these numbers are purely random, as there was no evidence of clustering beyond what is expected by the Poisson process[377].

Randomness is not uniform. It occurs in clusters [377].

The Poisson distribution can be applied to other areas of our lives: The number of mutations in our DNA as our cells age, the number of cars ahead of us at a traffic light, the number of typos we make while writing, and the number of births and deaths, marriages and divorces, or suicides and homicides in a given year. Randomness plays a more significant role in our lives than we care to admit. "Sadly, this fact offers little comfort when the cards in life fall against our favor" [377].

Dan kept wondering, "What do I make out of it? Can I still enjoy the randomness, or make use of it?"

# CHAPTER 24
## Chaos: A discipline for progress

To understand that randomness can help or be a basis for creativity, while remaining a practical person, Dan felt this would require learning some techniques. While randomness can be helpful, even when it is somewhat controlled, most of us do not want to live under chaotic conditions. Between the randomness, the chaos, and the quantum, is it possible to have some order?

Intuitively, we would say that chaos does not lead to progress. However, it is may be a crucial part of every structure [384]. We get up in the morning and find ourselves with a busy schedule. This includes our daily routines, family obligations, work schedules, calling our parents, and fixing our car. On some of these days, we find it okay to follow these routines, but at other times, we may get fed up with them and prefer to do something else or just nothing. Doing nothing, or focusing on things other than our obligations may seem chaotic. We do know of people who live what may seem to others as a chaotic life. Many people may feel that this is a wasteful way of living. But contrary to what they think, chaos may actually be productive and lead to opportunities that could in turn put one on the road to success. While chaos does not in itself lead to progress, it may become part of a process that leads there. [385].

Dan was looking into the chaos theory, which states that within the apparent randomness of complex chaotic systems, there are underlying patterns, constant feedback loops, repetition, self-similarity, fractals, self-organization, and reliance on programming at the initial point, known as "sensitive dependence on initial conditions" [386]. Dan already knew from his studies that there are varying interpretations of this theory.

There are many ways to look at chaos and randomness versus discipline. They can be viewed as enemies or opposites. Some view chaos, or randomness, as a step before discipline. Discipline is not a step between chaos and progress, but more of a structure into which chaos can be built. How about adding one or two or more hours per day into our daily schedule and calling it "my chaos time?" Unfortunately, we cannot reset and start our lives again. If we have lost time and did not do something that we wanted to do, we have lost that time. This does not mean we always have to do something. Doing nothing is also okay, as long as this is what we wanted to do. Does being disciplined mean that one should not waste time? We are all told to put our time in order. We are told when we need to get up and when to go to sleep, and what to do in between. Many of us may find this unpleasant, but most of us cannot avoid the routine. In fact, since childhood, many of us have been told not to waste time. What we were not told was that "wasting time" is not necessarily bad if we know how to use it as "productive chaos time."

Spark generation can be viewed as the ability to make the most out of events. A spark is not a genius thought or a unique gene, but rather, it is the ability to see an opportunity in a somewhat regular event. It is the skill to know which glasses to put on while staring at something. If we put the right glasses on, blurred sentences will suddenly seem very clear.

We may claim that our hectic daily routine of running from one place to another, fulfilling our obligations to our boss and our families, and paying taxes, does not leave us any time for sparks. Our hectic life has suppressed the "spark." How about viewing it as a prerequisite for success? Hard work or a boring daily routine could also present an opportunity for generating sparks.

Where and how do geniuses, top artists, scientists, top athletes, and super CEOs receive their sparks? Is it all about genetics and hard work combined with a bit of luck or coincidence?

Dan was searching for a way: if his path led him to success (or his definition of success), it would be an excellent outcome. However, just finding the right path to productive thought may be enough. Most importantly, Dan felt that he should be able to enjoy the journey even without reaching any targets.

Do we need to have goals?

Some people claim that not having a goal is also a goal. Others find it frustrating not to be able to close the gap between their goal and their inability to come up with the solutions they need to resolve problems in order to reach it.

This book is not about achieving goals. There are far too many books about this subject. It is more about finding the most fulfilling ways of reaching these goals. One may set a goal in order to determine the path you want to follow. We can sometimes learn more about our goals or change them just by the path we have chosen. A path is not necessarily a step-by-step process. It is better understood as jumping from one place to another or wandering in space.

To focus or not to focus.

Focusing on one thing is what we are all told to do. Concentrating on the aim is essential. There is no recipe to tell us how much of our time should be devoted to the aim and how much to other related or entirely unrelated things. For many people, doing things that are somewhat different or outside their "regular" tasks generate a personal "chaotic situation" that can lead to opportunities. This could include reading newspapers or books, listening to music, or engaging in athletics. It could also include talking to people that we don't interact with on a daily basis.

Many events occur in the course of our lives-some happy, and some less so. These events are not always what we want. We do not get up in the morning with the knowledge of everything that will happen to us on a particular day, and we cannot plan or prepare for all eventualities. Even when we do plan and prepare for things, we cannot control all the potential parameters that can affect the end result. Other events, people, and unpredictable factors could change our plans or create opportunities for us.

One of the most critical discussions Dan was having with his children, now that they were older, is "where should we set our bar?"

If we were all athletes preparing for a big contest, we would know where to set the bar for winning a gold medal. This bar may be beyond our current capabilities, but we know precisely what is required and also the current achievements of our competitors. We also know that while we are preparing for the contest, our competitors are doing the same. They are practicing so that they fare better than us, by attempting to set their bar at a level they think we will be unable to achieve. There are many bars that we all set for ourselves. How much money to make? How many pounds to lose this year? What courses to study? Passing tests. Having two kids. It's an endless list. Bars need to be set based on our capabilities, and then maybe one level above. If we want to run 100 meters, and we can do it in less than 9 seconds, stop reading now. If we can do it in 20 seconds, we are far from being able to win a gold medal, but it does not mean we need to set the bar at 20 or at 10. Put it somewhere in between.

Dan was looking into chaos to help him understand himself better.

# CHAPTER 25
## Chaos

How is chaos different from randomness? Dan had already understood that there are several types of randomness. He realized that randomness evolves on the basis of the initial conditions. There are systems whose behavior is very sensitive to small variations in initial conditions. Some of these conditions are described by the chaos theory.

Chaos is a state of total confusion with no order [387]. Chaos can also be defined as "stochastic behavior occurring in a deterministic system" [388]. Is chaos important? Some believe that "no other recent development in mathematics has made such an impact on scientific thinking as the theory of chaos" [389, 390]. In fact, some scientists believe that the chaos theory is at least as crucial as Newtonian physics and quantum mechanics [391].

Several rules have been developed for the application of the chaos theory to biology and medicine. "The importance of biological chaos is that the variables governing the spatial and temporal geometries of the system may be few in number, fractional in dimension, and thus enable low-energy control with complex deterministic consequences." The complexity of control that is inherent in chaotic systems may be necessary for the dynamics of many aspects of biology [391]. Thus, the chaos theory can shed light on the complexity of nature. The chaos theory can be viewed as a bridge between Newton's classical determinism, which claims that "the future is determined by its past," and the theories of probability, which claim that "the future depends in some random way on the past, but it cannot be determined by its past" [389].

Random behavior shows a sensitive dependence on the initial conditions and is sometimes termed "constrained randomness" [392]. In this respect, the word "chaos" is not used in the sense of a purely random process, but in the mathematical sense, and it implies "apparent randomness generated by a dynamical, deterministic process" [389, 390]. An essential element of chaotic, random-like systems is nonlinearity and non-proportionality. Non-linear regulatory systems are operating away from equilibrium. In fact, according to the chaos theory, the goal of physiological systems is not to maintain constancy, but to stay far from being fully balanced [393, 394].

Edward Lorenz, an American mathematician, meteorologist, and a pioneer of the chaos theory, introduced the "strange attractor" notion and coined the term "butterfly effect" [395]. The butterfly effect is based on the concept that "small causes can have larger effects." It explains how a small change in a deterministic nonlinear system in one state can lead to significant differences in a later state: "small causes can have larger effects"[396]. This concept was initially used in theories about weather prediction. Later, the term became a favorite metaphor in science writing, and it is now applied to many aspects of our lives [397]. A classic example that is commonly used to explain this effect is that a butterfly flapping its wings in Brazil can cause a tornado in Texas. Small differences in initial conditions, such as rounding errors in numerical computation, produce broadly diverging outcomes in these dynamical systems. This means that long-term predictions of these systems cannot be made [386].

Edward Lorenz came across the chaos concept accidentally through his work on weather prediction in 1961 [398]. He was using a simple digital computer for studying weather simulation. To view a sequence of data again, he started the simulation in the middle of its course to save time. He accomplished this by inputting the data that corresponded to the middle part of the original simulation. To his surprise, whenever he did this, the predictions turned out to be completely different from the previously calculated ones. His computer provided outputs with 6-digit precision, but the new printout rounded variables off to a 3-digit number. This is how he realized that small changes in initial conditions produced substantial changes in long-term outcomes [399]. This experience also revealed that even detailed atmospheric modeling cannot make precise long-term weather predictions.

Thus, the sensitivity of the initial conditions proved to be a crucial influencing factor for later outcomes.

The chaos theory can also be applied to deterministic systems, where future behavior is determined by initial conditions, without the involvement of random elements [400]. "Deterministic chaos" implies that even the deterministic nature of a system does not necessarily make it predictable[401]. A system in which the present determines the future, but the approximate present does not approximately determine the future can be defined as chaotic. Thus, the chaos theory concerns deterministic systems whose behavior can, in principle, be predicted. Such chaotic systems are predictable for a while, after which they "appear" to have become random [397].

A system may appear random, but on closer look, it may appear orderly. The overall behavior of a non-linear system is not the sum of the behavior of its individual components. It is complex and seemingly unpredictable. However, once we look into it, this so-called chaotic system may appear to have some order and can be predictable [402]. A dynamical, non-linear system is a deterministic mathematical sequence whose state is defined at a given time by a number of values of variables. Based on the knowledge of the initial conditions, the evolution of the system over time can be predicted. By working with these initial conditions and other parameters in mathematical equations, it is possible to alter the evolution of the system and induce it to operate in a particular direction.

The behavior of chaotic systems can be predicted for a certain amount of time, which is influenced by how much uncertainty can be tolerated in the forecast, how accurately the current state of the system can be measured, and a time scale based on the system dynamics (called Lyapunov time). In the case of chaotic electrical circuits, it is about 1 millisecond, and for weather systems, it could be a few days. In chaotic systems, the uncertainty of a forecast increases exponentially with the amount of time that has elapsed. A meaningful prediction cannot be made when the amount of time is more than two or three times the Lyapunov time. A system for which meaningful predictions cannot be made appears random [403].

Dan came across James Gleick's best seller *Chaos: Making a New Science,* which introduced the general principles of the chaos theory to the broad public [404]. Dan was looking into the history of chaos. The chaotic behavior of a system can be studied using mathematical models or through analytical techniques such as recurrence plots and Poincaré maps. Henri Poincaré, in the 1880s, proposed the existence of non-periodic orbits that are not forever increasing or approaching a fixed point[405]. In 1898, Jacques Hadamard described the chaotic motion of a free particle gliding frictionless on the surface of a constant negative curvature; this example is referred to as "Hadamard's billiards" [406]. Hadamard showed that all trajectories are unstable as all particle routes diverge exponentially from one another.

The chaos theory was formalized in the mid-twentieth century, when it was evident that the linear theory could not explain the observed behavior of specific experimental systems such as the logistic map. What had earlier been attributed to imprecision in measurements and pure "noise" was considered by chaos theorists as a component of the studied systems. This was a significant breakthrough, as it was finally shown that the "noise" in scientific systems was part of the system itself. Dan wondered whether this could also be applied to our everyday life. The real issue for him was the practical implications of this: how to deal with it, and how to make better use of it.

The mathematics of chaos theory involves the repeated repetition of simple formulas, which is impractical to perform manually. Electronic computers made these repeated calculations practical, while figures and images made it possible to visualize these systems. In 1961, Yoshisuke Ueda, who was working at Kyoto University, noticed what he called "randomly transitional phenomena" when he was studying analog computers. This finding was reported only a decade later, as his lab advisor had initially contradicted his conclusions [407].

Benoit Mandelbrot was a Polish-born, French–American mathematician with an interest in what he called "the art of roughness" of physical phenomena and "the uncontrolled element in life"[408]. He was looking into recurring patterns at every scale in the data on cotton prices [409]. He concluded that noise has a pattern: the ratio of noise-containing periods to error-free periods was found to be constant on all scales. This means that errors are inevitable and must be planned for by incorporating redundancy [410].

Dan was thinking beyond cotton prices. He was thinking, "Are noise, errors, unpredictability, all part of our life?" When we get up in the morning, we know that we cannot predict even the next hour with 100% accuracy. There are always factors, which we cannot control, which add much noise to our life. Noise is translated by most of us as a distraction to our daily routine, to our thoughts. Some of us will view this "unpredictable, chaotic noise" as having an anti-productive effect on our work, life, decision-making process, and relationships. However, if it is an inevitable part of our life, we can either just accept it or learn how to make better use of it.

While studying prices, contrary to the conventional belief that changes in price are normally distributed, Mandelbrot described the "Noah effect," wherein sudden discontinuous changes occur, and the "Joseph effect," wherein a value can persist for a while and then suddenly change afterward [411]. He published a statistical study entitled "How long is the coast of Britain? Statistical self-similarity and fractional dimension" [412]. His study showed that the length of the coastline varies with the scale of the measuring instrument. The coastline resembles itself at all scales and is infinite in length in the case of an infinitesimally small measuring device. In addition, the dimensions of an object are relative to the observer and may be fractional. An object that has constant irregularity over different scales ("self-similarity") is a fractal.

A classic example of a fractal object is the Menger sponge [413]. Dan was looking at an image of a Menger sponge and was amazed. He was thinking of how he could create it. He thought of gluing toy building blocks together to make a giant cube. The cube is three by three, which means that it has twenty-seven blocks in total (like a Rubik's cube), and each face has nine blocks each. If we remove the center block of each face, and the center block of the entire cube, we are left with an empty set of "lines," each made up of three blocks, defining the edges of the cube. Consider the blocks that make up each edge of the cube to be made of smaller building blocks; this means that these blocks are miniature versions of the original cube. Now, if this was done also to each of the mini-cubes, you will get a cube with a surface that appears pitted [414]. Because the edges of each cube, at all levels, are left intact, the structure maintains its shape even as holes are being drilled into the lower-level cubes increases. As the number of divisions reaches infinity, it turns into a structure that has no volume within, and is only made up of surfaces of infinitely pitted and thinned walls. This is a purely theoretical shape that has infinite surface area and no volume whatsoever. In fact, it does not have a specific number of dimensions, but manages to exist in what is called "fractional dimensions" [414].

In the Menger cube, each of the pitted walls is called a Sierpinski Carpet, a technique of subdividing a shape into smaller copies of itself, removing one or more copies, and continuing recursively. The construction of the Sierpinski carpet begins with a square. The square is divided into nine similar sub squares in a three-by-three grid, and the central one is removed. This process is applied recursively to the remaining eight sub squares, ad infinitum [415].

We were taught to think of things as having one, two, or three dimensions. However, the Sierpinski Carpet is supposed to straddle the division between a one-dimensional line and a two-dimensional plane. It occupies an area, but the surface is so pitted that it technically does not fill the area. Complicated calculations can be made to show that the Sierpinski Carpet has a fractional dimension of 1.89. Similarly, the Menger Sponge, which has no real volume, has a fractional dimension of 2.73 [414]. The Menger sponge is too big if it is measured two-dimensionally, but it is too small if it is measured three-dimensionally.

Mandelbrot wrote *The Fractal Geometry of Nature*, which is considered a classic book on chaos theory [416]. The first symposium on chaos was organized by the New York Academy of Sciences in 1977. It led to an advanced understanding of the universality in chaos, with many studies showing the applicability of chaos theory in many fields [415].

Can this concept be applied to biological systems? A mathematical model of the eye tracking disorder among schizophrenics was one of the first models in which the concept was applied in medicine [417]. It was also applied to the study of pathological cardiac cycles, and one of the standard examples is the branching of the circulatory and bronchial systems, both of which fit a fractal model [418].

Self-organized criticality(SOC), which is considered as one of the mechanisms by which complexity arises in nature, was first described in 1987 [419]. It was described under laboratory conditions and was then demonstrated in large-scale natural or social systems that display scale-invariant behavior. In physics, self-organized criticality (SOC) is a property of dynamical systems that have a critical point as an attractor [420]. These systems display scale invariance, which is a feature of the critical point of a phase transition, and do not require the tuning of control parameters to a precise value. This is because the system, effectively, tunes itself as it evolves towards criticality.

Self-organized criticality is typically observed in slowly driven non-equilibrium systems with extended degrees of freedom and a high level of nonlinearity. It is a mechanism by which the emergence of complexity from simple local interactions could be spontaneous and a source of natural complexity. This property demonstrates that complexity could be generated as a developing feature of extended systems with simple local interactions. It indicates that much complexity in nature could be described by particular ubiquitous mathematical laws. In the lab setting, a simple cellular mechanism was shown to produce several characteristic features observed in natural complexity in a way that is linked to the critical-point phenomenon. The complexity was found to emerge in a robust manner and was not dependent on the fine-tuning of the details of the system. Variable parameters in the model could be altered to a considerable extent without affecting the emergence of critical behavior; this is why it is termed self-organized criticality [420].

Many patterns observed in nature have been explained using self-organized criticality: for example, it has been applied to the statistical distribution of the size of earthquakes, which are a source of scale-invariant behavior, the frequency of aftershocks, and solar flares, as well as fluctuations in economic systems such as financial markets, landscape formation, forest fires, landslides, and epidemics [386]. Some have even suggested that this concept can be applied to the occurrence of wars.

There is no universally accepted mathematical definition of chaos, but the definition formulated by Robert L. Devaney is commonly accepted; it states that to classify a dynamical system as chaotic, it must be sensitive to initial conditions and be conducive to topological mixing, and it must have dense periodic orbits [421]. In continuous time dynamical systems, chaos is a feature of the spontaneous breakdown of topological supersymmetry. This is an intrinsic property of evolution operators of all stochastic and deterministic, partial, differential equations. Dynamical chaos works for deterministic models and also for models with external noise. In reality, all dynamical systems are influenced to some extent by their stochastic environments [422].

The concept of sensitivity to initial conditions implies that each point in a chaotic system is randomly approximated by other points with significantly different future paths. In such a system, an arbitrarily small change may lead to significantly different future behavior, as described in the "butterfly effect": Had the butterfly not flapped its wings, the trajectory of the system might have been vastly different. So, if we start with a limited amount of information about the system, then beyond a specific time, the system is no longer predictable. We may find this to be the case for many events in our life. But this is most evident in the case of weather, which is generally predictable only about a week ahead. However, this does not mean that we cannot predict anything about events far in the future, as there are, of course, some limitations in the system. With the weather, we know that the temperature will not naturally reach 100°C or fall to -130°C on earth, but we cannot precisely predict which day in a given year will have the highest temperature [423].

Sensitivity dependence on initial conditions alone does not give rise to chaos. We need something else. Topological mixing means that the system evolves over time so that any given region or open set of its phase space overlaps with any other given region. This mathematical concept of "mixing" corresponds with standard intuition. Mixing of colored dyes or fluids is an example of a chaotic system. A simple dynamical system produced by repeatedly doubling an initial value has sensitive dependence on initial conditions everywhere, since any pair of nearby points becomes widely separated. However, this example does not involve any topological mixing, and therefore, has no chaos. Indeed, the behavior of this system is straightforward: all points except for 0 tend to have a positive or negative infinity.

Dense periodic orbits in a chaotic system mean that every point in space is approached arbitrarily closely by periodic orbits [424]. Any one-dimensional system that exhibits a regular cycle of three periods also displays regular cycles of every other length and ultimately chaotic orbits. Under the right conditions, chaos can spontaneously evolve into a lockstep pattern. It means that there is some synchronization in a chaotic system [425].

Despite his knowledge of physics, all this information was confusing to Dan. Dan felt that he had now fallen deep into chaos. And as always, he started thinking about the best ways that it could be applied to everyday life, outside of mathematics.

# CHAPTER 26
## More chaos

Dan learned that while the chaos theory was born from observation of weather patterns, it has been found to be applicable in a wide range of other contexts. The availability of cheaper and powerful computers has extended the applicability of the chaos theory to many disciplines including mathematics, topology, physics, social systems, population modeling, biology, meteorology, astrophysics, information theory, and neuroscience [426].

Chaos-based cryptographic algorithms have evolved from similarities between chaotic maps and cryptographic systems. These algorithms are used in the design of cryptographic schemes using image encryption and secure pseudo-random number generators [427]. The majority of these algorithms use uni-modal chaotic maps, control parameters and the initial conditions of the chaotic maps as their keys [428]. Encryption can rely on diffusion and confusion modeled by the chaos theory [429]. DNA-type computing is also based on the chaos theory, and DNA-Chaos cryptographic algorithms for encrypting data have also been developed. Some were proven to not be secure [427, 430], which goes to show that not everything which seems to be chaotic is thoroughly efficient or secure in the sense that it can be used to hide information.

The chaos theory is applied in robotics for designing predictive models that replace the trial-and-error type of behavior used for improving their interaction with the environment [431]. These models are being used for the design of walking robots. Chaotic dynamics have been exhibited by passive walking biped robots [432]. They are also applied to population models, and are replacing the continuous methods. Chaotic behavior has also been described in population growth in the Canadian lynx [433, 434]

Chaotic models are applied in many areas of medicine such as in follow up of a lack of oxygen in the fetus[435]. Similar models are being developed in cardiology for a better understanding of heart function [436]. Chaos has also been described in ecological systems, such as in the field of hydrology [437]. In chemistry, too, chaos models are used for predicting gas solubility, which is essential for the manufacturing of polymers. [438]. Chaos theories are also applied to predict when asteroids will approach Earth and other planets [439]. Further, four of the five moons of Pluto have been found to rotate chaotically.

Consider a situation where a career choice has to be made. A chaotic model can be used to interpret the relationship between employees and the job market. This type of modeling can improve our decision-making process [440]. Studies of many companies and organizations have shown that there many internal and external forces that contribute to the chaotic type of structures generated. This "chaos metaphor" is based on mathematical models and psychological aspects of human behavior. It provides insights into the complexity of small and large workgroups. However, the implications go far beyond the simple description of "a chaotic workplace" [440].

Predicting the economy, promising stock options, and our health are highly challenging tasks. Chaos theories have been applied to such systems also in an attempt to improve the prediction ability [441]. Financial systems are fundamentally different from classical natural science systems, since they result from the interactions between people. Thus, the ability of purely deterministic models to provide accurate forecasts in this context is questionable. The results of studies that have investigated this are mixed. Not all of them were able to show that chaos theories can improve the ability to analyze economic data. This is attributed in part to the confusion between specific tests for chaos and more general tests for non-linear relationships [442].

Predictions of heavy traffic can be useful for preventing congestion. Using chaos theories for traffic forecasting has led to the generation of more accurate short-term prediction models [443]. The chaos theory has also been applied to modeling of group behavior in psychology. In this context, the assumption is that heterogeneous members share behaviors to different degrees. The group dynamics are a result of the personal dynamics of the members. Each person reproduces the group dynamics at a different scale, and the chaotic behavior of the group is reflected in each member [444]. This model can be applied to many of our everyday interactions with other people.

Despite the impressive results produced by all these studies, a major limitation to the application of this theory is that the methods used for detecting a chaotic signature were often relatively subjective. This has also resulted in contradictory results, for example, in the analysis of environmental water cycle data [445], which were found to be chaotic in earlier studies, but not so in subsequent studies [446].

A famous example of a chaotic system is the Tilt-A-Whirl found at amusement parks and fairs [447]. In this game, there are seven freely spinning cars containing three or four riders apiece, which are attached to a rotating platform at a fixed pivot point. As the entire platform rotates, parts of it are raised and lowered. As a result of the centrifugal and gravitational forces acting on the cars, they spin in different directions and at different speeds. The weight distribution of the riders further affects the spinning motion. Since there are multiple factors in this system, the result is unpredictable motion.

Another example is Atwood's machine, which was invented in 1784 by the English mathematician George Atwood as a laboratory experiment to verify the mechanical laws of motion with constant acceleration. It illustrates the principles of classical mechanics. A derivation of this machine is the swinging Atwood's machine, which resembles the simple Atwood's machine, with the exception that one of the masses is allowed to swing in a two-dimensional plane. This produces a dynamical system that is chaotic [448] [449]. The swinging version has two masses: a pendulum mass and a counterweight, which are at each end of an inextensible string suspended on two frictionless pulleys of zero radii. The pendulum mass can swing freely around its pulley without colliding with the counterweight [450]. The swinging Atwood's machine has large spatial conditions that lead to a variety of motions. Some motions are chaotic due to the pendulum's reactive centrifugal force counteracting the counterweight's weight.

For Dan, these examples showed that many "simple physical rules" which underline their movements have some chaotic nature embedded in them.

Consider a spot of dye injected into a river or stream. Contour advection is a method for simulating the evolution of one or more contours of the dye as it is stirred by a moving fluid. This method is used for studying chaotic mixing[451]. Even if the river moves quietly, the contours are likely to develop into intricate fractals. The tracer is typically passive, but may also be active, representing a dynamical property of the fluid such as vorticity[452]. Even for a phenomenon like this one that seems entirely unpredictable, there exists an equation that can be used to predict parameters such as vorticity.

Arnold's cat map is a chaotic map named after its creator, Vladimir Arnold, who demonstrated its effects in the 1960s using the image of a cat [453, 454]. In this map, the pixels of an image are randomly rearranged by chaotic transformation, but when the transformations are repeated for a certain number of steps, the original image appears again. The original image is sheared and then wrapped around itself in the first step of the transformation. After a certain number of duplications of this step, the resulting image appears random or disordered. With further repetition, the image appears to be moving closer to the original image of the cat, until it ultimately returns to the original image. The whole mapping process is a mathematics-based method. This map proves that may be some order in what sounds and looks chaotic.

Dan reviewed the physical behavior of the motion of a bouncing ball before, during, and after impact against the surface of another body. Accurate modeling of the performance of the ball is complex and is affected by many laws of physics, some of which are associated with chaotic modeling. This is relevant to many sports, such as tennis and basketball for example [455].

The Rössler attractor is defined as the minimum system for chaos: it is made up of three non-linear ordinary differential equations, which are used to define a continuous-time dynamical system that exhibits chaotic dynamics associated with the fractal properties of the attractor [456, 457]. An orbit within the attractor follows an outward spiral close to the display style plane around an unstable fixed point. Once the graph spirals out enough, a second fixed point influences the graph, causing a rise and twist in the display style dimension. With time, although each variable is oscillating within a fixed range of values, the oscillations become chaotic [458].

There are many chaotic maps in mathematics, each of which is based on different equations. Such maps are created with a pair of mathematical transformation equations that can be plotted on a two-dimensional graph. As is the case with all dynamical maps, the action represents the evolution of a real physical system in time. Such a map is actually a mathematical model that physicists use to understand and describe the phenomenon of chaotic motion. It displays many of the features of chaotic motion in a straightforward fashion. The map enables to understand better the conditions under which chaos occurs in mathematics [459]. A chaotic map in mathematics is an evolution function that exhibits chaotic behavior. These maps often generate fractals. The fractals may be built by an iterative process. Different iterative processes can generate the same fractals [460].

A horseshoe map is a dynamic structure that is created by first crushing a square, then stretching the resulting structure into a long strip, and finally folding the strip into the shape of a horseshoe. Most points eventually leave the square and move into the side caps, where they come together at a fixed point in one of the caps [461]. The squeezing, stretching, and folding of the horseshoe map are typical of chaotic systems. However, these are not sufficient for chaos[462]. In this map, the squeezing and stretching are uniform and compensate each other so that the area of the square does not change. The folding is precisely done so that only the orbits that remain forever in the square can be described. In this map, there is an infinite number of periodic orbits, some of which are of arbitrarily long periods. The number of periodic orbits increases exponentially as the number of periods increases [461].

The standard map in mathematics is an area-preserving chaotic map formed from a square with its side folded onto itself [463]. It is one of the most widely studied examples of dynamical chaos in physics. It is a two-dimensional dynamical map that is useful for studying the essential features of chaotic motion. The standard map is chaotic, but under the most basic minimalist conditions under which chaos can occur. The physical system of the standard map is called the "kicked rotor." This "rotor" is represented by a drop sliding along a circular wire in a frictionless way. The "kicked" component is represented by a force that hits the rotor at even intervals of time. This driving force always follows the same direction and is always of the same intensity. The amount of force absorbed by the bead depends on its position on the wire at the time that it receives the "kick." Accordingly, its speed may increase or decrease. This type of position-speed dependency is called phase space by physicists and is used for studying chaos.

We can set "minimal" physical conditions for chaos to occur [464].

Chaotic motion in a map is represented by the "mixing up" of initial conditions. If we set up different initial conditions, by using different colors, the chaotic motions are indicated by the mixing up of colors. If the kick strength happens to be set to a low value, the system is not chaotic at all. At some intermediate values, the system is chaotic for some initial conditions, but not for others. If the driving strength is increased, more and more initial conditions are chaotic. Yet, even at high levels of driving strength, there still remain initial conditions that are not chaotic. In fact, there is a certain critical value above which chaos appears [465].

In electronics, Chua's circuit is a simple electronic circuit that exhibits classic chaos theory behavior. It is a "nonperiodic oscillator" that produces an oscillating waveform [466]. In contrast with conventional electronic oscillators, Chua's circuit oscillator never "repeats" itself. It is a real-world example of a chaotic system, as a result of which it a considered to be "a paradigm for chaos" [467]. For chaotic behavior to occur, one or more nonlinear elements along with one or more locally active resistors and three or more energy-storage elements are required. Chua's circuit is the most straightforward electronic circuit that meets these criteria [3][468].

A coupled map lattice (CML) is a dynamical system that models the behavior of non-linear systems [469]. This system is used for the qualitative study of the chaotic dynamics of spatially extended systems. It includes the dynamics of spatiotemporal chaos, where the number of active degrees of freedom diverges as the size of the system increases [470]. Some features of the coupled map lattice are discrete time dynamics, discrete underlying spaces such as lattices or networks, and real numbers or vectors, as well as local, continuous-state variables [471]. The studied systems include populations, chemical reactions, fluid flow, and biological and computational networks [472]. While the value of each site in a network is strictly dependent on its neighbors from the previous time step, in the case of the coupled map lattice, each site is only dependent upon its neighbors relative to the coupling term in the recurrence equation [473].

Chaotic processes can be dependent or non-dependent on previous measures.

A double pendulum is defined as a pendulum that has another pendulum attached to its end. It is a simple physical system that exhibits rich, dynamic behavior with strong sensitivity to initial conditions [474, 475]. The motion of a double pendulum is governed by a set of equations and is chaotic. In the case of large motions, it is a chaotic system, but for small motions, it is a simple linear system [476]. We can drag the pendulum with our computer mouse to change the starting position. We can change parameters in the simulation, such as mass, gravity, and the length of the rods.

A billiards table is a dynamical system in which a particle alternates between motion in a straight line and specular reflections from a boundary [477]. When a particle hits the boundary, it reflects from it without loss of speed. Billiard dynamical systems are Hamiltonian idealizations of the game of billiards, except that the region contained by the boundary can have shapes other than rectangular, and even be multidimensional. The billiard particle moves in a straight line, with constant energy, between reflections from the boundaries. In the case of all reflections, the angle of incidence just before the collision is equal to the angle of reflection just after the collision. The sequence of reflections is described with the help of a billiard map that ultimately characterizes the motion of the particle. Billiards capture all the complexity of Hamiltonian systems, from integrality to chaotic motion [478]. There are many equations that can be used for analyzing these chaotic motions.

Chaotic scattering is a branch of the chaos theory that deals with scattering systems which show keen sensitivity to initial conditions [479]. In such systems, there are one or more impact parameters which cause a particle to be sent into the scatterer. It gives rise to exit parameters as the particle exits towards infinity. While the particle is traversing the system, there may be a delay time, which is defined as the time it takes for the particle to exit the system. In a chaotic scattering system, a minute change in the impact parameter may give rise to a substantial change in the exit parameters.

The Gaspard-Rice (GR) scattering system is known as the "three-disc" system. It consists of three hard discs arranged in a triangular formation. A point particle is sent in and undergoes perfect, elastic collisions until it exits towards infinity. The trajectories created by the collisions bounce around in the system for a while before finally exiting. If we consider the impact parameters to be the start of two entirely horizontal lines, the two trajectories are observed to be initially so close as to be almost identical. By the time they exit, they are entirely different, thus illustrating the strong sensitivity to initial conditions [479].

Dan was sitting at his desk and trying to imagine these maps, while looking again and again at the images on his screen. Although complex, these maps clearly showed how chaotic events could be analyzed with mathematical equations. David, his son, was coming for a short visit that evening. David liked history.

# CHAPTER 27
## Is history chaotic?

Dan had difficulty classifying his relationship with David. They were close, but not close enough. David had never been married. Although he had been in several serious relationships, none of them had led to marriage. Dan was not sure why. David was not a workaholic. He did care about people and was not too career oriented. He liked history, though.

That evening, Dan was telling David about his journey into chaos. "How about viewing history as science and applying some of the rules of chaos to history?" Dan asked. David never liked physics and was not sure how you could apply these equations to the real world.

Dan was telling him about an area of research that was integrating cultural evolution and economic history with mathematical modeling of historical processes[480, 481]. The concept was to develop theories that explain such dynamical processes as the rise and fall of empires, population booms and busts, and the spread and disappearance of religions [482]. David did not believe that one could actually apply models of mathematics to historical processes. To convince him, Dan told him that the theories had been tested against actual data. "You simply cannot ignore the facts," Dan said.

Historical processes are dynamic in the sense that they change with time. Populations increase and decline, economies expand and contract, states grow and collapse. One approach for looking into it is dividing it into steps and assuming that each one follows or interacts in some way with the other. This is the dynamical systems approach. The phenomenon is represented as a system consisting of several parts that interact and change dynamically over time. If we accept this notion, we may be able to apply mathematical methods for looking into these dynamical systems. These methods can be used to understand how subsystems interact with each other. Some researchers have attempted to use these formulations for predicting the future. Mathematical models are even used to explain macro historical events such as the rise of empires, social discontent, civil wars, and state collapse [483, 484].

The field of cliodynamics relies on data and evidence by using "digital history," which enables the analysis of large databases [485]. Several important historical events have been evaluated using these methods, through the creation of models of social complexity and warfare [486]. These methods have also aided research on revolutions [487] and the global distribution of languages. Such research has revealed that the geographic area within which a language is spoken shows the closest association with the political complexity of the speakers of the language as opposed to other variables [18]. Further, analysis of large quantities of newspaper content has shown how periodic structures can be automatically discovered in historical newspapers [481, 488].

It's quite exciting to think of the possibility of analyzing and maybe even predicting historical events using mathematical formulae. David discovered, and later told Dan, that cliodynamics methods have been critiqued by several academics, who felt that the complex social formations of the past cannot and should not be reduced to quantifiable data points, as one could overlook historical society's changing circumstances and dynamics in the process [489]. Their opinion is based on the notion that there are no generalizable causal factors that can explain large numbers of cases. This concept, in turn, is based on the notion that there is no time-invariant structure that can organize all the traditional mechanisms into one system [490]. In response to their critics, cliodynamicists claim that the historical dynamics of most known incidents can indeed be explained by large-scale, macrohistorical patterns. These patterns can be recognized through systematic, mathematical analysis[481]. However, these equations also need to be applicable to minor events that are associated with macro historical developments.

What about economic bubbles? An economic bubble, which is sometimes referred to as speculative bubble or a financial bubble, is trading in an asset at a price or price range that strongly exceeds the asset's intrinsic value [426, 491]. This represents a chaotic situation.

Tom Konrad wrote a few years ago about "Chaos theory, financial markets, and global weirding" [492]. He claimed that by studying chaos theories, he had realized the boundaries of the ability to predict, which is even more critical than making forecasts. His definition of the chaotic system goes back to the butterfly theory, and it states that it is a system in which any minor change in initial conditions can result in considerable changes in the results. He introduces the idea of looking at feedback in these systems. Chaotic systems are disordered because they contain positive feedback. This positive feedback amplifies trends over time, while negative feedback tends to reduce trends over time.

Dan and David were reading the examples Konrad uses for complex systems. Both climate systems and financial markets are characterized by both positive and negative feedback. In the case of climatic systems, positive feedback occurs when a series of hot, sunny days form a high-pressure system that keeps storms from moving in. When a storm does move in, positive feedback may help to cool things off. In stock markets, financial bubbles may occur due to positive feedback.

In his book "A Short History of Financial Euphoria: Financial Genius is Before the Fall" [493], John Kenneth Galbraith discusses the idea that when we see others make money in a stock market rise, we tend to think they were smart enough to know when to get in. If we make money in stocks, we tend to think that we are smart. In both cases, we tend to think that buying stocks is a smart thing to do. In most cases, it was most probably no more than just luck. This type of feedback leads to additional buying, which further increases prices. Although the increase in price could have been justified in the beginning, the positive feedback increases the prices to a point that is beyond the reasonable value of the underlying company. Wealth effect, relative valuation methods, and the increased ability to borrow against inflated asset prices are additional examples of positive feedback, which are known to occur in financial bubbles and bull markets. In contrast, negative feedback is created by value investors buying when prices have fallen and selling when prices have risen.

Galbraith, who is one of the most well-known economists, introduced in the 1960s a skepticism of markets and an unshakeable belief in the ability of a steady state to balance the market. This coincided with the peak of liberalism in the US [494]. He is considered by some to be less an economist and more a mixture of a sociologist, political scientist, and journalist. His argument is that bubbles are inherent in the free market system because of "mass psychology" and the "vested interest in error that accompanies speculative euphoria" [495].

Financial memory is very short. What seems to be a "new financial instrument" is inevitably nothing of the sort. Galbraith cautions, "The world of finance hails the invention of the wheel over and over again, often in a slightly more unstable version." Crucial to his analysis is the creation of debt in response to financial speculations, which "becomes dangerously out of scale in relation to the underlying means of payment." The financial crisis of 2008 is considered as a confirmation of his theory.

Tom Konrad takes it further by concluding that both in the analysis of weather and the financial market, external shocks to the systems can reverse self-reinforcing trends [492]. Does this mean that complex systems are always chaotic? His answer is that they are not. They tend not to be chaotic all the time, but instead, exhibit chaotic behavior only some of the time. This means that we can sometimes predict the behavior of a system that functions in a regular and systematic way. At the same time, these systems can shift to a different type of predictable behavior that follows a different set of rules, following a small change. Such behavior can be mapped to chaotic systems and may exhibit a pattern called *Strange Attractor*.

In dynamical systems, an attractor is a set of numerical values toward which a system tends to evolve, under a wide range of initial conditions [397]. System values that get close enough to the attractor values remain close even if slightly disturbed [496]. The only restriction on such a dynamical system is that its trajectory should always move forward in time in the direction of the attractor. The trajectory may be periodic or chaotic. When the flow of a system is away from a set of values, such a set is called a repeller. An attractor is strange if it has a fractal structure, and this often happens when it exhibits chaotic dynamics. But strange non-chaotic attractors can also occur. A strange attractor is chaotic and exhibits sensitive dependence on initial conditions. A dynamic system with a chaotic attractor is locally unstable, but it is still globally stable. Once a certain number of sequences have entered the attractor, nearby points diverge from one another but never depart from the attractor [497]. As the system moves through such a strange attractor, it will often stay in one set of the rings curves shown for an extended period, before jumping to another set after an irregular period of time [492].

"I am not sure if I am with you on that," David said. He was in a good mood and did not mind too much his father's new craze. Both of them decided to delve deeper into the financial bubble story over some Chinese food that they had ordered.

# CHAPTER 28
## Chaotic financial bubbles

It was somewhat easier for David to accept the implementation of the chaos equation in financial bubbles than in the fall of empires in history.

Chaotic bubbles occur in dynamic non-linear conditions that exhibit chaotic patterns. This is consistent with the chaos theory [498]. In most systems, chaotic bubbles arise when some kind of resistance or shear factor is applied to a forcing pressure. Nonlinear analysis of the dynamics of bubbles in liquids is a good example of these chaotic bubbles [499]. It can also be applied to acoustics, in which bubble dynamics play a crucial part [500].

The study of controlling chaotic bubble dynamics, from which the antithetic term "control of chaos" is derived, shows that periodic oscillations can be introduced in such systems. This type of chaos control has applications in many fields in physics.

Economic bubbles may arise as a result of speculations in asset markets. Richard H. Day and Weihong Huang described how the interaction between fundamentalists and trend-chasing traders evolves into chaotic dynamics in a speculative bubble [501]. A similar model was described for foreign exchange rate dynamics [502]. Economic bubbles are described as situations in which asset prices are based on implausible and unpredictable views about the future [503].

It was now David's turn. He told his father the story of The Dutch Golden Age's *Tulipmania* that occurred in the mid-1630s. It is considered to be the first recorded economic bubble. During that period, the Netherlands' otherwise sensible merchants, nobles, and artisans spent all the money they had on tulip bulbs. The bulbs changed hands hundreds of times in a single day, and some bulbs, sold and resold for thousands of guilders, never even existed. Tulipmania is an example of the gullibility of crowds and the dangers of financial speculation. It affected the transformation of Dutch society in the Golden Age [504]. Dan wondered whether much had changed over the years in terms of our behavior as human beings under similar conditions.

The association of the term "bubble" with financial crisis originated in 1711–1720 and the source is the company British South Sea Bubble. The South Sea Company, or The Governor and Company of the merchants of Great Britain, were trading with the South Seas and other parts of America. It was a British joint-stock company founded in 1711. It was created as a public-private partnership to consolidate and reduce the cost of national debt. The company was granted monopoly by the British government over trade with South America. However, Spain was in control of South America at that time, so there was no realistic prospect of any trade happening and no profits were actually made by the company. As the company expanded its operations, the value of its stock increased significantly till it peaked in 1720, before entirely collapsing [505].

In many cases, relatively small bubbles are only viewed retrospectively, once a sudden drop in prices has occurred. The terms "crash" or "bubble burst" are used with all the associated connotations. Going back to feedback loops in chaotic systems, we can consider a boom and a burst of a bubble to be examples of positive feedback mechanisms. This is in contrast to the negative feedback mechanism that determines the equilibrium price under normal market circumstances. Prices in an economic bubble can fluctuate erratically, and they can become impossible to predict based on supply and demand alone. Additional factors determine the chaotic nature of the system under these conditions.

There are economists who look at these chaotic bubbles from a different perspective. In "Cracking the enigma of asset bubbles with narratives," Preston Teeter and Jörgen Sandberg argue that periods of intense market speculation are driven by narratives. They suggest historical research as an alternative to crack the enigma of asset bubbles.

There are studies which show that bubbles could happen even without uncertainty, speculation, or bounded rationality [491, 506, 507]. Some call them non-speculative bubbles or sunspot equilibria, and attempt to demonstrate the rationale behind them. Such studies suggest that investors are adequately compensated for the possibility that a bubble might collapse. In the case of such non-speculative bubbles, the timing of a collapse should be predicted probabilistically, for which a prediction model could be used [508].

Conventional economists think that bubbles cannot be identified in advance and cannot be prevented, and that attempts to "prick" the bubble may cause a financial crisis. It is claimed that instead, authorities should wait for these bubbles to burst of their own accord, dealing with the aftermath via monetary policy and fiscal policy [491]. It is too chaotic, as there are too many factors that lead to marked changes. Nothing is predictable.

However, we have already learned that chaos could be predictable.

The economist Robert E. Wright from South Dakota is one of those to make the claim that bubbles can be foreseen [509]. In his book *Fubarnomics: A Lighthearted, Serious Look at America's Economic Ills*, Wright argues that major economic trouble has almost always been the result of a combination of both bad policy making and marketplace deficiencies. FUBAR is an acronym stemming from the World War II GI slang that means "fouled up beyond all recognition." Thus, "fubarnomics" could be used to describe the gloomy state of an economy. In this book, he provides his insights into the recent crippling recession, including the subprime mortgage meltdown, as well as the looming healthcare crisis and the perennial problem of social security. In his view, measures can be taken to prevent such crises by creating combined life-healthcare insurance policies, divorcing health care from employers, and many more such initiatives.

There are other models that have been proposed to explain bubbles [510]. One such model suggests combining the economic theory of rational expectation bubbles with behavioral finance theories on imitation and herding of investors, along with the mathematical and statistical physics of bifurcations and phase transitions. This type of modeling has been developed as a flexible tool to detect bubbles by considering the faster-than-exponential increase in asset prices decorated by accelerating oscillations as a diagnostic marker of bubbles. This model takes into consideration a positive feedback loop of higher return anticipations competing with negative feedback spirals of crash expectations. The model was tested in the Chinese stock market crashes between May 2005 and July 2009 and was able to predict time windows for crashes in advance. The same model was used to successfully predict the peak in mid-2006 of the US housing bubble and the peak in July 2008 of the global oil bubble [510]. There many additional models that use different parameters for the prediction of chaotic bubbles.

Bubbles may be rational, intrinsic, contagious, and spreadable [511-513]. There are several computer-based models which, for example, suggest that excessive leverage is one of the causative factors associated with financial bubbles [514]. Bubbles can be characterized by several parameters [491]. For example, asset price bubbles are often characterized by unusual changes in single measures and/or relationships among measures relative to their historical levels [515]. Additional examples of situations which can lead to bubbles are: In the case of stocks, the price-to-earnings ratio provides a measure of stock prices relative to corporate earnings; higher ratios mean that investors are paying more for each dollar of earnings; purchasing stocks on margin or homes with a lower down payment; higher risk lending and borrowing behavior, such as originating loans to borrowers with lower credit quality scores, combined with adjustable rate mortgages and "interest only" loans; Rationalizing borrowing, lending and purchase decisions based on expected future price increases rather than the ability of the borrower to repay "Levy Institute-Hyman Minsky-the Financial Instability Hypothesis-May 1992"; A high presence of marketing or media coverage related to the asset; and many more; Rationalizing asset prices by increasingly weaker arguments, such as "this time it's different" or "housing prices only go up."[491];

These bubbles may occur even in highly predictable markets, where most uncertainty is removed and market members are able to calculate the intrinsic value of the assets by examining the expected stream of dividends [506].

According to the greater fool theory, the price of objects is not determined by their intrinsic value, but by the irrational beliefs and expectations of market participants. This means that if you buy securities, irrespective of whether they are overvalued or not, you can always later sell them at a profit because there will always be someone willing to pay a higher price and is therefore a bigger fool [516]. The rationalization of the buyer is based on the trust that someone else is willing to pay an even higher price. This is what leads people to buy things even at "foolishly" high prices...the expectation that the object can be resold to a "greater fool" later on [517]. When will such a chain of transactions end? When the higher fool becomes the greatest fool and pays the highest price, after which they can no longer find another buyer [507].

It has been shown under somewhat artificial conditions, however, that speculative bubbles are not bound by rationality or assumptions about the irrationality of others, as assumed by this theory. Bubbles appear even when market participants correctly price the assets [518]. These bubbles appear even when speculation is not possible or when over-confidence is absent.

Bubbles are therefore just more complicated than some models assume them to be.

Some studies tend to look at economic bubbles as being sociologically driven [519]. If bubbles are indeed sociologically driven, the focus should move from "pure chaos" to our behavior. It is argued that market speculation is driven by culturally-situated narratives which are embedded in and supported by the prevailing institutions of the time [519]. Bubbles are formed during periods of innovation, easy credit, loose regulations, and internationalized investment. Under those conditions, narratives tend to have a more profound effect.

This brings us to the issue of chaos and narratives.

In purely economic terms, most economists agree that economic bubbles can occur when too much money is hunting too few assets. This results in the prices of both good assets and bad assets appreciating much beyond their actual value. Once the bubble bursts, the fall in prices causes the collapse of both speculative and not so speculative funds. Once we lose money, we tend to panic and to lose confidence in the system. We then pull out our money, and a vicious cycle of crisis occurs. Under such conditions, central banks and governments take measures that are aimed directly or indirectly at improving our confidence in the system. They want us to believe that the economy is stable, so they undertake monetary measures as well as psychological measures, which are another method for controlling chaos.

As human beings, we sometimes extrapolate. We look at an increasing price and predict that it will continue to increase. If prices have risen at a specific rate in the past, they will continue to rise at that rate forever [491]. We are willing to take a risk based on predictions based on past performance. This means that our "chaotic behavior" is not that chaotic, at least not all the time. One common behavior we all share is the "sheep behavior." We follow the crowd, assuming they know where they are going. In the market, this translates into buying and selling in the direction of the market trend [520].

Investment managers are often compensated and retained in part due to their performance relative to peers. In an attempt to maximize returns for their clients and keep their job, they may rationalize participation in a bubble that they believe to be forming, as the risks of not doing so outweigh the benefits [521].

In his article in the *Atlantic*, Henry Bodget wrote, "Live through enough bubbles, though, and we do eventually learn something of value. For example, I've learned that although getting out too early hurts, it hurts less than getting out too late. More important, I've learned that most of the common wisdom about financial bubbles is wrong…Most bubbles are the product of more than just bad faith, or incompetence, or rank stupidity; the interaction of human psychology with a market economy practically ensures that they will form. In this sense, bubbles are perfectly rational, or at least they're a rational and unavoidable by-product of capitalism. Technology and circumstances change, but the human animal doesn't. And markets are ultimately about people." [521]

Does he mean that we were born to generate chaotic bubbles and cannot actually control it?

What about all the experts, research, experience in this area? Bodget says, "In fairness to the thousands of experts who've snookered themselves throughout the years, a complicating factor is always at work: the ever-present possibility that it really might have been different. Everything is obvious only after the crash."

The moral hazard concept of bubbles is based on the view that if we are shielded from risk, we are likely to behave differently from the way we would behave if fully exposed to the risk. In the case of every rational behavior, we trust that we are responsible for the consequences of our own actions. Are we always rational in our behaviors in the market? Most of us are not. We always need to consider the option of making a return on our investment against the risk of making a loss. A moral hazard can occur when government regulations interfere with our ability to make these decisions. A good example is the intervention by the Dutch Parliament during the Tulip Mania of 1637, as also the U.S. President George W. Bush's Troubled Asset Relief Program (TARP), signed on October 2008 to provide a government bailout for many financial and non-financial institutions who made high-risk financial investments during the housing boom [491].

A laboratory bubble is defined as an experiment that is created under control conditions in the lab, where one can study causes and effect. Studies have shown it is easy to create a crash [506, 522]. There have been multiple attempts to mathematically model bubbles. A model was proposed for trading [523], but it did not consider two important assumptions. The first one was that supply and demand of an asset depends not only on valuation but also on price trend and other factors. The second assumption was that the available cash and asset are not in the "infinite arbitrage" that is generally assumed to exist. The model predicts that a bubble would be more significant if there was initial undervaluation. Moreover, when the initial value of the cash-to-asset ratio in a given experiment was increased, they predicted that the bubble would be more significant [523]. Many of these models are based on an equation which takes into account measurable parameters such as the amount of chase, timescale, and others.

It is more difficult, although not entirely impossible, to add into these equations our somewhat chaotic brains.

Both Dan and David were tired. They both agreed that chaos is essential for bubbles. Whether it can be modeled into equations or not is another story.

# CHAPTER 29

## Chaos is a necessity, but it's not necessary to fall over the edge

That evening, David went home somewhat bothered by the question of whether chaos is good or bad. While he had always been trying to show his father that the two of them were not alike and that he did not share his father's eccentricities, he knew that he also had a deep desire to lose himself in something he was passionate about and leave work behind. The only difference between his father and him was that he had never let himself reach that point. He usually suppressed issues that bothered him, and had never had the courage to explore and see where they led him. He kept telling himself that he did not have enough time. But this was far from the truth; he spent many of his evenings by himself.

This time, he decided to let himself into chaos. He did not enjoy so much the mathematics behind it, and he tried to focus on other concepts that might be of more relevance to him.

He quickly realized that the chaos theory could provide insights into processes that were previously thought to be unpredictable and random [524]. It delivers a set of tools that can be used to analyze many types of data. David found tutorials which use this theory for psychotherapy. One fundamental concept, which is apparently a doubtful one, is that the emotional experience of chaos is a necessary developmental step: "It is important for the therapist to recognize whether a client is avoiding this experience or is overwhelmed by this experience" [525] .

David came across the concept of the "edge of chaos," in the context of designing analytic techniques [526]. The "edge of chaos" sounded intimidating, and David thought that it was a place he would not want to be in. He was not sure sometimes that he was not already there though…

At any given time, we are in an emotional state that affects how we perceive the world around us, what we evoke from it, and what decisions we make. We may consider "chaos" to be a part of these emotions. Rather than treating emotions as undesirable forces that create disorder in our rational being, it is suggested that one use them to better shape cognitive processes in increasingly predictable ways [527]. The field of chaos theory provides concepts related to psychoanalysis that have implications for psychoanalytic techniques, for example, "the edge of chaos," emergence, attractors, and coupled oscillators. Such psychoanalytical methods are at the same time freer and more firmly based, and they can be used to manage obsessive-compulsive disorders[526].

David found himself looking into biological systems, which are connected to our emotions and probably form the same structure. Biological systems follow a hierarchical order that is based on dynamic bidirectional communication among their components. Imagine it like the Russian dolls, a set of wooden dolls of decreasing size placed one inside another. These dolls are also called matryoshka which means literally "little matron," and is a diminutive form of Russian female first name "Matryona" or "Matriosha"[528]. In addition to the compound inter-relationships between the different parts of biological systems, the complexity of each component spans several folds to make complex networks. Investigating the phenotypes associated with these networks is a difficult task, as it requires the integration of different approaches. Also, biological systems contain many types of "engines," which are actually molecules creating what is termed "molecular motors" inside our cells. These somewhat magical structures can perform multiple tasks while being immersed in a sea of chaos composed of many different organelles, molecules, and an almost indefinite number of networks, and so much more. Statistical physics is being used for analyzing these super complex systems [14].

MicroRNAs (or miRNAs) are a group of small, non-coding RNAs that can regulate the expression of certain target genes. They typically contain about 22 nucleotides, or building blocks, and are found in plants, animals and some viruses [529]. The majority of miRNAs are located within the cell, but some miRNAs, commonly known as circulating miRNAs or extracellular miRNAs, are outside of our cells and present in biological fluids [530]. MiRNAs are currently being researched for their potential application in therapeutic and diagnostic procedures. General patterns of miRNA signatures have been recognized in studies on single or multiple drug abuse; miRNAs are considered to represent a chaotic system that is found in normal versus disrupted states, particularly in substance use disorders. By analyzing these chaotic miRNA systems, one can come up with biological-signatures of clinical relevance [531].

The diversity of genome structures is due to variation in transposable elements and whole-genome duplication events. These are mediated by chromatin and epigenetic modifications [532]. Flowering plants have distinct genomes while also containing a similar suite of expressed genes. Some researchers consider the current structure of a genome to be the result of bursts of transposable elements and whole-genome duplication events. The silencing mechanisms and the chromatin structure of a genome are shaped by these events. This means that the mechanisms targeting chromatin modifications and epigenomic patterns vary among different species [532]. Whether these changes are fully ordered or whether there is some kind of "chaotic mechanism" underlying them is essential not only for the generation of more beautiful flowers but also for a better understanding of ourselves.

Heart rate variability (HRV) is the sequential beat-to-beat variation in specific intervals that is measured when we undergo an electrocardiographic (ECG) recording. This parameter reflects the regulation of heart rate (HR) by our autonomic nervous system (ANS). Models have been developed to use heart rate variability for risk stratification of patients with cardiovascular disease. Such models have been used as a noninvasive tool to predict mortality in patients with myocardial infarction as well as in patients without any heart conditions. It is based on the changes that occur with age in our nervous systems that affect this parameter. Nonlinear dynamics and mathematical concepts of chaos theory and fractals can allow for better interpretation of this parameter and also improve its prognostic significance in the elderly. [533].

When chaos concepts are used for modeling of our aging nerves, it opens up a whole new dimension of our understanding of our body.

Chaotic systems are deterministic but not predictable. They are characterized by sensitivity to initial conditions and strange attractors. Studies of menstruation and transition to menopause using these concepts suggest that menstruation is a result of a complex nonlinear, dynamical, and chaotic system. The chaos theory provides a clear framework that qualitatively accounts for confusing results from perimenopause research. It directs attention to variability within and between women, adaptation, lifespan development, and the need for complicated explanations. Whether the menstrual cycle is chaotic can be empirically tested [534]. This is just one of many studies, which are still in their early stages that are attempting to apply the chaos theory to biological systems. Such studies would help explain the occurrence of several diseases that do not fit the linear-reductionist paradigm, for example, fibromyalgia and chronic fatigue syndrome. An interesting disease in this realm is what is called Gulf War syndrome, also known as "Desert Storm Disease" or "Gulf War Illness." This condition is defined by a collection of symptoms reported by veterans of the first Gulf War since August 1990. Later, it was found that veterans from every country that made up the coalition forces had been affected, with more than 110,000 cases reported in the U.S. alone by 1999. In the UK, too, veterans of the 2003 conflict began reporting symptoms identical to those reported in the first war, shortly after they returned from duty. These symptoms include fatigue, persistent headaches, muscle pain, tingling and numbness in the limbs, short-term memory loss, poor concentration, depression, anxiety, insomnia, skin rashes, hair loss, persistent coughing, bronchitis, asthma, diarrhea, constipation, nausea, and bloating. Most of these symptoms are similar to those of chronic fatigue syndrome [535].

Through the recognition of chaos fractals and complex systems in our body, it might be possible to understand more complexes such as these.

Nonlinear dynamics theories propose that the essence of disease is dysfunction and not structural damage; this view is in conflict with the notion of homeostasis and disease. This implies that fibromyalgia and similar illnesses may be caused by degradation in the performance of our primary complex adaptive system. According to this view, health is perceived as resilient adaptation, and some chronic illnesses, as rigid dysfunction [536].

The complexity theory is an interdisciplinary theory that has evolved from research in the natural sciences that examines uncertainty and non-linearity [537]. This theory emphasizes on interactions and the accompanying feedback loops that continuously change systems. Systems are unpredictable. However, they are also constrained by order-generating rules [538]. The complexity theory has been used in the fields of biology, strategic management, and organizational studies, and many others.

In the field of strategic management and organizational studies, the complexity theory is called "complex adaptive organizations." This term is used for better understanding how organizations or firms adapt to their environments and how they cope with conditions of uncertainty. If we think of organizations and firms as collections of strategies and structures, we will find them to be complex. All such structures are dynamic networks of interactions, and their relationships are not simple aggregations of individual static entities [537]. In fact, most organizations are adaptive, and both individual and collective behaviors are continuously adapting to the changes that initiate micro-events or collections of events [539].

David was thinking of the law firm he was working for. The company always seemed very non-adaptive and super non-flexible to him.

In the past, organizations were viewed as determinist, closed systems, much like machines. This meant a high level of bureaucracy, hierarchy, and standardization [540]. "This is where I work," David was thinking to himself. We may still think that most of the organizations we know are such. Nowadays, most of us think of organizations as dynamic systems in constant states of change.

Initially, the methods employed for organizational change involved a planned approach. The goal was to make incremental improvements by focusing on one issue at a time [538]. The new approach to organizational change is based on the premise that change is both continuous and unpredictable. Change is now considered to be a continuous process that takes place through many small steps, rather than big significant events that take place at specific time points. In fact, organizations do not have the luxury of dealing with one significant change at a time. The punctuated equilibrium model claims that organizations evolve over time, with long periods of stability that are disrupted by short periods of substantial change. These disruptions set the stage for a new period in the life of the organization [538].

The application of the complexity theory to organizational change has been happening over the last two decades, and in the process, the concept that organizations are machines that require a planned approach to succeed is slowly being rejected. This theory supports the notion that power and constant change are crucial elements of organizational life. Organizations are considered as complex adaptive systems (CAS) that display characteristics such as self-organization, complexity, emergence, interdependence, space of possibilities, co-evolution, chaos, and self-similarity [537, 541, 542].

In complex adaptive systems, there are relationships between the system itself and the agent acting within it. This type of relationship may be in contrast with ordered and chaotic systems. For any ordered system, there is a certain degree of constraint, which means that agent behavior is limited to the rules of the system. In a chaotic system, the agents are not constrained in any way, and are susceptible to statistical and other analyses. In complex adaptive systems, both the system and the agents co-evolve, interact and affect each other. Thus, these systems mildly constrain the behavior of the agents, and at the same time, the agents change, too, through their interaction with it. This self-organizing character of the structure is what differentiates complex adaptive systems from chaos [543].

According to theories about complex adaptive systems, every agent within the environment attempts to get a better take, but most of the time, their outcomes are highly influenced by what other agents do. Most people are not working alone. Most of us are a part of teams. And most of us feel from time to time that others get credit for what we do, or at least, benefit from what we do. This points to the dynamic equilibrium of coevolution in these systems, which effect some changes in the end results. This goes well with the power law, which claims that there exists a functional relationship between two measures, such that a relative change in one results in a relative proportional change in the other. This is independent of the initial size of those measures. Thus, the changes in the power of one entity can change the power of another [544]. So, small changes in any component of an organization or system may lead to significant improvements or alterations in the system as a whole. This brings us back to the edge. Systems that are at the edge of chaos can defeat those that are not [545].

David was not sure what this meant to him. But he got the sense that the edge of chaos might just be an excellent place to be in.

If one accepts this concept, then we must also accept that the best-run companies succeed because they operate at the edge of chaos. For a company, this means persistently following a path of constant innovation. If a company keeps inserting novelty, freshness, change, or some chaos into their standard and regular operations, they continuously risk falling over the edge [538].

No one wants to fall over the edge, but we do want to be the "best run" company. So how do we do that? This calls for balance. A company should maintain an equilibrium between flexibility and stability to avoid failing [537].

"What about my life?" David was wondering. Many would say that there is no such balance in personal life, and that there is no way to maintain such a balance in a company, a family, or organization. However, even if such an ideal point of balance does not really exist, it does not mean that we should not aim at reaching it. David was wondering whether taking this path would be the perfect way to live his life from now on.

Concepts from complexity sciences are useful for understanding the strategy of organizations and can be applied to our personal lives. The complexity theory also recognizes new ways of project management [546]. It argues for the establishment of a "culture of trust" that "welcomes outsiders, embrace new ideas, and promotes cooperation" [547, 548].

Can we create such trust with ourselves?

David was reading a Harvard Business Review article that stated, "Culture is a community. It is an outcome of how people relate to one another. Communities exist at work just as they do outside the commercial arena. Like families, villages, schools, and clubs, businesses rest on patterns of social interaction that sustain them over time or are their undoing. They are built on shared interests and mutual obligations and thrive on cooperation and friendships [548]."

David never considered himself anti-social, but he realized that some of his colleagues thought him to be so.

He did agree with the concept that for business communities, the benefits of high sociability are clear. This means working in a more pleasant environment. Not less important, sociability promotes creativity. It also promotes teamwork, sharing of information, openness to new ideas, and the freedom to express and accept out-of-the-box thinking [548].

All of this sounds adorable, but even two decades ago, some authors had summarized the drawbacks of high levels of sociability: "The prevalence of friendships may allow poor performance to be tolerated. No one wants to rebuke or fire a friend." As friends are often reluctant to disagree with or criticize one another, they may end up with compromises and not the best solutions.

Another limitation of the complexity theory is the assumption that organizations are homogeneous. Just as one organization differs from another, so do units within them. But this is not necessarily bad. This could even help organizations to achieve better results. The complexity theory reveals that in an organization, individual behaviors and selections are more central than managerial plans. Individuals are very affected by their interrelations with other members of the organization. The complex adaptive system theory suggests that leaders focus on self-organization instead of management control [537].

David was happy that this theory did not involve equations. It could even be applied to his personal life, including his relationships with his family, friends and enemies. One of the implications is to pay attention to small changes and interventions that happen to us or around us, maybe even small events in the Antarctica. Remember the butterfly.

Another implication is to simultaneously encourage some conflict, some change, and some chaos. These are necessary. By pushing ourselves to the edge, or to instability, we can achieve improvement. This may actually be essential for upgrading. The edge of chaos is healthy [549].

The aim of research over the last two decades is to apply some part of the complexity theory to various aspects of our lives, for example, redesigning health care, education, and the economy [550].

Can we redesign ourselves based on some of these concepts? Not all view the complexity theory as calling for action all the time. In fact, in contrast to some of the old approaches of calling managers to fix problems continuously, the complexity theory recommends that a "wait and watch" approach be employed to see how the issue resolves itself [540]. This means that we, and of course our bosses, should stop looking for problems and trying to prevent them from deteriorating or fix them. As an alternative, we need to look for the balance between chaos and stability to promote creativity and innovation. While this point of balance may be hard to achieve, and it means having some instability, taking this path is not only more interesting, but it can upgrade us too.

Based on this notion, if our lives, our workplace, and our company, are always stable and entirely predictable, they are also motionless and very much stagnant. They are "frozen." There are even "comfortably frozen." Should we feel comfortable if we are stable? Some would call it boring. What is the trick? It is all about the non-existence of balance. Find a beautiful place on the edge of chaos.

Tensions, pressures, and forces always exist. Some believe that we need to "encourage tension, rather than fight it" [540]. An exciting article in Forbes puts it in these words: "Conflict resolution is about seeing opportunities that others don't see. When dealing with conflict resolution through the lens of opportunity, conflict can be a good enabler of growth for our business and professional growth for all of the people involved. Effective leaders know that the most authentic relationships with their employees, clients and external partners don't truly begin until they experience some form of tension with them." [551] In an excellent article in the Harvard Business Review a few years ago, David read about the concept of tension in teams. The claim is that conflict within teams is inevitable. It is also claimed to be essential to the process of creative collaboration. "Without differences of opinion, there can be no debate about important issues nor synthesis of ideas" [552].

Does this mean that constant conflicts are required in our lives, too? Is it better for use than sitting on the beach? William L. Wrigley Jr. was an American chewing gum manufacturer. He is quoted by Paul Hennessey, from BayGroup International, as saying, "If two people in business always agree, one of them is unnecessary." [553]

Encouraging tension is not the opposite of understanding the importance of the relationships of individuals within a family, an organization, or within ourselves. What it calls for is generating an environment of encouraging "care and connection." Why? Because it could potentially improve us, as well as our family's or organization's creativity, efficiency, and adaptability [549]. We do not necessarily have to think about tension in the negative sense: It sometimes means encouraging asking questions. We can ask ourselves questions. We can let our spouse ask us a question, or let our employees raise an issue. It is important for us to be active participants rather than observers.

We do not need to send others to the cliff. We need to find a beautiful spot, with a beautiful view and stand there.

# CHAPTER 30

## Standing at the edge, creating more tension, and artificial life

The next morning, David experienced what he believed his father had been going through from time to time. He did not feel like going to the office. He had the feeling that he had gotten into something that held much more meaning for his life. He wanted to learn more. He finished early that day, came home, and began reading about standing at the edge, balancing on a board.

The term "edge of chaos" is used to symbolize a transition zone between order and disorder that is assumed to exist within a wide variety of systems [554]. This transition area is a region of confined instability and variability that creates a continuous dynamic interplay between order and disorder [555, 556]. The mathematician Doyne Farmer, who is the founder of the Prediction Company, used this phrase to describe the transition phenomenon discovered by computer scientist Christopher Langton. This phrase originally refers to an area in the range of a variable, which was found to be diverse while examining the behavior of a cellular automaton. Langton, one of the founders of artificial life, began his work by studying one-dimensional cellular automata. This is a model studied in computer science, mathematics, and physics, which represents complexity and non-linear dynamics in a variety of scientific fields [557].

Cellular automata are abstract, distinct and comprise a finite or denumerable set of homogenous, simple units (atoms or cells). At each time point, the cells instantiate one of a finite set of states. They evolve in parallel at discrete time steps, following state update functions or dynamical transition rules. A cell state is updated based on the states of cells in its local neighborhood. This means that there are no actions that occur over a distance. Cellular automata can be specified in purely mathematical terms, and physical structures can be used to implement them. They can be used to compute functions and solve algorithmic problems. Cellular automata display complex emergent behavior that starts from simple atoms and follows simple local rules.

The concept of cellular automata can be applied in many other fields, such as for modelling reality, as well as to study the philosophical hypothesis that the physical world itself is a discrete, digital automaton. Thus, while cellular automata might seem like straightforward entities, some researchers have associated them with profound questions [558]. One such question is how living things arise in a world in which one of the governing principles is that entropy, or disorder, is always on the increase.

Some cellular automata are "boring" because all the cells die out in a few generations or because they quickly settle into simple repeating patterns. They are said to be highly ordered [558]. David found this to be analogous to what we call "the comfort zone." Even though we believe something to be comfortable, it is still somewhat mind-numbing. Not exciting. Life in the comfort zone is incredibly predictable and easy to describe, and can seem quite annoying. In the same way, artificial life can be annoying if it is predictable and repeats itself. However, there is an interesting claim made by the scientist David J. Eck that cellular automata can also be tedious because their behavior is random. Langton calls such cellular automata "chaotic" [558]. Their behavior is boring because it is entirely unpredictable. This sounded somewhat bizarre to David. "I can understand that full order, which repeats itself is boring, but if full chaos is also dull, what is left?"

The in-between zone. This is the "edge of chaos" zone.

Some cellular automata display unusual, complex, almost lifelike behavior. Langton said that these are near the border between order and chaos. If they were more ordered, they would be too predictable to be interesting; if they were less ordered, they would be too chaotic.

"Can I find this zone in my life?" David wondered.

Langton proposed a simple way for predicting whether a given cellular automaton is within the ordered territory, the chaotic one, or near the boundary or the edge of chaos. He proposed a number that can be computed based on the rules of cellular automata. This number is defined as the fraction of the rules according to which the new state of the cell is "living." He called this parameter *lambda*. The lambda value is a number between 0 and 1. If lambda is 0, then all cells die immediately, since every rule leads to death. 0 indicates that the cellular automaton is in the ordered zone. If the lambda value is 1, then a given cell that has at least one living neighbor will stay alive in the next generation and, in fact, forever. So lambda values close to zero indicate that the cellular automaton is in the ordered realm, while values close to 1 indicate that it is in the chaotic realm. The value for the edge of chaos is somewhere in between [559]. The difficulty with this method is that there is no lambda value that represents the edge of chaos [560].

If we start with a cellular automaton with a lambda value of zero, where all rules lead to death, and it is entirely ordered, and then we randomly modify the rules one by one to lead to life instead of death, the lambda value will increase. Thus, the sequence of cellular automata will have lambda values increasing from zero to one, and they will be moving from the ordered region to the chaotic region. The automata at the beginning of the sequence are thus highly ordered, but they get chaotic towards the end. Somewhere in between, at some critical value of lambda, there will be a transition from order to chaos. It is near this transition zone that the most interesting cellular automata with the most complex behavior will be found [558, 561].

The ideal lambda value is not a universal constant. It depends on the track selected through the space of cellular automata. To apply Langton's concepts in the search for "interesting cellular automata," we have to make such a path and wander along it, looking for the transition between order and chaos. Physicists and mathematicians are studying these concepts, in an attempt to better understand them.

In the book *Complexity and Organization* [562], it is noted, "nothing novel can emerge from systems with high degrees of order and stability. On the other hand, complete chaotic systems, such as stampedes, riots, rage, or the early year of the French Revolution, are too formless to coalesce.

Generative complexity takes place in the boundary between regularity and randomness." In other words, a system with no order cannot exhibit valuable behavior. We cannot benefit from it. However, a system with too much order is over constrained and, likewise, will not generate useful results [561]. Some believe that the edge of chaos is where life begins. The claim is that that evolution pushed systems towards the edge of chaos, where sophisticated, exciting behaviors such as life could occur [561]. The "ideal zone" at the edge of chaos is considered by some as a place where evolution takes place. It involves the collapse of local structures that give rise to new patterns of organization, creating a dynamic life-cycle [563]. "Some biologists find new rules for life at the edge of chaos"[564]. Several studies in biology have drawn an analogy between the computation/mathematical "edge of the chaos" zone and biological processes.

Based on these concepts, we can hypothesize that both organizations and humans are in a continuous process to organize themselves into conditions so complex that no practical functionality can result from it. The systems in between, i.e., at the edge of order and chaos, may exhibit more flexible and organized behavior.

In the sciences in general, the edge of chaos has come to symbolize the region between order and complete randomness or chaos, where the complexity is maximal, within which some physical, biological, economic and social systems operate in [554]. It is being used to symbolize real complexity. "Seeking the edge of chaos, therefore, is not seeking disorder or randomness but the right balance between order and flexibility" [565].

David realized that this ideal place, the edge of chaos, the in-between zone, may, in fact, be a highly comfortable zone to be in. The highest complexity along with flexibility and creativity result from being in this super calm and content zone. He also discovered that the generality and significance of the idea, however, has since been called into question. Melanie Mitchell, a professor of computer science at Portland State University, claims that the phrase "edge of chaos" is misused [554]. In fact, this phrase has been appropriated by the business community, too, and it is sometimes used in contexts that are far removed from the original scope of the term.

It may be ideal to use this phrase only symbolically and for the purpose of thinking.

The "ideal zone" at the edge of chaos is considered by some as a place where evolution takes place. It means that it involves the collapse of local structures that give rise to new patterns of organization, creating a dynamic life-cycle[563]. "Some biologists find new rules for life at the edge of chaos"[564, 566]. David was reading an article in Wired, where the trick of harnessing the capacity of small perturbations, such as proteins that are needed for the activation of a pathway or neuronal firing, is discussed. The idea is to produce significant effects without entering into a place where these inducers become overwhelming. We want to get as close as possible to chaos, but we do not want to go into the chaos. We want to be at the edge, but on the safe side. For example, imagine dropping sand grains one by one from a single point. For a long time, nothing much will happen: a conical pile will accumulate. Eventually, however, the pile becomes so steep that the addition of just one more grain can cause an unpredictable collapse[564]. So, the "ideal edge" in this case would be a pile containing the maximum number of grains, after which the addition of even one more would result in the collapse of the system.

If we look at networks of neurons in our brain, we will find thousands of cells that are connected directly or indirectly, by activator and suppressor molecules, to produce systems which may underlie cognition, memory, and many other of our brain activities [567].

For complex systems, excessive order and too much change will not cross rigid boundaries. On the other hand, extreme chaos may lead to the total collapse of a system [563]. If we are willing to apply this notion symbolically to complex systems such as ecosystems, societies, and economies, consider the following. All complex systems can be viewed as trying to maintain themselves between randomness and order at a point where they can use both to configure and reconfigure themselves. This means that complex systems can go through both integration and differentiation in the process of evolving to become more complex.

Mitchell Waldrop, in his book *Complexity. The Emerging Science at the*

*Edge of Order and Chaos* [568], says that "the edge of chaos is where life has enough stability to sustain itself and enough creativity to deserve the name of life." The edge of chaos is where new and innovative ideas occur. It is far from the edges of the status quo [563]. "The edge is described as a constantly shifting battle zone between stagnation and anarchy, the one place where a complex system can be spontaneous, adaptive and alive" [568, 569].

Looking at history, the edge of chaos is probably where slavery and segregation gave way to the civil rights movement, or where seventy years of Soviet communism gave way to political turmoil.

The economist Joseph Schumpeter presented the idea of creative destruction as the driving force within a market economy. It describes how new innovations are continually being generated by entrepreneurs in order to displace older ones in an unremitting cyclical dynamic [563]. "The same process of industrial mutation that incessantly revolutionizes the economic structure from within, incessantly destroying the old one, incessantly creating a new one. This process of creative destruction is the essential fact about capitalism" [570]. Schumpeter argued that capitalism exists in the state of ferment he dubbed "creative destruction," with spurts of innovation destroying established enterprises and yielding new ones [571]. He describes a stationary state, which can be considered as the classical economic equilibrium of order and predictability. The entrepreneur disturbs this equilibrium by introducing a transformation that leads to economic development. Based on this theory, capitalism is understood as an evolutionary process of continuous innovation and creative destruction [572].

In the context of human cognition, we would notice highly predictable and orderly states being created from those that are more unpredictable and chaotic. We all have these states and transitions in our minds [573]. In simple words, in chaotic regimes, network states are disconnected from those in the ordered regime. However, at the edge of chaos, the states can be seen to be maximally novel while still connected to states in the ordered regime and can present with the ideal combination of novelty and utility. This is one of the hallmarks of innovative thinking.

The edge of chaos is being studied in association with creativity too

[563]. In any system, there are forces pushing towards order and others introducing unpredictability and randomness. A genuinely creative idea can be viewed as a bridge between these two states. Genuinely creative changes and significant shifts occur at the edge of chaos [573, 574]. This edge is associated with the freedom to explore, increased engagement, and making more connections, which promote creativity under these conditions. At the same time, the creative process requires some structure [575]. An ability to inhibit the first thing that comes to mind in order to get to the higher hanging fruit in the cognitive tree is one of the cornerstones of creative achievement [563]. Many psychopathologies involve shifts in the regulation of stability and flexibility, which yield both increased redundancy and increased entropy within the same individual [573]. The "edge of chaos" concept would also explain exceptional creativity in individuals with mental illness, without an overall increase in creative achievement, often described as "madness." Increased creative achievement among relatives of people with mental illness, or people with milder syndromes, for whom the increased flexibility or stability is less disabling, has been shown [573].

We should not view order and chaos as being on the same longitudinal scale. The zone we are talking about is not halfway between them. It is not 50% order and 50% chaos. Not even 80/20. We can view it as two islands— the chaos island and an order island—with a bridge between them. This is a semicircular bridge, so that when we stand at the highest point on the bridge, we are much above both chaos and order. It does not mean that there are no places with part chaos and part order. There may be a road connecting the two islands, which is below the bridge, and is at the level of the two islands. Along this road, we can find a place with part chaos and part order. But the best place to be is at the highest point of the bridge. It is not only because we can get the best view from there, but also we have the best perspective of the world. Being above means not letting other issues distract you. It is a much more comfortable and much more enjoyable place to be in.

If we apply this symbolism to our life, we can think of many places, events, relationships and so on, where we can see almost pure order. Our daily routines. Or pure chaos. Our bedroom? Problems in our life? We need to find the highest point of the bridge. This zone is at a different level, not along the line between the two extremes. There are different levels of this zone.

If we understand this, we also realize that there is no equation that can direct us to an elevator that can take us to this zone. Even a basic understanding of this concept could open the door to new opportunities though.

David was thinking again about his relationships.

The concept of the edge of chaos is also being applied to understanding relationships between people, as well as society in general. It is all about interactions at the micro and macro level [563]. At the macro level, social structures, such as laws, religions, governments, and social institutions, offer the potential for order and stability. While we may not like them, they provide us with some stability and order. Sometimes, we feel that these institutions impose too much order on us. Some of us may feel that all these institutions and rules are limiting to some extent our personal development. All in the name of conformism, and solidarity with society. With no rules at all, it is most likely there will be some if not total chaos. Such a situation would end with a different set of laws. We cannot change this situation, even if we do not like it. Even if we feel that "stasis and lack of novelty are being imposed on us" by the world around, it is unlikely that we can change it. The solution is to explore ways for finding our paths to novelty and becoming better under those circumstances. Others are doing so. There is no reason we cannot do it.

At the micro level, there are many sources for constant disorder that "bother us" from the moment we wake up. Some are minor and are major, or some are minor and seem major to us. This leads us to feel that we are being pulled in different directions. Total chaos. Our train is late; our kid is sick; our spouse is moody; our neighbor is bothering us; our boss is crazy; we spilled our coffee…how can anyone be innovative in such circumstances? Well, there are people who can. We may also feel that there is some conflict between ours and other people's individual agendas, as well as with the agendas of special interest groups. We may also feel a conflict between micro chaos and macro order. Others may feel a conflict between the chaos in the world around them and the fully ordered life they have.

We could apply the concepts of chaos in the context of prosperous societies. A prosperous society is a one that maintains itself on the edge of chaos. On the one hand, it has stable macro institutions that maintain sufficient order, but at the same time, it also preserves the individual autonomy required for personal development.

If we are willing to take it to a somewhat philosophical level, we may accept the notion of Piero Scaruffi, an Italian-American freelance software consultant, who said "life only happens at the edge of chaos. The difference between life and death is minimal. It takes very little to kill a living being. Oxygen is one of the most toxic elements, but without oxygen, we do not survive more than a few minutes. We are made mostly of water, but we drown at the rate of thousands of individuals a year. The temperature of our body has to stay within a narrow margin, or we get sick. The slightest defect in the food we eat causes us to get poisoned. Life requires that a very high number of parameters remain within a narrow margin of values from birth to death." [576] The same notion is true for societies. Both successful individual life and successful societies have a narrow window of opportunity. The view is that effective statutory democracies maintain both social order and individual rights through laws while providing mechanisms for individual members to change those institutions when needed. As such, they "enable upward and downward interactions in a cyclical fashion that is characteristic of evolutionary processes, where new diversity comes from below while constraints and selection come from above to continuously generate new and relevant variants in response to changes in the environment" [563].

Components of the chaos theory are relevant in forecasting service outcomes and, consequently, the impact on the management of such services in nursing care. The ability to track the course of service and manipulate that trajectory by introducing new parameters can allow managers to put forth plans for service development and to evaluate the helpfulness of services [577].

The chaos theory offers new insights into physiological systems. We can apply some of the concepts of chaos into analyzing scientific data in order to better understand what is hard to explain. Autism is a triad of impairments that consists of impaired communication, impaired social skills, and over-regulated behavior. The over-regulation component is being explored through the rules of the chaos theory [578]. A migraine results in some dysfunction as a result of a mismatch between the complexity of the environment and the system that is seeking to regulate it. It may be a result of an incompatibility between the complexity of midbrain sensory integration and cortical control networks.

Biologists are rather cautious about making analogies between mathematical models of the "edge of chaos" transition zone and actual biological processes. In the pile of sand example, criticality is a global property, and it is the same at every point in a system. Biology could involve many critical networks, snuggled together in hierarchies that generate ever more complex phenomena [579]. The chaos theory provides a new perspective to explain the underlying physiological mechanisms [579]. As another example, polycystic ovarian syndrome is characterized by defects in primary cellular control mechanisms that result in chronic anovulation and hyperandrogenism, or an inappropriate increase in some hormones. The pathogenesis of this condition has not yet been clarified. Models of the chaos theory, which provide a particular approach for the interpretation of data, can help better understand the association of different parameters and their disturbances in the pathogenesis of polycystic ovarian syndrome [580].

David realized that if we could view the same data using a different pair of lens, the chaos lens, we would reach different results. It may also enable us to look at difficult issues in a different way.

How about aging? From time to time, novel ways of interpreting and modifying aging mechanisms are proposed. Many lead to dead ends. Using dynamical system chaos theories, new insights into aging are being reconnoitered. One prediction is that aging is associated with loss of physiological complexity from the molecular to the cellular level, and from the tissue to organismic levels. According to several theories, aging is associated with an increase in complexity, but the chaos theory looks at aging as a simplification of physiological dynamical complexity. In fact, based on the chaos theory, traditional pharmacological regimes for slowing aging have been challenged, and it has been suggested that medication should be given at irregular, pulsed or multiple intervals, and at continually changing dosage strengths, to ensure maximum benefit [581].

The chaos theory deals with deterministic systems that show complex, apparently random-looking behavior. Pharmacodynamics is the study of how a drug affects an organism. It is tightly associated with complex physiological processes. The use of the chaos theory in this field enables a new approach for viewing the data obtained from studies on drug therapies. This new tactic is fundamentally different from the classic approach [582].

A few years ago, David had dated a woman named Joan, who was an artist in the real sense of the word. She painted a little. David always had the feeling that she really understood art. He was not that type of a person. At some point, both of them felt that they could not continue with their relationship as they were broadcasting at different levels. He remembered Joan telling him about chaos and art. It started to make sense to him now: the random and chaotic elements in art from the position of both a scientist and a painter is of great interest. There is some debate around defining the possible use of the concept of entropy in art, and whether fractals and so-called chaos theory can play a useful and meaningful role in art [309].

Despite their complexity, they do make us think. And it is all about that.

# CHAPTER 31
## Creating chaos

David met his father that weekend and shared his thoughts about chaos. Dan was amazed. It was one of those rare moments when he felt that David was opening up to him, and he was even trying to get Dan's opinion on the topic.

Dan was telling David about a book he had just read called *Sapiens*, in which Yuval Noah Harari argues there are two types of chaos: first- and second-order chaos [583]. According to Harari, first-order chaos does not respond to prediction. With this type of chaos, we may end up with predictable behavior even if a phenomenon is chaotic. With the help of supercomputers and the appropriate models, we could make predictions in many cases of first-order chaos, which can also be defined as a "simple" type of chaos. The weather would be an ideal example of a system that exhibits first-order chaos. It is a complicated, chaotic system that is made up of so many factors; however, if one uses the right algorithms, it is possible to come up with a more or less accurate prediction model. Most of the time, the weather report is right about whether we need an umbrella or not. Clearly, meteorologists are able to understand and make predictions about this chaotic system.

Second-order chaos, on the other hand, is less predictable because it does respond to prediction. This type of chaos is resistant to prediction even when the results of the predictions are available to others to respond to. With this type of chaos, even super predictions may turn out to be incorrect [584]. Second-order chaos could be described as a much more sophisticated type of chaos. It is the type of chaos one would see in a multifactorial disordered system with one additional factor: the system responds to predictions made about it. If the weather was of this type and it were to listen to the news and hear a prediction about rain, it would change its mind and the sun would come out. Most historians believe that history is characterized by second-order chaos. The economy is another system with second-order chaos. Once we predict the economy, the economy will respond to us. The best example is the stock market. If the oil price increases today, we run and buy oil stocks. Our prediction is that the oil prices will go up. But this prediction may be accurate for today and not so for tomorrow. The market will respond to our prediction and the prices may go down. This type of chaos can be seen in war too. If we know what will happen in a war and our enemy knows it too, he will not behave as expected.

Second-order chaotic systems are unpredictable, and as per definition, they cannot be modeled. If we believe we have a model that can predict oil price, which as per definition is a second-order chaotic system, the model would not be reliable. The stock market involves making predictions about future events in the present. This is the reason why it's not possible to predict stock prices even a minute ahead, as the values keep responding to the predictions and change. This also explains why experts fail to predict crashes in the stock market, and similarly, fail to predict revolutions. If we are the ruler of a kingdom and we get to know of someone preparing for a revolt, we are likely to imprison them. As per definition, revolution is also second-order chaos, so it cannot be predicted in advance. This is the reason why revolutions and other significant events in our history are not predictable. By this definition, an economic crisis is not predictable. If it were predictable, it would mean that it is preventable. In which case it would then cease to exist. The existence of second-order chaos, therefore, implies that we cannot predict everything. The silver lining is that it provides us with several options, from among which we can select one or more and act accordingly [583].

The argument in support of second-order chaos is that there is nothing natural about our world, nothing deterministic about our history, and that it is all a combination of incidences. That is, random occurrences lead to events that are unpredictable. At each point of time in our history, there have been many options, and random minor events have led to the selection of one of them. Our history is therefore not deterministic. But not everyone will agree with this.

David was not sure how to associate this information with his findings. Dan tried to help him by telling him about Friedrich Nietzsche's famous words about chaos: "One must still have chaos in oneself to be able to give birth to a dancing star." There have been so many interpretations of this quote by experts and non-experts alike. Dan Blanchard wrote about this in an interesting blog: "I'm not sure what we came up with while thinking about the need of having chaos, but I think this means that we can't be content with our present circumstances. We have to be a little unsatisfied. Maybe we even have to be a little angry at our present circumstances if we want life to improve…I'm not talking about acting violently, but I am talking about the kind that drives us to take massive action and enables us to put a lot of sticks in the red-hot fire. In other words, I'm talking about creating a life of CHAOS!" [585]. What he means is that we always run away from chaos; we are unsatisfied with chaos. If we encounter problems, even minor chaos, we are always trying to resolve them and bring order. His suggestion is that we should try to absorb the chaos and benefit from it. This went well with David's insights from his readings about chaos.

How many of us want to become dancing stars? If we do not want to, we should continue with our regular lives. If, on the other hand, we want to become stars and we want to take his advice, we should not run away from chaos. Taking it one step further, we should look for chaos or even create chaos.

Maybe it is all about expectations. Blanchard says that he is sure that almost every one of us lives far below his or her real potential. This sounds disappointing [585]. If we have the ability and qualifications to become the greatest scientist, artists, or athlete, and we have not accomplished this, we may feel that we are missing something. Maybe we do not want to have this feeling, so we prefer staying in our comfort zone, looking at others making it. However, even if we are such a person, and we deliberately choose to not lift the bar to our potential, or what we believe to be our potential, we might still regret it at some point of time in our lives. David had repeatedly heard that "our true potential is so vast, encompassing, and empowering that we can't even begin to understand the worldly or universal powers that lie dormant in almost all of us" [585]. He had always been skeptical of this and similar quotes, but now he found that he was asking himself how it could be done. How could he achieve his so-called true potential?

There are so many cookbooks, and help books, and "gurus," and scientists, and artists, who believe that they can provide us with the answers. Chaos is now on the list of "answers." According to one writer, "maybe we all just need to have a little more faith in ourselves, and manage our chaotic lives just a little bit better and then just maybe we too can create something special." [585]

Both Dan and David felt like they had reached somewhere important. David left home that evening with a good feeling. He felt that while his father may be looking at it from a mathematician's or a physicist's point of view, he himself could reach the same conclusions without equations. It was not hard for him to symbolize and apply some of these thoughts to his own life.

# CHAPTER 32
## Adaptation

Olivia was 45. She was their daughter. Dan had always felt that she was the one to blame for Jenny's cancer; he was aware that it was a very potent and illogical thought, but he could not resist thinking it. Ever since Olivia was a little baby, she had never gotten along with Jenny. Olivia was a brilliant woman. Sometimes Dan thought that this was her primary problem. "She is just too smart for this world," he used to tell Jenny. Olivia rightfully thought that she was smarter than her teachers. While studying science in college, she used to tell Dan that she could not really find the answers to many of the questions she had in life by listening to "these endless courses." When she was finally done with college, she found work at a small biotechnology company. Dan never understood what they were trying to do. A few years ago, he even started exploring the topic of adaptation in order to understand her better.

Adaptation plays a vital role in all living organisms and systems [554]. All living organisms, us included, are continually changing their inner properties to better fit in with the current environment [586]. The self-adjusting parameters that are inherent in natural systems are in fact the most important tools for adaptation. We have so many stimuli to adapt to almost every minute of our day. To most of them, we adapt automatically. Most of them are simple to adapt to: we wear a heavy coat in cold weather and we take deep breaths (to calm ourselves) when talking to an angry neighbor.

Our environment always imposes on us the need to adapt. There are so many things happening at the same time. We must adjust [587]. Some of the constraints we need to adjust to are imposed by us. We do or say things which change the environment around us, which means that we need to re-adjust to the new condition that we actually forced on the environment around us.

But based on his discussions with David, Dan had started rethinking the whole concept of adaption.

Adaptation is essential for many natural systems. It is easy to understand that if we do not adapt, the result could be chaos. Systems with self-adjusting parameters are characterized by their ability to avoid chaos. This phenomenon is called "adaptation to the edge of chaos." [554] So, if we want to live on the edge of chaos, do we need to have good adaptation skills? Some researchers believe that adaptation to the "edge of chaos" is the notion that complex adaptive systems spontaneously evolve toward a regime near the boundary between chaos and order [588]. Physicists claim that this zone has the optimal settings for control of a system [589]. In physics, the edge of chaos is also an optimal setting that affects the ability of a physical system to perform functions for computations [590]. If we extrapolate this concept to human beings, the implication is that all of us are aiming to reach this zone. We may require an adaptation process to reach it, and a continuous adaptation process to remain there.

Was Olivia losing it because she was unable to adapt to the edge of chaos?

Plants, animals, and humans have adapted to their environments by means of genetic, physiological, behavioral, and developmental mechanisms. The process of adaptation also includes changes in both instinctive behavior and learning [587]. Some of the adaptations processes are spontaneous and intuitive, while some require thinking and more effort. Apart from dealing with physical changes in our environment, such as light, dark, temperature, water, and wind, adaptation also requires us to adapt to complex changes in our environment, one of the biggest being other organisms in our surroundings. This might be a lion that we meet in the street, but more realistically, they are "lions" that we meet at our workplace or even at home. We deal with enemies, competitors, parasites, but also with lovers. We are required to adapt ourselves to all of these. Sometimes simultaneously. The need to continually adapt to so many changes may lead to conflicting demands and all kinds of compromises [587].

Most environments have many niches. If a niche is "empty" and no organisms are occupying it, new species evolve to occupy it. This happens through the process of natural selection, which is a type of adaptation wherein species undergo gradual changes to adapt themselves to the niche [591]. If we become well adapted to the new environment, and if the environment does not change too much, we are likely to stay there for a long time. For example, giraffes have evolved to have very long necks so that they can eat tall vegetation, which other animals cannot reach. Cats have eyes like slits so that they can adjust to bright light (by narrowing the slits) and to very dim light (by opening up the slits) [591]. Behavior is another important adaptation method. We inherit many kinds of adaptive behaviors that help us survive. In southern Africa, meerkats, which are from the mongoose family, exhibit a peculiar group protection behavior: they take turns playing guard by standing on their hind legs and looking out for danger while the rest of the colony hunts for food [591].

Organisms are continuously changing as their environments change. These include physiological changes such as those that occur in acclimation, as well as behavioral, learning, and/or genetic changes, as well as evolutionary changes, depending on the timescale of the environmental change [592]. Birds cope with changing seasonal conditions by migrating to warmer places at lower latitudes where there is more food. Natural selection has endowed birds with a built-in biological clock, which they compare against day length, effectively giving them a built-in calendar. Changing the day length affects the pituitary gland of birds, causing it to secrete hormones that control avian behavior [587, 593]. In a similar manner, human beings who live in cold places are known to move to warmer places during winter.

Vestigial organs are examples of physiological changes resulting from adaptation. In dogs, the claw no longer serves any purpose because they run on the balls of their feet and four digits; so the claw is found on the inside of the leg in a position similar to the thumb in humans. In human beings, the appendix is a vestigial organ that was earlier used to store microbes that helped to digest plant matter and is no longer needed [591]. Such vestigial organs are evidence of the changes that species are still undergoing.

It is easier for us to adapt and cope with predictable changes. We listen to the weather report in the morning, and we are more or less prepared for what the day might bring. As long as these changes are not too extreme, most of us will manage them. What happens if the changes imposed on us by the environment are unpredictable, random, or extreme? Adaptation under such conditions is more difficult. Sometimes, the situation is so chaotic that it is impossible to adapt.

How do we try to adapt to random conditions?

Animals have developed the ability to undergo dormant stages, which allow them to survive unfavorable periods, both predictable and unpredictable. For instance, brine shrimp eggs survive for years in the salty crust of dry deserts. When a rare desert rain occurs, the eggs hatch and the shrimp develop into adults that later produce more eggs. Annual plants know when to fall asleep and when to wake up, as they cannot merely adjust to all weather conditions [587].

Small and undirected changes in the environment can help improve our level of adaptation, but significant changes can be detrimental. Changes in the environment that reduce our overall level of adaptation are explained by Fisher's model of adaptation and undirected environmental deterioration [592]. Such changes cause directional selection and result in accommodation to the new environment. However, other types of changes in the environments, for example, changes in the hunting efficiency of an organism's killer, may reduce the level of adaptation [587]. The concept behind this model is that no organism is "perfectly adapted." This means that we fail to conform to all the changes in our environments [592]. Fisher's model is based on the assumption of a hypothetical, perfectly adapted organism. It is a mathematical argument that is expressed as an infinite number of "dimensions" for adaptation.

Imagine an adaptation space with three coordinates, which represent the competitive, predatory, and physical environments. An ideal "perfectly adapted" organism lies at a particular point in this space. Any given real organism is at another point which is some distance away from the point of perfect adaptation. The distance between the two points represents the degree of conformity between the organism and its environment, or the level of adaptation. Fisher noted that minimal undirected changes in either the organism or its environment have a 50:50 chance of being to the organism's advantage and reducing this distance [592]. If marked changes occur in either the organism or its environment, even if the direction is favorable, they "overshoot" points of closer adaptation and therefore always lead to maladaptation. Fisher explains this using the analogy of focusing a microscope: wonderful changes are as likely as not to improve the focus, but gross changes will almost invariably throw the machine further out of focus [592]. So small changes around us might help us to adapt, or sometimes not, but marked changes are most probably not going to be easy to deal with.

Any genetically based, physiological, or behavioral feature that enables an organism to cope adapt, and survive in its environment represents an adaptation. Some traits may not be adaptive but are leftovers of traits that once were adaptive. A given trait can also be "pre-adapted" if it was formerly adaptive under some prior set of conditions. It can serve as a basis of a new adaptation under new environmental conditions [587]. Once there are changes and adaptations in response to the new conditions, there are reciprocal counter-responses that are within us, or in the environment around us. In evolution, this is termed co-evolution. Organisms with narrow tolerance limits, for example highly specialized organisms, experience more significant fitness loss due to environmental deterioration than organisms with more versatile requirements [592].

It was clear that being more tolerable or being able to adapt quickly did not necessarily mean more accessibility to the point of perfect adaptation or comfort zone.

Fisher's model applies only to non-directed changes in either party of the adaptation complex—the organism or the environment. It mainly applies to mutations, climatic fluctuations, and other random events. But many environmental changes are nonrandom and directional. For example, changes in other associated organisms can reduce an organism's degree of conformity to its environment. Directed changes in competitors can either increase or decrease an organism's level of adaptation. This depends on whether they avoid competition or improve their competitive ability. Directed changes in mutualistic systems usually tend to improve the overall level of adaptation of both parties [592]. Every individual is simultaneously a member of a community, and therefore, must be adapted to cope with others [587]. An individual's fitness is influenced by its status within its own population.

"Arms race" is a term used to describe any long-term escalating competitive situation where each competitor focuses on outdoing the other. Individuals must adapt and evolve as their environments change. Natural selection acting on natural enemies results in a deterioration of an organism's environment, diminishing fitness. Targets that are better able to escape from their hunters, or hosts that can better resist infection by parasites, will enjoy a fitness advantage. However, better hunters and better parasites can sometimes be favored by natural selection, guaranteeing that the "arms race" will continue to escalate indefinitely [587]. In practical terms, this means that we are continuously forced to adapt. Our adaptation induces changes and counterchanges, so more adaptations are needed. At the same time that we are being affected by our hunters and parasites, we keep affecting others too. But many interactions between different species are mutually beneficial, resulting in increased fitness for both parties.

Dan realized that this concept could be used to understand the function of cellular automata: their rules are constantly adapting so that they can move towards or remain at the boundary of chaos and order [554, 594].

A simple model for chaotic dynamics is the logistic map. The logistic map is a polynomial map of degree 2, and it depicts how complicated, chaotic behavior can arise from elementary non-linear dynamical equations [397]. The self-adjusting dynamics of the logistic map displays adaptation to the edge of chaos [595]. One can predict the location of the small parameter rule near the boundary towards which the system evolves [596]. Physicists have shown that adaptation to the edge of chaos occurs in many systems with feedback [597]. The concept of adaptation to the edge of chaos has also been shown in ecology [555], business management [598], psychology, political science, and other domains of social sciences [554], all of which are known to have feedback loops.

Using adaptation strategies, whether they are voluntary or involuntary, to keep ourselves in this ideal zone, the edge of chaos, seemed very appealing to Dan. He decided to have a talk with Olivia about it.

# CHAPTER 33
## Minus: Fractals, biology, and disease

Dan invited Olivia to dinner. Olivia was living with her boyfriend for many years now, and they had a child. His sole grandson. Dan was sharing with her everything that he had learned about chaos and the edge of chaos. Olivia was very interested. Working in an artificial intelligence company, Olivia was very much into studies that bring together biological process and physics. She told Dan about a short review by Dr. Ary Goldberger from Beth Israel Hospital in Boston, about non-linear dynamics for clinicians: "Chaos theory, fractals, and complexity at the bedside" [367]. In this review, he attempted to explain the concept of chaos in a way that was understandable to biologists and physicians.

Dan asked Olivia if she had heard the one about the doctor, the engineer, and the programmer who were arguing about what the world's oldest profession was. The doctor said that it was medicine because the Lord had surgically removed Adam's rib to create Eve.

The engineer countered this by saying that before that act, the Lord had performed great feats of engineering by creating the earth and heavens from nothing.

The doctor conceded.

Then, the programmer interjected by saying that programming was even older than that. But both the doctor and the engineer disagreed with this by saying that before the Lord created the earth and heavens, there was nothing but the Great Void, only chaos!

The programmer smiled and said, "And where do we think the chaos came from?"

There are many versions of this story, and we can create more just by changing the professions, like this:

A surgeon, an architect and a lawyer are having a heated discussion at a bar about which of their professions is the oldest.

The surgeon says, "Surgery IS the oldest profession. God took a rib from Adam to create Eve, and we cannot go back further than that." The architect says, "Hold on! In fact, God was the first architect when he created the world out of chaos in 7 days, and we cannot go back any further than THAT!"

The lawyer puffs on his cigar and says, "Gentlemen, Gentlemen...who do we think created the CHAOS?"

Dr. Goldberger rightfully said more than two decades ago that clinicians are aware of the increase in interest in non-linear dynamics, also known as the chaos theory.

Linear systems are well behaved, with the magnitude of their responses always being proportionate to the strength of the stimuli. They are understood and predicted by dissecting out their components. The subunits of these systems add up. In most of them, there are no surprises or anomalous behaviors [367]. In non-linear systems, on the other hand, proportionality does not hold. Small changes can have noticeable and unexpected effects. Non-linear systems cannot be understood by analyzing their components individually, because their components interact with each other and with other systems. Their non-linear coupling generates behaviors that are difficult to explain based on traditional linear models [367].

Bifurcation is a class of abrupt, non-linear transitions. This term is used to describe situations in which a minimal increase or decrease in the value of parameters controlling the system lead to an abrupt change from one type of behavior to another [599].

Biologists define adaptation as conformity between an organism and its environment [600].

If we take the example of the heart, the sudden appearance of regular oscillations that alternate between two values is a common type of bifurcation. Goldberger claims that chaos consists of only one subtype of nonlinear dynamics, which is a random type of variability that arises from the processes of even the most simple non-linear system [367]. However, equations that are used to generate erratic and unpredictable behavior do not contain random terms, and the resulting chaos is called "deterministic chaos." This chaos is different from the term "chaos," observed in everyday use, which is used to describe unfettered randomness, with catastrophic implications.

In the field of biology, it was earlier assumed that chaotic fluctuations were produced by issues in pathological systems, such as problems with heart rhythms. This initial presumption has been challenged. Irregularity in the heart does not represent deterministic cardiac chaos [600]. Under normal conditions, beat-to-beat fluctuations in heart rate display the kind of long-range correlations typically exhibited by dynamical systems which are far from equilibrium. In contrast, heart rate time series from patients with severe heart failure show a breakdown of this long-range correlation behavior. This means that heart-rate fluctuations seen during normal rhythm in healthy individuals, even at rest, are attributable in part to "deterministic chaos." Diseases, such as those associated with heart failure, may be associated with a decrease in this type of non-linear variability.

When we think of fractals, we may think of a tree with many branches. This structure also corresponds to our arterial and venous trees, the branching of individual cardiac muscle bundles, as well as the ramifying tracheobronchial tree in the lungs [367]. Tree-like fractals have self-similar branching such that the small-scale structure resembles the large-scale form. A fractal process such as heart rate regulation generates fluctuations on different time scales that are statistically self-similar. Why do we need these complex structures? These self-similar structures all serve the common physiological function of rapid and efficient transport over a complex, spatially distributed system. Our nervous system contains fractal structures that serve functions related to information distribution. Our bowel contains fractals required for nutrient absorption, and our kidney has fractals needed for collection and transport of different molecules.

The concept of fractals is evident in irregular geometric or anatomical forms lacking a specific scale, and it is also evident in elaborate processes that lack a single time scale. Fractal scale-invariant processes generate irregular fluctuations on multiple time scales, analogous to fractal objects that have a wrinkly structure on different length scales. The heart rate of a healthy individual shows an irregular wrinkly appearance, suggestive of a coastline. The irregularity seen is not visually distinguishable, but is an observation confirmed by statistical analysis [600]. Complex fluctuations with the statistical properties of fractals have been described for heart rate variability, as well as for fluctuations in respiration, systemic blood pressure, human gait, and white blood cell counts [601-603].

Scale invariance is a feature that does not change if scales of length, energy, or other variables, are multiplied by a common factor. Thus, it represents a universality. If scale-invariance is the rule underlying the physiological structure and function of these systems, we can predict what might happen when these systems are disturbed. If a functional system is self-organized in such a way that it does not have a characteristic scale of length or time, a breakdown of scale-free structure or dynamics with disease might be anticipated [367].

How does a system behave after a pathological transformation? In contrast with a healthy scale-free fractal system that has multiple scales, a pathological system has one dominant frequency or scale. These types of systems are periodic, and they repeat their behavior in a highly predictable and regular pattern. The appearance of highly periodic dynamics in disease states is an example of loss of complexity in a disease. Complexity refers to a multiscale, fractal-type of variability in structure or function. Disease states are marked by fewer complex dynamics than those seen under normal conditions [367]. This decomplexification of systems is a standard feature of many diseases, as well as of aging. The decomplexification of physiological systems leads to the degradation of their information content, and they consequently become less adaptable and less able to cope with the exigencies of a continually changing environment [366]. The output of pathological systems has a nearly sinusoidal appearance [604].

Both Olivia and Dan were fascinated by this: A healthy state is complex, while a disease state is less complex and less flexible.

Fractals are irregular. However, not all irregular structures or irregular time series are fractals. In biological systems, fractals are a characteristic type

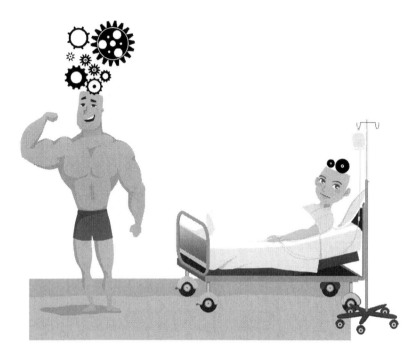

of long-range order that generates correlations that extend over many scales of space or time. For complex processes, long-range fractal correlations are the mechanisms underlying a memory effect. The value of a variable, such as the heart rate at a particular time, is associated with its previous values, and with historical fluctuations [367]. Diseases are marked by a breakdown of this organization property, which results in uncorrelated randomness.

Olivia was trying to draw an association between Goldberger's studies and what Dan was telling her. She noted that Goldberger had predicted two decades ago that several indices derived from the chaos theory would be useful in predicting those at high risk of electrophysiological or hemodynamic instability [605]. More exciting than this is the use of these concepts for therapeutic interventions [367].

Biological systems are complex. They involve cross talks among themselves, and with other systems in the body. These interactions occur over a wide range of temporal and spatial scales. The findings from studies on non-linear dynamics have challenged the conventional belief about physiological control that healthy systems seek to attain a constant steady state. By contrast, non-linear systems with fractal dynamics behave as if they were driven far from equilibrium under basal conditions. This kind of complex variability, rather than a single homoeostatic steady state, seems to define the free-running function of many biological systems [367].

Dan was thinking now about the "edge of chaos" zone. It seemed clear to him that being in this zone, which may seem less balanced, is also much healthier. Both of them went home that evening with much to think about.

# CHAPTER 34
## Chaos in adaptation

Olivia was working for a company that was attempting to develop algorithms to explain aging. Now that her father had introduced her to the edge of chaos, she was looking into how it would fit into what they were doing. Deep inside, she felt that last night's dinner was about her. She knew that both her parents had not been very happy with her. When she was younger, she tried to fight their lack of acceptance, but in the last few years, she had left it as is. She was bothered by the question that the "lack of her adaptation" as her parents used to tell her, meant that she could not be in that "ideal zone," if it did exist.

While surfing the web the next morning at her office, she came across some interesting papers by Kyriazis.

Marios Kyriazis is a biomedical gerontologist who thinks and writes about anti-aging processes. He helped formalize the concept of anti-aging medicine, and has even founded several non-profit societies for the same [606]. One of his notable works is the concept of "practical applications of chaos theory to the modulation of human aging" [389]. Specifically, he discusses the idea that nature prefers chaos to regularity. This went well with what she had discussed with her father last night. The premise is that aging is associated with a loss of physiological complexity from the molecular to the cellular level, and from the tissue to organismic levels. Kyriazis claims that aging is a simplification of dynamical complexity. This is in contrast with the claims of those who believe that there is an increase in complexity during aging and dysfunction.

During the course of our life, we are introduced to and are required to maintain interactions with multiple interacting stimuli that preserve the dynamical complexity of our output signal. During the early years of our life, we are exposed to multiple stimuli that result in dynamically rich outputs, and this explains the low levels of disability or dysfunction observed in younger age groups. From middle age and beyond, the amount of stimulation is reduced, as a result of which the output signal becomes less complex and more regular, consequently increasing the level of disability.

Olivia found out about The National Academy of Sciences meeting on complexity and chaos, "Self-organized complexity in the physical, biological, and social sciences," which was held at the NAS Beckman Center, Irvine, CA, on March 23–24, 2001. The meeting presented examples of complexity in subjects ranging from fluid turbulence to social networks [607]. She found out that the definitions for self-organizing complexity were vague. Further, the signs of systems that exhibit self-organizing complexity include fractal statistics and chaotic behavior [607]. Some systems that exhibit self-organizing complexity are entirely deterministic, but others have a random or stochastic component.

Additional areas in physics that are related to self-organizing complexity include the study of complexity and robustness [607] [608]. Highly optimized tolerance is a conceptual framework that is used to study the fundamental aspects of complexity. It is based on highly structured, non-generic, self-dissimilar internal configurations, and robust yet fragile external behavior. These are believed to be the essential features of complexity and not accidents of evolution or artifices of engineering design. They are inevitably intertwined and mutually reinforcing.

Olivia's primary interest was in applying the chaos concept to health and disease. Intuitively, it may seem that any alteration in a physiological system may result in a pathological condition. However, a change in a system could also lead to an improvement or normalization; the change may even be a cure. This depends on the direction of the alteration or the intervention [389]. The term "dynamical disease" describes alterations in the dynamical properties of physiological systems that lead to diseases [609]. In dynamical diseases, there are sudden changes in the qualitative dynamics of physiological processes, which result in a pathological condition [610]. This involves the application of the mathematical concept of nonlinear dynamics to medicine, and diseases are now being studied from the perspective of nonlinear dynamics.

Nonlinear dynamics is the division of physics that involves systems ruled by equations more complex than the linear, aX+b form. Nonlinear systems, such as the weather or neurons, may appear chaotic, unpredictable or counterintuitive, and yet their behavior is not random. Normal heartbeat intervals are considered to be fractional noise, and deviations from this normality are considered to be indicative of pathologies such as heart failure [367, 393] and changes in protein levels [611] and in dynamical variables related to neurobiological functions [612]. The transient synchrony of the action potentials of a group of neurons is indicative of the "recognition" of a space-time pattern across the inputs the neurons receive. Appropriate synaptic coupling produces synchrony when the inputs to these neurons are nearly equal. In the case of other input circumstances, the neurons are unsynchronized or only weakly synchronized. When the input is from timed events in the past that show decaying delay activity, the pattern of synaptic connections can be set such that synchronization occurs only for select spatiotemporal patterns.

Olivia was looking into examples of dynamical diseases. For her, the beauty of mathematics is its ability to generalize concepts from one state to another, even when they seem to be unrelated[613]. The chaos theory predicts that it is possible to manipulate and control diseases by applying the laws of nonlinearity. The use of non-linear models has been demonstrated for "dynamical diseases," Parkinson's disease being one of them [614]. Dopamine plays an important role in the pathogenesis of Parkinson's. The secretion of dopamine is controlled via negative feedback loops. Studies that use mathematical equations integrated this feedback component into a model in which the rate of dopamine release is a function of the quantity that is bound. This model demonstrated that competitive antagonists augment release, whereas competing agonists reduce such release. Based on this model, studies for designing better therapies for Parkinson's have been conducted.

In the case of heart rhythm irregularities [615], analysis of rhythmic changes in blood pressure can explain the underlying control network. Circulatory variations are non-linear and do not consist of rhythmic components. The variations are analyzed by non-linear techniques that are adopted from the chaos theory.

Menopause signals the end of menstrual cyclicity in a woman's life; this phase is characterized by abnormalities in estrogen release [616]. Concepts from the chaos theory are being applied to hormonal cycles, in order to enable an understanding of the parameters that control the process and develop strategies for alleviating the negative aspects of menopause.

In epilepsy, too [617], the role of chaos in EEG findings are well proven. EEGs reflect the electrical activity of the brain. They are produced by a nonlinear system. A nonlinear system with some degree of freedom can exhibit chaotic behavior. The brain has many types of chemicals called neurotransmitters that carry information through millions of synapses within it. Each of these neurotransmitters acts through many receptors; these transmitters manifest chaotic patterns in the nervous system of healthy individuals [618]. The structures in the nervous system have multiple steady states that are directed by "chaotic" attractors. In chaotic systems, an infinite number of unstable periodic fixed points may occur. These are found in spontaneously active neuronal networks in epilepsy [618]. Deterministic chaos enables a better understanding of the findings in the brain and EEG data, even though different factors limit the use of nonlinear measures to characterize brain dynamics. The correlation dimension or the Lyapunov exponents can be used to characterize different states of normal and pathologic brain function [617]. Concepts from the chaos theory enable analyses of interactions between the epileptogenic zone and other brain areas, and detection of features predictive of seizure activity. These techniques enable localization of the primary epileptogenic area in the brain and testing of new treatments. For example, a precisely input electrical stimulus can control an epileptic seizure [619].

The chaos concept can also be applied to aging [620]. Mathematical models are used for following age distributions in a population and some aspects of aging. The applicability of these models to stem cell dynamics has allowed investigation into the issue of age-related telomere loss, which is a process that is closely associated with aging.

Olivia was looking into examples in other fields. Working in a medical company, she had never viewed biological processes as being different from other processes going on in the world.

Turbulence, weather, and climate clearly exhibit deterministic chaos. Exact certainty cannot be expected in the case of these entities [607]. In physics, the classic problem in self-organizing complexity is fluid turbulence [621]. The small-scale turbulence structure concept was described for bifurcations and pattern formation in the atmosphere and oceans [622]. Approximate limits to atmospheric predictability showed that the details of atmospheric flow fields are lost after about 10 days. Specific gross flow features repeat, however, after time periods in the order of 10 to 50 days; this shows that there is some hope for their prediction.

There have been attempts to model the prediction of recurrent features that involve increasing spatial resolution and physical faithfulness. This includes theoretical attempts to analyze the phase space of large-scale atmospheric motions. Two separate approaches were used in these studies. One of them was an episodic/alternate approach which describes multiple-flow or weather regimes, their persistence and recurrence, and the Markov chain of transitions. The second approach is the oscillatory/periodic method for studying intra-seasonal oscillations, with periods of 15 to 70 days, and their predictability [622]. Most climate models are large dynamical systems involving a million variables on big computers[623]. Given that they are nonlinear and not perfect, what can we expect to learn from them? How can we determine which aspects of their output might be useful and which aspects are noise? Chaos prevents accurate weather forecasts, and model error precludes accurate forecasts of the distributions that define climate, yielding uncertainty. In physics, uncertainty is quantified within a given modeling paradigm.

The predictability of catastrophic events is of high importance, as most of them seem to be unpredictable [624]. Some researchers claim that catastrophic events are "outliers" with statistically different properties from the rest of the population, and that they are a result of mechanisms involving amplifying critical cascades. Models for predicting these catastrophic events or "ruptures" are based on the concept of viewing them as sudden transitions from a quiescent state to a crisis. Such ruptures involve interactions between structures at different scales. These concepts may be used for prediction of the rupture of composite materials, earthquakes, turbulence, abrupt changes in weather regimes, financial crashes, and human birth rates.

But why is earthquake prediction so difficult? [625] The "critical point" concept in the case of large earthquakes is examined within the framework of "finite time singularities." The singular behavior associated with accelerated seismic release is a result of the effect of positive feedback about the seismic activity on its release rate. In models for positive feedback, the stress shadow cast by the last massive earthquake is progressively fragmented by increasing tectonic stress.

Threshold systems represent some of the most critical nonlinear self-organizing systems in nature. Self-organization occurs in leaky threshold systems, and it is evident in earthquakes and neurobiology and computation systems [626]. These systems are dynamic and are correlated in space and time. They typically display a multiplicity of spatial and temporal scales. The physics of self-organization in earthquake threshold systems can be viewed at a "microscopic" laboratory scale, in which results from simulations lead to dynamical equations that originate from sliding friction experiments. There is also a "macroscopic" earthquake fault-system scale, in which the physics of strongly correlated earthquake fault systems uses time-dependent state vectors similar to those used in the mathematics of quantum mechanics.

Olivia was thinking about the prediction of wild forest fires, the evolution of shorelines, signatures of complexity for the Old Faithful geyser, and complexity in financial markets [607], [627]. And what about the earthquakes we have in our personal lives? We live in a world that exhibits seasonal dynamics rather than a state of equilibrium. We are all in a position where we feel the need to better understand the impact of "ruptures" in their multiple forms [624].

She was now looking into economic systems.

Some models seem to be universal and hold for widely different economies as well as for different time periods. These include models for fluctuations in prices in any stock market, which are characterized by a probability density function. These models are based on a simple power law that is analogous to the Gutenberg-Richter power law for describing the histogram of earthquakes. This histogram shows how the size of an organization is inversely correlated with fluctuations in its size across a range of economic organizations. Whether this law can be applied to everything in nature is under debate; however, it may be possible to extrapolate this symbolically to other areas.

Self-organization has been described for social networks too [628]. Models for simple unipartite networks, such as acquaintance networks and bipartite networks, such as affiliation networks, have been described. In some cases, the models show remarkable correspondence with real-world data. But the correspondence may be poorer in other cases; this may be attributable to additional social structure in the network that is not captured by the random graph. Olivia knew that not all models are an ideal fit for the real world. But this does not mean that all of them are useless.

Engineers try to impose structure on systems that are generally not self-organizing. Think about cars, airplanes, highway systems, and airline-route networks. Some engineered systems become so complex that they become self-organizing by default; for example, when an electrical transmission system reaches its capacity limit, it can exhibit chaotic behavior and failure. The World Wide Web is considered to be one such a system [607] that has evolved into a self-organizing complex system. In the case of the internet, self-similar scaling has been observed in the burst patterns of internet traffic and, in some contexts, a scale-free structure in the network's interconnection topology has been shown [629]. Concepts such as fractals, chaos, and self-organized criticality are associated with scale invariance and power laws.

Fractal structures assist in understanding human processes too. For instance, we can assign a numerical value to DNA, proteins, and every molecule in our body [613], and with the help of mathematical equations, we can calculate the fractal dimension of any molecule based on its molecular surface area and probe radius. The surface area can be measured with a mechanical probe. If we go up one level to cells, we can assign fractal numerical values to cells, too, for quantifying age-related changes or any change associated with specific pathologies [368]. This concept is also applicable to a situation such as screening of breast cancer. While conducting mammography, the radiologist is required to differentiate between benign and malignant lesions. Earlier studies have indicated that lesions considered to be "suspicious" by radiologists may prove to be malignant only in less than 30% of cases. Fractal analysis has been proposed as a method for quantifying the difference between the shapes of benign and malignant lesions. Similar calculations based on fractal analysis have been suggested for understanding drug response in older people [618]. Nonlinear/chaotic interactions have also been studied in depression to identify which neurotransmitters act on the different receptor subtypes. A mathematical approach using fractal concepts has been developed for analyzing the interactions between certain parameters and nuclear estrogen receptors [630]. The binding of the compounds to these receptors and their dissociation were analyzed using nonlinear equations.

Kyriazis was one of the first to demonstrate the potential role of randomness in aging [631]. He suggested that some of the concepts from the chaos theory can be applied to molecular gerontology. The idea is to use mathematical modeling for improving the function of our body in a way that can alleviate age-related damage [632]. It is known that genes control our lifespan to some extent. In fact, models for gene regulation have shown that these control systems are in many ways chaotic. Aging is therefore chaotic at the level of genetic control. This means that the state of health, which is caused by fluctuations, only has weak nonspecific influences on the system.

Kyriazis proposed that there is a loss of complexity in aging [631]; that is, a degradation of physiological complexity was suggested to underlie aging and age-related diseases. The concept of "complexity," which is derived from the field of nonlinear dynamics, was adapted to measure the output of physiologic processes that generate highly variable fluctuations resembling "chaos" [633]. Loss of such complexity leads to impaired ability to adapt to physiologic stress. Age-related loss of complex variability in physiologic processes including cardiovascular control, hormone release, and electroencephalographic potential in the brain has been shown [633]. This explains why we gradually lose the ability to adapt as we grow older.

Can we overcome this decline in our adaptive capacity?

In medicine, physiological and pathological models are based on the principles of formal logic, which provide clear answers that are positive or negative[634]. It has been proposed that the more relevant "logic of conditioned possibilities" be applied, along with what is termed "fuzzy logic" and "more truth values." Fuzzy logic is used for better analyzing information about biological phenomena [634]. For example, fuzzy logic can be used to demonstrate how glycemic data in healthy individuals is in the form of an unbroken continuous stream of set partials. In aging, the structures of automatic control systems are associated with a reduction in dynamic stability and an increase in dissipative phenomena and entropy [635]. Functional exhaustion of homeostatic systems, which is associated with the linearization of the system, is not compatible with life unless a substitute system takes on its function.

The laws of thermodynamics suggest that in systems that are moving away from equilibrium, processes can emerge so that the system organizes in a way that reduces the effect of the applied slope [636]. If dynamic conditions permit, self-organization processes can be expected. If we apply this to our body, it means that whenever there is a state of non-equilibrium, we try to minimize the damage in an attempt to reach a state of equilibrium. In complex biological systems, there is more energy flow, an increase in cycling activity, and more diversity, as a result of which more hierarchical levels are continuously being generated. During aging, this process slows down. Once it stops altogether, it is assumed to be incompatible with life. Species which survive in particular ecosystems are those that pipe energy into their own production and contribute to processes which increase the total dissipation of the system while at the same time surviving within the constraints of their changing environment [636]. This concept has also been applied to neurodegenerative disorders [637].

The breakdown of fractal and non-linear physiological properties leads to an increase in regularity and uncorrelated randomness: Does this mean that there is a decrease in real randomness during aging and disease? [389]. According to classical concepts, healthy systems are believed to be self-regulated in a way that reduces variability and maintains physiologic constancy. Contrary to this notion, however, a wide variety of systems, such as the normal human heartbeat, show complex fluctuations even under resting conditions. This suggests that nonlinear regulatory systems are operating in a state that is far from equilibrium and that maintaining steadiness is not the goal of physiologic control [393]. In patients at high risk of sudden death, it is believed that fractal organization and nonlinear interactions break down. Fractal analysis can thus provide new approaches to assessing cardiac risk and forecasting sudden cardiac death. As explained earlier, it has been applied to aging too [393].

Olivia was working for a company that was striving to come up with algorithms that tell us what we should do if we want to stay young. She now realized that their basic notion that people need to be in a state of equilibrium to stay healthy and young might be wrong. Do we want to stay in equilibrium, or should we stay away from it? Do we need to diversify or not? The last few hours had opened up a whole new way of thinking for her. Sometimes, she did feel a strong fondness for her father.

# CHAPTER 35

## Staying young but complex. A new perspective on our food and medications.

Olivia was preoccupied with aging—personally and professionally. In fact, her team's mission statement as stated on their company website was to design algorithms for staying young—this is what their investors were also being told. They were trying to develop the algorithms by using genetic data as well as behavioral data they received from several academic centers they were associated with. The truth was they had not made much progress since the company had been established. But as long as someone was paying them to think about it, they kept trying.

Jacob, one of her colleagues, was always telling her different versions of the following story.

Andy's wife, in an attempt to fight the effects of aging on her skin, buys a new line of expensive cosmetics guaranteed to make her look years younger. After a lengthy session with the "miracle" products, she asks her husband, "Darling, honestly, if you didn't know me, what age would you say I am?"

Andy observed her carefully and replied, "Judging from your skin, twenty; your hair, eighteen; and your figure, twenty-five."

"Oh, you flatterer!" she gushed.

And just as she was about to announce Andy's reward, she is interrupted by Andy, who says "WHOA, hold it sweetie! I haven't added them up yet!"

So, what should we do in order to control the aging process?

Olivia was reviewing Kyriazis's concepts of reversing the loss of the required increase in randomness. According to him, we can restore physiological complexity by applying multiple external physiological stimuli [389, 638]. Under basal resting conditions, most healthy physiologic systems demonstrate profoundly changing, complex dynamics that represent inter-acting regulatory processes operating over multiple time scales. These pro-cesses prime the organism for an adaptive response, making it ready and able to react to sudden physiologic stresses [638]. Olivia was thinking about something she had heard her father say: "Randomness is good for us." This was in opposition to some of the concepts which underlined the algorithms they were working on. Maybe this was the reason why they were not so successful?

"It may not seem intuitively right, but on second thought, I accept it," she was telling herself.

The inability of an organism to restore its original complex physiological state is believed to be the cause of disease and degeneration. A healthy organism is able to return to this original physiological state after an injury or disease.

According to a physiological law of mortality, insults cause oscillations around a mean physiological state. If a system is weak, it means that it oscil-lates beyond a critical boundary, leading to death. In other words, when there is deviation from a given set of boundary conditions, closed-loop respons-es that operate over relatively short periods of time are activated to restore equilibrium. This mechanism is called "reactive tuning," and it transiently alters the dynamics of a less complex, dominant response mode. This means that equilibrium is not the ideal state, but rather, a state the body tries to reach as an escape mechanism from a stressful situation. "This is the mistake we are making," Olivia was telling Jacob, who was sitting at the desk next to her, not understanding why she was re-reading the same paper. "If we accept that aging and disease are associated with a loss of complexity in resting dynamics and inability to adapt to changes, it means that they are associated with a functional decline and fragility. We should use nonlinear mathemati-cal techniques to quantify physiologic dynamics and predict the onset of this decline," Olivia was reading to him. "Our concepts need to be turned upside down. Randomness is good. Equilibrium should not be our aim." She was now rethinking what her father was telling her about the edge of the cliff.

Kyriazis simplified his concept by using the example of a branch of a tree: when it is cut off, the complexity of the geometrical shape, or of the fractal dimension, of that tree, is altered. The tree then grows new branches in an attempt to return to its original state, or re-establish the degree of its physiological complexity, or its "healthy" status [389]. In humans, if there is blockage of a vascular branch, the response is usually to re-establish the complexity of vascularization around that area through the placement of shunts [639]. Healthy physiologic control of cardiovascular function is a result of complex interactions between multiple regulatory processes that operate over different timescales. For example, the nervous system regulates parameters such as heart rate, blood pressure, body temperature, and sleep. Interactions between these control systems generate highly variable fluctuations in continuous heart rate and blood pressure. Age-related changes occur within the spectrum of the amplitude and frequency of heart rate. They are characterized by a decline in the approximate dimension and approximate entropy of both the heart rate and blood pressure time series. This means that there is a decline in the "complexity" of cardiovascular dynamics, which reflect the breakdown of the regulatory systems with aging. It signals an impairment in the ability of the cardiovascular system to adapt to external and internal changes [639]. The simplification of physiological complexity with aging affects our body at all levels: molecular, cellular, organismic and behavioral. We lose the complexity of integrated inputs, and this leads to a chain of dysfunctional events [389].

Open-loop and closed-loop control mechanisms are involved in the regulation of many of our body systems [640]. For example, aging is associated with changes in the dynamics of the postural control system. The steady-state behavior of the **open-loop** postural control mechanisms in the elderly is positively correlated and unstable. The output of the system has a tendency to drift away from the equilibrium point over the short term. In contrast, the steady-state behavior of the **closed-loop** postural control mechanisms in the elderly is negatively correlated over the long term. They are more stable and occur over a more extended period. This means that any movement away from the equilibrium point is counterbalanced by adjustments back towards an equilibrium position, which is not good. It means that with aging there is a more considerable delay before closed-loop feedback mechanisms are functioning[640].

If the original complexity is restored, an organism is considered to be healthy again; an inability to do so indicates disease [641]. Analysis of 24-hour heart rate behavior in elderly subjects based on the power-law relationship could predict mortality better than the traditional risk markers in elderly subjects. The altered long-term behavior of heart rate implies an increased risk of death caused by vascular conditions rather than frailty leading to a loss.

Adaptive reactions enable an organism to respond quickly to changes, physiological demands and stress. The more complex the system, the better is its adaptive capability, and the higher is its functionality [633].

"Perhaps her mother was intuitively right in calling her a non-adaptive person," Olivia thought. This felt like she needed a break; her mother's death had affected her quite deeply. Mostly, she felt that she had not met her mother's expectations. She had never been able to have a real discussion with her mother. Following her dinner with her father, she made a decision not to repeat the same mistake with him. She also had newfound respect for him, as she realized that he might know more about the science of randomness than he had already revealed. He had also mentioned his meetings and discussions with her brother. Olivia had never been close to her brother. He had always seemed to her as a very "regular" person who just lived by the rules. The only nonconformity was that he had never been married.

It was clear to Olivia that we should aim towards being more complex, more chaotic, and abler to adapt and adjust. However, being more complex means greater susceptibility to malfunction [389]. It means getting out of the "comfort zone," as her father had put it. But complexity is essential not only for slowing down aging, but also in other situations. The complex and irregular dynamics of physiological systems allows for a response that is more efficient in times of stress and challenges. When it comes to answering problems and performing tasks, such a system provides an organism with more choices for a valid answer.

An age-depended reduction in the complex dynamics of physiological systems or loss of complexity means that an organism has to work in a less than optimum state. Complexity is altered during aging by the loss of coupling functions between different elements of physiological systems. We lose structural elements as we age, such as neurons and some of the neurotransmitters in our brains. This results in a loss of functional connections between the remaining structural elements. It compromises the dynamics of communication between neurons, and thus reduces our response capabilities. Also, with age, there is a decrease in the rate of formation of dendrites in the brain [642]. These cells, as Olivia learned, are facilitators of the brain networks. With age, electrical activity in the brain, as measured by EEG, also becomes more simplified and less complex [643, 644]. As explained earlier, both our heart rate and blood pressures have built-in variability or randomness, which is healthy. A decline in this variability occurs when we age [645].

Lethal heart arrhythmias or epileptic seizures are significant problems. Chaotic systems such as the nervous system can be quantified by determining the correlations in a sample of the data generated by the system. Biological systems have an advantage in that they do not presume the stationarity of the data. Algorithms tend to follow transient non-stationarities that occur when systems change state. Non-stationarities arise during normal functioning as well as in pathological states, such as an epileptic attack and cardiac arrhythmias. Standard methods of data analysis are associated with poor sensitivity and specificity. Further, while a reduced standard deviation in heartbeat intervals in indicative of increase in mortality in cardiac subjects, it cannot be used to determine which individuals will or will not manifest lethal arrhythmias. This is possible with the help of equations based on the chaos theory, which can be applied to the very same data to predict which patients will manifest severe arrhythmias and sudden death [643]

A degradation of complexity with aging and in disease states is exemplified by reduced complexity in the range of movements in the case of arthritis, stroke, and Parkinson's disease [646]. A study evaluated how changes in neural parameters that result in the weakening of synaptic abilities between network units affect inhibitory neural networks. The findings of this study indicate that transitions from irregular to periodic dynamics are frequent in such systems. Further, the weakening of synaptic abilities results in a decrease in the number of units that drive the dynamics and thus results in more straightforward behavior. The hypothesis that formed the basis of this study was that multiple interconnecting loops of the brain's motor circuitry, which involve many inhibitory connections, exhibit such transitions. Tremor in Parkinson's disease is a result of weakening of the synaptic efficacies of neurons in specific sites in the brain. Thus, the nervous system model also supports the notion that healthy physiological systems are regulated by strongly connected feedback networks with complex dynamics.

If loss of complexity in the feedback structure is associated with disease states, can we restore parts of it that are lost? To Olivia, this seemed to be the key.

Fluctuation is used as a measure of complexity. Fluctuation analysis has been used to analyze the inter-breath interval time series, as well as to compute fractal scaling exponents that quantify power-law correlations. Aging is associated with erosion of fractal properties and with a reduction of complexity of respiration dynamics [647]. There is a fractal organization in physiologic human breathing cycle dynamics, which is gradually lost with aging. Similarly, patterns of hormone secretion become less complex in the elderly. This is associated with reduced ability to respond to challenges and narrowing of functional responsiveness [389].

Fractal dynamics are believed to be at play in the "noisy" variations observed in intervals recorded during walking in human beings. Dynamical analysis of these step-to-step fluctuations revealed a self-similar pattern: fluctuations at one-time scale are statistically similar to those at multiple other timescales. The stride interval fluctuations exhibited long-range correlations with power-law decay. In contrast, during metronomically paced walking, these long-range correlations disappeared. Variations in the stride interval were random, uncorrelated, and non-fractal. This shows that the fractal dynamics of spontaneous stride intervals are usually quite robust and intrinsic to the locomotor system [648].

Oxidative damage is an example of a pathological process. With aging, some of the defense mechanisms against this type of damage are partially broken. Loss of the ability to repair damage also occurs. A telomere is a region of repetitive nucleotide sequences at each end of a chromosome. It protects the end of the chromosome from deterioration or from fusion with neighboring chromosomes. Oxidative damage may affect the somatic DNA fractal architecture, which becomes less complex following shortening of telomeres. Shortening of the telomeres is known to play a role in aging [649]. While our germinal DNA maintains its fractal complexity and physiological functionality, age-dependent reduction of somatic telomere length occurs [650]. This explains the age-related changes observed in cell structure and physiology in many organs. Once cells in our body lose their standard healthy complexity and their information-rich variability of function, they become regular and rigid; that is, they become less adaptive. This limits their ability to respond to demands or difficult conditions. For example, autoimmune diseases, chronic inflammation, cancer and frequent infections are a result of the reduced capability of our immune cells to recognize antigens, on account of a reduction in the complexity of their individual sub-components [643].

Olivia also came across studies which do not agree that loss of complexity is associated with physiological functioning [651]. As a non-biologist working on biological systems, she had already realized that modeling is difficult in biological systems. However, in the case of opposing ideas, it is not necessary that one of them is wrong. It has been suggested that either an increase or a decrease in the complexity of a behavioral or physiological system output could occur with aging, as changes in both directions would be associated with impairment of function. The direction of change is dependent on the confluence of constraints that control the system dynamics [652]. A system can be said to be malfunctioning if it is too simple or too complex [653]. The outcomes of decrease or increase in the measured entropy are calculated as a function of changes in several parameters. The variety of elements in these systems decrease with age, as a result of which it can show less complexity or become more entropic.

So, do we need complexity or not?

It is argued that an increase in complexity observed with aging is dependent on the value of individual parameters, which may be abnormally high. It is also believed that the increase affects only some systems and not others [389]. This means that it is important to have the right degree of complexity. Going back to the cliff, it means not crossing the red line. Things began to finally make sense to Olivia.

With regard to the methods used to calculate complexity, some of them can separate healthy systems characterized by long-range correlated noise, from pathologic systems carrying uncorrelated noise, i.e., actual randomness. Such methods have been used to show that there is a decrease in complexity with aging [389]. Several age-related processes can be quantified, and the effects of the treatment can be measured. Even if both a decrease and an increase in complexity are bad, at least with regard to some functions, a decrease is clearly undesirable. With regard to the reversibility of these processes, Kyriazis and others have tried to come up with ways of overcoming the decrease in complexity. Some believe that at least some dysfunctions can be reversed [654, 655]. For example, age-related loss of complexity can be reversed by increasing the amount of integrated physiological inputs, which will result in the widening of functional usefulness. This notion can also be applied to drug therapy. However, most people seem to believe that the aging process is irreversible.

In the case of patients with stroke who have paralysis of the arm, the aim is to regain the original range of movement of the arm joints. In terms of the chaos theory, this implies an increase in the fractal, space-filling dimension of the movement, and not just an increase in muscle strength. Similar concepts have been applied to many fields in medicine, at both the cellular and behavioral levels [631]. Random events which damage DNA, proteins and other macromolecules are associated with aging [652]. Age-related DNA damage is linked with many complex and redundant mechanisms which are altered as a result of time-dependent injury; such mechanisms may considered to represent non-beneficial randomness [656].

Olivia realized that genuinely stochastic events, which are entirely random, contribute to aging and are difficult to control [657]. Non-stochastic events, which are random but in reality, self-regulated, follow the rules of the chaos theory and also contribute to aging. Such events may be open to intervention through mathematical analysis and could be controlled [658, 659]. Different regimes of activities by nerve cells, neural assemblies and behavioral patterns, the linkage between them, and their modifications over time, require methods based on the chaos theory for their understanding. These models suggest that while chaos can be controlled, notoriously, the randomness couldn't. This can be explained better if we take a look at various types of randomness.

In Alzheimer's disease, there is a loss of physiological complexity at the molecular level that causes wide-ranging cognitive changes [660]. Diurnal variation in the secretion of many hormones in our body follows the rules of the chaos theory and is reduced with age [661]. The secretion of many hormones oscillates, and the frequency and amplitude of this oscillation changes with age [662]. Both quantitative and frequency losses occur. These oscillations of rhythmic processes demonstrate a fractal-like, power-law relationship [638]. Depending on the fractal dimension, the complexity of the system increases or decreases. A particular value of a parameter may indicate true randomness and complete unpredictability of the system, or "white noise." A different value may be related to real chaos in the mathematical sense, indicating long-range correlations and maximum complexity, or normality.

The current practice of prescribing medications is based on a linear concept. We are told by our physician to take our medications on a regular, same-strength, daily basis. This is based on the pharmacological concept of keeping drug levels constant in the blood, and their anticipated effects on a molecular basis. Applying the concepts of chaos theory to medication calls for increasing the effectivity of drugs by administering them at more complex, pulsed or irregular intervals. In terms of preventing age-related disability, this means that it is necessary to introduce and maintain a multiplicity of external and internal physiological stimuli, such as variable physical and mental exercise regimes [389].

Consider hormonal therapy. The chaos theory implies that the quantitative loss of hormonal secretion is not as significant as the loss of frequency. That is, loss of variability is less relevant than the loss of complexity [638]. An increase in amplitude, which means an increase in dosage during hormonal replacement treatment, is indicative of uncorrelated randomness, which is not beneficial for maintaining complexity. On the other hand, if a lower dose is given at a higher frequency, the dynamical complexity of the system can be maintained. In other words, a linear increase in the dose of a replacement hormone that is administered at regular, monotonic intervals would not have as much impact as administering a lower dose at irregular intervals. This means that the linear approach adopted in conventional hormone replacement treatment aims at re-establishing deficiency in a hormone. It contributes little to the synchronicity of secretion. If the frequency of the stimulus is inappropriate, the results will also be suboptimal.

Pharmacodynamics is the study of the variability in the relationship between the intensity of the pharmacological effect and drug concentration. What happens to a drug following its administration is dependent on complex physiological processes? Medications should not be administered according to rigid, monotonic, and periodic dosage regimes. Maintaining periodic elements results in an increase of predictability and loss of complexity [663] [664].The introduction of irregularity into the regime forces the system to operate aperiodically in a non-linear way [582]. It is expected to improve the clinical efficacy of the drugs. There are many inter-individual differences and some intra-individual differences that can affect these dynamics. Better modeling of the pharmacodynamics of different drugs may help establish better treatment regimens [665]. Currently, analysis of gastrointestinal absorption is based on the concept of homogeneity. However, drug dissolution, transit, and uptake in the gastrointestinal tract are highly heterogeneous processes. The high variability of whole bowel transit and the unpredictability of drug absorption require the use of models based on fractal processes [666].

The concept of chaos can also be applied to diets. It has been suggested that we are not designed to consume all our dietary supply at regular and rigid intervals, in the same amounts, two or three times a day. As scavengers, hunting for food and eating irregular quantities of nutrients at irregular, opportunistic, intervals is what we have evolved to do. This means that food intake should be non-linear and follow the rules of the chaos theory [389].

Reversing the progress of dysfunction and restoring physiological integrity means interfering with the initial conditions and control parameters of a system. This approach contradicts the conventional linear model in which the therapeutic stimulus is correlated with proportionality [389]. Pharmaceutical models exhibiting the chaotic behavior of drugs have been described. Several types of mathematical models for applying these concepts into pharmacodynamics have also been developed [667, 668].

Dynamical behavior has been described in systems where drugs have been administered orally at variable doses [669]. Scaling affects these results. Depending on the value of the parameters, a system of drug administration can be stable or unstable, effective or ineffective. According to the mass action law, the local concentration of an endogenous ligand that binds to a particular cell receptor is bound within the range that contains the basal point. However, based on the chaos theory concepts, new models of specific ligand-receptor interactions are being developed [670, 671, 672].

Do not change your medications. These are just theories.

Olivia met David for dinner that evening. It was the first time she had ever called him for dinner. He was surprised. While having dinner, he told her that their father had gotten him interested in randomness and chaos concepts. "That does not sound like you," she said laughing. "Well, that was what I thought, too. But I found it to be extremely interesting." David was smiling back at her. At this point, Olivia told him about everything she had found out. David was surprised to see that their father had gotten both of them interested in the same topic. This was surprising because their parents had always emphasized on how different the both of them were; not only were they different from each other, but they were both also very different from their parents.

"I have started thinking that our parents were wrong. They were judging us based on superficial features. Deep inside, we are made of the same genes. How else can you explain how each of us got so hooked to this topic?" Olivia was saying.

"For you," David said, "it seems to make sense with regard to your work."

"I am just trying to apply some of these concepts to my life," he continued.

They had both learned that sensitivity to initial conditions is crucial in chaos theory. Olivia was telling David about how this concept has been used to explain the dynamics of aging and pharmacological therapies.

If the initial conditions are unstable, the system forms an infinite sequence of the values. This sensitivity to the initial conditions of the system is reflected in the different variables involved in drug absorption and eventually in the effect of drugs [673]. After we take a drug, its absorption, interaction with cells, and its final effect follow the laws of non-linearity [582]. That is, administration, absorption, and interaction of a formulation with cell receptors are dynamical processes that obey non-linearity laws and are liable to manipulation [582, 674]. For example, if medicines are administered at irregular intervals, irrespective of whether a subject is fed, the absorption, concentration, and interaction with target organs may differ accordingly. Such a regime will stimulate the system to operate in a more complex state and will therefore maximize the clinical effect of the drug [389]. Increasing drug concentration by increasing the dose has a non-linear relationship with its effect.

It has been claimed, although not always through controlled clinical trials, that using single pluripotent medication may have a more beneficial effect than using several unipotent formulations [638, 675, 676]. Treatment regimens that are based on complex and aperiodic routines, in which the medication is taken at irregular intervals and at irregular strengths, without any change in the total dosage, leads to improved effects [389]. Kyriazis conducted small trials in which he showed that constant daily administration of a drug did not have a better effect than irregular administration [389]. It is important to understand that the regimen is much more complicated than just taking irregular doses, as there are safety margins for many drugs. If we take them too often, or at inappropriate times, we may experience severe side effects or even lose the effects of the drugs.

Drugs that are based on pluripotent molecules target several mechanisms simultaneously. They force the system to operate in a complex state by introducing elements with a multiplicity of interacting stimuli. Medications that affect multiple targets simultaneously stimulate many interactions between different organs, different cells, and different pathways. These types of drugs force coupling and connections that are non-trivial. Even for simple associations between organs, these drugs promote increased linking between all elements. When the drug we are taking is unipotent and works only on one target, its overall effect on the body may be more limited [677, 678].

If we take a constant daily dose of a medication, the concentration of the drug increases in our blood until it reaches a peak level, and then gradually decreases until we take the next dose. This process repeats itself several times a day for most drugs; it follows a monotonic cyclic pattern. Some call this an "information-poor regimen" [389]. If we apply a model based on the chaos theory, the medication would have to be taken at various dosages, at different times, according to a fully irregular pattern. We can change the intervals between the dosages, and the dose we take every time to create a complex dynamic system, where the levels of the drug in the blood and in target organs are going up and down throughout the day in a fully chaotic manner. In such a system, the initial condition is constantly being changed, and parameters that can be controlled such as the dose, timing of drug administration, frequencies, time in relation to meals, sleep, and many other factors, are all being altered.

Both Olivia and David were struck by the same question: If a chaotic system results in a high-information, high-energy in, is it better for the overall effect of the drug?

The multiplicity of external stimulation refers to the addition of stimulation to increase complexity. Olivia and her team, who were evaluating data on behavioral therapy for aging, were using this concept as a basis for understanding the possible benefits of maintaining a heterogeneous and entirely diverse lifestyle. This does not mean an entirely randomized life though. It means having multiple and interacting experiences, different physical and mental exercise regimens, complex social, spiritual and artistic activities, non-monotonic nutrition, and drugs or supplements at multiple intervals [389].

David was wondering if there was a reference here to the hippie years of the 70s. The "hippie subculture" started as a youth movement in San

Francisco during the early 1960s and then spread throughout the world [679, 680]. But some believe that this culture actually originated way before the European social movements, Bohemianism, and Eastern religion and spirituality. Olivia felt that the concept of a chaotic lifestyle went beyond the ethos of harmony with nature, communal living, artistic experimentation in music, and the use of recreational drugs, and it was not exactly about the practice of unconventional lifestyles. She also mentioned to David that there is a whole debate centered on whether these lifestyles actually add to complexity, as some claim that they oversimplify things and work in a way that is contrary to what complexity is all about.

Olivia said, "the way I look at it, complexity does not mean the opposite of easy. It does not mean making our lives more difficult. It also does not mean sitting on a beach whenever we feel like it. It is all about making our lives more interesting, stimulating, motivating, exciting, and fascinating."

Kyriazis uses a simple example of maintaining multiplicity in nutrition [389]. Most nutritionists recommend that we consume a wide variety of foods and a mixed diet, rather than restricting our diet to certain foods that are eaten regularly. Such a diet would expose us to many interacting nutritional inputs, and if these multiple correlated inputs are sustained, our physiological state is maintained at a higher complex, chaotic, and functional level [681].

Theories about aging that are based on the notion that aging occurs due to negative factors or regulation disorders are now considered to be erroneous. Aging is now considered as a multifactorial process that involves both external factors (such as material, energy and information) and internal factors (such as the genome), and the process of senescence may be determined by the information level of the organization [681]. There are many levels of information that are relevant for the regulation of all systems. If the complexity theory is applied to aging, factors which decrease the information level of an organism can be said to act against aging and maybe even specific diseases, and vice versa. That is, elements which deteriorate the state of the information system could contribute to the acceleration of the aging process [681].

External stimulation, such as the diversity of foods in our diet, reading, meeting people, pleasant and unpleasant, events, surprises (good or bad), all increase complexity by increasing the level of information. Any loss of stimulation reduces the complexity of the response, and is therefore detrimental to health [393, 638]. Consider what happens to us during the course of our life. During the early years after birth, we are exposed to multiple new stimuli every day. This high level of input results in a complex dynamic rich output. From middle age and beyond, the amount of stimulation is gradually reduced. The output signal therefore also reduces. Everything becomes regular, less complex. As this continues, our level of disability increases. This means that we are required to keep maintaining a high level of stimuli throughout our life. If we do so, we can preserve the dynamic complexity of output signals, thus reducing the level of disability [389].

Both Olivia and David were wondering if these concepts could be translated into more practical terms. "If I go to work every day, does it mean that I age more quickly?" David was smiling at her. "Not if your day is full of surprises. Just keep fighting with your bosses." Olivia was laughing.

Olivia was telling David about several conclusions her company had already come up with. There was nothing new about them. The aging of our brain is associated with harmful changes in our physiology and function. Intellectual and behavioral activities, diets, sports, gaming, and meeting people, are all interrelated interventions which boost neuroprotective mechanisms and result in improvement in mental health [682]. Neural cells may respond to these changes adaptively, thus preventing disorders such as Alzheimer's and Parkinson's. Thus, increasing complexity, by increasing stimuli, may assist in maintaining the integrity of our nerve cell circuits, which facilitate responses to environmental demands and promote recovery of function after injury. This is because such stimuli induce the production of neurotrophic factors and cytokines, expression of various proteins important for cell survival, preservation of genomic integrity by telomerase and DNA repair proteins, and mobilization of neural stem cells to replace damaged neurons and glia [682]. Glial cells are those cells in our brain which support neurons and facilitate interactions between the neuronal circuits.

Genetic and environmental factors superimposed upon the aging process influence the effects of aging on the brain. Mutations in genes may cause inherited forms of Alzheimer's disease, Parkinson's disease, and other diseases of the brain. Still, neuroprotective mechanisms can be strengthened by dietary interventions, including caloric restriction, nutrient supplementation, constant changes in dietary habits, and adjustment of behavioral (both intellectual and physical) activities.

Should we go play bridge already? Let ourselves have some basketball breaks from time to time?

The effectiveness of applying multiple interacting interventions in an attempt to improve age-related dysfunction is well known. For example, multiple interventions are known to be better than single ones in reducing the risk of falls in older people [683]. In fact, group-based exercise regimes were found to be the most potent intervention for the reduction of falls among elderly and is associated with improved balance. In the case of delirium, too, interventions consisting of a combination of standardized protocols to treat the six risk factors for delirium were found to be successful, the risk factors being cognitive impairment, sleep deprivation, immobility, visual impairment, hearing impairment, and dehydration. These protocols resulted in significant reductions in the number and duration of episodes of delirium in hospitalized older patients [684]. For patients with chronic depression, too, combination therapy with multiple interventions is superior to cognitive-behavioral psychotherapy or drug therapy alone [685].

This was the first time that David and Olivia were getting into such a profound discussion about her work. He felt sorry that they had not done it before. On the other hand, he was not sure whether he would have been able to absorb some of these concepts at a younger age.

They were now talking about stress, and Olivia was telling him that, indeed, mild stress has been shown to be beneficial for slowing down aging [686]. Different types of moderate physical exercises help if they are accompanied by a continually changing daily routine [687]. Exercise increases physiological complexity. It increases the short-term fractal correlation properties of heart rate dynamics, which is related to changes in the balance between low- and high-frequency oscillations in controlled situations [688]. Blood flow following exercise can be described using fractals [689]. High correlations for fractal dimensions among various muscles has been described using this method.

Brain and sensory exercises broaden the range of integrated inputs to the brain, increase the complexity of information processing, decrease linearity and monotonicity, and reduce the rate of age-related cognitive decline [690]. Integrating new information and learning new tasks is related to power-law growth and increased complexity [691]. External stimuli increase brain complexity [692]. Any type of cognitive challenge, such as listening to music and solving problems, increases the dynamical parameters of the brain [693]. Patterns of interdependency between different brain regions have been observed during the performance of tasks that require higher cognitive function, as they are accompanied by an upsurge in complexity. The electrical activity of different parts of the brain while listening to various types of music has proven this. Also, subjects with musical training were found to possess significantly higher degrees of interdependencies than those without musical training while listening to music. Both the number and the diversity of the connections, and their overall integrations contribute to complexity. Neurons in our brains show enhanced survival capabilities when appropriately stimulated. Odorant stimuli are known to rescue olfactory sensory neurons from death [694]. Conversely, when the electrical activity of neurons is reduced, they are more likely to die.

Cognitive stimulation through an enriched environment increases neurogenesis and integration of neurons in adults, and also increases the number of neurons, their dendritic length, and projections [695]. That is, environmental enrichment enhances neuronal survival [696]. This has been shown in the early postnatal period, where extrinsic factors have been shown to be important for the modulation of neurogenesis during critical time windows of hippocampal development. If we consider social relations, we all aim to build connections with well-accepted individuals and to abandon connections with less famous people. But in order to continue to grow and maintain fitness, we need to disturb the system, which may mean being more random in our choice of company [697]. More diverse information ultimately leads to better survival. Both the fitness and the lifespan of individual components in a system increase if the components provide useful functional feedback to the system [698, 699]. Higher levels of mental stimulation require the use of more independent neural processes, which contribute to the complexity of brain dynamics [700]. When the complexity of brain activity was measured under resting conditions, during a periodic finger opposition task, and during a finger opposition task alternated with mathematical serial calculation, a direct relationship between complexity and the difficulty of the task was shown. This implies that higher levels of mental load require a more significant number of independent neural processes, which contribute to the complexity of brain dynamics.

They were getting done with their dinner. Both of them were surprised at

how much they had learned from each other. "John is waiting for me with little Andy," Olivia said. "He is playing tonight, and I promised to get home early." John, her partner, was a pianist who played at jazz clubs from time to time.

On the way to the parking lot, David was asking her, "Should we start running while listening to music? Playing bridge with our left hand? Solving questions in algebra with our right hand, all at the same time?"

Olivia told him, becoming serious, "What about social bonding? These are really complex sometimes, are not they?"

"You sound like our parents," David said.

"We should definitely do this more often," Olivia answered.

She did not tell him about the studies which suggested that strong social bonds and having a big circle of friends reduces the risk of dementia [701]. Also, avoiding monotonous and dull social activities and choosing to attend variable and changeable ones have a positive impact on health by improving the dynamics of social interaction [607]. Even active spirituality, including religious involvement, can improve health [702]. Addressing the spiritual needs of a patient is associated with better health outcomes, including longevity, better coping skills, and better health-related quality of life.

Both Olivia and David went home that evening feeling grateful to their father for drawing them into this fascinating story.

# CHAPTER 36

## Technology creates more randomness in our lives. Do not lose your smartphone.

Dan was going through a dull phase at work. It had happened to him several times over the years. He was not sure if it was the time to quit. In most cases, things usually changed when a new customer came in. New challenges were always the turning point. Now, he decided to take a short vacation. He knew that the only thing he was really interested in was to visit Jeremy and Edna. It had been a while since they had met. He got himself invited for a long weekend.

He took the flight to Arizona from LaGuardia airport on Wednesday night. He planned to come back on Sunday so that he could be back at work the following Monday. Interestingly, he was thinking while taking off that sometimes, the people you feel the most connected to are not necessarily those that are considered friends in the usual sense or those that you meet most often.

Dan was in a good mood. The lady next to him on the plane was a sixty-year-old blond who had been visiting her son in New York. She had lived all her life in Arizona. She was working as a salesperson for a small computer store chain in Phoenix. Dan was telling her a funny story he had once heard.

Jesus and Satan were engaged in an ongoing argument about who had better computer skills. They had been going at it for days, and God was tired of hearing all the bickering.

Finally, God said, "Cool it. I am going to set up a two-hour test on computers, and I will judge who's better."

So, Satan and Jesus sat at the keyboards and typed away. They moussed, they did spreadsheets, they wrote reports, they sent faxes, they sent e-mails, they sent out an e-mail with attachments, they downloaded, they did some genealogy reports, they made cards, and they did every known job.

But ten minutes before their time was up, lightning suddenly flashed across the sky, thunder rolled, the rain poured and, of course, the electricity went off. Satan stared at his blank screen and screamed every curse word known in the underworld. Jesus just sighed.

The electricity finally flickered back on, and each of them restarted their computers. Satan started searching frantically, screaming "It's gone! It's all gone! I lost everything when the power went out!"

Meanwhile, Jesus started printing out all of his files. Satan observed this and became irate. "Wait! He cheated, how did he do it?"

God shrugged and said, "Jesus saves." [703]

Having shared this story and gotten a few laughs out of it, Dan got back to reading. Incidentally, he came across some of the studies that Olivia had mentioned.

Kyriazis has published a study on technological integration and hyper-connectivity, which suggests that they can be used as tools for promoting extreme human lifespans[704]. Evolution is characterized by increased complexity that is driven by non-equilibrium processes which increase both the entropy and the information content of the species [705]. Artificial, neuro-biological, and social networks are complex adaptive systems (CASs), each containing discrete processing units composed of nodes, neurons, and humans, respectively. Connections between these components underlie many of the events in our daily lives. There are models for each of the three and for combinations of the three. A complex adaptive system (CAS) exhibits properties that are dependent on the network of connections between its components [706].

Information with some kind of organization increases complexity and functionality. An information-rich environment can grow and incorporate progressively more information. This is a positive feedback loop, which keeps nourishing itself and leads to a stable entropy state. By contrast, information-poor systems shrink with time, stop growing, and do not adapt well to their environments [707]. Genomic complexity is associated with the amount of information a sequence stores about its environment. A system moves to a low- or high-information state depending on its energy status, as the benefit of information in maintaining and increasing order is balanced against its energy cost. Living systems achieve a stable entropic state by maintaining an extreme level of information [708]. Kyriazis has proposed the "law of requisite usefulness" to explain these behaviors. This law states that the length of retention of an agent within a complex adaptive system is proportional to the agent's contribution to the overall adaptability of the system[704]. That is, the more "useful" an agent is within a system, with respect to the system's adaptability and function, the more likely it is that this agent will be retained within the system, and thus survive longer.

Dan was rethinking the concept of adaptation. Interestingly, both Olivia and he were troubled by the question of whether humans can take control of these "adaptation" processes themselves.

For organisms to increase their own complexity, they must increase their information content. This is important for health and survival in more complex and less predictable environments [709]. This applies to our everyday lives, as much of the stimuli around us are unpredictable and random. In particular, in this age, technology is continually impacting our activities. When we interact with the growing technological environment around us, we are exposed to a wide variety of stimuli and challenges [710]. These modulate our stress response, changing the way we respond and adapt. Almost every minute or second of our life is affected or controlled by technology. We cannot imagine living without a smartphone. Just think of what happens when it is broken. Some of us feel like we have lost a leg or two. Technology is attempting to insert more order into our lives. With the help of all the applications available, we can order food online and practically organize all the activities in our lives. However, at the same time, we are continuously being bombarded with random stimuli through various social media platforms, emails, news forums, etc.[710, 711]. We are now continuously being exposed, whether we want it or not, to a huge amount of data. Much of the information is not relevant to us. But it is claimed that exposure to information via digital communication technologies creates positive stress which upregulates neuronal function [710]. Technology helps us to gather information. In fact, most of us cannot imagine how to get data without using digital equipment.

In addition to providing information, wearable technological devices can help us monitor our health status. Sensors in such devices identify early signs of medical emergencies, such as heart rhythm abnormalities, and initiate appropriate response [712] [713]. Brain-machine interfaces use neuronal activity recorded from the brain to establish direct communication with external actuators, such as prosthetic arms. These brain-machine interfaces restore the standard sensorimotor functions of the limbs. Further, brain-machine-brain interfaces can control the exploratory reaching movements of an actuator and allow signaling of artificial tactile feedback through intra-cortical microstimulation of the primary somatosensory cortex in the brain; this technology has been tested in animals with much success [714]. Monkeys operated this interface to search for and distinguish between three visually identical objects, using the virtual-reality arm to identify the unique artificial texture associated with each. As a step further, "brain to brain" technology can be used for direct exchange of information between brains without the need for language or keyboards [714]. Communication from one brain to another may be implemented through wireless methods [715]. An all-chain-wireless brain-to-brain system that enables control of a cyborg cockroach (made up of both organic and biomechatronic body parts) by a human brain has been developed. Further, a steady-state visual evoked potential-based brain-computer interface has been used for recognizing the intentions behind human motion. Through Bluetooth communication, specific electrical pulse trains were triggered in the micro-stimulator through brain-computer interface commands and were sent through the antenna nerve to stimulate the brain of the cockroach [715].

All this is viewed by Kyriazis as evidence that our brain is a participant of increasing relevance in the technological environment, shifting the emphasis from a physical lifestyle to a more cognitive one. This is viewed as a beneficial process that is dependent on cognition, self-generated thinking, a tendency to engage in creative, imaginative, abstract behavior, and enhanced brain activities. Being in front of a computer screen for hours every day and spending time browsing for exciting information—while Dan liked these concepts, he was not sure if they were the most beneficial. Does spending hours a day in front of social media sites help our children's brains? (He did not like how Olivia let Ron watch television for hours a day) Does continuous exposure to millions of bits of information in a random manner actually help our brain? Is it a useful type of randomness?

The magnitude of information burden and the increased knowledge we are exposed to create new biological situations which have a profound impact on many aspects of our life. Initiating stress responses is viewed as a potentially useful aging modulator. [716, 717] Such exposure was suggested by Kyriazis to affect our somatic repair processes and resource allocation mechanisms [718]. This may upregulate our biological function directly, in a way that is different from Darwinian evolution processes that occur by natural selection. According to this theory, more information, or more randomness, results in improved somatic repair and a progressive reduction in age-related degeneration [710, 719].

Dan came across the following figure of speech in the context of neurobiology: "neurons that fire together, wire together." This means that the formation and maintenance of synapses are promoted by the activation of those synapses. This is comparable with the effects of stress induced by exercise on muscle cells; neurons respond to action by activating signaling to stimulate cellular stress resistance. Fasting, exercise, and an intellectually challenging lifestyle protect neurons against the dysfunction and degeneration that they otherwise suffer in acute brain injuries such as stroke and head trauma, and neurodegenerative disorders such as Alzheimer's, Parkinson's and Huntington's [719]. This is because such activities stimulate the stress response [720]. A continuously changing environment requires adequate stress responses to maintain an internal dynamic equilibrium of the body and mind. A successful stress response requires energy in an amount that is proportional to the severity of the stressor and the type of response.

Cell death is triggered as part of the normal oogenesis program and is increased in response to various stresses. There are types of stresses at the cellular level which can enhance cell death. Cognitive information originating from the internet up-regulates neuronal endoplasmic reticulum stress response factors, which regulate cell death [710]. Neuronal stress is a potent apoptosis-initiating factor in germ line cells, thus affecting mechanisms of cell death [721].

Degeneracy refers to the structural diversity underlying functional plasticity. Degeneracy is a system property observed within individual brains or across different brains. Dementias result from a diverse range of cellular "faults." It is an example of degeneracy because the symptoms are similar despite the different underlying mechanisms [722]. Dan was considering plasticity in the broader term. Living in an entirely random environment, continuously being bombarded by random digital improves our brain plasticity. This requires the brain to continuously adapt to the changes and to the stimuli around us. Is it a beneficial type of plasticity? Developing brain plasticity may be important for improving our brain; in addition, it may also be viewed as a simple defense mechanism.

His plane had landed. He retrieved his bag and took a taxi to Jeremy's house.

# CHAPTER 37
## Randomness for better brain plasticity?

*Chaos in the midst of chaos isn't funny, but chaos in the midst of order is.*

**Steve Martin**

Phoenix was hot. Dan arrived at Jeremy's house. Edna was at work. He took a shower and was resting. They had made plans to go out for dinner. Dan was updating them about his work, his thoughts about leaving. He was not sure what his plans were. Both Edna and Jeremy told him that they planned to never retire. They could not imagine sitting on a beach in Miami for more than a week.

Gradually, Dan was moving the discussion from family, plans, and work, to chaos.

Being a biologist and a quantum physicist, both Edna and Jeremy were interested in his story.

That evening, Edna was telling Jeremy that, on first thought, she got the impression that Dan had just gotten himself involved with something to keep himself from thinking about his wife, or to keep himself from feeling lonely.

Jeremy usually counted on his wife's instincts. He also agreed that Dan seemed to be really into his research.

The weekend was spent at their house, mainly talking and resting.

Edna was talking about brain plasticity.

Brain plasticity or neuroplasticity refers to the brain's ability to undergo changes at any age, and under any type of challenge [723]. It reflects the flexibility of the nervous system, and is vital for brain development. Some believe that it is one of the mechanisms by which our personalities are shaped. Brain training exercises are based on this feature of neuroplasticity [723]. The gray matter in our brain can shrink or thicken, and the neural connections in our brain can be forged and refined or weakened and disconnected. Changes in the physical brain manifest as fluctuations in our abilities. When we learn a new dance step, it creates changes in our physical brains, as it leads to the creation of new "wires" or neural pathways that provide our bodies with instructions on how to perform the step. Why some of us cannot learn to dance is another story. Each time we forget someone's name, it also reflects a change in our brain. The cables in our brains that once connected to the memory are probably degraded, or even disconnected[724].

Brain plasticity has significant implications for healthy development, learning, memory, and recovery from brain damage [724-726]. If we look at the brain as a multi-wired organ, plasticity can be viewed as changes in the number and type of connections between these wires, our neurons. This is termed synaptic plasticity. Non-synaptic plasticity refers to changes in the intrinsic excitability of each of the wires, or neurons. Neuroplasticity is a continuous process, with synaptic connections being continually removed or re-formed. The process depends on the degree of action of the neurons. Dan told Edna about his findings on the activity-dependence of synaptic plasticity: "neurons that fire together, wire together; neurons that fire out of sync, fail to link" [724]. Whether this is an organized or somewhat random process is unclear.

Edna told Dan that the brain is sensitive to a wide range of experiences. It shows a remarkable capacity for plastic changes that impact behavioral outcomes throughout life. Factors which can modulate the developing brain include early sensory, motor, and language experience, early stress, caregiver interactions, peer interactions, psychoactive drugs, diet, microbiome, and the immune system [727]. With regard to exercise, some believe that the effects of exercise are long-lasting, and that they can even affect future generations. The effect of exercise on epigenetic regulation of gene expression seems central to building an "epigenetic memory" to influence long-term brain function and behavior [728]. This means that if we start exercising today, even our grandchildren may benefit from the cognitive benefits.

Many molecules in our body support these processes. Why can't we just buy these molecules and inject them so that we can improve our brain function? Dan was laughing.

Brain-derived neurotrophic factor (BDNF) is one such molecule [729]. This protein regulates the development of our neuronal and glial cells, as well as both the wires and the cells that support them. Brain-derived neurotrophic factor contributes to neuroprotection, assisting in keeping our wires working correctly. It is also associated with modulation of our short- and long-lasting synaptic interactions, which are critical for cognition and memory.

The wires (neurons), in our brain are being assisted by a support system in the form of microglia cells, which are immune cells that permanently reside in the central nervous system. These cells are critical for proper brain development, actively maintain health in the mature brain, and adapt their function to physiological or pathological needs. They are important for our brains to adapt, to change, and maybe, to get better. Microglial cells are essential for brain development, plasticity, and cognition [730]. Abnormalities in these cells are associated with various disease states, as well as impaired learning, memory, and other essential cognitive functions. The diversity of microglial phenotypes across a person's lifespan, between compartments of the central nervous system, and sexes, as well as their crosstalk with the body and external environment, are a part of their essential functions. Understanding what defines particular microglial phenotypes is imperative for the development of innovative therapies to control their effector functions, and thereby improve our brain function. This has consequences for cognition in chronic stress, aging, and neuropsychiatric and neurological diseases [730].

Most of us want to stop dementia from happening to us. A better understanding of the cells, molecules, processes, and cross-talks happening inside our brain, and between the brain and other organs of our body, may help us find ways of increasing brain plasticity and improving higher cognitive functions [731]. The potential for adaptation, plasticity, and perceptual learning exist, and if we are able to understand them better, we can improve our cognitive function.

In contrast to our visual system, our motor system is highly flexible. The chances for restitution in the primary visual cortex are limited [732]. Recovery from certain types of visual field loss patterns after stroke is common, but it seems to be impossible in other patterns of visual field loss. This implies that certain brain areas have better plasticity than others. Compensatory mechanisms are used for some of our brain function, and they occur spontaneously. Further, some functions can be enhanced by training. They are based on distinct relationships between perception and action, and between cognition and action [732].

Edna remarked about how "the healthy adult brain can learn new functions. It is essential for our living."

Brain plasticity is described as an inherently dynamic biological capacity of the central nervous system to undergo maturation. It can undergo both structural and functional changes in response to experience, stimuli, and environmental events, and make the required adaptations following an injury. This plasticity is a result of genetic, molecular and cellular mechanisms. These influence the dynamics of synaptic connections and neural circuitry formation. The final results are gain or loss of behavior or function [733].

There are several patterns of neuroplasticity expressed by the developing brain. One type is developmental plasticity, which is classified into normal and impaired plasticity, as observed in autism. Another type is adaptive, experience-dependent plasticity that occurs after intense motor skill training. We all benefit from this type of plasticity, as it helps us gain more skills. A third type is reactive plasticity, which occurs in response to injury to the central nervous system or sensory deprivation. This may also be relevant throughout our lives. A fourth type is what some people call "excessive plasticity" or the loss of homeostatic regulation. This may underlie some diseases such as dystonia and refractory epilepsy. In both, overexcitation of the brain occurs. This means that the brain becomes vulnerable under certain conditions such as lack of oxygen in stroke and stress in epilepsy.

Neuroplasticity is essential during critical and sensitive periods. Pre- and postnatal brain development are considered as "critical and sensitive periods." If the concept of critical and sensitive periods of brain development in health and disease are right, it may mean that we have "windows of opportunity" for neuromodulatory interventions, especially in children, but also in people who are in their later stages of life. Such periods enable augmentation of plasticity and improving function [733].

If the brain is observed after periods of deprivation of input, it will show late activation in response to stimuli. Such studies have been conducted in animals before and after amputation of the third digit. Before amputation, five distinct areas of the brain that corresponded to each digit of the experimental hand were observed. Two months after amputation of the third digit, the area corresponding to the third digit was invaded by the adjacent areas that corresponded to the second and fourth digits [734]. This demonstrates that behavioral manipulations have an impact on brain plasticity.

Similarly, when a stimulus is cognitively associated with the strengthening of one brain area, its cortical representation is enlarged. Cortical representations increase two- to threefold in one or two days when a new sensory-motor behavior is acquired, and the changes are finalized within a few weeks. These changes are not the result of the sensory experience alone. They require learning about the sensory experience, and they are most reliable for stimuli that are associated with reward. These changes occur with equal ease in the case of operant and classical conditioning behaviors [724].

An interesting phenomenon involving brain plasticity is the phantom limb sensation. It is experienced by people who have undergone amputation of the hands, arms, and legs, but it is not limited to the extremities. These people can sometimes still feel the missing appendage. This phenomenon is associated with a type of brain plasticity or reorganization [735].

Plasticity can be classified into adaptations that have positive or negative behavioral consequences. An organism that recovers after a stroke and reaches normal levels of function exhibits "positive plasticity." In contrast, excessive neuronal growth leading to spasticity or tonic paralysis or excessive neurotransmitter release in response to injury, which result in nerve cell death, are examples of "negative" plasticity [724, 736]

Modifiable lifestyle factors, including physical activity, cognitive engagement, and diet, are a vital strategy for maintaining brain health during aging. Physical activity and diet are associated with common neuroplasticity substrates, such as neurotrophic signaling, neurogenesis, inflammation, stress response, and antioxidant defense, whereas cognitive engagement enhances brain and cognitive reserve. Relationships between lifestyle factors, brain structure and function, and cognitive function have been shown in aging adults [736].

Dan felt that he had a very good understanding of neuroplasticity. But he now wanted Edna to help him understand the relevance of randomness in all of this. Whether all these processes were organized or random processes was unclear. More importantly, whether randomness can improve plasticity is a significant question. If brain plasticity is good for us, and if randomness does increase plasticity, it means that we may want more randomness.

Our brain is not completely "hard-wired" with fixed neuronal circuits. Cortical and subcortical rewiring of neuronal circuits does occur in response to training, stimuli, and injuries, and experience can influence the synaptic organization of the brain. Neuroplasticity may help with memory and learning via experience-driven alteration of synaptic structure and function [724].

A study compared the effects of high-intensity interval training (HIT) and moderate-intensity aerobic training (MOD) on functional recovery and cerebral plasticity during the first two weeks after cerebral ischemia. The high-intensity training was more useful in terms of improving endurance performance; it resulted in fast recovery of the impaired forelimb grip force. Low-volume high-intensity interval training seems to be more effective after cerebral ischemia to improve aerobic fitness and grip strength and to promote cerebral plasticity [737].

A study of healthy astronauts before, during, and after the Neurolab Space Shuttle mission was performed based on observations of controlled breathing and apnea. The sympathetic burst frequencies observed after the mission were higher than the preflight, space, and landing day frequencies. Further, the astronauts' abilities to modulate both burst areas and frequencies during apnea were diminished. The conclusion of this study was that spaceflight triggers long-term neuroplastic changes that are reflected by reciprocal sympathetic and vagal motor neuron responsiveness to breathing changes [738]. In a study of healthy astronauts on earth, in space on the 1st and 12th or 13th day of the 16-day Neurolab Space Shuttle mission, on landing day, and 5–6 days later, they were asked to follow a fixed protocol comprising controlled and random frequency breathing and apnea. It was observed that their sympathetic mechanisms had changed. After the mission, the burst frequencies during fixed frequency breathing were greater than the preflight, space, and landing day frequencies, but their control during apnea was altered. The astronauts had increased their burst frequencies from already high levels, but they could not modulate the burst areas or frequencies appropriately. All these findings mean that space travel provokes long-lasting sympathetic and vagal neuroplastic changes in healthy humans [738].

Thus, behavior, environmental stimuli, thoughts, and emotions contribute to neuroplastic change through activity-dependent plasticity, which can help alter many aspects of our brain function [739].

Another study determined how the timing of stimulation influenced neuroplasticity in relation to practice in aged people. The participants completed several sessions of intervention with robotic movement trials using sub-threshold, single-pulse transcranial magnetic stimulations (TMS) delivered during the late reaction time (LRT) period, when muscle activity exceeded a threshold, or randomly. The direction of the transcranial magnetic stimulation-evoked movements significantly changed after practice. The amplitude of movement was significantly increased after the late reaction time and random conditions. When combined with robotic reach practice, stimulation during the late motor response period had a positive effect on the responsiveness of the motor cortex, while stimulation during the early movement period had a negative effect [739]. The sensitivity of the activated motor cortex to additional stimulation is dynamic, and the randomness of the stimuli seems to affect plasticity [739].

Perceptual learning is a manifestation of neural plasticity. Research on brain plasticity during learning using noninvasive transcranial electrical stimulation has shown that different types of transcranial electrical stimulations (tES) have different effects on the nervous system and result in different patterns of plasticity. For example, different plasticity effects were generated using direct current stimulation and random noise stimulation during the execution of a visual perceptual learning task [740]. Random noise stimulation was found to improve neuroplasticity during perceptual learning.

A surprising consequence of neuroplasticity is that brain activity associated with a given function can be transferred to a different location. This occurs during recovery from brain injury. Rehabilitation techniques, such as constraint-induced movement therapy, functional electrical stimulation, treadmill training with body-weight support, and virtual reality therapy, support these changes and lead to reorganization. Robot-assisted therapy may also bring about its effects through neuroplastic changes [741].

Several companies offer cognitive training software programs for improving neuroplasticity and assisting with learning disabilities. But a systematic review found very little evidence supporting any of the claims of these products [742]. This means that not all stimuli are effective; further, different people may require different types of stimuli for achieving positive plasticity.

There are techniques for which there is some evidence of improved plasticity though [724]. A number of studies have associated meditation to brain plasticity and to positive changes in cortical thickness or the density of gray matter [743-745]. Also, aerobic exercise promotes adult neurogenesis by increasing the production of neurotrophic factors such as brain-derived neurotrophic factor (BDNF)[746], and exercise is also known to improve memory [747]. Consistent aerobic exercise over a period of several months induced clinically significant improvement in the cognitive control of behavior. It increased gray matter volume in multiple brain regions, particularly those that are important for cognitive control [748].

Dan asked Edna whether it would be possible to improve some of these methods by introducing some elements of randomness into them. Can we improve plasticity by adding some chaos into the stimuli? Dan was convinced that randomness would indeed be helpful.

# CHAPTER 38
## Do we want to live longer?

Before leaving for Arizona, Dan had a lengthy telephone conversation with Olivia. He wanted to hear what more she had learned about the topics they had discussed. He asked her whether she thought that some of the randomness concepts are applicable to her topic of interest—aging.

The human lifespan receives a lot of attention in science, medicine and among the general public. Demographic forecasts suggest that most babies born after the year 2000 will survive to their 100th birthday. However, several studies suggest that human biology precludes survival to the age of 100 for most people [749].

Kyriazis described a model of aging that he termed "third phase science" [750]. This model represents an integrative concept based on an inclusive worldview. It looks into the relationship between humans and their environment, the integration of humans with technology, and the biological consequences of an increasingly techno-cognitive ecosystem. He makes the claim that the entire research into aging is biased towards reductionism, and relies on simplified concepts in terms of a physical object [751]. While there are many drugs and supplements which reduce age-associated damage, there is currently nothing that can eliminate it completely and dramatically extend lifespan [749].

Dan told Olivia a joke that he had once heard:

A patient approaches his doctor and asks him this pertinent question: How can I live longer than 100 years?

The doctor asks him the following questions.

Do you smoke?

Do you eat too much?

Do you go to bed late?

Do you have affairs with promiscuous women?

He replies in the negative to all these questions. The doctor then promptly asks him, "Why would you want to live more than a 100 years?"

Kyriazis suggests that instead of searching for a drug, injection, or procedure to reduce mortality, we should examine how the human organism aligns itself in relation to society and its environment.

The "First Phase Science" model was shaped by Descartes, among others, who imagined a distinction between an objective world and a subjective one, with a detached observer separated from the object he was studying by a distinct mental barrier [752]. This model views object-based therapies as separate from the patient. It cannot be applied in complex situations.

In the "Second Phase Science" model, the observer is immersed in the observation. Here, observing refers to a participating variable that causes the system under study to react to this observation. An example of this model is the reciprocal relationship between psychoanalysts and their patients, and unblinded clinical trials, in which the patient and/or the physician know what drug is being administered [753]. Under these situations, the interventions are shaped following feedback from the patient himself, and the properties of the observed "object" are reduced to individual elements that are expected to be valid across domains. This model is applied to current research, which believes that aging is a process that can potentially be reduced to individual components [750].

If we accept the concept that aging-related mechanisms adapt, change and respond to effects originating from the environment including cultural, social, and technological stimuli in addition to biological changes, then the Second Phase model may be unsuitable [750, 754].

In the third-phase model, Kyriazis claims that rather than looking at an individual patient, we should consider interactions between people, and between each person and each of the stimuli around him. The "Third Phase science model views human beings a part of a broader ecosystem, and looks at their adaptations and responses to different situations [755]. The complexity lies in the fact that the views of the observer interact with those of other observers to create a diversity of viewpoints that may form a more inclusive concept. These systems are non-additive. That is, the properties of such a system are not predictable by the sum of its components [756, 757]. This model emphasizes on the importance of a multilevel, integrative approach to the study of behavioral phenomena in the decade of the brain. This is therefore an integrative and dynamic model that is closer to real life.

Kyriazis describes an experiment in which the effects of the administration of amphetamine or a placebo to animals showed no effect when the effect was evaluated on each animal. However, when social hierarchy was considered, amphetamine administration was found to amplify dominant behavior in high-ranking animals and increase passive behavior in low-ranking animals [758]. This proves the importance of evaluating phenomena or scientific variables within the context of the environment. The interaction between biological and social factors is not evident when only the biological or only the social aspect of the behavior is considered [757]. The approach needs to be inclusive and consider biological, cultural, environmental and other factors [759].

Social genomics is a new field of science, in which extensive alterations in the expression of human genes have been observed across different social environments. The science is founded on the notion that our genome has "social programs" to adapt molecular physiology to the changing patterns of threat and opportunity associated with changing social conditions [759]. Certain types of genes are sensitive to social regulation, the biological signaling pathways that mediate these effects, and the genetic polymorphisms that modify their individual impact[759].

If our genes are being altered by the environment, it means that we should be careful about where we choose to be, which stimuli we choose to be exposed to, people we select to interact with, and much more. This goes well with the notion of viewing aging as a "time-and place related dysfunction" [750].

Dan had briefly heard from Olivia about drugs that are used for alleviating age-related disorders. The pharmacodynamics of therapies obeys the rules of non-linearity. This means that the result of the treatment does not necessarily depend on the modality of the therapy. In fact, biological systems usually display chaotic behaviors that are sometimes hard to evaluate [760]. We are therefore unable to calculate the effects of treatment, because of the inherent complexity and non-linearity of biological systems. Repairing or replacing a gene or molecule, for instance, has unpredictable effects on the entire organism. There are multiple, inherently heterogeneous, interacting processes which may lead to a disease, and these processes affect individual patients in unpredictable ways [761].

"Each of us is different," Olivia said. "That is the reason why it is so difficult to come up with good models." Treatment modalities must therefore be tailored to individual patients and cannot be developed as a generic, fit-all treatment [762]. This means that even if we believe in the environmental stimulation theory, the effect of each stimulus on a said person may be completely different. Each of us is expected to respond differently to different stimuli. Each patient has unique pathogenic processes resulting from various cellular genetic and epigenetic alterations [762]. The interactions between cells, organs, responses to stimuli, and exposures to dietary, environmental, microbial, people, and lifestyle factors are different. So even random stimuli, or "organized random" stimuli, will exert a different effect on each of us. The perception of the randomness of the stimuli may also differ. What seems random to someone may not necessarily be random to another person. But this means that there cannot be accurate recipes, list or algorithms.

Olivia left the phone conversation wondering whether her father was right. Would all the work they put into building algorithms for the prevention of aging prove to be useless?

Molecular pathological epidemiology (MPE) is an integrative transdisciplinary science based on a unique disease principle and the disease continuum theory. It enhances causal inferences by linking etiologic factors to specific molecular biomarkers as outcomes. Biorepository and biobank networks and worldwide population-based databases are used for this purpose. This in in keeping with the goals of the Big Data to Knowledge (BD2K), Genetic Associations and Mechanisms in Oncology (GAME-ON), and Precision Medicine initiatives [761]. So perhaps big data is the answer to creating accurate algorithms and recipes.

This was precisely what Olivia was trying to do in her company.

Science can analyze disease risk factors and develop statistical methodologies to maximize utilization of big data on populations and disease pathology. Molecular pathological epidemiology (MPE) can be used to associate the data to exposures to molecular pathologic signatures, and thereby improve inferences and help identify potential biomarkers for clinical impact [762]. The integrative social molecular pathological epidemiology model goes a step further to include sociology, economics, precision medicine, global health disparities, and inequalities, and elucidate the biological effects of social environments, behaviors, and networks.

But Olivia was still bothered by the randomness.

Much of the stimuli we are being exposed to continuously is electronic. This phenomenon is referred to as "living in a techno-cultural environment" or "the human-computer merge" [716, 750]. Much of this exposure is random. We have limited control over the type of stimuli we receive. It is suggested that these types of stimuli could be associated with the epigenetic phenomenon of altering cells in our body [763]. It can also be seen in the light of theories that human evolution is substantially influenced by the interactions between our cultural and genetic systems. The application of this culture-gene co-evolutionary approach to understanding human social psychology and other fields in our lives has generated novel insights into the understanding of human cognition and behavior [750] [763]. This "gene-culture" coevolution requires continuous adaptations to the technological surroundings [764]. If we observe carefully, it seems that we are developing relationships with technology: we often find ourselves talking with our computer or with our smartphone. These relationships have an effect on our biology and could result in unprecedented changes in the human body [765] [766].

Our thinking and behavior are related to how perception and action subsystems are integrated during coordinated goal-directed activity. Degeneracy is a neurobiological system property which explains how skilled individuals functionally adapt their perception and action to interacting constraints during their performance [767]. Improved coupling of information and movement could lead individuals to explore functionally degenerate behaviors. Degeneracy can support plural-potentiality as a way toward refinement in performance [767]. It may also lead to innovation. Given all this information, a passive brain-computer interface framework is therefore a promising construct for assessing cognitive and affective states [768].

To summarize everything, the interactions we experience with electronic devices add information which affects our brains. This type of stimuli, many of which are random, as mentioned before, can affect our body's repair abilities, improve neuron response in our brain, and alter the generation of stress molecules, among many other things [750].

Olivia came to the conclusion that an algorithm could be improved and be more inclusive if it were based on big data. Such an algorithm would represent both one's body as well as the external environment.

# CHAPTER 39

## Quantum: a meaningless word or the clue to generating certified randomness?

Dan was sitting with Edna and Jeremy over lunch.

He realized that the concept of randomness is essential in many disciplines. He put forth the question of whether the existence of random processes is essential for our understanding of nature. He knew that Jeremy was into quantum physics, and that randomness and quantum physics are associated.

Randomness is being used as a resource for cryptography, algorithm generation and simulations [16]. Standard methods for generating randomness rely on assumptions about the devices that are often not valid in practice. This is where quantum physics comes in. Quantum methods provide new ways of generating certified randomness, based on the violation of Bell inequalities. These methods are device-independent because they do not rely on any standard models [16].

Quantum theories describe an event at the subatomic levels, which are determined by virtue of statistical probabilities, and not by the laws of certainty. Walter Isaacson, in his book *The Innovators: How a Group of Hackers, Geniuses, and Geeks Created the Digital Revolution* [769], provides a simple explanation. In science, it has been traditionally assumed that if we know everything about the universe at a given moment, we could predict what will happen from then on for the entire future." This idea is consistent with the success of many prediction theories. However, modern science has discovered that when we deal with atoms and electrons, we do not actually have the ability to read their precise state. Our instruments themselves are made of atoms and electrons, so the possibility of knowing the exact state of the universe doesn't exist when reduced to such a small scale.

Does this mean that the theory that our actions can be predicted just like the weather is no longer valid? Does this mean that we cannot determine the action of atoms in a small part of the brain?

Before the age of quantum physics, it was believed that a physical system had a determinate state that uniquely determines the values of its measurable properties. Conversely, the values of its measurable properties uniquely determined the state of the system. This belief was countered by quantum indeterminacy, which is defined as the apparent essential incompleteness in the description of a system [770]. According to this concept, a system can be quantitatively characterized only by a probability distribution of the set of measured outcomes of its observable properties. It is therefore the distribution, and not the properties, that is uniquely determined by the system state. Quantum mechanics provides a recipe for calculating this probability distribution. In quantum mechanics, indeterminacy is of a much more fundamental nature, having nothing to do with errors or disturbance.

Can apparent indeterminacy be construed as in fact deterministic, but dependent upon quantities not modeled according to the current theory, which would, therefore, be incomplete? What about the possibility of hidden variables that could account for statistical indeterminacy in an entirely classical sense? Can indeterminacy be understood as a disturbance in the system being measured? [770]

Isaacson describes the life of Alan Mathison Turing, an English computer scientist and mathematician who studied the mathematics underlying quantum mechanics. Turing described how events occurring at the subatomic levels are determined by virtue of statistical probabilities, and not by the laws of certainty [769] . According to this concept, quantum indeterminacy is exemplified in the case of a particle with a measured momentum, for which there must be a limit to how correctly its location can be specified. Explained in terms of the quantum uncertainty principle, this means that for a particle with definitely measured energy, there is a fundamental limit to how precisely one can specify how long it will have that energy. For a given quantum state, each measurable observable has a determinate value. The values of an observable can only be obtained non-deterministically in line with a probability distribution that is determined by the system state, and the state is destroyed as a result of a measurement. When referring to a collection of values, each measured value must be obtained using a newly prepared state [770].

Einstein believed that a quantum state could not be a complete description of a physical system. Einstein, Podolsky, and Rosen showed that if the concept of quantum mechanics is assumed to be correct, the classical view of the world, at least after application of the special relativity theory, is no longer justifiable [771]. A measurable property of a physical system whose value can be predicted with certainty is actually an element of reality [770].

Dan was not sure he got it. He came back to the question of how randomness and quantum physics are related.

One of the significant challenges facing modern science is understanding the nature of randomness. The relationship between quantum indeterminacy and randomness is elusive. [772] Quantum indeterminacy is viewed as information or lack of information, which exists in individual quantum systems prior to measurement. Quantum randomness is a statistical manifestation of that indeterminacy.

In classical physics, experiments of chance, such as coin tossing and dice throwing, are deterministic, in the sense that perfect knowledge of the initial conditions render the outcomes predictable. The "randomness" stems from ignorance of physical information in the first toss or throw. In contrast, quantum randomness does not stem from any physical information [773-775] [770]. Quantum randomness is exclusively the output of measurement experiments whose input settings introduce logical independence into quantum systems [776]. Logical independence refers to a null logical connection that exists between mathematical propositions that neither proves nor disproves one another. There is a statistical link between quantum randomness and logical independence. One can correlate predictable outcomes with logically dependent mathematical propositions, and random outcomes with propositions that are logically independent.

Jeremy was now referring to an MIT review on the association between randomness and quantum ideas. [777] Many scientists believe that all physical processes can be thought of in terms of the information they store and process. This means that information is the basic unit of existence in our world. This line of thinking implies that reality is a kind of computation in which the primary processes at work merely grind their way through a broad basis of information. [777]

Information can be defined as an ordered sequence of symbols, but in contrast to it, randomness is the opposite of order—it is the absence of pattern. Further, true randomness is that which cannot be produced by a computer. Otherwise, it wouldn't be random. This is a real challenge, because "if all physical processes in our world are ongoing computations, how does randomness arise?"

Mathematicians study randomness generated by classical physical processes such as coin tosses or computer programs which generate pseudo-randomness. Since it is difficult for physical processes like coin tosses to be unbiased, random number generators and programs such as Mathematica use the properties of cellular automata to generate pseudorandom sequences of numbers. Another method is just to choose a sequence of numbers from the digits of an irrational number such as pi. This looks and feels random, but because it can be computed, maybe it is not random. "Mathematicians treat it with suspicion." [777]

In the last decade, a new source of randomness that cannot be produced by a computer program called algorithmic randomness was discovered. This is considered to represent the real absence of order. This randomness is part of the quantum world. It comes from exploiting quantum processes such as whether a photon is transmitted or reflected by a semi-silvered mirror [777]. It produces sequences that can never be created by a computer.

Cristian Calude at the University of Auckland in New Zealand compared several kinds of the random sequences generated by diverse methods. The sequences were obtained from a quantum random number generator called Quantis [778, 779]. He studied the possibility of distinguishing between quantum sources of randomness, which are proven to be theoretically incomputable, and some well-known computable sources of pseudo-randomness. It was shown that incomputability is necessary, but not sufficient, for "true randomness." [780] Algorithmic random sequences are incomputable, but the converse implication is false. The algorithmic information theory characterizes algorithmic random sequences in terms of the degrees of in-compressibility of their finite prefixes. Tests of randomness were conducted on pseudo-random strings of finite sequences of length generated with soft-ware such as Mathematica and Maple: some strings were cyclic and com-putable, while some strings, such as those containing the bits of π, and were computable but not cyclic. Strings were also produced by quantum mea-surements with the commercial device Quantis and software by the Vienna IQOQI group. Four different tests were used to compare the sequences; these included tests based on the algorithmic information theory, statistical tests involving frequency counts, a test based on the information theory, and a test based on random walks. The results indicated that there were quan-titative differences between computable and incomputable sources of "ran-domness" [780]. The sequence generated by Quantis was distinguishable from the other data sets, but quantum randomness was incomputable [779]. This indicated that the sequence could not have been being generated by a computer [777]. This is in itself controversial: Quantis produces random sequences that cannot be generated by a computer; yet, Quantis is a machine that must work by manipulating information in a way that is in keeping with the laws of physics. It must be a computer of sorts. This discrepancy means there is something wrong with the way we think about randomness or information or both [777] .

The solution lies within the nature of information in the quantum world. It's easy to define information classically as an ordered sequence of symbols. But this definition becomes obsolete once symbols become quantum in nature. If each bit can be both a 1 and a 0 at the same time, what does order mean in the case of such a sequence? Equally, what would the absence of order look like in such a quantum sequence?

A paper published in Nature called "Certified randomness" discuss-es when a given process can be said to generate "good" randomness [16]. The most reliable definition of randomness or "perfectly random" is being unpredictable, from the perspective of both the user of the device and an observer. However, unpredictability from the perspective of an observer may not be needed for some applications, such as Monte Carlo simulations. We cannot argue that a process is random if there is an observer who is able to predict its outcomes. The requirement that the results should be unpredictable by any observer assures that the generated randomness is private. If the process is run in a secure location, the user is confident that nobody else knows what the results are. Such private randomness can safely be used for cryptographic purposes. This means that the generation of randomness from scratch is impossible. This notion challenges the hypothesis of the existence of a super-deterministic model in which everything, including the entire history of our universe, was pre-determined in advance and known by the external observer [16]. All protocols for randomness generation are based on assumptions. The appropriateness of the assumptions may depend on the application.

A physics-based approach to randomness generation means that the random numbers are unpredictable by any physical observer. Any observer whose actions are constrained by the laws of physics, as well as the device generating the randomness should obey the laws of quantum physics.

How can a user certify that the numbers produced by their device are random?

Random bits should follow a uniform probability distribution and be uncorrelated to the environment. Statistical tests can be used to certify the randomness of sequences generated by the device [781]. Even if these statistical tests prove the randomness of a sequence, it is impossible to certify with limited computational power that a given sequence is random. The guarantee of privacy may be even more difficult.

Consider a situation in which the provider generates a long sequence of good random numbers, stores them into a memory stick and sells it as a proper random generator to the user. The sequence will pass any statistical test for randomness; however, they are not adequately random because they can be correctly predicted by the challenger [782].

To summarize, it is difficult to be really random. But quantum physics may help.

# CHAPTER 40
## Being really random is difficult

While it seems easy and intuitive to be random, generating real perfect randomness is hard. Dan was reviewing with Jeremy the three types of approaches for generating random sequences [16].

The first approach involves the use of pseudo-random number generators (PRNGs) which use an algorithm to process an initial random seed. These types of generators are fast, cheap, and good enough for some applications. The random character of the output of these generators and their privacy are based on assumptions about the computational power of the adversary. However, true randomness requires unpredictability by any observer, independently of the computational power.

The second type of approach uses a true random number generator (TRNG) to exploit physical processes that are hard to predict, such as meteorological phenomena or the mouse movements of a computer user.

The third type is the quantum (QRNGs) random number generator, which exploits a quantum process that is thought to be substantially random. An example is the clicks observed after single photons impinge a beam splitter. However, this idealized set-up is based on many assumptions that are vital to guarantee the match between the ideal theoretical situation and its implementation [16].

The sequences generated by quantum random number generators are certified by statistical tests, but these are problematic. This means that the only guarantee that a user has that the symbols have a quantum origin is the word of the provider. The user cannot test the privacy of the symbols. Trusting the provider is the only option. It is difficult to achieve a satisfactory level of trust between the provider and user because in many situations, especially in the case of cryptographic applications, it is convenient to reduce trust in the provider. Even if the provider is trusted and has constructed the devices in the best possible way, uncontrolled drifts and changes in the devices are unavoidable and could deteriorate the quality of the generated randomness.

Device-independent QRNGs (DIQRNGs) quantum random number generators offer a solution for some of these obstacles. They provide protocols for generating certified randomness in a way that is in keeping with the laws of quantum physics. These generators function as quantum black boxes processing classical information, and no assumptions need to be made about their inner working. Such generators may provide better insights into real randomness.

Randomness certification without assumptions about the inner working of the devices can be achieved by exploiting the quantum violation of Bell inequalities. Device-independent quantum random number generator protocols make use of the correlations observed when measuring entangled particles that violate a Bell inequality and therefore do not have a classical analog [783].

A user needs at least two separate devices to run a Bell test. The devices receive inputs and produce outputs. After several rounds of collecting the input and output data, the user calculates the relative frequencies of the outcomes based on the inputs, which can be estimated without making any assumptions about the internal working of the devices. A Bell inequality is a linear function of these relative frequencies. Violation of the Bell inequality implies the presence of non-classical correlations between the two devices.

For device-independent quantum random number generators, if a user observes the violation of a Bell inequality, they can be confident that an unknown quantum state in the devices is entangled and pure. The purity of the quantum state certifies that the two devices are not too correlated with the environment or with the external observer. The entanglement certifies that the local state of one of the devices is mixed, and that measurement of this state can generate random outcomes. The Bell certification of randomness is intrinsically quantum because classical devices always satisfy a Bell inequality. Further, the randomness is device-independent because only the observed statistics are needed for its computation [16]. Because the state is pure, it cannot be correlated with the environment. The local measurements on half of it produce perfect random bits according to the equation, which is certified by the observed Bell violation.

It is possible to design device-independent quantum random number generators that do not satisfy the quantum theory. They are based on the no-signaling principle, which is based on the non-feasibility of faster-than-light communication between devices. According to the no-signaling principle, the violation of a Bell inequality guarantees the random character of the outputs [784-787]. The conditions for generating such randomness are as follows: (a) the inputs should have no correlations with the devices, (b) there should be no communication between the two devices during the generation of the two distant sequences, and (c) the measured quantum state should be independent of the inputs and outputs. This means that the product and the measurements on one device do not depend on the input of the other. The protocols for such generators that have been proposed involve two or more devices, each having an input and an output.

One way of satisfying the first condition is to select the inputs using a random seed that meets specific "independence" requirements depending on the protocol. Protocols designed to optimize the trade-off between initial and final randomness are termed randomness expansion protocols [788-791]. Good randomness can be generated in Bell set-ups using sources of imperfect randomness and running them with "randomness amplification" protocols [792-795]. A non-perfect seed ensures the security of a protocol. For most applications, we assume that the seed is uncorrelated to the adversary and devices. Thus, the expansion rate is a more practical value.

Can we generate device-independent private randomness under a minimal set of assumptions and with minimal resources?

Bell-certified randomness is a resource for device-independent crucial quantum distribution [796-799]. It generates randomness and establishes a secret key between two distant users using a Bell violation observed between their devices. The devices are in two different locations, and the channel joining them is accessible to a spy. But this may be contradictory to the case of randomness generation.

Implementation of the DINING protocols requires the observation of a Bell inequality violation. It is required to prepare an entangled state of two or more particles, which are distributed to several devices where they are subjected to local measurements. A challenge for the observation of Bell inequality violations is that a high detection efficiency is required to close the detection loophole [800]. This means that for low enough detection efficiencies, the statistics of a Bell experiment can always be described by a model, which makes it deterministic. Thus, no randomness certification is possible for such an experiment [801]. Closing the detection gap is demanding because it results in losses in the set-up. Complete closure of the gap also requires a high detection efficiency [802, 803]. Contrary to the detection gap, the presence of locality, collapse-locality and free-will gaps is detrimental to the validity of the model [804, 805]. These gaps can never be strictly closed, but their credibility can be enforced by making physically motivated assumptions about the experimental arrangement.

The standard approach to closing the detection gap is based on Einstein's theory of relativity and involves arranging the measurements so that they define events that are separated in a space-like way such that no communication can take place between the two devices [16]. There may be scenarios in which it is possible to assume the validity of a model without space-like-separated measurements. If a low level of trust is placed on the provider, it would be safe to assume that the devices do not signal to each other when producing the outputs in response to the inputs [16]. A level of shielding, essential for any cryptographic use of the generated numbers, may be assumed to avoid any unwanted communication between the devices. The space-like arrangement that is adapted to close the locality gaps assumes that there is precise knowledge about when the local measurements start and end, when inputs are defined and outputs are produced. If there is no information on the timing of the generation of inputs, it is possible that the information exists before the entangled state is produced [16]. A proposed theoretical way to avoid this dependence is to assume that the inputs are generated by humans. The more practical approach to close the gaps is to use a standard QRNG56 quantum random number generator. However, it is questionable whether such a generator is preferable over those of classical origin [806].

Several other methods for certified quantum randomness generation are being developed. They keep part of the device-independent spirit and make only mild assumptions about the set-up, without modeling of the devices [16]. Randomness certification is believed to a purely quantum process with no classical analog. Standard quantum random number generators do not fit into this category because they require modeling and randomness certification with statistical tests.

Information protocols under a dimensional constraint are considered to be semi-device-independent [807]. This model is different from a Bell test and consists of a device that prepares a system in different quantum states and a measuring device that performs measurements on it. The states prepared by the first device are measured by the second device. Randomness certification is obtained based on the violation of the dimension witnesses [808]. It does not require the generation of entanglement. The preparation and measuring device share no correlations, and the devices do not display memory effects, which certifies the presence of randomness for any value of detection efficiency [809].

An asymmetric scenario is one in which one trusts the preparing devices but not the measuring devices. These scenarios are considered in the context of navigation [810]. It is defined in the same set-up as non-locality. It means that the two parties perform measurements on two distant quantum particles, and one of the devices is fully trusted. The detection of steering provides a quantum certification which guarantees randomness [811] [16].

Connecting randomness and non-locality is relevant for applications of quantum technologies. Protocols that achieve full randomness amplification against non-signaling spies are the most powerful form of certification using quantum physics of the existence of random events in nature [16]. However, it is impossible to certify randomness from scratch. Under the assumption of no-signaling, violation of Bell inequalities certifies the presence of randomness but requires some initial randomness. Full randomness amplification protocols are not able to completely break this circularity [16]. The violation of Bell inequalities implies that quantum predictions cannot be reproduced by a deterministic theory without violating the no-signaling principle [792, 812].

The quantum theory allows for maximal randomness certification [16, 813]. Full randomness amplification protocols against no-signaling are viewed as proof of the incomputability of the quantum theory.

Dan was still not sure he got it. It was clear to him that quantum randomness is better. It may not be the ultimate type of randomness though. The ultimate goal would be to design a robust, secure protocol that achieves an infinite randomness expansion rate, by using original sources of arbitrarily weak public randomness with only two devices and assuming only the validity of the no-signaling principle. This goal may be unreachable.

He would continue this discussion with Jeremy later.

# CHAPTER 41

## Making sense of randomness through quantum physics

Dan felt that his visit to Arizona had been enlightening. Not only had he gotten to meet Edna and Jeremy, who he considered to be his true friends, but they had also helped him understand randomness better. In fact, getting them to think about randomness, much like he did with Olivia and David, was unexpected. He realized that he might be crazy to spend hours and hours in pursuit of this randomness, but how come those around him were falling into the trap one by one?

He was glad.

It was his last day, and he was to fly home in a few hours.

Under some circumstances, there may be some disagreement about whether a physical phenomenon is a *quantum* phenomenon or a phenomenon with *chaotic* behavior [814]. It is also unclear whether our universe is *deterministic* or not, and whether everything that happens is essentially predetermined [814].

Quantum physics describes the universe at the atomic and subatomic levels. Random number generators are based on the quantum physics concept that subatomic particles appear to behave randomly under certain conditions. There appears to be no information about what causes these events, and they are therefore believed by many to be nondeterministic. Supporters of random number generators of the quantum variety argue that systems governed by the laws of quantum physics are inherently nondeterministic, whereas systems governed by classical physics laws are fundamentally deterministic [814]. In contrast, chaotic systems are those in which tiny changes in the initial conditions can result in dramatic changes in the overall behavior of the system. This, as discussed several chapters ago, is called the butterfly effect. So, chaos can be deterministic, but systems that follow quantum physics laws are not.

Dan felt that he had finally understood it. His major issue now was how to make use of it.

Jeremy and Dan were browsing random.org, a website which offers true random numbers to anyone who needs them [814]. The randomness is derived from atmospheric noise, which for many purposes is believed to be better than pseudo-random number algorithms used in computer programs. People use this website for holding drawings, lotteries, and sweepstakes, to drive online games, for scientific applications and for art and music. The service has been available since 1998, and it was built by Dr. Haahr of the School of Computer Science and Statistics at Trinity College, Dublin, Ireland. It is operated today by Randomness and Integrity Services Ltd.

The atmospheric noise that is used as the source can be considered as a chaotic but deterministic system. Hence, if we knew enough about the processes that cause atmospheric noise, such as thunderstorms, we could potentially predict the numbers that are generated. However, to do this, we would need knowledge of the position and velocity of every single molecule in the planet's weather systems. Because this is not infeasible, as weather forecasts are often inaccurate. For the same reason, it is unreasonable to predict the random numbers generated by this website, even for a determinist.

Dan asked Jeremy that since there is disagreement about the appropriateness of chaotic phenomena for creating randomness, why not use only quantum physics? That would seem to be the safe bet. Using the laws of quantum physics would enable the generation of real randomness.

Jeremy told Dan that quantum generators are also being criticized. Nothing is perfect. According to determinists, the behavior of subatomic particles is not really random but rather precisely predetermined, as everything else in the universe has been since the Big Bang. These specific particles seem to behave randomly to us because no human laws or measurements have been able to explain their behavior. This means that subatomic events have a prior basis which is yet to be discovered. It is thus claimed that while subatomic events seem to be random, they are not so, and thus quantum physics is as suitable for random number generation as atmospheric noise or lava lamps [814].

This conundrum also has to do with how one defines randomness.

The random.org website suggests that the most meaningful definition of randomness is that which humans cannot predict. Whether randomness originates from unpredictable weather systems, lava lamps, or subatomic particle events is an academic question. It does not really matter, as long as we cannot predict it. Quantum random number generators produce actual random numbers. If we accept this definition, it means that this type of randomness generation is no different from all other approaches which are based on complex dynamical systems.

Does this mean that we may not need to understand quantum physics in order to achieve randomness?

John Matson describes in his paper published in the Scientific American [815] his view on Antonio Acín, a physicist at the Institute of Photonic Sciences in Spain and author of a paper published in the April 15 issue of Nature, which states that true randomness is elusive [17]. "If we go to a casino and play roulette, or we flip a coin, if we had access to the initial position and speed of the ball or coin, we could predict the result with certainty," he says. "The randomness that we have in our world is because of lack of knowledge." In this study published in Nature, it is claimed that random numbers are difficult to characterize mathematically, and that their generation must rely on an unpredictable physical process. Inaccuracies in the theoretical modeling of such processes or failure of the devices, due to adversarial attacks, limit the reliability of random number generators. Using non-locality and device-independent quantum information processing, it was shown that the non-local correlations of entangled quantum particles could be used to certify the presence of genuine randomness [17].

The answer to all this controversy would be to design a cryptographically secure random number generator that does not require any assumptions about the internal working of the device. Using a system of two entangled atoms separated by approximately one meter, the observed Bell inequality violation, featuring near-perfect detection efficiency, guarantees that 42 new random numbers are generated with 99 percent confidence. This is proof for the association between two fundamental concepts of quantum mechanics—randomness and the non-locality of entangled particles. The violation of a Bell inequality certifies the generation of new randomness, independently of any details of the implementation. This quantum-based real and robust randomness is certified by a Bell inequality violation and is believed to represent true randomness [17]. Quantum physicists claim that true randomness does not exist in classical physics, "where randomness is necessarily a result of forces that may be unknown but exist." The quantum world has an intrinsically true randomness. But this is difficult to prove as it is not much different from noise and other uncontrollable factors.

In quantum physics, the study of large arrays of Josephson junctions benefitted greatly from the chaos theory [386, 425]. So perhaps chaos could contribute to randomness generation. This was something to think about.

Dan was thanking Jeremy and Edna. He had much to think about during the long flight back to New York. One thing that he was sure about was that he needed a vacation. Not a vacation, but a break. The next morning, he bought a ticket to Paris.

# CHAPTER 42
## Dadaism with some constraints

He had two weeks left before his trip to Paris. Both David and Olivia were surprised when he told them. More surprising was the fact that he had not asked Diana to join him. He had, however, told her about his trip to Arizona, and that he had decided to take off for two weeks. His boss had already realized that he might need to look for a replacement. He had worked with Dan for many years, and he understood that it was different this time. His distraction may have begun with the loss of Jenny, but had become more of an issue than just that.

His plane landed early in the morning at Charles de Gaulle airport. He had a few hours to kill, as the check-in time for the small hotel that he had booked was 2 PM. The plane had been full and noisy, and Dan was tired. He was sitting at a small café not far from the hotel. The last time he had been in Paris was almost 15 years ago, when Jenny and he had spent a week doing all the typical touristy things. Jenny loved to follow the guidebooks, so they had spent their time hopping from one place to another. "This time I'm taking it easy," he thought.

The next morning, he was looking at some brochures at the hotel desk and decided to visit The Museum de l'Orangerie, one of the most beautiful museums in the world. It is small, with a unique collection of masterpieces. One of its highlights is Claude Monet's Water Lilies.

In 2017, there had been a unique exhibition about Dadaism in Africa in The Museum de l'Orangerie. Dan got interested.

Dadaism is a European avant garde art movement that started in the early 20th century. Its first few centers were in Zürich, New York, and Paris [816]. Most art experts view it as an anti-constraint movement, the goal of which is to expand boundaries to a point where none exist. Dadaists felt that art should have no boundaries. The movement consisted of artists who rejected the logic, reason, and aestheticism of modern capitalist society. They focused on portraying nonsense, irrationality, and anti-bourgeois protests. [816].

The term anti-art, a precursor to Dada, was coined by Marcel Duchamp to describe works that challenge the accepted definitions of art [817]. Cubism and the development of collage and abstract art would inform the Dada movement's detachment from the constraints of reality and convention. The work of French poets, the Italian Futurists, and the German Expressionists influenced Dada's rejection of the tight correlation between words and meaning [818].

Many Dadaists of the time were of the opinion that the reason and logic of middle-class capitalist society had led people into war. They expressed this in the form of art, which appeared to reject logic and embrace chaos and irrationality [819]. While rejecting reason and logic, Dada prized nonsense, irrationality, and intuition.

By 1924, in Paris, Dada was melding into surrealism, and artists had gone on to other ideas and movements, including social realism and other forms of modernism. Several important retrospectives have examined the influence of Dada on art and society [816]. Some of the Dada artists criticized mainstream painters and artists, claiming that they were narrow-minded. Analyzing art can be difficult, as the same product can be interpreted in many ways. Many who have a first look at these works view them as entirely random. Some think that they are too random to the point that they are worthless.

What if I try looking at these pieces of art not via entirely random glasses, but via the glasses of randomness with some constraints? Randomness within boundaries. Can Dadaism be viewed as randomness with some constraints? Or does this go against the idea of Dadaism?

Kristin Brenneman discusses in *Chance in Art* that "chance must be recognized as a new stimulus to artistic creation" [820]. She claims that the Dadaists embraced chance as an avenue to expression in their works of art. They eventually merged random occurrence with conscious creation, attaining a balance between art and "anti-art." This may seem paradoxical, but it is not a new concept. The attractive character of a random design captivates some and gives others cause for contempt. There are many such forms of modern or abstract art. Many of their viewers question the merits of such nonrepresentational works. If, on the other hand, we are willing to view abstractions, randomized as they may be, as art, we may wish to derive meaning from them. Under such an assumption, we need to explore the methods of modern artists, when they relate to chance [820].

During the eighth century, randomness was already seen in Chinese paintings. These artists stated that they had "intended the unintentional." The teachings of Taoism led some of them to believe that chance images could be better explained as symbols of the artist's harmony with the cosmos.

How does randomness create this so-called harmony with our surroundings? Dan was puzzled.

Kinesthetics played a large part in Oriental calligraphy. These artists would suspend their bodies over their scrolls and mobilize their whole body, collecting momentum which they could then drive through their tools to make designs. However, there was some control. There were controlled actions which result from setting a canvas in front of the body, when only the wrist and arm, hopefully following the brain, actually perform the action of creating art. The motion of the whole was important to these artists of old, and this concept was later visible in the works of the American artist Jackson Pollock in the 20th century [820].

When one looks at modern art, many immediately think of chance. People tend to view abstract art not as a part of more representational, not as one texture among many, but as the image itself. Pollock has been quoted as saying, "when I am in my painting, I'm not aware of what I'm doing. It is only after a sort of 'get acquainted' period that I see what I have been about. I have no fears about making changes, destroying the image, etc., because the painting has a life of its own. I try to let it come through. It is only when I lose contact with the painting that the result is a mess. Otherwise, there is pure harmony, an easy give and take, and the painting comes out well." [821]

Dan thought that this could be translated to chance, randomness, or to some type of control at a higher level. Regardless of any opinion to the contrary, Pollock never intended a "mess." Dan thought, "If it is not a mess, then it is somewhat organized."

Pollock said, "the source of my painting is the unconscious" [822]. For Dan, this did not indicate a mess or pure chance. "I can control the flow of paint; there is no accident, just as there is no beginning and no end" [823]. We may accept the notion that Pollock achieved a state of "letting go," enough to allow his painting to "live for itself," and not enough to let it control him [820].

Matthew Rohn, in his book *Visual Dynamics in Jackson Pollock's Abstractions, Studies in the Fine Arts: Art Theory*, talks about the abstractions made by the artist: "Genuinely random, freely generated strokes of paint would have produced uninteresting, static imagery rather than anything resembling the verve and life of a Pollock." The idea is that an abstract artist cannot be compared to a monkey and his random designs because the animal performs with "no clear visual intent." Though some critics may disagree, he argues that even the human artist's least work will show much more profound imagination than that of a monkey. So randomness and chance cannot be used in the pure sense of the terms under these settings.

How many modern artists does it take to change a light bulb?

Four. One smashes bulbs against the wall, one piles hundreds of bulbs in a heap and spray paints it orange, one glues them to a bull dog, and one fixes it in the socket to light up the room so that the critics and buyers can watch the performance of the other three.

Though Pollock remained a master of his canvas, some aspects of his drip methods contradict his concept of complete control, no matter how much he believed that there was "no accident." [820] We may ask ourselves how he could know whether the paint would form a puddle or how viscous it would be.

What about the random quality of Jackson Pollock's work?

It is claimed that he did vary his method from thoughtful to thoughtless, achieving improvisation in his work [820]. Sometimes he chose where to pour his paint and in what type of stroke; at other times, he relinquished his painting tools to the wiles of the irrational, allowing his body to become automated[824]. Rohn says in his book about Pollock that he controlled his parameters while welcoming "the dynamics of spontaneity and flow."

For Dan, it meant some type of what was now called "controlled randomness."

Let us go back to Dada. Hans Richter, Dadaist and author of *Dada: Art and Anti-Art* [825], says "Chance became our trademark. We followed it like a compass." Henri-Robert-Marcel Duchamp was a French-American painter, sculptor, chess player and writer whose work is associated with Cubism, conceptual art, and Dada [826]. He is not considered by all to be directly associated with Dada groups, but there are some who think of him as the founder of Dadaism in America [820]. Along with Pablo Picasso and Henri Matisse, Duchamp is also considered to be one of the artists who shaped the revolutionary developments in the plastic arts, which resulted in significant changes in the fields of painting and sculpture.

In particular, Duchamp experimented with chance in his work "3 stoppages étalon." Duchamp glibly writes that this work was "a joke about the meter" [827]. However, he presents his basis as a theorem: "If a straight horizontal thread one-meter-long falls from a height of one meter onto a horizontal plane, twisting as it pleases; it creates a new image of that unit of length." To create this work, Duchamp dropped three threads that were one-meter-long from a height of one meter onto three canvases. The threads were tied to one end of their respective canvas to preserve the random curves they assumed upon landing. The canvases were cut along the threads' profiles, creating a template of their curves, and creating new units of measure that retain the length of the meter but undermine its rational basis. For Dan, this was far from "pure randomness" or "pure chance." He felt that Duchamp had planned out the problem and had only "invited chance" to the execution of the plan [820].

Jean Arp was a German-French sculptor, painter, poet, and abstract artist in other media such as torn and pasted paper [828]. He is considered a premier Dadaist. He tore up paper, let it fall from his hands to scatter upon a surface, and then he glued down the design. He discovered what he had unsuccessfully been striving for in his conscious works of art. He considered such chance patterns to be fate's work, correlating this to Dada's premise of the artist trusting in an outside, "mysterious collaborator." Dan thought that this could represent a particular type of randomness, or chance, in the form of an outside mysterious collaborator or pure fate. However, these pieces of paper have meaning, at least in the eyes of some people.

Can we give meaning to randomness? Would it then still be truly random?

Dan was attempting to take it one level above and view it as a something that was far from pure chance. Organized randomness.

Arp was one of the first artists to make randomness and chance part of his artwork. In fact, he viewed chance as a collaborator in his process. This concept is considered to be a turning point in the visual arts. Until that point, Western artists had always striven to achieve a skilled level of control. Rather than starting with a specific topic, as artists had always done, Arp first generated the form and then captioned his works after their completion. He thus sought to minimize any intervention of the conscious mind [829].

Referring to the laws of chance, Arp said, "The law of chance, which embraces all other laws and is as unfathomable to us as the depths from which all life arises, can only be comprehended by complete surrender to the unconscious. Maintain that whoever submits to the law attains perfect life" [820, 830, 831]. The concept of chance and the concepts associated with it have been a part of the artistic debate since the last century [831].

Paul Klee was a German artist who was influenced by art movements such as expressionism, cubism, and surrealism, and abstraction. He worked in isolation from his peers and interpreted new art trends in his own way [832]. At the beginning of Klee's *Pedagogical Sketchbook*, he describes what a line is: "An active line on a walk, moving freely, without a goal is. A walk for a walk's sake. The mobility agent is a point, shifting its position forward" [833, 834]. Is it pure randomness, or pure chance? Is my line going to be different from the one my spouse or neighbor will draw? Is my line expected to be different under new circumstances? Klee claimed that a line might have no goal. But if I draw a line, I may have had to relinquish its purpose, just because as a human being I couldn't avoid thinking about the role of the line [820]. Kristin Brenneman concludes that Klee had a value of chance in his artwork, yet his status of control over each piece cannot be ignored.

Many of the artists who were part of Dadaism or abstraction viewed randomness as a creative ideal. Perhaps chance itself in the general sense, cannot constitute art, but these abstractionists verify that they used it to the benefit of their art. They allowed fate or chance to take its course, often instead of using their minds to plan out a pattern. They formulated no rules because that would defy chance.

Is it really pure randomness in the symbolic sense? Dan was sure that this pure randomness is controlled, whether or not we admit it. He then came up with the term "sophisticated randomness." He knew that pure randomness could never be controlled. But can I take it to a higher level and make it more sophisticated in a way that we can use it for making something, a human being or anything, better?

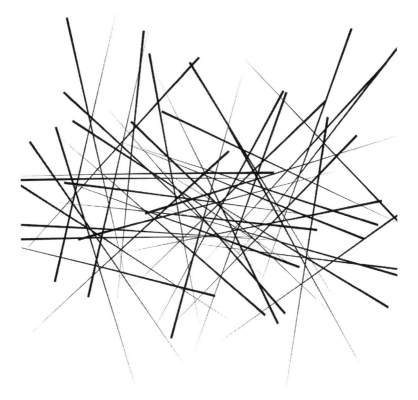

# CHAPTER 43
## Formulating chance

Dan was sitting in his hotel room and asking himself whether "sophisticated randomness" can be defined as randomness that can be controlled. Could there be a formula for this type of randomness? Can chance meet a formula? [820]. He was looking at an example of how randomness, when properly modelled, could be used to our benefit.

Coal mines are dangerous places where frequent natural gas leaks cause many deaths. Until recently, there was no reliable way to predict when they would occur. But these gas leaks have chaotic tendencies that, when correctly modeled, can be predicted with reasonable accuracy.

The term "stochastic" refers to something that was randomly determined[835]. Stochastic processes and random processes are considered interchangeable [73]. Stochastic processes can be found in almost every field including biology, chemistry, ecology, neuroscience, physics, technology, engineering, image processing, signal processing, information theory, computer science, cryptography, telecommunications, and financial markets [48].

The definition of a stochastic process as one with a "sequence which combines random components with a selective process so that only certain outcomes of the random are allowed to endure," [820] is not be accepted by all mathematicians. But Dan already realized that these terms are sometimes used more symbolically.

Chance may be counter to most people's conceptions of real art. It seems to not require skills. Many do not look at randomness in art as real creativity. We are likely to hear this comment at every modern art museum: "My 5-year-old can do it." Dan was thinking of the torn pieces of paper Jean Arp saw on his floor. They appeared in an array he never would have chosen, though captivating nonetheless.

Michael Eckersley, who leads a design research and innovation center at The University of Kansas, wrote *Randomness, Rules and Compositional Structure in Design* [836]: in this book, he states, "random graphical arrays, almost without exception, exhibit striking examples of dynamic asymmetry; localized sections of large arrays can be isolated and appreciated as powerful compositions...The design process can be viewed as a cybernetic machine in which the rules define the capabilities of the machine, randomness provides the input, and the design product is the output" [836, 837]. Dan noticed that the words "randomness" and "rules" appeared together in the same sentence. Randomness can create exciting and beautiful compositions. But does it adhere to rules once they are set by the human mind?

For Pollock, it was the creator who controls while chance gives distinct, ultimate life to the image [820]. So, can randomness have rules?

Fred Lawrence Whipple published an article on stochastic paintings [838]. His idea was to formulate a set of rules for this type of art. In his introduction, he wrote, "Stochastic paintings are those in which shapes and/or colors are structured randomly. The reader immediately asks why? Can there be any creativity or self-expression in random processes? Can there be any beauty, charm, or interest in a painting that is not planned or organized and does not spring from some internal need for expression or communication on the part of the one who paints it?" [839] [840]. Whipple's position was that there must be rules for the chance: "A stochastic painting must be based on a set of rules governing the nature of the randomness. Establishing a set of rules is a creative process and, of course, the actual application of the colors is a type of expression in texture, shading or structuring of the application. In painting or coloring in shapes chosen by randomization, a human hand applies the colors or shading; thus, stochastic painting does involve creativity and self-expression, although not of the classical type" [839].

"Random processes can produce form and pattern, although not repetitive. Most people confuse irregularity with randomness, which are different concepts, although related. Out of an aggregate of random numbers, random colors, or random distributions of colors, there is a high probability of structured patterns, which do not repeat but may be conspicuous. The monkeys with the typewriters will indeed compose poems, even though one must look over considerable manuscripts to find them" [839].

To elaborate, a random design may very well display some regularity, though it goes against our notion of chance as something that happens without cause. A regular pattern is just as likely to occur as an irregular one. The probability of the sequence *HTHTHTHTHT* is the same as that of the sequence *HTTHTHHHTT*, even though the latter may seem "more random." It seems that we all believe in certain myths about chance that are difficult to ignore [820].

"Random numbers by means of rules can produce forms and color distributions. The question of beauty arises next...If to be beautiful, a painting must express feelings, moods or ideas, or communicate them; then stochastic paintings cannot be beautiful. If these traditional assumptions are discarded...then stochastic painting may be 'charming, attractive, beautiful, and ugly' according to diverse viewers. If the purpose of a painting is only to produce an emotional response in the viewer, then stochastic paintings qualify along with many other modern efforts." [839]

Whipple also offers a more philosophical view: "Is nature, is a planet, or is the man himself anything more than the consequence of a set of physical rules carried out by random processes in the physical universe?"

Whipple proposes a set of rules which can be followed to create a random design for these types of "chance paintings": (1) The first step is to write down random number pairs. (2) In the next step, the first pair should be used as the *x* and *y* values on a canvas coordinate system and be used to determine the starting point. (3) The first of the second number pair, taken as a decimal of 360°, provides the direction from the starting point, and the second number multiplied by a unit distance (for example, a centimeter or half an inch) provides the distance from the starting point in this direction. (4) From the end of the first line, the first number of the third number pair represents the distance, and the second number multiplied by 15 indicates the angle in the counterclockwise direction from the tip of the previous line. (4) Successive lines are developed by successive number pairs from the ends of the previous lines or from the outer sides of the closed areas. (5) We now must have a rule for closing the areas and so on.

Whipple suggested that creating such rules is art.

Dan felt that as human beings who have the capability of reasoning and discerning, we want to find patterns in everything.

Stephen Jay Gould was an American paleontologist, evolutionary biologist, and historian of science [841]. In his book Triumph and Tragedy in Mudville: A Lifelong Passion for Baseball [842], he attempts to explain how it is human nature to try and find a pattern in everything we see. In his essay about Joe DiMaggio's hitting streak, Gould explained why the human brain often finds it difficult to understand the scientific data of a random universe: "We see a pattern, for pattern surely exists, even in a purely random world...We think we see constellations because the stars are dispersed at random in the heavens, and therefore clump in our sight...Our error lies not in the perception of the pattern but in automatically imbuing pattern with the meaning" [843]. We see a "constellation" in the first ten tosses of a coin, though its stars are just as randomly placed as those of the second. What the eye finds pleasing is not always planned. A pattern pleases the eye, and even if a creator/artist has planned no pattern, the eye will find one [820].

Kristin Brenneman discusses in *Chance in Art* how she followed Whipple's rules: "I experimented with a simpler method of randomizing color for a static set of shapes, small squares as part of a larger square. I was thinking of Mondrian's color block paintings, and I, in fact, achieved something very similar. I controlled virtually everything but the colors" [820].

For Dan, this seemed to be proof that there may be rules for chance. "This proves one extreme of chance in art: the work is hardly random at all." [820]

Brenneman continues, "using True Basic programs to create very random designs with line and color, I ran this program over 30 times and noticed that within each separate run, the most common area to fill was the background. Often it would change colors many times before anyone space inside the figure would be colored...I replaced those equations with 'and,' and I started the program with 'randomize,' and I discovered the resulting designs to be random and intriguing. I found the work of David Bomberg, an English painter to look very similar."

So, if we give a set of rules to a computer, will it produce abstract art? Would it be different from that produced by an artist? A computer cannot think in the broader meaning of the word. It can only follow rules that we program into it. A human mind, through the controls of the program, can instruct a computer on how to randomize an image.

Randomness holds much power in this world [820]. Chance holds power in the world of art.

For Dan, randomness was power and creativity. He started looking into examples of how it can be used. His short art course in Paris was about to finish. He would soon head back to the airport and home.

# CHAPTER 44

## Randomization is saving lives. Have a safe flight

Dan did not believe in accidental events. But while waiting for his plane, he came across studies about airport security.

As a result of limited security resources, full security coverage is not possible at all times. This means that adversaries can observe patrol and other security patterns and use the information to plan an attack. Using randomized security patrols is one method to make this more difficult for such parties. However, getting humans to generate random security protocols has drawbacks because humans are not good at generating true randomness. All of us can quickly fall into the trap of generating predictable patterns [844, 845]. Game theories are currently being used for developing models and solution algorithms to determine randomization strategies. Game theory is a well-established paradigm for reasoning about situations with multiple self-interested decision makers [846]. Models based on game theory have been used in a variety of homeland security settings, such as protecting critical infrastructure [847, 848].

The Stackelberg leadership model is a strategic game in economics in which the leader firm moves first, and then the follower firms move sequentially. This model was first described by the German economist Stackelberg, who wrote about it in his book *Market Structure and Equilibrium* (Marktform und Gleichgewicht) in 1934 [849, 850]. In game theory terms, the players take on the role of a leader and a follower who are in competition with each other. The goal is to sustain the Stackelberg equilibrium. The rules are that the leader must know that the follower observes their actions, the follower must have no means of committing to a future non-Stackelberg follower action, and the leader must be aware of this. In fact, if there was a chance for the follower to commit to a Stackelberg leader action and the leader was aware of this, the leader's best response would be to play a Stackelberg follower action. It is also important that the leader have commitment power. Moving observably first is the most obvious means of commitment. Once the leader has made a move, it cannot be undone and the leader must stay committed to that action. A leader can move first if they have incumbent monopoly of the industry and the follower is a new entrant. Having excess capacity is another means of commitment [849]. Games are a simplified way of representing strategic interactions among multiple players. The goal of each player in such games is to maximize their own utility function. Hence, the aim is always to reach an equilibrium solution. This calls for a joint strategy, where no agent has an incentive to deviate. [851]

Security problems have been studied using game-theoretic analysis, from computer network security to terrorism [852, 853]. Several applications have been designed to assist security forces in randomizing their operations based on fast algorithms for solving large instances of Bayesian Stackelberg games [854]. Also, several software programs designed for the randomization of security patrols are based on Stackelberg games between the defender, the security forces, and the attacker, usually a terrorist adversary [854]. These games gauge the ability of an attacker to gather information about the defense strategy before planning an attack. These theories specify different payoff values for both players in the event of an attack on every potential target. By extending these games to Bayesian Stackelberg games, uncertainty about the payoffs can be captured in the game model. Solutions to these games can provide a randomized policy for defense strategies, which can be used to schedule security patrols.

The ARMOR system, Assistant for Randomized Monitoring over Routes has been successfully set up at Los Angeles International Airport (LAX). It is used by airport police to randomize the placement of checkpoints on roads leading to the airport and the routes of canine unit patrols at the airport terminals. Another example is the Intelligent Randomization in Scheduling or IRIS system, which is designed to randomize flight schedules for the

Federal Air Marshals Service (FAMS). IRIS has been used in a pilot program by the Federal Air Marshals Service to randomize the schedules of air marshals on international flights [854]. Both these systems are based on Stackelberg game models that weight the randomized schedules and use efficient mixed-integer programming formulations of models to enable solutions for massive games. These systems allow for interactive manipulations of the domain constraints and parameters by the users [854]. Real randomization is crucial to their success. However, relatively simple programming may be sufficient for achieving the level of randomization that is required. For many purposes, a somewhat lower, although high enough level of randomization may be sufficient for achieving the aim of randomization.

A guard and a janitor were having a conversation about their jobs.

*Guard:* The problem with our job, buddy, we keep on removing the dirt, and yet others keep putting it back..
*Janitor:* Sure, pal, but if there wasn't any dirt, I would be jobless. But our job is more onerous, we search and search for it, and people out there keep on hiding it.
*Guard:* Oh, that's OK. If there were no prohibited items, I would also be jobless.

A critical question in randomizing security operations is how different actions should be weighted. One obvious approach is to "roll the dice" efficiently using a consistent random strategy where all possible targets or entry points are treated the same. However, this method fails to take into account that some targets are more attractive or vulnerable than others. As a result, valuable security resources are under-utilized for relatively unimportant targets. This is why even a simple randomization problem becomes more complicated than it seems at first glance.

Another complicating factor is that some of the methods provide a randomization strategy for the defender but do not take into account the fact that the adversaries can make adjustments according to the observed actions. This can be countered by using methods based on learning, Markov Decision Processes (MDPs) and Partially Observable Markov Decision Processes(POMDPs) [855].

The Hypercube Queueing Model is based on the queueing theory and shows the detailed spatial operation of urban police departments and emergency medical services. This model does not consider the possibility that an intelligent attacker will observe and exploit patterns in security policy. Further, if the policy is based on a history of previous attacks, it is mostly a reactive policy that can easily be cracked by an intelligent attacker [854, 856].

Stackelberg games have also been used for screening visitors entering the U.S. The U.S. government leads the process, and specifies the biometric identification strategy to maximize detection probability with finger print matches. The follower is the terrorist, who can manipulate the image quality of the fingerprint [857]. Similar models have been developed for border patrol strategies, too. [858]

A more efficient version of the Stackelberg games better suited to complex real-world situations has been proposed. This model incorporates domain limitations, such as scheduling constraints, for better applying randomization to everyday life situations [854].

In a security game model, a defender must continually defend the site, whereas the attacker is able to observe the defender's strategy and attack when success seems most likely. This fits into a Stackelberg game model if the attackers assume the follower's role and the defender assumes the leader's role [847]. The defender has many possible resources to schedule in the security policy. This may end with a combinatorial explosion in a standard normal-form representation. If a leader has $x$ resources to defend $y$ entities, there are many options in terms of how the resources can be allocated. Consider the entities or targets to be defended as flights, and the resources as federal air marshals. Each target is associated with payoffs that define the possible outcomes of an attack. The payoffs depend only on whether the target is attacked and whether the target is covered by the defender. The payoffs do not depend on other scheduling aspects, such as whether any non-attacked target is covered or which specific defense resource provides coverage [854].

Both the LA airport and Federal Air Marshals Service are security scenarios which have a leader/follower dynamic between security forces and terrorist adversaries. Both are concerned about surveillance and insider threats. In both cases, the resources available are limited, so it is not possible to provide complete coverage [854].

In the case of LAX, airport police have designed a security system based on the concept of multiple rings of protection. These rings include vehicular checkpoints, police units patrolling the roads to the terminals, patrolling inside the terminals with canines, security screening and bag checks for passengers. As there are resource limitations on the vehicle checkpoints and canine units, randomization is used to increase the effectiveness of these resources while avoiding patterns in the schedule. The different terminals at the airport have varying physical size, passenger loads, and levels of foot traffic, all of which contribute to the assessments used in creating a security policy. Models are used for developing optimal coverage probabilities for each target. By sampling according to these probabilities, one can obtain an exact schedule for the security forces. The models need to allow enough flexibility to regularly change the input parameters [854].

Game-theoretic randomization that appropriately weighs the costs and benefits of different actions and randomizes with appropriate weights can improve the efficiency of such security models. Instead of asking people to make numerous and unnecessary changes, computerized programs can minimize complexities. Comparing the random schedules generated using these game theory-based methods against a uniform random policy, which is the most obvious alternative for randomization, shows that the former has many advantages. According to the uniform random policy, each defender action has an equal probability regardless of payoff. Solution quality is measured by calculating the highest expected payoff attainable by the defender, based on the assumption of a strong Stackelberg equilibrium that the attacker chooses an optimal response and breaks ties in favor of the defender. Using the data from LAX, with the uniform random strategy, canines would be randomly assigned to terminals with equal probability. Software-based randomization with even fewer resources provides better results than uniformly random strategies in the same domain with more resources [854].

With simple pattern recognition techniques, an attacker can easily figure out the cyclic and restricted uniform strategies. These patterns can be avoided with the use of uniformly random strategies. But a uniform random strategy does not take into account the preferences of the defender with regard to the targets. ARMOR provides weights for the different targets such that the average defender reward is the highest when compared to both "cyclic" and "restricted uniform" strategies. ARMOR strategies are not just weighted random strategies; they also account for the fact that the adversary observes the defender's strategy and then makes an informed, rational choice.

"Ladies and gentlemen thank you for flying *xyz* airlines. We hope you enjoyed our flight as much as we enjoyed taking your money. Please remember to take all your belongings. Anything that is left behind will be distributed fairly among crew members. Have a safe flight."

The plane was taking off.

Mass Rapid Transit using rail is a favorite mode of transport employed by millions of people in most big cities across the world. These are popular targets for criminals. Randomized patrols are being used to improve the security of such rail networks. Stackelberg game theories were used to provide an approach called RaPtoR for computing randomized strategies in patrol teams, which guarantee a strong Stackelberg equilibrium and are optimized in terms of distance traveled by the patrols, despite scheduling constraints. [851]

Models for the probabilities of attacks on train stations have been prepared based on various parameters obtained from geographical information, criminology analysis, and intelligence sources [859]. The integer linear program was developed by employing new inequalities and calculating tighter linear program relaxation bounds, thereby improving the computation performance. The concept was to maximize the coverage of most crowded stations at the most populated hours and minimize the total distance traveled by patrol teams. The schedules were determined automatically and optimally by using the integer linear program. There are certain limitations to this approach however. Firstly, the optimal schedule generated is deterministic. Secondly, the scalability of the model is limited. Applying it to more stations resulted in several problems. This led to the employment of the Stackelberg representation and the new approach, the RaPtoR or Randomized Patrols for Rail networks algorithm [851], [860] .

RaPtoR is divided into two phases: In Phase 1, coverage distributions are computed based on a strong Stackelberg equilibrium, for each decision made for all the targets. In Phase 2, the execution plans for individual patrolling groups over the entire distance are executed based on the coverage samples generated from the coverage distributions in Phase 1. Connecting the equilibrium coverage strategies of each decision can help generate execution plans and increase scalability [851]. When this model was applied to Singapore train stations, it was not found to be optimal, but it retained a beautiful property of the optimal algorithm. As more resources were provided, the phase 2 algorithm was able to find better execution plans with respect to distance traveled by the patrols [851].

Dan was falling asleep during the flight. "Randomization is taking good care of me," he thought to himself, laughing.

# CHAPTER 45
## Randomization can prevent disasters

Back home, he made the final decision to quit work.

His boss was very understanding about it, and the team gave him a lovely going-away party at a nearby bar.

This was the first time that Dan felt entirely sure that randomness is beneficial.

In his paper "Big Data, Social and Behavioral Sciences, and National Security," Fred S. Roberts discusses how the age of big data has revolutionized the social and behavioral sciences, and how it is now possible to derive conclusions from information in ways that were hitherto thought to be impossible [861]. Dan remembered his discussions with Olivia, who had told him that her company was trying to solve the aging problem by using big data. "Big data is gradually becoming our big brother," she said.

Can big data be combined with randomization?

The theory of decision-making is based on methods developed in the social sciences. According to this theory, we all have enormous amounts of information, occasionally too much…and are often required to make decisions based on it. New technologies, all the information available on search engines like Google, the significant number of data sources, and the sharing of information from various sources, are all available to us and can be used very quickly nowadays. But do they always lead to better decisions?

Traditional social science tools based on the decision theory are often found to be inadequate in this new big data age. However, the new tools that have been developed based on the decision theory also have their limitations, especially when it comes to matters of national security, which presents complex new challenges. Despite the availability of significantly large quantities of data, the data itself is often incomplete, unreliable, unevenly distributed, or uncertain. Sometimes, it is difficult to see the whole picture on the basis of too many pieces of information. We now have at our disposal multiple sources of data which we need to merge to make a decision. There are a few efficient algorithms available to support decisions under these settings, and these are based on algorithmic decision theory [862].

With the growing amount of data and the high speed with which decisions need to be made, it is often necessary to make choices according to feedback from earlier decisions before we can access all the relevant data. Such consecutive decisions arise in scenarios where the outcome of one examination is used to determine which inspections should be carried out next. Sequential decision-making processes require a different type of modeling, and the traditionally used algorithms are not sufficient [861].

Roberts talks about a decision algorithm for inspecting containers at a port, which classifies containers using a Boolean decision function [863, 864]. What about protecting critical infrastructure such as electric power stations? This requires decisions about design, operation, and repair of grid systems [865]. The limitations of the algorithmic decision theory in terms of the management and control of such networks include the scale of the problem, inherent uncertainties in monitoring its stability, and the potential to cause cascading blackouts. Algorithms in such contexts would need to combine multiple data streams into forms suitable for action and human interpretation, quantify and balance the risk of acting on insufficient information against delay in the action to get more data, and determine when it is advisable to "break" the network and isolate instability to avoid cascading failures [861].

Dan remembered a story he had once heard.

A chemist, a biologist, and an electrical engineer had all been sentenced to execution by electric chair.

The day of their sentence arrived. The chemist was first in line. As he strapped the chemist in, the executioner asked him, "Do we have anything we want to say?"

The chemist replied, "No." So the executioner flicked the switch, but nothing happened. According to the law of the State, if an execution attempt fails, the prisoner has to be released. So the chemist was unstrapped and allowed to walk free.

It was the biologist's turn next.

As he was being strapped in, the executioner asked him, "Do we have anything we want to say?"

The biologist replied, "No, just get on with it." So the executioner flicked the switch, but once again, nothing happened. So, just like the chemist, the biologist was released.

Finally, the electrical engineer was brought forward.

The executioner asked him, "Do we have anything we want to say?"

The engineer replied, "Yes. If we swap the red and the blue wires over, we might just make this thing work."

Classical work in game theory provides some rich equilibrium concepts [866]. Scaling up of game theory concepts to large complex systems requires methods for computing the solution to a game with a massive and changing number of players [867, 868]. A player might use early rounds to learn about an opponent's strategy. In the same way, a terrorist might spend early "rounds" observing. Repeated rounds allow players to modify their strategies based on the results of earlier rounds. This is a standard approach in today's transnational criminal organizations. Some of these methods even challenge the basic notions of rationality [869]. Studies in behavioral economics have shown that human subjects frequently deviate from traditionally accepted notions of self-interest and greed [870]. They seem to do this in ways which are predictable, repeatable, and amenable to mathematical modeling and analysis. The notion that everything we think and do can be predicted by a computer is frustrating and even quite alarming. Interestingly, it's being revealed that even concepts such as altruism, revenge, and envy can be quantified and measured [869, 871].

The Ebola outbreak in West Africa in 2014 showed us that the world is not prepared for epidemics on such a large scale. Infectious diseases seem to emerge and re-emerge more frequently and spread over greater distances. They even seem to be passing more easily between humans and animals and evolving into more virulent strains. Some of the reasons for this are increased disease risk, global connections via transportation, and increases in migration, tourism, and trade. Analysis of the Ebola outbreak provided an understanding of the role of funeral practices, hospitals, social contact, and population mobility in the spread of epidemics [865]. Using mathematical conceptualizations about the interplay between economics, human behavior, and disease ecology can improve our understanding of the emergence, persistence, and spread of infectious agents [872]. Models based on such conceptualizations can help in making decisions about health interventions and public policies. Models of the spread of disease require analysis of both group and individual behaviors. They should also consider the cost and impact of alternative disease treatment strategies and the allocation of resources for prevention and treatment strategies [861].

A challenge of growing importance in the field of homeland security is the radicalization of individuals outside of terrorist groups. Many models are based on the characteristics of people who are vulnerable to violent ideologies, the structural and social characteristics of systems that enable such spread, and the impact of the extreme behavior of terrorist groups on vulnerable populations [873]. Models for responsible behavior in the face of both natural and man-made disasters assume a fixed social landscape with passive bystanders and rational actors who comply with authorities. Past examples suggest that episodes of mass panic or hysteria are rare and localized, while actions based on perceived self-interest, evacuation, queries from the worried-well, antibiotic stockpiling, are widespread. Acts of spontaneous altruism and mutual aid, criminal opportunism, and civil disruption are also known to occur [861].

Dan gave it another thought: Things that look random may actually be predictable.

He was reading about studies which have shown that people follow typical sequences when communicating in emergency situations. One of them was a study of Hurricane Sandy that analyzed 6.5 million geo-tagged Twitter posts. Community resilience in the face of natural disasters is important. Anecdotal evidence indicates that the sharp rise in social media complaints/ emergency calls lasts for a shorter time once community training is provided, as it improves community resilience [874, 875]. However, the responses of different groups are diverse, and social behavior varies among cultures.

Roberts talks about the 2015 Paris attacks, following which security professionals placed increased emphasis on making decision-making more difficult for terrorists, and specifically using randomization techniques for this purpose. The purpose of randomization methods in national security strategies is to confuse the enemy, make them work harder to understand defensive tactics, and make attacks more expensive and risky. [861] When secondary inspection resources are limited, randomization can provide increased security. The 2015 and 2017 attacks on the Stade de France and the Manchester Arena were a warning about the vulnerability of stadiums and other public arenas. Since then, randomization has been described as the "best practice" for many aspects of stadium security [876].

Can safety strategies that employ randomization be run by robots?

Robot teams have been used for daily patrol tasks in which the robots are required to repeatedly visit a target area based on the point-visit frequency criterion in order to detect any penetration [877] . The aim of such models is to maximize the robots' chance of detecting penetrations in the patrol area [878]. The efficiency of the patrol strategy remains the same for any number of penetration attempts. However, the robots do not change their behavior once penetration is detected. Another limitation is that requiring the robots to inspect penetration attempts physically has consequences on the performance of the patrol algorithm. It creates vulnerability points along the patrol path that a knowledgeable adversary can take advantage of.

What about coordinated attacks, in which the adversary initiates two attacks in order to maximize its chances of successful penetration, assuming a robot from the team will be sent to examine the first penetration attempt? In realistic settings, the robot that detects the penetration has to handle it as well, for example, by confining the penetrator or examining the penetration using additional sensors. Thus, the penetrations will necessarily influence the remaining team's ability to handle the task, which makes the patrolling team more vulnerable to coordinated attacks. When the adversary initiates a coordinated attack, it will try to penetrate one location, and then try to penetrate again through vulnerable points generated by the handling of the first penetration. This means that it is necessary to create an algorithm that can compute the optimal robot strategy for handling such attacks. Despite its exponential time complexity, the reasonable runtime of the algorithm can be significantly reduced without harming the optimality of the strategy [877].

One of the difficulties in devising robot strategies is that one needs to compute specific strategies for each agent. This is in contrast to the constant phase where all agents follow the same strategy. In addition, there are vulnerability points of the patrolling robots. A recent study proposed an algorithm for the optimal patrol strategy for robots based on a probability distribution over all the possible paths for each robot [877, 878].

The game-theoretic domain can be applied to a single robot in the patrol, but it would formulate their problems as non-linear optimization problems [879]. Alternatively, modeling the problem as a Stackelberg game can also help formulate strategies. Another proposed method was to represent an exponential number of paths for patrol [880]. Removal of robots due to failure requires the rest of the robots to adjust to the new state with one less robot as quickly and efficiently as possible, by adopting a deterministic behavior [881]. Patrol algorithms require the robots to be spread out uniformly. Phase I is the steady-state prior to the extraction of the robot for handling the penetration; Phase II is the reorganization phase, where the team's composition changes from several patrolling robots to one less; and Phase III is the steady-state of patrolling with one robot less. When a robot is extracted from the team to handle the first penetration, the remaining robots need to be organized uniformly around to achieve optimal behavior, while the extracted robot remains close to the location of the initial penetration [877, 882]. A naive approach would be for each robot to assume its final position and wait for the reorganization phase to end, thus minimizing the time required for reorganization. But such an approach would create vulnerability points, as there are segments that will not be covered at points in time. A knowledgeable adversary would be able to easily penetrate the weak points.

So even if we have an army of robots, we would need a good and reliable randomization algorithm to make the most out of them.

# CHAPTER 46
## Managing randomness

Dan realized that randomness, chance, and luck influence our lives and our work more than we realize. He was reading *Fooled by Randomness: The Hidden Role of Chance in Life and in the Markets* by Nassim Nicholas Taleb, which deals with the unreliability of human knowledge [883, 884]. Taleb proposes the idea that we are often unaware of the existence of randomness, as random outcomes are often described as non-random. If this is so, it means that we are misled by our unawareness, and that we overestimate causality. A typical example is how we look at randomly shaped clouds and see animals and other forms. In other words, we tend to look at the world as more explainable than it really is, and we try to look for explanations even when there are none. To avoid this tendency, we need to accept that some things are random and need to be accepted as such.

Not having any work obligations felt weird to Dan. But it gave him more time. Somehow, he found himself even busier. He did not have to take the train every morning, but was reading and thinking much more. Diana told him that they should meet more often, now that he was freer. "We only live once, and God knows how many years we have left," she was telling him. Dan was not bothered by this thought. For him, every day was just one more day, and not the last day of his life that he needed to make the most out of.

Diana had also read Taleb's book. She told Dan she was not really into it, and that while there were many people who liked it, there were also many others who were critical of the idea [885] [886].

Of the several "misunderstandings" about randomness which Taleb discusses, some are described as "apparent traps" that many of us fall into. For example, survivorship bias occurs when we look at a few winners and try to learn from them while forgetting about the vast number of losers. Another common misunderstanding is how we treat real-life phenomena as 50:50 bets (akin to tossing a coin), when in actually they exhibit various unusual and counter-intuitive distributions. For instance, in a 99:1 bet, we almost always win, but when we lose, we lose all our savings [883, 884]. Because of hindsight bias also known as the knew-it-all-along effect, which is an inclination, after an event has occurred, to see the event as having been predictable, despite the lack of any objective basis for predicting it. There is also survivorship bias, where we forget the many who fail, remember the few who succeed, and create reasons and patterns for their success even though it is mostly random. Mild success can be explainable by skills and hard work, but any wild success is usually attributable to variance and luck too [887]. "Remember that nobody accepts randomness in his own success, only his failure."

The James Clear site shares some of the ideas from Taleb's book [887]. Taleb claims that we are inherently flawed, and that our cognitive biases are a result of how our brains function and the way we are naturally built. Sometimes, these biases are useful to us. There are many biases that we all need to deal with. Many of us grasp the first piece of information we get and build a general theory around it. This is the anchoring bias. For most of us, our brain will use the last experience we've had to force conclusions on other events. This is called a reservation bias. We reach a point where our mind is already equipped with certain stereotypes about the how to behave. In many cases, we just try to match or enforce our pre-programmed stereotypes on whatever we have in front of us. This is known as a reference bias. The problem is that even if we know about randomness and cognitive biases, most of us are just as likely to fall victim to them.

Taleb also talks about randomization in the markets. We are quickly fooled by statements like "I won this bet 50 times." In relation to this, he says that "option sellers eat like chickens and go to the bathroom like elephants." This means that while they do stand to earn a steady but small income from selling options, they also stand to lose a fortune in the face of disaster.

It is claimed that we cannot look at the odds of something happening and be able to correctly estimate the payoff we would receive if it works and the price we would have to pay if it fails. A bet on something improbable can be smart if the payoff is enormous, but we also need to have rules to limit the many small losses that are likely. Minor stalemates in life can be solved by selecting randomly. In many cases, it doesn't matter as long as we choose something and move forward [887].

When we encounter randomness, how do we make sure that it is indeed random?

Diana was reading to him from "four-minute books" [888]. According to the analysis of the book by Taleb, our life is non-linear, which makes the rewards of continued effort disproportionately big. This means that life isn't fair, because many of the systems in our life behave in a linear fashion. With every day at work, we get closer to the next promotion. We hope that with every exam in school, we get closer to graduation. We hope that with every dollar we put into our retirement plan, we get closer to being able to retire with the same lifestyle. The events of our everyday life seem to show us that things are all linear. The problem is that they are not so. At least not all of them.

Darwin's rule of "survival of the fittest" means that the best-adapted organisms will survive on average. However, that doesn't stop unfit organisms from surviving, at least in the short run [888]. According to this theory, if life was non-linear, we would not end up with the same results if we were to start over. There are many tipping points which are hard for us to see in advance. Our intuitive feeling is that incremental changes only have an incremental impact. But one grain of sand can bring down an entire sand castle, and that one extra blog post, one extra day in the lab, one extra phone call can lead to vast rewards in a short time. This shows that the size of rewards is not always in balance with ongoing efforts. But because progress on the extra mile is not clearly visible, most of us give up too early, as we do not see the extra mile.

Diana was making a point. She was getting into randomness. The important point as she saw it, was that "although it is more random than we think, not all of it is random." Chance favors alertness, but it is not caused by preparedness [888A]. Unlike Diana, Dan was more focused on our ability to use randomness, and also ways of creating randomness. Both of them realized that they might be onto something important.

Dan had developed a habit of writing down his thoughts and maintaining them in a file on his computer. In the case of most of them, it took him a few months, or sometimes several years, to realize that there was nothing significant in them. These realizations usually made him feel that he was not as smart as he thought himself to be. Several times, it had happened after reading or listening to someone say the same thing. But the idea of creating useful randomness seemed different. The fact that even Diana, who came from an entirely different background, was saying that we can make ourselves "ready for randomness," made Dan think that this might be one of his most viable ideas of all time.

One of the take-home messages from Taleb's book is that we need to make decisions based on our irrational emotions [888]. Emotions are "lubricants of reason." To make decisions, we need to "feel." Emotions energize us to think and are important for our day-to-day life. It is important that we do not analyze everything based on perfect logic, in the manner of a robot [887]. However, we tend to consider the risk of specific occurrences to be greater than general risks: for example, we consider the risk of dying in a terrorist attack while traveling to be greater than the risk of dying on our next trip, even though the second is inclusive of the first. Intuitively, however, we overvalue those things which trigger an emotional response and undervalue the things that aren't as emotional. We are being thought to use rationality for making decisions, but it is claimed that without our irrational emotions we are unable to make decisions at all. We need irrationality. If we were to make every single one of our decisions based on rational reasoning, we would cease to exist. We also need to understand that some choices are indifferent: neither outcome will leave us better or worse off. A common example used is this context is that of a donkey that is equally hungry and thirsty and is placed between a stack of hay and a bucket of water, at a point that is equally distant from both. The tendency of a donkey is to reach for whatever is nearest to him, but because they are equidistant, he's just as hungry as he is thirsty and would starve to death as a consequence.

Making a purely rational decision is sometimes impossible. In such cases, a little irrationality or randomness can help us make up our minds. **Our emotions are the metaphorical coin flip in this regard**, which get us to stop deliberating. The idea is to just decide and move on. Our emotions serve a critical purpose in our decision-making process [888]. The problem is that our emotions can also lead to us behaving irrationally in situations where we really need to use logic and reason.

Both Diana and Dan accepted the notion that in life we need to use both. The solution is to enjoy randomness when it is harmless and use stoicism to deflect it when it's harmful. The problem is that we do not always know when and how to differentiate and how to "use and enjoy" randomness. Taleb attempts to help us eliminate and deal better with the randomness in our lives. He also says that "randomness can be beautiful when it's harmless." We should let ourselves be fooled by it, but only by the right kind.

To deal with the wrong kind of randomness, Taleb suggests we take on a stoic attitude. When life deals us one of those unexpected, random, horrifying blows, stoicism should be our weapon of choice, without self-pity, laying blame on others, complaining and taking responsibility [888]. The only entity that we have complete control over that can never be subject to randomness is, after all, our own behavior. The only aspect of our life that fortune does not have control over is our behavior.

So how do we overcome the biases associated with randomness? We need tricks. We are just animals, and we need to restructure our environment to control our emotions in a smart way. "Most of us know pretty much how we should behave. It is the execution that is the problem, not the absence of knowledge."

"Things that happen with little help from luck are more resistant to randomness." Repetitiveness is critical for determining if we see skill or randomness at play [887]. Randomness means there are some strategies that work well for any given cycle, but these cycles often lead to short- to medium-term success. More importantly, the strategies that work for a given cycle in the short term may not be the best in the long run. They are suboptimal strategies for winning a randomly beneficial short-term cycle, but they are unsustainable and suboptimal for the long term. Thus, suboptimal strategies and traits seem desirable in the short run even though they will be resoundingly defeated in the long run [887].

Much of what seems to be random is actually based on timing. Therefore, the best method for success for a particular period is often not the best one overall. Also, specific phases of a given cycle may carry more risk than others, and some trading strategies might be more fruitful than others. If we find ourselves doing something extraordinarily well in a random situation, then we should keep doing what we do while trying to limit our risks. While trying to reap the benefits of randomness, we need to protect ourselves from random adverse events too.

Dan was sure that randomness can be helpful if we learn to use it for our benefit. His mantra for this was to "enjoy randomness when it's harmless and use stoicism to deflect it when it's harmful." However, he did want to take it one step further. His next goal was to learn how to prepare himself for randomness or to program randomness in a way that works in our favor.

He knew that Diana, not being into physics, would not be able to understand this. For her, the preparation part was all about her emotions.

# CHAPTER 47
## Turning to our brain in times of uncertainty

Diana met Dan the next morning with the book *The Social Animal: The Hidden Sources of Love, Character, and Achievement*, in which New York Times columnist David Brooks talks about our brains and success [889]. It reveals some of the social aspects of our minds and exposes the bias in modern culture that overemphasizes rationalism, individualism, and IQ [889].

Diana told Dan that according to the rationalist view, we philosophize to be more moral. The intuitionist view, on the other hand, suggests that we interact with others. It is difficult to impossible to be more moral alone, as this requires constant environmental stimuli [889]. Our brain tends to make immediate judgments about all the sensory details it receives and to file new data based on pre-programmed assumptions. People hate uncertainty, and this is why they are in a rush to judge. Studies have shown that in circumstances that do not allow people to calculate their chances of success, the centers of fear in their minds turn on. Then, in an attempt to put an end to fear, people try to come to a conclusion, any conclusion, about the patterns in the situations so that their fears are alleviated.

Diana asked Dan, "What happens in our brain during so-called random events?"

Much is known about how people make decisions under varying levels of probability. But less is known about the basis of decision-making when probabilities are uncertain because of missing information. According to the decision theory, uncertainty about probabilities does not affect choices. Using functional brain imaging, it was shown that the level of ambiguity in choices correlates positively with the activation of specific areas in our brain, and negatively with the activation of other areas. Further, activity in specific areas was correlated positively with the expected reward. This suggests that, contrary to the decision theory, there are specific brains areas which respond to different degrees of uncertainty [890].

In an exciting story in Forbes magazine, Matthew Herper talks about some of the studies that look into our brain [891]. He describes studies by the brain scientist Brian Knutson from Stanford, who used MRI (magnetic resonance imaging) scanners to look inside people's heads as they experienced intense emotions. He showed volunteers pictures of nude and decapitated bodies. But those reactions paled in comparison to what happened when he offered people cash. "Ha, ha, ha," Diana giggled.

In 2000, Knutson published a study using MRI to photograph what goes on in the brain when people deal with money. Activation of brain areas was studied in volunteers as they anticipated and responded to monetary incentives. Significant activation of many areas was noted in response to both monetary rewards and punishments. Further, in trials involving punishment, activation of other areas that are associated with incentive-driven behavior was found [892].

Using event-related functional MRI, the effect of anticipation about an increase in monetary rewards and punishments was determined. Whereas the anticipation of increasing rewards elicited both an increase in self-reported happiness and activation, the anticipation of increasing punishment elicited neither. However, the anticipation of both rewards and punishments activated different brain regions. At the highest reward level, activation was correlated with individual differences in self-reported happiness elicited by the reward cues. The findings suggested that whereas certain brain areas may code for expected incentive magnitude, there are other brain regions which code for expected positive incentive value [893].

Traditional economics predicts that people use money to acquire things that make them happy. But money by itself does not make people happy. Offers of cash caused a surge in the hormone dopamine in a tiny piece of neural machinery in the brain. The surge wasn't caused by the cash already in people's back pockets, but by the opportunity to make some easy money [891].

Investors are known to systematically deviate from rationality when making financial decisions. Using event-related MRI, it was studied whether one can predict optimal and suboptimal choices in a financial decision-making task. Based on the optimal rational risk-neutral strategy, two deviations were analyzed: risk-seeking mistakes and risk-aversion mistakes. The activation of specific brain areas preceded risky choices as well as risk-seeking mistakes. The activation of other areas preceded riskless choices and risk-aversion mistakes. These findings suggest that distinct areas are linked to the prevention and promotion of different types of financial choices, and that excessive activation of these circuits may lead to investing mistakes. Thus, consideration of preventive brain mechanisms adds predictive power to the rational actor model of economic decision making [894].

Dan was thinking of aging. He was wondering whether his brain function was the same as it was in his thirties. The effects of aging on decision making and associated brain areas have been studied, and it was shown that aging, among many other factors, alters our decision-making abilities [895]. With the aging of the population, older decision makers will need to be more responsible for their own physical, psychological and financial well-being.

Temporally specific changes in activity within specific brain areas occur during anticipatory periods preceding consummator behavior. These are viewed today as an opportunity for intervention. However, no available therapy is capable of spontaneously sensing and therapeutically responding to this vulnerable moment in time when anticipation-related brain signals are present. Increased activity was detected during reward anticipation, which can efficiently trigger neuro-stimulation and reduce consummator behavior in animals sensitized to highly palatable food. Similar oscillations were observed in the human brain during reward anticipation, highlighting potential translational interventions [896].

Every day, we make dozens of choices between an alternative with higher overall value and a more tempting but ultimately inferior option. Optimal decision-making requires self-control. Some of our decisions are random. Goal-directed decisions have their basis in a standard value signal encoded in specific brain areas. Exercising self-control involves modulation of this value signal by other areas. MRI monitoring of brain activity in dieters who were engaged in making real decisions about food consumption showed that some areas in our brains correlate with goal values regardless of the amount of self-control [891].

Dan was thinking, "Does this means that we can intervene in the decision-making process even when they seem to be random decision-making processes? Perhaps we should all have some electrodes in the right areas in our brains which are connected to our cell phone, so that we can push the right buttons at the right time for making decisions."

The economist Colin Camerer tried to understand why people are afraid to invest in stock markets outside their own country. To investigate this, he designed the following experiment: Participants were presented with two decks of cards: one comprised ten red cards and ten blue cards, and the other comprised an unknown number of red and blue cards. They were told that there was a prize of $10 for guessing the color of the first card drawn from either deck. Most of the participants chose the deck with the equal number of red and blue cards. This was a rather odd case in which logic goes against common sense, because the chance of drawing a red or blue card is 50% in the case of either deck [891, 897].

This experiment presents a conundrum to our brain, because a certain area of the brain is used for decision making when the odds are already known and the risk can be evaluated, while decisions about ambiguous odds (as in the case of the ambiguous deck) are made in a completely different part of the brain. People, irrationally, tend to favor markets where they think they know the risks and stay away when they don't know the risk [891].

It was becoming more evident to Dan that there are some brain areas which may be related to random things. This made him feel more confident about the possibility of programming these areas. Can we use brain plasticity to program randomness in our favor? For Dan, programming it meant maintaining its randomness or maintaining the right kind of randomness.

# CHAPTER 48
## Making random decisions


Dan was amazed at how interested Diana was in the whole issue of decision making. He was quite happy about it, mainly because the approach she took was entirely different from his. Her literature background made her look at the same problems from a different angle. The real surprise for him was that sometimes, while talking and quoting from different sites, she came up with similar conclusions. Or at least that was what he was hearing.

Diana was telling Dan about an interesting character from Greek mythology.

Metis in ancient Greek religion is a mythological character who belonged to the Titans [898]. By the era of Greek philosophy in the 5th century BC, Metis had become the mother of wisdom and deep thought [899]. The Greek word "metis" refers to a quality that combines wisdom and cunning. David Brooks in his book *The Social Animal*, mentions that a man with metis has a mental map of his own reality [889]. He has a collection of metaphors that organize activities and situations. He has acquired some practical skills that allow him to predict a change. In this book, Brooks suggests that perception is a multi-dimensional process. It involves not only observing what is going on, but also almost simultaneously weighing the meaning of what is happening, evaluating it, and producing some feeling about it. "Think about what happens to us when we put new food in our mouth. We do not have to decide if it's disgusting. We just know it." Similarly, when we look at a mountain landscape, we do not have to decide whether it is beautiful. We just know that it is. Some of our moral judgments are, in some ways, made along these lines. These judgments are quick and intuitive assessments [889]. Researchers at the Max Planck Institute for Psycholinguistics in the Netherlands found that even on complex issues such as euthanasia, evaluative sensations can be identified within 250 milliseconds of the reading of any sentence dealing with the issue. It just seems to happen spontaneously [900] [889]. Dan asked Diana, "Are they random? Or are our intuitive and spontaneous decisions and actions which seem to be random, not random at all?" Maybe these super quick decisions are entirely pre-programmed.

Joshua Greene is an American experimental psychologist, neuroscientist, and philosopher, and a professor of psychology at Harvard University. The focus of his research is moral judgment and decision-making [901]. Greene, along with some colleagues, proposed the dual process theory of moral judgment, which states that moral judgments are determined by both automatic, emotional responses and controlled, conscious reasoning or deontological judgments. So the dual theory comprises rights- or duty-based moral theories that are preferentially composed of automatic emotions, and consequentialism or outcome-based theories that are supported by conscious reasoning and allied processes of cognitive control[902].

Are these seemingly random automatic responses predetermined?

Greene showed that when it came to "personal" moral problems, such as whether to sacrifice one person to save the lives of five others, many brain areas associated with emotion were activated. These brain regions were not activated in the case of more "impersonal" decisions, such as turning on a switch in order to kill one person instead of five people [903]. The cognitive load seems to be greater in the case of utilitarian moral decisions, which seem to take a longer time as a result. But the response time was much shorter in the case of non-utilitarian decisions [901, 904].

Greene says that like cameras, people also have automatic settings for "face image," "activity picture," or "landscape," which determine the shutter speed and focus. These settings are fast and efficient but are not flexible. Sometimes, we abandon the automatic setting and use manual tuning, setting our own shutter speed and focus. Manual tuning is slower, but it allows us to do things we would not have been able to do in the usual, automatic way. Greene implies that just like the camera, our brain has automatic moral responses. But at critical moments, one can bypass them and move to a slower process of conscious reflection [905, 906]. If this theory is correct and can be applied to our everyday decision making, can we control random, automatic, or maybe not so random decision or actions? If they need to be random, how can they also be controlled? Diana was smiling at Dan.

We may accept the notion that while our intuition is constantly at work or always ready to pop in when asked for, or not asked for, our unconscious and conscious minds are functioning in parallel. According to Brooks, our mind transitions naturally between various levels. Our intuition keeps identifying different stimuli that may or may not be random. "One of our levels continues to work vigorously. It continues to merge data and search in a consistent way for similarities and rhythms. It develops some sense of this new landscape: how does the light fall? How do people greet each other? What is the pace of life? The unconscious is not only trying to distinguish between people but also between their patterns. How close is the cooperation between them? What are the concepts of authority and their individuality, even if they do not explicitly state this? The point is not only to describe the fish in the river, but also the nature of the water they swim in. At one point there is a moment of peace and separate insights that integrate into a coherent whole" [889]. This continuous process, whether random or not, creates all kinds of maps, such that the outlines of our brain fit harmoniously with the contours of reality in every new place. Sometimes, this synchronicity is achieved gradually. Occasionally, there are bursts of inspiration, and the map becomes clear at once. After these moments, the brain will interpret every piece of information in a new and radical way. What seems inseparably tangled will now look beautiful in its simplicity [889]. This seems to imply that our mind is adapted to a disorganized world, not to a harmonious world. For Dan, it meant that we might be more adapted to randomness than we think we are.

We certainly have a strong urge to be as moral as possible or to justify ourselves when our morality is questioned. We also want to do the right thing for ourselves and for those we care about. The fact that we have a universal sense of morality does not mean that we always, or even often, act in good and virtuous ways. Many of our decisions and acts are intuitive, and seem to be based on random stimuli, random facts, people we randomly meet, and many other random events. What pleases us is often more important than what we do—our judgments are more fundamental than our ability to meet them ourselves. And yet, we are genuinely motivated to be moral, to do the right things and to be seen as moral [889] [907].

Diana was beginning to make sense of it: For many of us, we feel like wanderers who live in ambiguity about many of our decisions. As wanderers, we manage to overcome many of these uncertainties. The wise wanderer knows how to restrain himself. She told Dan about Brooks Atkinson, a theatre critic who said that the perfect bureaucrat is the one who manages to make no decisions and escape all responsibility.

"Negative capability" was a phrase first used by Romantic poet John Keats in 1817 to characterize the capacity of some of the most significant writers, such as Shakespeare, "to pursue a vision of artistic beauty even when it leads them into intellectual confusion and uncertainty." It describes the conflict between philosophical certainty and artistic beauty [908]. The term is used by philosophers to describe the ability of an individual to perceive, think, and operate beyond any presupposition of the predetermined capacity of the human being [909]. This "negative ability" is the ability to live in "uncertainty, mysteries, doubts, without any frantic pursuit of facts and reason." The more complex the landscape, the more the wanderer relies on his patience. The more confusing the sight, the more cautious his point of view. He is aware not only of his ignorance but also of his helplessness in the face of this ignorance [889]. This term (negative capability) seems to imply an acceptance and even indulgence of randomness.

Dan was led back to the issue of making randomness happen. Randomness or this lack of full certainty may have advantages under some circumstances. Diana felt that life in a world where everything was pre-determined would be boring. This seemed to concur with what Dan was saying: We need randomness. We need to make use of it, and we need to generate it.

# CHAPTER 49
## Generating randomness


Dan's focus now was on how randomness could be generated. He went back to some of his notes from a few months ago when he had just started to dive into his research on randomness. Now, he was more convinced than ever that he can indeed make use of random number generators to generate randomness in his personal life.

Random number generation is defined as the creation of a sequence of numbers or symbols that cannot be reasonably predicted, except by random chance; the sequence is usually generated through hardware called random number generators [910]. Random number generation can be performed by humans by collecting various inputs from end users and using them as a randomization source. Most studies have found that human subjects use some degree of non-randomness when attempting to produce a random sequence of digits or letters. They may alternate too much between choices when compared to a good random generator. Thus, this approach is not widely used[845].

This means that things which we create ourselves and believe to be random may not be all that random. We would need a real random generator for doing so.

While people are not suitable randomness generators upon request, they do generate random behavior in the context of playing mixed strategy games [911]. To explore this possibility, some researchers constructed a game suitable for randomness extraction, in which the playing patterns were analyzed. The results showed that in less than two minutes, a human being can generate 128 bits that are close to random. Based on this experiment, a complete working software that generates random sequences based solely on human gameplay was designed [912] .

Dan had already learned that many applications require external methods to generate randomness. As we are all biased, we need better systems than ourselves. This has led to the development of various methods for generating random data. Some of these are ancient, such as rolling of dice, coin flipping, shuffling of playing cards, and the use of yarrow stalks [910]. Random number tables were also used in the past. Nowadays, computerized random number generators are used for government-run lotteries, slot machines, security, gambling, statistical sampling, computer simulation, cryptography, and other areas and for various other purposes [910]. In the context of cryptography and specific numerical algorithms, a considerably high degree of apparent randomness is needed as opposed to certain operations that require only a modest level of unpredictability. Therefore, random number generators for which the seed is kept secret are used in cryptography. In such applications, the sender and receiver can generate the same set of numbers automatically for use as keys [910]. The process of random number generation in games is frequently referred to as being controlled by a "Random Number God" or "RN-Jesus." The term was created by players of some games, with the belief that certain actions can appease or anger the "God," leading to number generation that is seemingly skewed in favor of or against the player[913]. Dan was wondering what level of randomness we would require for our "life."

There are two principal methods used to generate random numbers.

The first method measures a physical phenomenon which is expected to be random and then compensates for possible biases in the measurement process. For example, one can measure atmospheric noise, thermal noise, radioactive decay, shot noise, avalanche noise in Zener diodes, clock drift, the timing of actual movements of a hard disk read/write head, radio noise, and other external electromagnetic and quantum phenomena. Cosmic background radiation or radioactive decay measured over short timescales also represents a source of natural randomness. But these physical phenomena and the methods used to assess them are usually characterized by asymmetries and systematic biases, as a result of which their outcomes are not uniformly random. The speed at which randomness can be harvested from natural sources is dependent on the underlying physical phenomenon being measured. Sources of naturally occurring "true" randomness are believed to be of the "blocking" type, as they are rate-limited until enough randomness is harvested to meet the demand[914-916].

Dan learned about a physical random number generator that is based on random atomic or subatomic physical phenomenon, whose unpredictability can be traced to the laws of quantum mechanics. Wide-band photonic sources of randomness such as chaotic laser beams and amplified spontaneous emission noise are used to create physical random number generators. Laser chaos produces fast, physical random numbers on account of its high bandwidth and large amplitude [917, 918]. Various methods for collecting this information have been developed [910].

Another method for generating randomness is to use computational algorithms that produce long sequences of apparently random results, which are entirely determined by a shorter initial value, known as a seed value or key. The entire seemingly random sequence can be reproduced if the seed value is known. These are pseudorandom number generators and do not depend on sources of naturally occurring entropy, though they may be periodically seeded by natural sources. This generator is of the non-blocking type, so it is not rate-limited by an external event, making vast bulk reads a possibility [910]. Most computer-generated random numbers are generated through pseudorandom number generators. The algorithms used automatically create long runs of numbers with good random properties, but eventually, the sequence repeats [919]. To avoid this non-random property, several single linear congruential random number generators can be used in parallel instead of using a single linear congruential generator, with a "master" random number generator that can choose from among the different generators [910].

Most computer programming languages include functions or library routines that provide random number generators. They are designed to provide a random byte or word, or a floating point number uniformly distributed between 0 and 1. The quality of the randomness generated by these methods varies widely from utterly predictable outputs to cryptographically secure ones. Several library functions have poor statistical properties, while there are others that repeat patterns after only tens of thousands of trials. They are initialized using a computer's real-time clock as the seed, since such a clock generally measures time in milliseconds, far beyond a person's precision. While these functions are adequate for specific tasks such as gaming, they do not provide the high-quality randomness that is required, for example, in cryptography applications, statistics or numerical analysis [910].

Generation of weak forms of randomness or pseudo-random numbers is a common task in computer programming. A method that "randomly" selects music tracks for a background music system can only appear random, as it may actually have ways to control the selection of music. In contrast, a truly random system has no restriction on the same item appearing two or three times in succession. The computational random number generation methods do not produce true randomness, but they do pass some statistical tests for randomness that measure the unpredictability of their results or the discernibility of their patterns.

There are hybrid methods for generating randomness, too, which include the collection of data from natural sources when available and from periodically re-seeded software-based secure pseudorandom number generators when required. When the desired read rate of randomness exceeds the ability of the natural harvesting approach, random number generating software is used. This approach avoids the rate-limited blocking behavior of random number generators that are based on slower and purely environmental methods [910].

There are also methods that generate random numbers based on a probability density function. They convert a uniform random number into a sequence of random numbers. These methods can generate pseudo-random and genuinely random numbers equally well [920].

It is important to understand that there are many limitations to these random number generation methods. For example, with a quantum mechanics-based generator, the results are often affected by temperature, power supply voltage, the age of the device, or other outside interference. Further, it is difficult to detect bugs in software or hardware used for random number generation. Therefore, these methods are sometimes statistically tested before running them in order to ensure that the underlying source is still functioning, after which the sequence is post-processed to improve the statistical properties of the methods. The TRNG9803 is an example of a random number generator that uses an entropy measurement and then post-processes the random sequence with a shift register stream cipher [921].

Dan felt that he was now on the right track. The next step was to find the best way of generating randomness.

# CHAPTER 50
## When good randomness goes terribly wrong

Dan was looking into how he could turn randomness generation into reality. From time to time, he felt that he had bitten off more than he could chew, and that at his age he should just read and dream. However, last night, while sharing some of his thoughts with Diana, he was surprised when she told him, "Dan, at some point in your life you just need to do what you want to do. Even if it means taking a risk. Even if the risk is high. Your age has nothing to do with it. In fact, your age is in your favor. You have not started your own business in your life. However, you are somewhat smarter than a 30-year-old who is making his first steps in the wild business world."

Dan was sitting at his desk and looking deeply into quantum sources of randomness.

Entanglement and non-locality are two defining features of quantum mechanics. Both have a profound and far-reaching connection with randomness. Quantum non-locality improves the quality of sources of randomness[922]. The non-local correlations obtained by measuring two entangled quantum systems can be used to transform an imperfect source into a perfect source of randomness while certifying that the transformation has indeed occurred [792]. This might sound like gibberish to non-physicist "normal" people. When put in lay terms, it simply means that it is possible to improve the degree of randomness.

Randomness plays a role in classical and quantum information processing. In computer science, one makes a distinction between deterministic algorithms and randomized algorithms, or algorithms that have access to a perfect source of randomness[922]. For cryptographic purposes, the quality of randomness needs to be much higher, but this is impossible using classical post-processing methods [923]. A source which produces either a perfectly random bit or a bit that is perfectly correlated with the environment and can be interceded by a potential hacker or enemy. It is impossible, using standard post-processing, to improve the quality of this source.

Born's inspiring work on the interpretation of quantum mechanics showed that the outcomes of quantum measurements are intrinsically random [924]. This has led to the recognition of quantum random number generators, some of which are commercially available. Devices that are based on the time at which radioactive nuclei disintegrate or the direction a photon takes at a beam splitter are examples of what Dan was able to find.

Do these devices solve the issue of real randomness generation?

Quantum random number generators produce digital outputs, but they are intrinsically analog devices and therefore face the limitations of analog information processing. The operations carried out by the components may drift in time, or they may start to malfunction. Their output could thus become less and less random, or even become entirely deterministic, without the user becoming aware of the malfunction[922]. These limitations can be overcome by using entanglement and non-locality to generate randomness[17]. The concept behind this is to entangle two quantum systems and then randomly choose one of several measurements to carry out on each system. If the correlations between the measurement settings and measurement outcomes are non-local, then the measurement outcomes are necessarily random[922]. Such quantum random number generators have the advantage of a "digital" approach because they involve manipulating digital values to select measurement settings and to record the measurement results. It is no longer necessary to model the internal workings of the devices used: a decrease in the Bell violation immediately sends off a warning when the devices start to malfunction. It will be further discussed later. This is known as the "device-independent" approach to quantum information processing, which improves the security of quantum key distribution and ensures that a quantum computer works correctly[17]. It is necessary that the measurement settings of these devices be chosen at random. Therefore, some initial randomness is necessary. For this reason, it is more precise to talk about "randomness expansion" rather than "randomness generation"[922].

Randomness-expansion schemes require the amount of initial randomness to be lower than the total amount of randomness produced [925]. The first bits need to be entirely random and utterly uncorrelated with any potential enemy. Dan discovered that the device-independent approach to randomness generation also works with an imperfect randomness source [792, 926].

The possibility of certifying the production of new randomness using quantum non-locality is fascinating from a fundamental viewpoint, with important practical applications. In the world of information security, statements such as "secured by 128-bit AES" or "protected by 2048-bit authentication" mean that these algorithms are difficult to break. They are organized in protocols that protect our identity and the integrity and confidentiality of data. These algorithms are used when we buy a book at Amazon, or when we connect to our bank account to transfer money [927]. We rarely see statements about the strength of the random number generator used by a security system.

If I am going to develop a randomness-based algorithm, do I need to be concerned about the level of randomness, about data security?

System designers are more concerned with the power consumption and bit generation speed than with the actual degree of randomness of the bits generated. This is strange, given that the quality of the random number generator directly influences how difficult it is to attack the system [927]. In fact, random number generators are a weak link in the secure use of cryptography. Encryption and signing can fail in the face of predictable or repeated randomness, even when proper keys are used [928]. Therefore, the security of an operation relies on having good randomness. A random number generator takes measurements and produces bits that are uniform. But failures can occur at any level. [929]. The security of routine cryptographic operations such as encryption, key exchange, and randomized signing rely on access to good, unpredictable and fresh randomness.

Dan learned that unfortunately, the random number generators used in practice frequently fail. This is due to poor design, implementation bugs, early exposure of randomness, and the inability to find sufficient

368 | CHAOS ME!

randomness in a system's environment [930, 931, 932, 933]. Several methods have been developed to hedge routine cryptographic operations against lousy randomness, in order to mitigate the damage caused by failure in randomness [928].

Attacks can be indicators of the general fragility of cryptographic operations with repeated or predictable randomness. Cryptographic operations fundamentally rely on good randomness to achieve the desired security level, so repairing random number generators is the only solution. However, the complexity of their design, the frequency with which failures occur, and the significant damage that results, imply that the solution is to design cryptographic operations such that lousy randomness has as little ill effect as possible [928]. That is, the operations should not rely entirely on the randomness that is generated, and they should provide a satisfactory level of security even when the randomness generated is less than optimal or lousy.

There are two important layers when it comes to generating cryptographically secure random numbers[934, 935].

The first layer is where entropy is generated. For this, sources of unpredictable events are sampled, for example, temperature variations, clock drift, interrupt timings, mouse movements or keyboard clicks, and network packet arrivals. This involves the encapsulation of the physical processes from which entropy is harvested [928].

The second layer is sampling from the entropy layer to measure events and generate digital descriptions of them. This involves extracting uniform random bits from variable data and maintaining a pool of such bits. The uniform bits are provided for applications that require randomness in the consuming layer [928]. Every layer above the first can store randomness.

From the point of view of an application, randomness is classified as follows. (a) Fresh randomness: This refers to new, private, uniform bits. (b) Reused randomness: This is represented by private, uniform bits, but these bits might have been provided to the application before. (c) Exposed randomness: This refers to uniform bits that attackers are later able to crack. (d) Predictable randomness: This means random bits that can be predicted by an adversary. (e) Chosen randomness: This refers to adversarial-chosen random bits [928].

For Dan, fresh randomness seemed to be the right kind of randomness, and the other four were not ideal. Certain vulnerabilities lead to the applications using one of the four kinds of "bad randomness" instead of the first one [929]. In order to avoid these vulnerabilities, the system should be designed in such a way that its security depends solely on the critical material. This is why the "cryptographic strength" of security algorithms and protocols is expressed as the number of key bits that an attacker needs to crack in order to enter the system [936]. The "effective strength" of an algorithm is diminished when better attacks against it are found, and more necessary bits can be derived from looking at a limited amount of output data. Security protocols require random bits to remain secure, even though the protocol description will employ the word "unpredictable" to refer to a random value that an attacker would find difficult to guess.

True random numbers are required if the application uses one of the following: keys and initialization values for encryption, private keys for digital signature algorithms, values to be used in entity authentication mechanisms, values to be used in crucial establishment protocols, PIN and password generation, and other critical randomness-based technologies [927].

Dan realized that creating truly random numbers is hard.

Digital hardware and deterministic software are designed to behave predictably, each and every time. Therefore, hardware and software designers attempting to generate unpredictability need to look outside their healthy operating environment. True random number generation is surprisingly tricky. Dan was going through a list of questions. If I have found a proper source of unpredictability, how much "unpredictability" does my source generate? How do I translate this unpredictability into random bit streams or numbers? How efficient is this translation? Am I losing unpredictability? Is the resulting data biased or not? Does the data contain more zeroes than ones? Do I get sufficient unpredictable output for my purpose? Are all the output bits I am getting unpredictable, or only a portion of them? [937]. Statistical tests can be run on the output of a random number generator to provide answers to some of these. But they do not "prove" that a source is random. At best, they determine that a source is not, or only partially, unpredictable. For example, it is possible to create a module that creates a bit string that passes all statistical tests but still generates a predictable bit stream [927].

Sources of randomness can be internal or external. When selecting a source of randomness, it is essential to understand whether the randomness of the source is caused by a fundamental property of the system itself, called "intrinsic" randomness. Sources of intrinsic randomness cannot be influenced by an adversary. An external source is "just" a measure of events external to, and unpredictable by, the system itself. In this case, the "signal" in question is not part of the "desired" operation of the system. It is termed "external noise" [927]. Sources using external noise are usually influenced by an adversary. It is desirable that a random number generator use purely intrinsic sources of randomness, but unfortunately, this cannot always be guaranteed.

The boundary between external and internal sources of randomness is not black and white. Sources of external randomness are often easily recognized. However, they may often not be too easily ignored. Thermal noise is present in all semiconductors, but an adversary can still have influence over it by changing the temperature of the semiconductor. Despite this, he does not have total control over it, so thermal noise is still considered a source of intrinsic randomness. An application wishing to extract unpredictable bits of thermal noise current or voltage also has to deal with the voltage noise on the power lines, which is predictable and controllable by an adversary. Thus, it is important to ensure that the intrinsic randomness is not "drowned" by the external noise [927].

Compared with true random number generators, pseudo-random number generators provide unpredictable output very fast and are much easier to construct in terms of the digital hardware. As long as their internal state is unknown to an attacker, their output is unpredictable by the attacker. Well-designed pseudo-random number generators only leak a limited amount of data about their internal state through the output they produce. If their internal state is often restored by new, unpredictable data, their output remains unpredictable. One can generate unpredictable data from a limited amount of truly random data as long as it keeps its internal state secret [927]. Hybrid random number generators are those in which a random bit generator is constructed from a combination of a source of true randomness, which is used to seed the internal state of a pseudo-random number generator.

Most sources of random data generate "biased" output; i.e., the chance that an output bit is 1 or 0 is not equal to 0.5. The source could generate more 1's than 0's, or vice versa. In such cases, the output should be post-processed such that it has an equal chance of being 1 or 0. This post-processing method is termed "whitening," and it transforms the output to a bit stream with a mean of zero and "normal" distribution [927]. Several national and international bodies have set up certain criteria for the construction, testing and use of random number generators, in order to ensure the randomness of the output [938-940].

Random number generators can be deterministic or non-deterministic random bit Generator, DRBG and NDRBG, respectively. There are also different requirements for deterministic- and non-deterministic random number generators. For example, the internal state of a deterministic generator is considered as a Critical Security Parameter, and it needs to remain confidential [927, 941, 942].

The AuthenTec SafeXcel-IP-76 True Random Number generator uses current noise, present in the channel of a MOSFET transistor, as its source of intrinsic randomness. This noise causes uncertainty in the transition time of an inverter cell when it switches from low to high. This uncertainty is accumulated by placing an odd number of inverters in a ring to create a Free Running Oscillator (FRO). The uncertainty of individual inverter transitions increases with time, until it cannot be predicted whether a certain point in the free running oscillator has a value of 0 or 1. An output generated at such a point in time cannot be predicted and is considered as a single bit of randomness [927].

When using a true random number generator, there are a number of things to consider. How many random bits does our application need per time unit? How much "randomness" is needed in the application? Is it enough if the pseudo-random number generator is re-seeded from time to time to create unpredictable data? How much power can a true random number generator consume? More entropy requires a greater number of free running oscillators to be working simultaneously, which means that there is more power consumption. How much power would each free running oscillator consume? Higher frequencies mean that entropy data can be collected faster, but it carries the risk of the oscillators getting damaged and not running at all. Is such a generator testable? Probably not, because a true random number generator contains constructs that violate typical design criteria, especially those for testability. It is therefore important to devise mechanisms by which true random number generators can be tested with regular scans [927, 943].

Dan met Diana that evening. He told her he was seriously considering transforming some of his ideas into real-world products. But he was not sure how. There was still much that he needed to do. Much to read and learn. It would probably take him some more time. A few more months perhaps. Diana was happy to see that she had encouraged him to take these steps. She was not sure why he needed more time though. She was not sure of what products could be created out of all this information about randomness. But Dan seemed much more focused, and even more relaxed in a way, so she was happy about it. She decided to extend her full support to him.

# CHAPTER 51
## Entropy: We can't unscramble an egg

What is the difference between thermodynamics and a stick?

A stick has two ends and no beginning. Thermodynamics has two "beginnings," the first and the second law, and no end.

Dan realized that he had to learn much more about physics before he could translate some of his ideas into reality.

Entropy means a lack of order or predictability. It signifies a gradual decline into disorder[944]. Entropy is derived from the principle of thermodynamics, and it is based on the notion that everything in the universe eventually moves from order to disorder. Entropy is believed to be a measure of that change [945]. Alternatively, entropy is considered as a measure of uncertainty or randomness [944], or a measure of the number of possible arrangements the atoms in a system can have. Thermodynamic entropy includes a heat energy component. It is a measure of how organized or disorganized energy is in a system of atoms or molecules [944].

The word "entropy" finds its roots in the Greek word "entropia," which means "a turning toward" or "transformation." A typical example of entropy is that of ice melting into water. The resulting change from a fixed form to a free form, from order to disorder, is accompanied by an increase in entropy [945]. In physics, entropy is a thermodynamic quantity that represents the amount of thermal energy in a system that is unavailable for conversion into mechanical work. In other words, the entropy of an object is a measure of the amount of energy that is unavailable for work. As stated above, entropy is a measure of uncertainty or randomness. The higher the entropy of an object, the more uncertain we are about the states of the atoms making up that object because there are more states to select from [944]. According to a

374 | CHAOS ME!

law of physics, the entropy of an object or system can only be reduced with work [944].

Diana asked Dan a philosophical question in relation to this: "If everything slowly goes to disorder. What happens if someone or something tries to impose order on us?"

In 1803, the French mathematician Lazare Carnot proposed that in any machine, accelerations and shocks in the moving parts represent loss of the moment of activity. For any natural process, there exists an inherent tendency towards the dissipation of useful energy [946]. In 1824, his son, Sadi Carnot, stated that in all heat engines, when there is a temperature difference, work power can be produced from the action of its transition from a hot to a cold body. He explained this using the analogy of water falling in a water wheel: some calories are always lost in the motion cycle. This can be considered as ground work for the second law of thermodynamics[947]. In fact, Sadi Carnot is considered as the "father of thermodynamics."

The first law of thermodynamics expresses the concept of energy and its conservation in all processes. However, in the 1850s, German physicist Rudolf Clausius objected to the notion that no change occurs in the working body. He provided mathematical evidence of this "change" by questioning the nature of the inherent loss of usable heat when work is done. This is the heat produced by friction [948]. He described how to measure the entropy of an isolated system in thermodynamic equilibrium along with its parts. Clausius described entropy as the transformation content or the amount of dissipative energy of a thermodynamic system or a working body of chemical species, during a change of state [946].

In 1877, Boltzmann visualized a way to measure the entropy of ideal gas particles: he showed that entropy is proportional to the logarithm of the number of microstates an ideal gas can occupy. Boltzmann showed that according to this definition, entropy was equivalent to the thermodynamic entropy constant, which is known as Boltzmann's constant [949].

There are two related definitions of entropy: the thermodynamic definition and the statistical mechanics definition. Classical thermodynamics describes the state of a "system" in terms of the average values of the thermodynamic variables of the system or its parts. Some common examples of thermodynamic variables are temperature, pressure, and volume. A "system" is any region of space containing matter and energy: A cup of coffee, a glass of ice water, or an automobile. However, thermodynamic variables by themselves do not provide a "complete" picture of the system. Further, the microscopic nature of the system, such as the positions and velocities of the individual atoms and molecules that make up the system, is not described. Thermodynamics deals with systems at a macroscopic level, and it provides little insight into what is happening at a microscopic level [946] [950]. The early classical definition was based on the assumption of an equilibrium state. But this definition of entropy has also been extrapolated to non-equilibrium thermodynamic states.

Classical thermodynamics is unreliable for predicting the final state of a system that is subject to processing; this is where statistical mechanics comes in [946]. Statistical mechanics explains thermodynamics at the microscopic scale; based on the assumption that the macroscopic thermodynamic variables are known, it describes the possible "microstates" of the system. Many different microstates can make up a macrostate. Statistical mechanics does not define temperature, pressure, or entropy, as they are already defined by thermodynamics. Statistical mechanics serves to explain thermodynamics in terms of the microscopic behavior of the atoms and molecules in the system. That is, the entropy of a system is described by the number of different microstates that could give rise to the macrostate of that system [950]. If we assume that each microscopic configuration is equally probable, the entropy of a system can be calculated as the natural logarithm of that number of configurations, multiplied by the Boltzmann constant. Statistical mechanics provides an alternative definition to entropy in terms of the statistics of the motions of the microscopic constituents of a system. Entropy is modeled by the particles constituting a gas, and quantum mechanically by photons, phonons, and spins[951].

Entropy may be understood as a measure of disorder within a macroscopic system. Think of gas in a container with a known volume, pressure, and energy. The individual gas molecules contained within it can be in an enormous number of possible configurations. At equilibrium, each instant configuration of the gas may be regarded as random [946]. Statistical mechanics demonstrates that entropy is governed by probability, thus allowing for a decrease in disorder even in an isolated system. Although it is possible, such an event has a small probability of occurring, making it unlikely[951].

The idea of "irreversibility" is central to the understanding of entropy [950]. If a working body, such as a body of steam, is returned to its original state at the end of a cycle, then it is assumed that "no change occurs in the condition of the working body." If you had to watch everyday life in its normal direction and then play it backwards, it would easy to distinguish between the two. The latter would show impossible things…water jumping out of a glass and into a pitcher above it, smoke going down a chimney, water in a glass freezing to form ice cubes, and crashed cars reassembling themselves. The intuitive meaning of expressions such as "we can't unscramble an egg" or "we can't take the cream out of the coffee" is that these are irreversible processes [950].

In thermodynamics, one says that the "forward" process of pouring water from a pitcher is "irreversible." That is, all real physical processes involving systems in everyday life are irreversible. Entropy never decreases in an irreversible process in an isolated system, or a system that is not subject to outside influence [950]. In everyday life, an increase in entropy is practically unobservable, and in many cases it's almost zero. Reversing such processes will not seem impossible. If we made a one-second-long video of two billiard balls colliding, it would be hard to distinguish between the forward and backward playbacks because the increase in entropy in such a short time frame is very small. In thermodynamics, this process is practically "reversible," with an entropy increase of practically zero.

The concept of irreversibility stems from the idea that if we have a system in an "unlikely" macrostate, it will soon move to the "most likely" macrostate and its entropy will increase. Increase in entropy results in irreversible changes in a system, because some energy is used up as waste heat. This also limits the amount of work that a system can potentially do [952, 953]. The concept of entropy has also evolved to explain why some processes occur spontaneously while their time reversals do not. [954]. Further, it is implied that time and entropy move in the same direction.

Consider the following system: A glass of warm water with an ice cube in it. This system, which is most likely to have been recently created and not just have spontaneously appeared, will not remain in the same state. It will shift to a more likely macrostate, probably one in which the ice cube has partially or completely melted and the water has cooled [950]. The change in entropy that occurs here is determined based on the initial and final states. This applies to both reversible and irreversible processes. However, irreversible processes increase the combined entropy of the system and its environment [946].

The thermodynamic properties of a system are a function of the state that it is in. At a particular thermodynamic state, not to be confused with the microscopic state of a system, these properties have a specific value. If the value of two properties are determined, then it is possible to determine the state of the system as well the values of the other properties. Thus, for a single-phase system composed of a pure substance that is at a specific uniform temperature and pressure, and is therefore in a specific state, the entropy value of that state is also specific and can be determined for that particular state. If this system were to undergo changes and then return to its original state at the start of the cycle, the line integral of any function, including entropy, would be zero in the case of this reversible cycle.

Entropy is conserved in a reversible process and is not conserved in an irreversible process. An irreversible process results in an increase in entropy[955]. A reversible process is one that does not deviate from thermodynamic equilibrium while producing the maximum work. Any process that deviates from thermal equilibrium cannot be reversible. In irreversible processes, energy is lost as heat, the total entropy increases, and the potential for maximum work is lost[956].

Heat flow from a hot reservoir to a cold reservoir represents an increase in entropy. In such a system, the total entropy change is still zero at all times, if the entire process is reversible [946].

Heat transfer along the isotherm steps of the Carnot cycle is proportional to the temperature of a system. This relationship is expressed in increments of entropy that are equal to the ratio of incremental heat transfer to temperature, which was found to vary in the thermodynamic cycle. Eventually, it returns to the same value at the end of every cycle. It is a function of the state, explicitly, the thermodynamic state of the system [946].

Dan knew that he must dig into the second law of thermodynamics for better understanding of randomness.

In 1915, the physicist Arthur Eddington wrote, "The Second Law defines the ultimate purpose of life, mind, and human striving: to deploy energy and information to fight back the tide of entropy and carve out refuges of beneficial order. An under appreciation of the inherent tendency toward disorder, and a failure to appreciate the precious niches of order we carve out are a significant source of human folly" [957].

Dan was telling Diana that the second law of thermodynamics is acknowledged in everyday life, in sayings such as "Ashes to ashes," "Things fall apart," "Rust never sleeps," "Shit happens," "We can't unscramble an egg," "What can go wrong will go wrong," and "Any jackass can kick down a barn, but it takes a carpenter to build one." [957]. Diana was not sure what all this had to do with physics. She had her own interpretation of the "we can't unscramble an egg" phrase.

Dan told her that in the late 1940s, German theoretical physicist Arnold Sommerfeld, having previously written a series of books in physics, was asked why he had never written a book on thermodynamics. The following is his frequently quoted answer: "Thermodynamics is a funny subject. The first time we go through it, we don't understand it at all. The second time we go through it, we think we understand it, except for one or two small points. The third time we go through it, we know we don't understand it, but by that time we are so used to it, it doesn't bother us any more" [958, 959].

This seemed to aptly sum up Dan's experience with entropy too.

# CHAPTER 52
## The second law and entropy

Diana was beginning to accept that the second law may be worth understanding. At least, Dan had gotten her to the point where she was willing to try and understand it.

According to the first law of thermodynamics, which states that energy cannot be created or destroyed in an isolated system, loss of heat causes a reduction in the internal energy of a thermodynamic system. Thermodynamic entropy is a comparative measure of the decrease in the internal energy of a system and the corresponding increase in the internal energy of the surroundings at a given temperature.

The second law of thermodynamics is considered as a foundational concept of chemistry, and it is one of the fundamental laws of our universe. It states that the entropy of a closed system will never decrease. That is, the second law states that the state of entropy of the entire universe, as an isolated system, will always increase over time. It also states that the changes in the entropy of the universe can never be negative [960]. A simple interpretation of the second law is that energy changes from localized forms to more dispersed forms in the absence of any constraints. An entropy change is defined as the quantitative value of such a process: it is a measure of how much energy has flowed or how widely the energy has spread out at a specific temperature [950]. Systems spontaneously evolve towards thermodynamic equilibrium, the state with maximum entropy. For instance, heat will always flow from a region of higher temperature to one of lower temperature until the temperature becomes uniform.

According to the second law, entropy increase can be quantified to determine the reduction in the capacity of a system for change. Such quantification could help determine whether a thermodynamic process may occur. Entropy is essentially a quantitative measure of what is described as the dispersion of energy until it is evenly distributed [944].

Entropy cannot be directly observed; it needs to be calculated. Entropy is measured as the standard molar entropy from absolute zero, absolute entropy, or the difference in entropy compared to a reference state defined as zero entropy. The dimension of energy is divided by temperature [946]. There are two methods of calculating entropy. In the first calculation, the assumption is that of a sub-system within the system of interest. The sub-system here transfers heat to its environment, which is within the system of interest. Here, the calculation of entropy is based on the macroscopic relationship between heat flow into the sub-system and the temperature at which it occurs, summed over the boundary of that sub-system.

In the second calculation, the absolute entropy of a system is determined according to the microscopic behavior of its individual particles. For this, the thermodynamic probability is calculated, which is the natural logarithm of the number of microstates possible in a particular macrostate. This corresponds to the probability of the system being in that particular state. It effectively defines entropy independently from its effects due to changes which may involve heat, mechanical, electrical, chemical and other types of energies. It also includes logical states such as information states [950]. In systems where the temperature varies, the equation needs to be integrated over the temperature path. For such a system, the absolute value cannot be determined, and only differences in the values can be calculated. In this context, the second law of thermodynamics needs to be extended to non-isolated systems as well [950].

An ice cube left at room temperature begins to melt. We grow older but never younger. Rooms that are cleaned get messy again. Certain things move in one direction only; this is called the "arrow of time." The thermodynamic arrow of time, or entropy, is the measurement of disorder within a system. Changes in entropy indicate that time is asymmetric with respect to the order of an isolated system. A system will become more disordered as time increases [960].

According to the second law of thermodynamics, the total entropy of a system can decrease only if the energy that is lost by that system is used to increase the entropy of another system. In a system isolated from its environment, the entropy of that system tends not to decrease. Heat cannot flow from a colder body to a hotter body without the application of work, or the imposition of order, to the colder body. It is impossible for a device operating on a cycle to produce a network from a single temperature reservoir. The production of the network requires the flow of heat from a hotter reservoir to a colder reservoir. Thus, there is no possibility of a perpetual motion system. A reduction in the increase of entropy in a specific process, such as a chemical reaction, means that it is energetically more efficient [946]. The entropy change of a system at a specific temperature absorbing an infinitesimal amount of heat in a reversible way can be calculated [961].

An air conditioner reduces the entropy of air in a room by cooling it down. The heat from the room that the air conditioner discharges outside makes a more significant contribution to the entropy of the environment than the cooled air in the room with decreased entropy. Thus, the total entropy of the room increases along with the entropy of the environment, as per the second law [946].

The applicability of the second law of thermodynamics is limited to systems which are near or in an equilibrium state [962]. For systems which are far from equilibrium, one can use the maximum entropy production principle, which claims that non-equilibrium systems evolve such as to maximize entropy production[963, 964].

Diana was trying to get out of the heat examples. "Did not you mention information before?" She asked Dan.

In order to understand and apply the second law in other contexts, it is important to understand how and why that information changes as the system evolves from its initial to its final state. Entropy is defined as an expression of the disorder or randomness of a system, or of our lack of information about it. According to the statistical mechanics definition, entropy is the amount of additional information required to specify the exact physical state of a system, provided the thermodynamic parameters are known [946]. In the context of information theory, the entropy state function is the amount of information that would be needed to specify all the microstates of the system. Information entropy is defined as a measure of the information communicated by systems that are affected by data noise. Entropy is a measure of the amount of information that is missing before reception [965]. Information entropy takes the mathematical concepts of statistical thermodynamics into areas of the probability theory that are unconnected with heat and energy [950, 966].

# CHAPTER 53
## Entropy in everyday life

How does entropy apply to everyday activities like eating food? Here are some answers from a physics blog [967].

"I was eating a plate of food one day and thought of entropy. As I understand the definition of entropy, it is the logarithm of the number of arrangements or states the object in question can be in, where the object is composed of a number of particles/food particles.

So, I'm eating a plate of food, and I have diced up chicken, rice, and vegetables on the plate all mixed together. I thought, the current system I have, the food is arranged in a state that is of high entropy because this arrangement is common compared to the number of other rarer arrangements: 1/3 chicken, 1/3 vegetables, and 1/3 rice in a pie chart fashion. I like to eat neatly, and naturally, I've conditioned myself to pick up the food with my fork such that while I pick up chicken and rice, rice falls off one side of my work in a particular direction. As I eat, I sometimes end up with a neater, higher entropy state than what I began with. I didn't spend extra energy making it neater; I just pick up my food in strategic ways because that's how I usually eat.

My question is, how is this possible? I end up with a neater arrangement on my plate than I started with. I know food gets eaten, so the number of particles decreases with time. So because the number of food particles decreases, the number of arrangements also decrease!!

Can someone continue my chain of thought and correct me if I'm wrong? What do I need to think of next? Why is it that it appears that the entropy of my plate of food seems to lower with time?

In order to answer this question, we need to understand that a plate of food is not a closed system. The closed system here comprises the plate and the person eating it. Entropy increases in closed systems. Otherwise, could DNA exist, or the whole caboodle of organic life? However, we are factories that defy entropy until we die because we are open systems. In inorganic systems, crystals crystallizing out of a solution are highly ordered, but they are not a closed system. When the solution is considered to close the system, entropy increases [967].

"Entropy is the measure of the disorder or randomness in a system. If we drop a box of matches on the floor, the matches will fall all over the place, and this represents an increase in entropy. In contrast, if we build a house that we are bringing to order, and not chaos, the entropy or disorder of the system is decreased" [967].

Diana asked Dan, "If everything is going towards entropy, why are we busy all our lives in trying to create order?"

Increase in entropy, as per the second law of thermodynamics, is also characterized by a stochastic property. That is, entropy is on the increase, say, 99.99% of the time or in 99.99% of the system, but there could be instances where it decreases for a short time, and then increases shortly thereafter to previously observed values at any point of time. This is proposed by the Poincaré recurrence theorem, which states that a closed system goes back to a point very close to its current state at a later time. This time might be extremely long, so we can basically summarize it as "never." Zermelo noted that this contradicts the increase in entropy concept [967].

Research on the relationship between entropy and the evolution of life began at the turn of the 20th century [968]. The American historian Henry Adams wrote A Letter to American Teachers of History, in which he proposed a theory of history based on the second law of thermodynamics and on the principle of entropy[969].

In 1863, Rudolf Clausius published his noted memoir On the Concentration of Rays of Heat and Light, and on the Limits of its Action, wherein he outlined a preliminary relationship between his newly developed concept of entropy and life [968]. The Austrian physicist Ludwig Boltzmann, in 1875, stated that "the general struggle for existence of animate beings is not a struggle for raw material-these, for organisms, our air, water, and soil, all abundantly available-nor for energy which exists in plenty in anybody in the form of heat, but a struggle for [negative] entropy, which becomes available through the transition of energy from the hot sun to the cold earth".

In 1876, American engineer Richard Sears McCulloh, referring to the first law of thermodynamics and the second law of thermodynamics stated, "When we reflect how generally physical phenomena are connected with thermal changes and relations, it at once becomes obvious that there are few, if any, branches of natural science which are not more or less dependent upon the great truths under consideration. Nor should it, therefore, be a matter of surprise that already, in the short space of time, not yet one generation, elapsed since the mechanical theory of heat has been freely adopted, whole branches of physical science have been revolutionized by it...the body of an animal, not less than a steamer, or a locomotive, is truly a heat engine, and the consumption of food in the one is precisely analogous to the burning of fuel in the other; in both, the chemical process is the same: that called combustion. Heat of the body generally and uniformly is diffused instead of being concentrated in the chest." His conclusion was that "everything physical being subject to the law of conservation of energy, it follows that no physiological action can take place except with expenditure of energy derived from food; also, that an animal performing mechanical work must from the same quantity of food generate less heat than one abstaining from exertion, the difference is precisely the heat equivalent of that of work"[970].

The physicist Erwin Schrödinger stated in his book published in 1944, what is Life?, that life feeds on negative entropy or negentropy. In a later edition, he corrected himself in response to complaints and stated that the actual source is free energy. In his theory, he proposed that life, contrary to what the second law of thermodynamics states, decreases or maintains its entropy by feeding on negative entropy or free energy[971]. "This is what is argued to differentiate life from other forms of matter organization. ... although life's dynamics may be argued to go against the tendency of the second law, which states that the entropy of an isolated system tends to increase, it does not in any way conflict or invalidate this law, because the principle that entropy can only increase or remain constant applies only to a closed system which is adiabatically isolated, meaning no heat can enter or leave. Whenever a system can exchange either heat or matter with its environment, an entropy decrease of that system is entirely compatible with the second law" [972] [968].

The problem of organization in living systems increasing despite the second law is known as the Schrödinger paradox [973]. In 1964, James Lovelock was among a group of scientists who were requested by NASA to make a theoretical life detection system to look for life on Mars during the upcoming space mission. He is quoted as saying "I'd look for an entropy reduction since this must be a general characteristic of life."[974] [968]

In 1882, the German scientist Hermann von Helmholtz defined "affinity" as the highest amount of work possible under reversible conditions. Maximum work is defined as the diminution of the free, or available, energy of the system [975]. Until Helmhotz published this view, it was commonly accepted that all chemical reactions drive the system to a state of equilibrium in which the affinities of the reactions vanish. The term "affinity" was later replaced with the term "free energy" [975, 976].

In 1873, Gibbs published *A Method of Geometrical Representation of the Thermodynamic Properties of Substances by Means of Surfaces*, in which he described the principles of his new equation based on which it was possible to predict or estimate the tendencies of various natural processes that ensue when bodies or systems are brought into contact [975]. He defined three states of equilibrium-"necessarily stable," "neutral," and "unstable"-and the changes that may or may not follow these states [977]. He defined "available energy" as the highest amount of mechanical work possible with a given amount of a certain substance in a given initial state, without any increase in its volume or exchange of heat with the external environment [978]. According to Gibbs, the initial state is that from which "the body can be made to pass from its states of dissipated energy by reversible processes."

Biological processes on earth take place at a roughly constant temperature and pressure. Thus, the thermodynamic interpretation of evolution in relation to entropy is based on the concept of Gibbs free energy, and not entropy. Gibbs free energy is as the thermodynamic quantity required to perform the maximum amount of reversible work by a thermodynamic system at a constant temperature and pressure [975]. It is a useful way to express the second law of thermodynamics under these conditions[979]. The minimization of Gibbs free energy is a form of the principle of minimum energy. It follows from the entropy maximization principle for closed systems. The Gibbs free energy equation, in modified form, can be utilized for open systems when possible chemical terms are included in the energy balance equation.

Gibbs free energy is the maximum amount of non-expansion work that can be extracted from a thermodynamically closed system, one that can exchange heat and work with its surroundings, but not matter. This maximum amount of work can be achieved only if the process is completely reversible. When a system moves from its original state to its final state via a reversible process, the decrease in Gibbs free energy is equivalent to the work done by the system on its surroundings minus the work of the pressure forces[975, 980]. Gibbs free energy is also defined as the thermodynamic potential that is minimized when a system reaches chemical equilibrium at constant pressure and temperature. Its derivative with respect to the reaction coordinate of the system vanishes at the equilibrium point. According to the second law of thermodynamics, for systems reacting at a fixed temperature and pressure, there is a general tendency to achieve the minimum value of Gibbs free energy. In traditional use, the term "free" was added in "Gibbs energy" to mean "available in the form of useful work" [981].

A chemical reaction spontaneously occurs if the change in the total entropy of the universe that the reaction has the potential to cause is nonnegative. Under fixed temperature and pressure, Gibbs free energy is considered as a negative proxy for the change in the total entropy of the universe. It is "negative" because it moves in the opposite direction to total entropy. A reaction with positive Gibbs free energy will not occur spontaneously. However, in biological systems, energy inputs from other sources are "coupled" with reactions that are not entropically favored and have a Gibbs free energy above zero. If all the coupled reactions are included, the total entropy in the universe tends to show an increase. Such coupling of reactions is required for endergonic reactions, such as photosynthesis and DNA synthesis, so that they can take place without causing a decrease in the total entropy of the universe. In this way, biological systems also function in a way that is in keeping with the second law of thermodynamics [975].

This was important for Dan. As a physicist who was thinking more and more about biological systems, he had to make sure that the laws he was reading about are also applicable to biological systems. According to the concept of Gibbs free energy, while energy from nutrients is necessary to sustain order in an organism, the Schrödinger prescience should also be taken into account: "An organism's astonishing gift of concentrating a stream of order on itself and thus escaping the decay into atomic chaos-of drinking orderliness from a suitable environment—seems to be connected with the presence of the aperiodic solids..." [972].

It was clear to Dan that biological systems also obey the rules of physics. He needed this in order to extend some of his ideas about randomness to the human body.

# CHAPTER 54
## More physics

Olivia had never been too much into physics, but these days, it was she who brought up the topic. Dan was surprised. He had the feeling that their discussions about randomness had triggered something inside her. He felt that she had also started thinking about the same issues that he was discussing with himself. But he also knew that she would never share this with him.

Olivia asked him about the law of thermodynamics.

The first law of thermodynamics is that energy is always conserved in an isolated system.

The second law states that the entropy of such a system is always on the increase.

The third law is that a temperature of absolute zero is unreachable.

To sum them up, closed or isolated systems inevitably become less structured, less organized, until they move into a state of equilibrium.

Dan was thinking about the aging process. This issue had been bothering him since his discussions with his daughter.

DNA and other macromolecules in our body determine an organism's life cycle from birth to maturity and death. Nutrition is necessary for the growth and maturation of an organism, but it is not sufficient. Genetics or the information contained in DNA is one of the governing factors in this regard [968]. At some point, every person dies even while remaining in environments that contain sufficient nutrients to sustain life. This supports the notion that a controlling factor is internal, and that DNA must be the prime operative with regard to these characteristics [968].

If we apply Boltzmann's perspective of the second law, the change of state from a more probable, less ordered and high entropy arrangement, to one of less probability, more order, and lower entropy as seen in biological ordering is a DNA function. In biology, the information in our DNA represents the resolution of the paradox posed by life and the entropy requirement of the second law [982, 983].

Dan was looking up research on entropy and aging.

In 1982, the American biochemist Albert Lehninger proposed that the order produced within cells as they grow and divide is more than compensated for by the disorder they create in their surroundings in the course of their growth and division: "living organisms preserve their internal order by taking from their surroundings free energy, in the form of nutrients or sunlight, and returning to their surroundings an equal amount of energy as heat and entropy" [972, 984]. In his book *Information Theory and Evolution*, he describes the phenomenon of life, its origin, and evolution, and human cultural evolution, on the basis of concepts related to thermodynamics, statistical mechanics, and information theory. The paradox between the second law of thermodynamics and the high degree of order and complexity produced by living systems, according to the chemist John Avery, can be resolved by "the information content of the Gibbs free energy that enters the biosphere from outside sources"[985]. The local increase in order is a result of natural selection, and it is mathematically derived from the second law equation for connected non-equilibrium open systems [972, 986].

In a study titled "Natural selection for least action" published in the Proceedings of the Royal Society, Ville Kaila and Arto Annila use the second law of thermodynamics to devise an equation of motion for evolution. They show that natural selection and the principle of least action can be connected by expressing natural selection in terms of chemical thermodynamics. According to this view, evolution explores tracks to level differences in energy densities, thus increasing entropy most rapidly. A living organism plays the role of an energy transfer mechanism, and beneficial mutations allow for transfer of more energy to the environment [972, 986, 987].

In 2013, Azua-Bustos and Vega argued that all lifeforms decrease their internal entropy through free energy obtained from their environment. As entropy is a measure of the degree of disorder, any lifeform must have a higher degree of order than its supporting environment. They demonstrated a method to quantify the degree of difference in the structural complexity, or entropy, of living processes as distinct entities separate from their similar surroundings [968]. However, entropy is defined for equilibrium systems, while living systems operate far from equilibrium. Based on this discrepancy, there are objections to the extension of the second law and entropy to biological systems and the theory of evolution[988]. Another objection is based on the premise that living systems cannot persist in isolation. However, the second law of thermodynamics does not require that free energy is transformed into entropy along the shortest path. Live organisms absorb energy from sunlight or from energy-rich chemical compounds and return part of such energy to the environment as entropy, heat and low free-energy compounds such as water and $CO_2$ [968].

Both Olivia and Dan did not have a background in biology. However, both were now in the process of trying to apply the rules of physics and mathematics to biology.

From a macroscopic perspective, in classical thermodynamics, entropy is a state function of a thermodynamic system. It is a property which depends on the current state of the system, independent of how that state came to be achieved. In a thermodynamic system, pressure, density, and temperature become uniform over time. The equilibrium state has a higher probability, and thus has more possible combinations of microstates, than any other state. In classical thermodynamics, entropy can only be measured for a system that is in thermodynamic equilibrium [946]. Dan decided to go with statistical mechanics instead, as it was easier for Oliva to accept this version of entropy. In statistical mechanics, entropy is defined as a measure of uncertainty. For a given set of macroscopic characteristics, such as temperature, pressure, and volume, entropy is a measure of the degree to which the probability of the system is spread out over different possible microstates. The macrostate characterizes observable average quantities. The microstate specifies all the molecular details about the system, including the position and velocity of every molecule. Entropy is proportional to the number of possible microscopic configurations of individual atoms and molecules of the system, its microstates, which give rise to the observed macroscopic state, macrostate, of the system.

Entropy represents the number of arrangements that are possible for a system, or a measure of "disorder." The more the number of states with substantial probability, the higher is the entropy [946]. The higher the entropy, the higher is the disorder[953, 989].

Both Dan and Olivia realized that they were now moving towards randomness.

Entropy can be more generally interpreted as a measure of the uncertainty or randomness of a system. The equilibrium state of a system represents maximum entropy because it is the state wherein all information about the initial conditions are lost except for the conserved variables. Thus, maximizing entropy maximizes ignorance about the details of the system [990]. In physics, the model or system used has a central role in determining entropy. If two observers use different sets of macroscopic variables, they see different entropies. The set of macroscopic variables one chooses must include everything that may change in the experiment. Otherwise, one might see decreasing entropy [946, 991].

Consider a glass of ice placed at room temperature. In this system, some heat from the warmer surroundings is transferred to the cooler system of ice and water at a constant temperature, which is the melting temperature of ice. The entropy of the system increases as the entropy of its environment decreases. The entropy of the surrounding room decreases to a lesser degree than the degree to which the entropy of the ice and water increases. This is true for all natural events that occur in a thermodynamic system. The final net entropy after such an event is always higher than the initial entropy, as the total degree of disorderliness is higher. This thermodynamic system therefore shows an increase in entropy, as energy spontaneously got more dispersed than in the initial condition wherein the glass of ice and water was just introduced [950].

Entropy is not a conserved quantity, as it changes with the state or the disorderliness or randomness of the system.

It was clear to Dan and Olivia that there is much confusion between the terms *disorder*, *randomness*, and *chaos*. These terms have different meanings in physics and when used figuratively.

"Disorder" is defined in physics as the Shannon entropy of the probability distribution of microstates in a particular macrostate. Under these conditions, the association between disorder and thermodynamics is clear. Frank L. Lambert defines entropy as energy dispersal, but the meaning of the term "dispersal" in physics is different from its meaning in daily use[992]. An increase in entropy is often associated with a spatial reduction in the concentration of the energy density, and never with an increase. But there are counterexamples in which "dispersal" is not apparent. For example, if the dispersal includes the space of quantum energy levels it contradicts the definition of entropy as energy dispersal [950].

Entropy can also be viewed as a measure of energy unavailable for work. But this definition only holds true for cyclic reversible processes. For example, in the case of a gas container, all its internal energy may be converted to work. The amount of work would be close to the total amount of internal energy. For an isolated system comprising two closed systems at different temperatures, in the process of equilibration, the amount of entropy lost by the hot system is a measure of the amount of energy lost by the hot system that is unavailable for work [950].

Diana pointed out an interesting article entitled "Entropy: Why Life Always Seems to Get More Complicated," in which James Clear describes some implications of entropy [993]. His claim is that problems in life arise naturally on their own, while solutions require our attention, energy, and effort. "If anything, our lives become more complicated and gradually decline into disorder rather than remaining simple and structured." Clear hypothesizes that there is one force that governs everybody's life: Entropy. Entropy is a measure of disorder, and there are always far more disorderly variations than clean ones. In explaining this, he cites the example of a puzzle: Imagine dumping a box of puzzle pieces onto a table. In theory, it is possible for all the pieces to fall at the right place and create a completed puzzle as we dump them out of the box. But in reality, that never happens, because the odds are overwhelmingly against it [993]. While there is only one possible state where every piece is in order, there is an infinite number of states where the pieces are in disorder. An orderly outcome is therefore incredibly unlikely to happen at random. A second example is that of a sand castle being built on the beach, which is no longer there a few days later. While there is only one arrangement of sand particles that resembles our sand castle, there are a nearly infinite number of arrangements that don't look like it. In theory, it is possible for the wind and waves to move the sand around and create an arrangement that resembles our sand castle. But in practice, it never happens. This is because systems tend to progress in the direction of increasing entropy[994, 995]. Entropy always increases over time. Symbolically, and also not symbolically, it is the natural tendency of things to lose order. Our lives are not an exception. Life will always become less structured. The inevitable trend is for things to become less organized [993].

These theories do not agree with the "loosing of disorder" idea about aging that was being discussed before.

The British scientist Arthur Eddington claimed, "The law that entropy always increases holds, I think, the supreme position among the laws of nature...if our theory is found to be against the second law of thermodynamics I can give us no hope; there is nothing for it but to collapse in deepest humiliation."[996, 997]. This means that nothing escapes the second law of thermodynamics. Entropy and disorder always increase [998]. This can be viewed as ongoing decay, but disorder and randomness may not necessarily be so. If nature wants disorder and randomness, it might be good.

Based on the concept of entropy, the universe naturally moves toward disorder. Those that think that entropy is terrible, and that disorder is associated with deterioration suggest we need to fight back against it. "Solve a scattered puzzle; pull the weeds out of our garden; clean a messy room; organize individuals into a cohesive team" [993]. Any process for dealing with disorder requires the investment of energy to create stability, structure, and simplicity. "Successful relationships require care and attention. Successful houses require cleaning and maintenance. Successful teams require communication and collaboration. Without effort, things will decay" [993].

If we believe that disorder is evil, we need to expend energy in order to counteract this tendency. Creating order requires energy to resist the pull of entropy.

According to John Brockman's online scientific roundtable Edge, if closed systems inevitably become more disordered and less organized, does it mean that they are less able to accomplish exciting and useful outcomes until they move into equilibrium? Or does it mean that this type of equilibrium is gray, tepid, homogeneous, monotonous and permanent? [957].

Diana was trying to look at it from a philosophical perspective. The second law implies that misfortune may be no one's fault. The instinct that the universe is saturated with a purpose and that everything happens for a reason is proven invalid by the second law. When bad things happen, such as accidents and disease, people tend to think that someone or something must have wanted them to happen. This impels people to find a defendant, demon, scapegoat, or witch to punish [957]. Hundreds of years ago, both Galileo and Newton replaced this universal morality with a clockwork universe in which events are caused by conditions in the present, not goals for the future. The second law extends this notion: "Not only does the universe not care about our desires, but in the natural course of events, it will appear to thwart them. There are so many more ways for things to go wrong than to go right" [957].

It seems that in a world governed by entropy and evolution, houses burn down, ships sink, battles are lost, and poverty is the default state of humankind. It is an under appreciation of the second law that traps people into seeing every unsolved social problem, any bad thing that happens, as a sign that their country is being driven off a cliff. Problems, in fact, represent the very nature of the universe. Nonetheless, it is always better to fight back, by using our information and energy to expand beneficial order [957].

Carl von Clausewitz, a Prussian military analyst, explained in 1832 that "three-quarters of the factors on which action in war is based are wrapped in a fog of…uncertainty." The best military commanders seemed to see through this "fog of war," predicting how their enemies would behave on the basis of limited information. But even the most talented generals made mistakes. They were divining a signal through the fog when no such signal existed. Their mistake was endorsing the law of small numbers. They concluded that the patterns they saw in a small sample of information would also hold for a much more significant sample.

The law of small numbers explains the act of stereotyping. We make conclusions that all people with a particular trait behave the same way. We rely on a single interview when choosing job or college applicants. We tend to see short-term patterns in financial stock charts when stock movements almost never follow predictable patterns. The answer, then, is to consider not just the pattern of data, but also the amount of data [957].

This brings us back to big data. Big data can probably be used to overcome some of these problems. However, Dan was sure that the answer did not lie in big data. He also felt that Olivia was aware of this. After all, she had been working with big data in an attempt to resolve aging but had had no success so far. There was clearly another missing link. Dan knew that he could figure it out. If only he could properly integrate these concepts with his knowledge of biology.

# CHAPTER 55

## Molecular mechanisms and thermodynamics

Dan was looking into a review by Hoffman[14]. He knew that he had to make some sense of all the concepts he had read about in the context of biological processes if he wanted to move forward with translating the laws of physics into everyday life.

"I want to turn these laws into products," he was telling Diana. She was lost. She understood the words, but not what they meant.

The molecular machinery in living organisms performs purposeful tasks while surrounded by thermal chaos. As Hoffman says in his review, "Molecular motors take on a number of tasks in our cells, including moving cargo, re-arranging the cell's cytoskeleton, transporting organelles, moving chromosomes during cell division and helping cells change shape"[14, 999]. Dan learned that molecular machines are of great importance in biology. They also have a significant impact in physics. Models conceived to explain how motors operate in the presence of significant thermal fluctuations tell us about statistical physics, the emergence of the second law of thermodynamics and connections to information theory. These studies show that noise is not "bad," and that it is an essential element of functional nanoscale systems. Hoffman shows that the study of molecular motors relates statistical mechanics to a fundamental understanding of how life works. "Nature has been building 'nanobots' for billions of years—and now we have the opportunity to learn how she did it. Theoretical studies of natural and artificial machines will continue to enrich our understanding of statistical physics and guide further research"[14].

How can a single molecule create a directed motion in the presence of substantial thermal fluctuations? Or more precisely, how can a molecule, immersed in thermal noise, but provided with some kind of low entropy energy, in the form of chemical or electrostatic energy, perform directed work? How does chemistry turn into "clockwork"?

Answering these questions involves an understanding of many elements of fundamental physics, including entropy, free energy and the second law of thermodynamics at the single molecule level. It requires the application of statistical mechanics and information theory to biological systems[14].

A molecular machine is a molecule or small molecular assembly that performs a function. This function increases free energy or performs work at the expense of chemical energy in the presence of thermal fluctuations. The thermal fluctuations are of similar magnitude as the chemical energy used and the work produced. Molecular machines are capable of transforming one form of energy into another while using random thermal motion as part of their energy input[14]. Molecular motors are machines that convert chemical energy into directed mechanical work. A well-known molecular machine, ATP synthase, converts electrical energy into mechanical energy, which is then transformed into chemical energy[1000]. ATP synthase incorporates mechanical motion as part of its working cycle and increases free energy by "recharging" ADP to ATP. Strong thermal fluctuations make molecular motors very different from macroscopic motors. They cannot be described by macroscopic thermodynamics but can be described statistically. Molecular machines are subject to random forces, and the "natural state" is random diffusion. At the nanoscale, a force must be applied to keep an object from moving[1001].

Hill performed experiments on isolated muscle tissue to measure the work and heat output under various load conditions, from no load to isometric load, which is a load large enough to prevent the muscle from contracting. Based on these studies, he designed the "Hill curve," which relates applied load to the speed of contraction. The heat generated was independent of the load, and was only dependent on the length of the contraction. This suggested that a fixed amount of chemical energy was transduced for each "step" of muscle contraction[1002].

Andrew Huxley showed that molecular motors function outside the simple thermodynamics and mechanics of macroscopic machines[1003]. Huxley claimed that muscles transduced random thermal motion into directed mechanical motion and that chemical energy merely served to reset the molecular machine to its starting position. His model showed that the chemical energy used up by muscles was not used to move the fibers relative to each other. Instead, "the sliding members can combine temporarily with sites on adjacent actin filaments, the connection being formed spontaneously but broken only by a reaction requiring energy to be supplied by metabolic sources." This means that energy is required to break the connection between myosin and actin, but not to move the myosin and actin fibers past each other. A change in the conformation of the myosin occurred as it relaxed to allow the chemical energy from a metabolic source to be transduced, and the myosin would detach from the actin to repeat the cycle[1004]. This machine was capable of spontaneously rectifying random thermal motion due to its asymmetric construction; an attachment point was present at an offset location from the equilibrium position of the molecule. This seems to be in violation of the second law. However, the cycle could be repeated only after the "machine" was detached[14]. Detachment requires energy. Externally supplied energy must be supplied to "reset" the machine and allow it to repeat the cycle. The energy is converted into heat in accordance with the second law. The second law does *not* prohibit the existence of some mechanism that can directly convert heat into usable work under isothermal conditions, or the use of a lower temperature reservoir. However, it prohibits a mechanism that can do this continuously[1005].

Huxley showed that molecular motors work by switching between states with low energy barriers, which allow diffusion, and states with high energy barriers, such as active binding to a filament, which "fixes" the location of the motor from time to time. Breaking the high-energy barrier states requires an external input of energy. This led to a new understanding of the statistical nature of the second law[14].

Dan liked the concept that molecular machines can rectify random thermal motion. The mechanical motion of these motors is caused by thermal motion as they traverse energy barriers. Hoffman raised the question of how they convert random thermal motion into a directed motion. How does the time asymmetry of the second law apply at the molecular scale, given that molecular collisions are time reversible?

How the deterministic laws of thermodynamics emerged from statistical laws was explored by the Gedanken experiments? It is explained through "Maxwell's demon"[1006]. The demon, which is a thought experiment, is described as a microscopic creature which controls a trapdoor that separates two chambers filled with gas. Initially, the two chambers are at the same temperature, but the speeds of the gas molecules are statistically distributed according to the Maxwell-Boltzmann distribution. The demon can open and close the trap door to sort slow and fast molecules into different chambers. Heat can be made to move from a colder to a warmer body without the expenditure of energy. This violates the second law of thermodynamics. For Maxwell, the second law was not a law inherent in matter, but rather a statistical law[14].

Smoluchowski proposed a ratchet-based model as an example of a Maxwell's demon to support the statistical basis of thermodynamics. He developed a machine in which a small particle is suspended via Brownian motion by virtue of being attached to a linear ratchet. The ratchet allows the particle to move up but not down. This is achieved by having a spring-loaded pawl pressing into the asymmetric teeth on the serrated vertical shaft of the ratchet. The asymmetry of the teeth makes the force required to move up less than the force required to move back down [14, 1007]. In order to rectify thermal motion and work against gravity, the random thermal force on the small particle should be large enough to overcome the spring force of the pawl of the ratchet. That is, the ratchet mechanism needs to be weak enough to be moved by thermal energy and to be subject to the same thermal fluctuations. The fluctuations allow the pawl to open from time to time, letting the particle slip back down. Statistically, the position of the particle would follow a Boltzmann distribution, with or without the ratchet. The difference is an additional energy component originating from the potential energy of the ratchet's spring[14].

Richard Feynman, the American theoretical physicist, converted the linear ratchet to a rotating ratchet attached to a paddle wheel through a shaft. The ratchet and the paddle wheel are in different compartments. The ratchet does not move directionally if the wheel and the ratchet are at the same temperature. When the temperatures are different, the ratchet mechanism rectifies the random thermal collisions acting on the paddle wheel. The thermal fluctuations of the ratchet are reduced by keeping it cool, while the paddle wheel receives enough energy from collisions, by keeping it hot enough to push the wheel forward against the force of the spring. When the ratchet is hotter than the wheel, the machine runs backwards [1008].

Two essential ingredients were suggested for the Brownian motion to occur: asymmetry and out-of-equilibrium conditions. Asymmetry is required, as in a completely symmetric situation there is no preference for either direction, and the motor would randomly diffuse. Smoluchowski and Feynman showed that a simple ratchet in a regular temperature bath would not be able to rectify motion. All parts of the ratchet would be thermalized equally and perform random motions[1009]. In fact, Feynman's ratchet only worked in the presence of a thermal gradient. This gradient is maintained "artificially" to keep the machine working. That is, the system has to be kept out of equilibrium.

In a real molecular motor, the desired temperature gradients cannot be sustained. Over the small distances involved, the molecular motors cannot be based on temperature gradients. Any temperature gradient would be equalized in a time much shorter than the cycle time of the motor. For molecular motors, thermal gradients are not possible to keep them out of equilibrium[14]. In chemical systems at equilibrium, the forward and reverse reaction rates are equal. This represents "detailed balance." If we apply this balance to a molecular motor, it means that forward and reverse motions would proceed at the same average rate during equilibrium. However, a chemically driven molecular motor would make no progress, even in the presence of an asymmetric potential. For the system to be work, it has to be kept out of thermodynamic equilibrium, as non-equilibrium conditions provide asymmetry. The evolution of the system in one direction moves the system closer to equilibrium, and its evolution in the opposite evolution moves it further away from equilibrium. A microscopic system can spontaneously fluctuate in a direction away from equilibrium. Thus, a machine such as Huxley's myosin model converts heat into work in a way that is not in keeping with the second law[14].

Jarzynski equality states that the Boltzmann-weighted routine work performed by a "one-shot" machine is equal to the Boltzmann-weighted free energy difference[1010]. But according to the second law, the work performed during a process is *less* than the available free energy difference. This is true on average, but occasionally, the work equals or succeeds the available free energy difference. For molecular motors, this means that, given sufficient spatial asymmetry, a motor that could rectify thermal motion can be made only in a unique fashion [1011]. As explained in the myosin model, a reset step is required for repeated rectification, and this step requires external energy input into the system. This confirms that the second law is a statistical law and that a "one-shot" deviation is not a violation of the law. As long as external energy is required to reset the machine, the second law is upheld[14]. A violation only occurs if the machine could rectify thermal motion repeatedly without any external energy input.

Spatial asymmetry is achieved by the asymmetric potential energy of the track on which the motor operates, or by internal conformational changes which bias the motion in a specific direction. Temporal asymmetry through out-of-equilibrium conditions is achieved by applying an oscillating force, by subjecting the motor to an oscillating potential, or by immersing the molecule in correlated, non-white noise[1001, 1012]. The Huxley's model for myosin exhibits temporal asymmetry. The machine only works if ATP hydrolysis is correlated with the conformational state of the machine. Hydrolysis only occurs when the machine is attached and has pulled the actin filament and not at any other time during the cycle. There is a mechanism to "gate" the hydrolysis that happens at a particular time. In a real machine, this is achieved by conformational changes, i.e., allostery. A reverse process is avoided by maintaining a large, out-of-equilibrium supply of ATP and a small concentration of ADP. Thus, asymmetric structures, gating and non-equilibrium concentrations of energy-supplying molecules are necessary for the working of molecular machines[14] [1013].

A ratchet is implemented when a particle, placed in an asymmetric periodic potential, is subject to a correlated noise in addition to the uncorrelated thermal noise. In the presence of "white" thermal noise alone, an asymmetric potential is not sufficient to impose directed motion. However, in the presence of any correlated noise with time correlations longer than molecular relaxation times, a directed motion emerges in the presence of an asymmetric potential. It creates directed motion "for free," as no particular energy input is needed as long as there is a source of correlated noise[1001].

Correlated noise suggests low entropy noise, and, in a real physical system, such noise is produced by degrading a low entropy energy source. Correlated noise can be generated by a chemical cycle, such as the binding and hydrolysis of ATP and release of ADP. This chemical cycle serves as a "correlated noise generator." It does not drive the motion directly though. A molecular motor works by "gluing together" a chemical cycle and a mechanical cycle. The chemical cycle "eats non-equilibrium chemical energy" and produces "correlated noise," while the mechanical cycle "eats correlated noise" and produces directed motion. In this system, chemical energy consumption is separated from the mechanical cycle. The mechanical cycle does not consume any energy, and energy is consumed by the noise-generating chemical cycle[1014]. The ratchet model represents a "continuum" version of a machine operating through a "reset" step. Low entropy energy is used to create correlated noise, but not to drive motion directly. This means that some kind of mechanochemical coupling driven by chemical, correlated noise is sufficient to drive directed motion on an asymmetric energy landscape[14].

The term "Brownian ratchet" is used to refer to all molecular ratchets, as well as polymerization motors, where Brownian diffusion and biased monomer binding lead to the unidirectional extension of a polymeric filament such as actin[1015].

The two models of molecular motors are the fluctuating potential or "flashing" ratchets and the fluctuating force or "tilting" ratchets. In the case of flashing ratchets`, the height of the periodic potential fluctuates. This simulates a molecular motor which switches between weak and strong`, or attached and detached`, binding states. In the weak binding or detached state`, the motor can diffuse before reattaching tightly to the track. The tilting ratchet is based on a fluctuating force. The potential is the integral of the force`, and the entire periodic potential is tilted up and down during the fluctuations. This ratchet better corresponds to a power stroke-driven molecular motor [14, 1016].

Dan liked Hoffman's idea that molecular machines have deep connections to information theory. Hoffman had managed to describe quite aptly how the import of information in the form of reset steps (in the discrete picture of the machine) or correlated noise (in the continuum picture) lead to the transformation of thermal chaos into directed motion[14].

The ratchet machine tells us something profound about the second law of thermodynamics: A thermodynamic cost is exacted when a bit of information is erased[14]. This means that a Maxwell demon would have to erase its immediate measuring memory to make a new measurement. Even if it uses a permanent memory to keep track of all measurements, it would need to move the information from the measurement memory to the permanent memory, which involves erasure[1017]. The idea of erasing information is evident in a flashing ratchet. The potential at which the ratchet diffuses alternates between a non-zero asymmetric potential and a low, vanishing potential. It corresponds to a situation where the motor detaches, diffuses freely and reattaches to a track periodically. In this scheme, the motor "forgets" its position relative to the potential when it detaches. When the motor re-attaches to the track, the particle "takes a measurement" of the potential, which is erased again in the next cycle. Such a motor would not be able to operate for "free."

An extreme case would be to run a machine by destroying information directly, with no energy transformation. A recent paper suggests that this may be possible[1018]. That is, a machine could be run via the degradation of any conserved quantity, not just energy. In this case, the correlated noise is information-rich, low entropy noise, whose creation requires energy input[14].

Real molecular machines are more efficient than the diffusing ratchet model though. This is probably because they have much better "gating," which helps avoid back-slapping via a combination of internally conformational changes. Consider the motion of a kinesin molecule, for which the energy is supplied by the hydrolysis of ATP. Unbinding a kinesin head from the microtubule requires energy [1019-1021]. However, there are other energy barriers to consider. The potential is assumed to be spatially periodic, piece-wise linear and continuous, but at the same time asymmetric, with linear slopes representing the "teeth" of a linear ratchet. As a kinesin motor domain dissociates from the microtubule, the potential it "sees" is diminished in height. The energy supplied by ATP is more than sufficient for dissociation. The fluctuations in potential are a result of the energy provided by ATP hydrolysis. The time dependence of the fluctuations is described as a dichotomous symmetric Markov process. Using these parameters, we can simulate the motion of kinesin molecules[14].

High-frequency noise approaches random white noise when correlation times approach molecular collision times. At high frequencies, the motor does not have time to diffuse from a minimum of the potential to the next nearest maximum during a single cycle. This suggests that the critical time corresponds to the average time it takes for the motor to diffuse far enough. At low frequencies, the tilting ratchet shows massive displacement speeds, as the motor drifts while the potential is tilted. Since the potential is asymmetric, the drift is stronger in one direction than in the other. For the flashing potential, low frequencies are associated with long periods of diffusion over a flat potential, and therefore random diffusion dominates, reducing net speed. In the case of flashing ratchets, optimal speed is achieved when the motor diffuses just far enough to reach the next peak of the potential when the potential is weak or zero, and then drifts down the incline of the potential, when the potential is stable again[1022].

Molecular machines operate in a system where thermal, chemical and mechanical energies are of comparable magnitude. If the machine is too large, thermal energy will be too small to effect any mechanical deformations of the machine. All types of energy become similar to the available thermal energy only if the system size is in the 1–100 nm range. Thus, autonomous, thermally driven machines can only be built at the nanoscale level[1023].

A distinguishing feature of biological molecular motors is that they operate in one dimension. They move along a linear polymeric track. They originate from proteins diffusing along polymers, such as DNA, RNA, actin or microtubules. One-dimensional diffusion is common in biology. DNA and RNA provide a way to perform fast searches for matching sequences, which are impossible with random 3D diffusion. To make a simple diffusing molecular motor, an asymmetric track is needed, as well as a source of correlated noise from the binding and dissociation of molecules. Most biological polymers are asymmetric. Enzymes, which bind and dissociate various substrates, when bound to a polymeric molecule, could turn into a real directional motor[14].

It was clear to Dan that the basic structure of a molecular motor consists of a motor domain or "head," which includes the catalytic domain where ATP is hydrolyzed by ATPase, and a neck linker that connects the head or heads to a stalk, which is usually in the form of a "heavy chain" with a "coiled-coil" or α-helix configuration. The stalk connects the heads to a cargo or another head, or it forms a filament, as in the case of myosin II. Essential for the function of real molecular machines are chemically induced conformational changes, i.e., allosteric mechanisms[14].

Allostery describes the primary mechanism by which chemistry is translated into mechanics. Microscopically, allostery is associated with changes in the local conformation of a binding pocket. Via a molecular lever mechanism, this change is amplified and acts on a distal part of the molecule. In the case of enzymes, allostery is used to regulate their activity. For molecular motors, multiple allosteric changes help "gate" the motion to bias the motion forward and avoid backsliding. They also time the different motions and binding events in the correct sequence. Allostery is used in molecular motors to regulate their function by confirming that they only attach to a filament and start walking when they are attached to a cargo[14, 1024].

The typical cycle of a molecular motor is as follows: (1) ATP binding, hydrolysis, phosphate release, and ADP release; (2) Binding and dissociation from a polymer track or filament; (3) Internal conformational changes caused by and causing feedback. Conformational changes control the order of these events and provide mechanochemical coupling. An association exists between the chemical and mechanical cycles of the motor. Conformational changes are both caused by and result in different chemical and mechanical states; they provide feedback loops that gate the motion and ensure dynamic fidelity and consistency[14].

The relevant timescales and speeds of real molecular motors are determined by molecular friction, translational energy barriers, and cooperative conformational changes. The molecular relaxation times are in the order of picoseconds, and typical cycles in molecular motors are longer, in the order of 1–10 milliseconds[14].

Molecular motors exhibit *tight coupling* between ATP hydrolysis and stepping. Motors like kinesin or myosin V take one step per one ATP hydrolyzed [1025, 1026]. Stepping is associated with highly coordinated conformational changes that allow the motion to be highly choreographed and gated. This is suggestive of a pure "powerstroke" model.

This is not the whole story of molecular motors though[1027].

Molecular motors do not directly convert chemical energy and release it into mechanical motion. The chemical cycling of ATP does not correspond to the mechanical cycling of the motor. There is no direct association between ATP hydrolysis and the powerstroke. This essential role is played by thermal diffusion. Thermal energy and conformational diffusion are involved in helping the motor through the various transitions and finding consecutive low-energy conformations[14].

ATP hydrolysis often causes conformational changes that are not directly associated with propelling the motor forward, such as "pre-strokes" or dissociation of a head from a track. The relation between the chemical ATPase cycle and the mechanical cycle is different in different motors. ATP dissociation occurs in several distinct steps: ATP splits into ADP and phosphate (P), P is released, and finally, ADP is released. Thus, the energy from ATP hydrolysis may be used over several conformational steps of the molecule and possibly stored over this time as elastic energy[1028].

It is argued that a pure powerstroke model which does not take into account thermal motion is as inadequate as the strong thermal fluctuations themselves. Any conformational change of the motor involves a transition state and corresponding energy barrier. Significant conformational changes effected by distal binding events are involved. For the motor to overcome energy barriers and find the next accessible complex low energy state, thermal fluctuations are vital. The search for different conformational states during the cycling of the motor is a diffusional process in a multidimensional configurational space on a complex energy landscape[14].

The ratchet model provides a robust conceptual framework that is used in more realistic models of molecular motors. While applying this model, it is important to understand that some machines are more tightly coupled than others, with some exhibiting significant amounts of diffusional randomness and loose coupling between ATP hydrolysis and mechanical stepping [1029].

There are many different types of molecular motors. The best known are kinesin, myosin, and dynein. Each of these has many different subtypes, which vary in function, structure, processivity, and speed. Molecular motors are divided into processive and non-processive motors. Processive motors are motors that stay attached to a filament for a long time while moving along it, thus covering significant distances. Processivity requires that the motor stay connected to the track at all times. Kinesin is one such motor. It works alone and has to move cargo over vast distances in a cell. Kinesin is a high-duty ratio motor. Similar to tight coupling, processivity does not imply that the motor cannot work via a diffusive ratchet mechanism. This means that during the diffusion, there must be some method of keeping the motor from diffusing away from the filament. Myosin II is a non-processive motor. It attaches, tilts and detaches. It works in collaboration with large numbers of other myosin motors and is attached to a myosin bundle. It grasps, moves and releases periodically. Myosin II is a low-duty ratio motor[14].

Beyond molecular motors, there is a vast array of molecular machines, many of which use a chemical or electrical energy source together with thermal energy to effect motion. For example, the bacterial flagellar motor is a fascinating rotary machine in its own right[1030]. In fact, cells are full of molecular machines: active pumps that pump molecules against their chemical potential gradients[1031], machinery for DNA replication and transcription[1032], ribosomes for RNA translation[1033], machinery to divide the cellular chromosome[1034] and machines for membrane fusion[1035]. Kinetics studies performed on most molecular motors, such as kinesin, have confirmed that molecular motors are mechanically coupled enzymes that obey Michaelis–Menten kinetics[1036, 1037]. Slow product release seems to be a universal feature of molecular motors. There are also structural studies and motility studies which further shed light on these motors[14].

Dan realized that despite significant progress in our understanding of molecular motors and machines, there is still much to be learned. "Biology is a science of diversity and complexity," as Hoffman said[14]. Every type of molecular machine works differently: their work cycles, regulation, and structure are all be different. Further, the question of whether molecular machines have evolved to maximum efficiency, and if not, why not, is unresolved. There are also the questions about how these machines are regulated[1038] and how they work collectively[1039], their role in disease and aging[1040], and their role in the gene repair and cell division machinery. Determining their role in gene expression could help explain why oncogenic mutations occur or why the fidelity of gene replication seems to degrade with age[14].

Dan was also interested in the construction of artificial molecular machines [1041] and the applications of such molecular machines[14, 1042, 1043]. For Dan, it was fascinating. He realized that if he could apply some of the physics concepts he had in mind to biological processes, he could improve life itself.

# CHAPTER 56

## Mother Nature is a bitch, as explained by Murphy

Dan had a lengthy discussion with Diana about the possible connections between concepts in physics, biology, and psychology. For her, it seemed to be a matter of intuition that all these subjects were connected. "You must be right," Dan said. "I am too much into mechanisms, and at this point, there is so much that we know, yet we cannot understand all the associations and links."

Diana was reading to Dan a piece by Edge Steven Pinker, a cognitive psychologist and linguist, which described the significance of the second law for our understanding of the universe and our place in it:

In a biological sense, the second law describes why we humans must obtain food, water, and oxygen to continue living. We cannot continue for as long as a closed system does and we must have many inputs of energy [1044]. In Pinker's words, "The second law defines the ultimate purpose of life, mind, and human striving: to deploy energy and information to fight back the tide of entropy and carve out refuges of beneficial order." The concept presented is that entropy increases quickly as our body slides inevitably toward deterioration [1044].

One could also consider how the second law informs descriptions of human actions and interests, including human meaning. The second law implies that human life is a process full of self-expression and affirmation. It is viewed as a stream of activity in search of our interests and desires, with constant learning and adaptation. Our lives are filled daily with inputs to our cognitive and emotional systems. We are engaged in multiple modes of self-expression and action. The fundamental understanding is that there is no need to resist the tide of increasing entropy. Instead, the striving that Pinker talks about is the deploying of energy and information to create beneficial order.

Creating order from chaos is not easy. Entropy will always continue to increase. So the only way to bring order is to add energy. This requires effort.

Diana raised the question, "Why does it feel like we are attempting to fight nature? If the universe wants disorder, why do we want to fight back?"

Yvon Chouinard is an American rock climber, environmentalist, and outdoor businessman. His company, Patagonia, is known for its environmental focus [1045]. He once said, "The hardest thing in the world is to simplify our life because everything is pulling us to be more and more complex" [993]. But is order really simpler and better?

The collection of atoms that make up our body could be arranged in a virtually infinite number of ways, and nearly all of them would lead to no form of life whatsoever [993]. So, mathematically speaking, the odds are overwhelmingly against our very presence. In other words, we are an improbable combination of atoms. And yet, here we are. If this is indeed so, then in a universe where entropy rules the day, the presence of life with such organization, structure, and stability is stunning.

"Can we view the disorder as the order?" Diana asked. If the universe is indeed based on entropy and prefers disorder, then this disorder should be viewed as "the order" that we need to look for and get back to, and it also means using less energy.

"To be happy we need some degree of success in each major area. Thus, all happy families are alike because they all have a similar structure" [993]. Does this mean that we need order to be happy? This idea seemed defective to Dan.

Given what we know about entropy, what are the odds that the environment we happen to grow up in is optimal for our talents? It is doubtful that life will present us with a situation that perfectly matches our strengths. Out of all the possible scenarios we could encounter, it's far more likely that we'll encounter one that does not cater to our talents [993].

Human behavior always needs to be explained in reference to the situation the person is in. Failure is doing so is known as the Fundamental Attribution Error. We are confident that people behave honestly because that is their virtue. That is, people are considered to be open and friendly on account of a virtue called "extroversion," while those who behave in an aggressive way do so because of "hostility." Under different conditions, a person is expected to behave in a similarly honest or extroverted way [957]. Evolutionary biologists use the term "mismatch conditions" to describe when an organism is not well suited for a condition it is facing. Common expressions for mismatch conditions in our everyday lives are "like a fish out of water" or "bringing a knife to a gunfight." "When we are in a mismatch condition, it is difficult to succeed, to be useful, and to win" [993].

Diana asked, "Can we become more creative or talented under such 'disorder' conditions?"

We all face mismatch conditions in our life. It is far more likely that we all live in such a state than in a well-matched one. This does not mean that such a state is necessarily wrong. One way of thinking will tell us that you "must take it upon yourself to design your ideal lifestyle. We have to turn a mismatch condition into a well-matched one. Optimal lives are designed, not discovered" [993]. On the other hand, we may take advantage of such a mismatch. Rather than trying to change it or investing energy in fighting the entropy, we can think of ways of making the most out of it.

Diana suggested a compromise. Whether we decide to fight entropy or accept it, what is most important is that we find the best way for us to progress in the way we think we should. Whether we accept the notion that entropy is terrible, or that it is right, we can select the path that is optimal for us.

Cesar Hidalgo is a Chilean statistical physicist, writer, and data visualization designer. He is an Associate Professor of Media Arts and Sciences at MIT and the director of the Collective Learning Group at The MIT Media Lab, and is the author of Why Information Grows [1046], in which he writes about criticality and how it is fundamental to understanding complex systems. Dan was not trying to think of compromises. He was into clear solutions, equations.

In physics, a system is in a critical state when it is suitable for a transition phase. Water that is in the process of turning into ice or a cloud that is bursting with water vapor are examples of physical systems that are in a critical state. There is no difference between cold water and water that is about to freeze, because water that is just about to freeze is still liquid. Cold water that is about to freeze contains tiny ice crystals which are so small that water remains liquid. It is water in a critical state, a state in which any additional freezing will result in these crystals touching each other, generating ice. However, freezing is not a result of these last crystals, which only represent the instability needed to trigger the transition. The real cause of the transition is the criticality of the state [957].

Murphy's Law states that "anything that can go wrong, will go wrong." The concept of entropy seems to be in keeping with Murphy's law, and this explains why this law pops up so frequently in different life situations [993]. It is true that there are more ways things can go wrong than right, as disorder seems to be the nature of nature. This is essentially entropy. But the important question is whether disorder necessarily means that something has gone wrong. The difficulties of life do not occur because the planets are misaligned or because some cosmic force is conspiring against us. Neither is it because entropy is at work. It is nobody's fault that life has problems. "It is simply a law of probability. There are many disordered states and few ordered ones" [993].

**These phrases are commonly used by believers of Murphy's Law:**

Mother Nature is a bitch.

The universe is not indifferent to intelligence; it is actively hostile to it.

If everything seems to be going well, we have apparently overlooked something.

If in any problem we find ourselves doing an immense amount of work, the answer can be obtained by simple inspection.

Never make anything simple and efficient when a way can be found to make it complicated and wonderful.

If it doesn't fit, use a bigger hammer.

If we believe the opposite, start thinking that the disorder which is part of our universe can be used to our favor. The disorder is something we can learn how to benefit from. It does not necessarily mean harm to us. Mother Nature does not hate us.

Further, Murphy's law is self-proving for the following reasons [1047]:

1. It states that "If anything can go wrong, it will."
2. If it is held true, then Murphy's Law itself can go wrong.
3. If Murphy's Law can be disproven sometimes, it means that things can sometimes go right.
4. Things do sometimes go right, as proved by experience.
5. Therefore, Murphy's Law can go wrong.
6. Therefore, Murphy's Law holds true.
7. Therefore, Murphy's Law is self-proving.

Brian G. Thomas, a Professor of Mechanical Engineering at Colorado School of Mines said, "If it can be shown that something that could have gone wrong did not go wrong, then subsequent events will prove that everything would ultimately have turned out better if that thing had gone wrong." [1048]

Diana said, "as long as you believe that the path you select, under certain circumstances, is the right one for you, it is the right one."

Dan was not sure. He wanted to find a way that would help choose the appropriate path in life. In fact, his idea now was to create the right circumstances for making it happen.

# CHAPTER 57

## Randomness as a method of learning

Dan was thinking about parenthood. He was telling Diana about an incident between a parent and a child.

Linda entered her daughter's room. Her daughter Julia had returned home early from school saying that she was not feeling well. Linda remembered how she had made up stories to tell her own mother so she could leave school early or be excused from doing her chores. Julia was sitting on her bed surrounded by millions of toys, books, papers, pieces of her puzzles, all scattered about in what looked to Linda like a crazy mess. Linda already knew that it was a lost cause. If she asked Julia to tidy up her room, Julia would cry, and Linda would then ask her to stay in her room and not watch TV that afternoon. At the end of the day, Linda would have to fix the mess herself. It was a grey day in Cleveland, and she was not in the mood for a fight.

"Julia, would you like to have soup for lunch? It will make you feel better," she said quietly.

Julia looked at her, surprised. She was expecting the usual comments about how her life would be destroyed if she did not keep her room in order and how her grades would go down if she did not arrange her toys and books on the shelf. She believed her mother was right, but never could understand why her mother got so angry about it. In fact, the room did not seem so disorganized to her.

So, why do we keep telling our children to keep their rooms neat? Why do our teachers tell us to work and learn in a certain way? Why is the learning process we are all used to, always so orderly? We all learn mathematics, literature, languages in a specific structure. We are asked to follow a particular outline.

If our goal is learning, communicating an idea to our boss, or teaching others, are the "fully organized" methods actually the ideal ones?

In *Sources of Insight*, an article on different methods of teaching, randomness is described as one of the styles of teaching [1049]. For becoming a better teacher, having a better influence on others, and communicating our ideas better, there are many methods that we employ to reach our goals. In fact, all of them may be right, as well as not so effective. There is no one winning formula. It is all about how we sequence information and how we relate to it. One of the keys is to know our own preferences, and then understand others.

There are four methods people tend to use: (a) Concrete: This involves processing information based on what we see, hear, think, feel, and taste ("It is what it is"). Such learners look out for real-life examples to understand information. (b) Abstract: This method involves looking for patterns. It requires learners to be more cerebral in their analysis and use their intuition and imagination ("Things aren't always what they appear to be"). They create abstractions from examples and use it to improve their approach to learning or sharing information. (c) Sequential: In this method, chunks of information are processed in a linear way. These learners prefer a plan or set of steps to follow. They typically go line by line, building upon what they already know. (d) Random: Chunks of information are processed in a random way. Such learners hop around random bits of information with ease, in the manner of bouncing around or skimming bullets [1049].

Based on these four methods, there are several schemes of learning:

Concrete sequential: The information is presented sequentially with concrete facts and data. Students who use this method learn well when one example or concept follows another in a linear way. Hopping around is a problem and can create frustration and confusion

Abstract sequential: Abstractions are great as long as they follow a sequential flow. These students are satisfied if a linear method is used.

What about randomness?

Concrete random: The sequence of the information is not important, as long as it's concrete and relatable. These students can skip chunks of information around quickly, but they need examples to latch on to an idea. They are good at cutting through fog and finding where the rubber meets the road.

Abstract random: Abstractions are tremendous, and the sequence does not matter. Such students have the most uncomplicated time learning because the sequence does not matter to them. They have a hard time sharing what they know though, and they get bored when information is sequential and detailed [1049].

Most of us have mixed preferences for the best method to learn something. These may change with time or under different circumstances. But these methods demonstrate that we can use randomness for studying, interacting with others, and communicating ideas.

You need to know yourself, and also those you teach, talk to, or communicate with. Distinguish your preferences and theirs for processing information. If they don't like hopping around, create a path for them. If you are

moving too slow for them, try skipping to the main points, even if it is out of sequence [1049].

Our preferences may change every day, throughout the day, and under various circumstances. Figure out if you prefer concrete or random, random or sequential. Test the different styles to determine what works for you and for those you interact with under different conditions. Perhaps we will find that we can achieve better results if we add a dollop of randomness when studying history, mathematics, or languages.

# CHAPTER 58

## Is it really randomness that we chase?

Diana was trying to convince Dan to go on a short vacation. She was worried that he was compulsively studying this randomness for almost 24 hours a day. When he quit his job to focus on it, she had realized that it was very important for him. But she felt like he might be overworking himself.

"Maybe a short vacation will do you right?" she suggested.

Dan was telling her, "How many times have you heard someone say 'I really need a vacation to clear my head so that I can forget about my problems or daily routines'? Do we want to go on vacation to induce some randomness into our life? Life is pretty chaotic and random, and this is what really makes it so hard. So maybe we need a vacation to get more routine into our life?"

There is a famous joke that calculates our vacation days:

So, you want a day off. Let's take a look at what you are asking for.

There are 365 days per year available for work. This equals 52 week per year from which you already have 2 days off per week, leaving 261 days available for work.

Since you spend 16 hours each day away from work, you have used up 170 days, leaving only 91 available days. You spend 30 minutes each day on coffee break, which adds up to 23 days each year, leaving only 68 available days. With an hour for lunch each day, you use up another 46 days, leaving only 22 days available for work. You usually spend 2 days per year on sick leave. This leaves us only 20 days per year available for work. You are off another 5 days per year, so the available working time is now down to 15 days. We generously allow 14 days of vacation per year, which leaves only 1 day available for work, and I'll be damned if you are going to take that day off!

We need to get up every day at the same time, take the train, drive our car, work, or at least pretend we are working, drive home, have dinner, pick up our kids, talk with our spouse, pay our bills, and go to sleep... Is this the routine that we want to get out of? It does not sound too chaotic. In fact, it is so well ordered that it is pretty dull. But, of course, there are so many random issues that could pop up in the course of such "routine" life. It could be a small issue such as missing a train, being late to work, or having to deal with a grumpy or upset spouse or a nagging customer. But it could be a bigger issue such as our car breaking down, our child falling ill, or our boss driving us crazy. In either case, we find that our routines are suddenly disrupted. The order is interrupted. We panic. We spend energy on solving these problems. We crave the order that we had. The unexpected things are those that make our life more difficult, and not necessarily the routines. We may now shout out, "but I just want to sit on a beach and do nothing for a few days."

But such a vacation may replace chaos or randomness with a new routine of lying on a beach for a few hours a day.

Two very weary office workers had been working very hard for many days in a row. It was a very busy time of the year, and it was difficult for any of them to take time off. One of them was struck by an idea. He whispered to his friend, "I've found a way," and saying this, he quickly jumped up onto his desk, removed a few ceiling tiles, hoisted himself up onto the ventilation pipe and then swung himself upside down.

Within seconds, their manager emerged from his cabin and asked him what he was up to. "I'm a light bulb," he answered.

"And I think you need some time off," said his alarmed supervisor. "It's an order. I want you to take at least two days off and rest properly!"

"Yes sir," the worker replied, and then jumped down and quickly turned to exit the office.

His friend was close behind.

"Where do you think you're going?" the manager asked.

"Home," he said matter-of-factly, "You don't expect me to work in the dark, do you?"

So, why do we need a vacation from our routines or from the chaotic lives we lead?

"Diana," Dan said, "I really do not need a vacation. I am doing what I want to do. I just feel like I do not have enough time to do it."

# CHAPTER 59
## Randomness as a higher level of order

Does this paradox make sense? Can randomness really represent a new level of order?

Dan was telling Diana about routines and vacations, but what he really wanted to discuss was planning.

Many books, blogs, podcasts, self-improvement talks tell us about the importance of planning. Most of us have calendars. Some of us have a time-table divided into hours, some even to 15-minute time-blocks. Everything is so planned. If Plan A fails, there are 25 more letters.

Diana did not like planning.

How many times have we read blogs like "Skilled for Life: Why planning our lives is important" [1050]. "There are so many varying opinions on the keys to success and leading a meaningful, happy, and fulfilling life. Working hard, having discipline, and sacrificing are just a few examples. However, I believe that one of the integral factors necessary to be successful at anything is planning" [1050]. The concept is that while all of us have desires and dreams, very few of us have actually taken the time to write down a specific plan detailing how to go about achieving them. This is the explanation given by most of our teachers, parents, and mentors. The common slogan is "dream, plan, take action."

Most books and mentors ask us to use a worksheet for planning the steps we need to take in order to get where we want to be. "Planning our life is one of the most powerful and effective ways to attain what we want" [1050]. The more detailed our plan, the higher are our chances of accomplishing the task. Some of us plan on a piece of paper what to buy at the supermarket, and most of us plan our weddings to the last detail. Many of us neglect to plan our lives though. Some of us are then disappointed when we do not achieve what we want.

Planning our life is equivalent to having a roadmap that helps us reach our desired destination. Unless we have already been to the place we want to go numerous times and already know how to get there, we will need a good map [1050]. This always means diving into details. But while some people like to plan their vacation down to each hour, others like to get lost in a place without a proper plan or schedule.

Planning is also about taking control. Avoiding randomness. The more planning, the less randomness, and the more control we have. "Planning our life gives us control. If we create a plan, then we get to make choices and decisions, rather than leaving things up to chance, or worse yet, letting others make decisions for us" [1050]. Another advantage of pre-planning and living life in proper order is that it provides us with better balance [1050]. "It is much easier to establish and maintain balance in our life when we make a plan." Not only is planning expected to get us where we want to be, but it is also a way of living. It is claimed that planning can make our life more comfortable, more balanced and stable.

Planning does not involve ignoring the distractions we all face. We meet people who do not behave as we expect them to. We have a flat tire. The train is late. Our child is sick. So many things can affect our plan and take us off the track. Planning is expected to help us get past these distractions, to help us get back on track as quickly as possible and make sure we reach our target. "Without our plan, we may soon find ourselves off track and our life out of balance because we won't know when to say enough is enough." [1050]

Diana then made the point, "how about if these distractions can be of assistance? Are all random events unfortunate in the sense that they distract us from our final goal? Can they help us redefine goals or discover better ways of reaching these goals?"

Dan liked the idea. He felt that Diana was now much closer to his idea of making randomness useful. Randomness may indeed represent a higher level of order. Does planning help us reach a higher level? A better target? Or is it merely a marker indicating the average altitude?

So what benefit can I derive from a flat tire, a broken train, or a sick child?

"Reality distortion field" (RDF) is a term that was first used by Bud Tribble at Apple Computer in 1981, to describe company co-founder Jobs' charisma and its effects on the developers working on the Macintosh project[1051, 1052]. The term referred to some of the insights from Job's speeches. Andy Hertzfeld, an American computer scientist and inventor who was a member of the original Apple Macintosh development team during the 1980s, [1053], also used the term to describe Jobs' ability to persuade himself and others of almost anything with the help of a healthy mix of charm, charisma, marketing techniques, appeasement, and persistence. This quality was said to distort a person's sense of proportion and the scale of difficulties and make them believe that it was possible to achieve the task [1054]. Some also claim that Jobs used this as a method to appropriate others' ideas[1052]. In the movie Star Trek, this term was used to describe how the aliens created their own new world through mind power [1055, 1056]. The use of this term has extended to other industry leaders who try to convince their employees to become passionately committed to projects without paying attention to the details of the product or competitors [1054].

Reality distortion field is a dream. It has nothing to do with planning. Many view it as contradictory to the concept of thinking in an organized or linear way.

Bill Clinton's charisma has also been described as a reality distortion field[1057]. The term has also been associated with Donald Trump's approach to running his 2016 United States presidential campaign[1058]. The Financial Times has used the term when describing Elon Musk [1059]. These successful people, whether we like them or not, use a method that is in many ways considered to be counterintuitive to planning. They had a big dream that seemed unreachable, but reached it nonetheless. But the "planners" will always say, "if we feel like our dreams are always beyond our reach, it might be because we have never tried to develop a plan on how we can actually reach them. Once a realistic plan is in place, we will be amazed at how achievable our dreams really can be" [1050]. The only problem with this concept is that being realistic is not in keeping with the concept of the reality distortion field. In many ways, being realistic means lowering the bar.

424 | C<sub>HAOS</sub> M<sub>E</sub>!

"A planned life will give us a sense of peace. We will no longer have to worry about whether or not we are making the correct decisions. So long as our choices are in line with our plan and bringing us one step closer to where we want to be, then those are the right choices to make. The peace of mind we will feel is extremely satisfying" [1050].

Do really successful people live in peace though?

"Having a plan will make us feel more powerful…We will feel confident in our abilities and powerful enough to achieve what we want" [1050]. Is it because we put in front of us a more realistic and achievable target? In other words, we plan to reach an easy target, and we achieve it by planning.

"That is not necessarily bad," Diana said.

"Not it is not," Dan agreed. He has been working most of his life in a company that always set targets, most of which had been achievable. His team planned accordingly and usually reached the bar.

"The real issue is whether it prevents one from reaching a higher-level target," Dan said.

Katie Berbert had an article published a few years ago in The Elite Daily called "Five reasons it's all the little things in life that make for the happiest journey" [1060] . Many of these little details appear in a random way, and they are not planned, she wrote. Every moment of every day, we encounter these innumerable "little things." It is very easy to get lost in the big picture and forget the small stuff [1060]. Whether we've missed our bus or stubbed our toe, paying attention to the little positive things can help us shift our focus away from the negative things. Have your favorite lunch, but at the same time, enjoy a random event, a random beautiful view. Paying attention to details, even those that come randomly, may teach us more about ourselves and the world. Think about relationships with family, friends, customers. Big things matter every once in a while, but it's the little things that keep our relationships alive on a day-to-day basis. Bring them flowers. Littler moments, many of which are unexpected, unplanned, are those we tend to remember most. Someone smiling at us may give us a moment of joy. These moments are not epic, but they are precious, and they deserve our attention. Our monumental moments in life are all the results of a lot of little things that led up to them. Our marriage is a result of a lot of little moments of laughter and love. Our job is the result of a lot of little moments of working hard and making sacrifices. If we live our life just looking forward to the big moments, we'll lose a lot of those little things along the way [1060]. Many of these little things, small events, minor actions, are random. They led to the big things. So, what meaning does this have for the virtue of planning?

Ralph Waldo Emerson was an American essayist, lecturer, and poet who led the transcendentalist movement of the mid-19th century. A supporter of individualism and critic of the countervailing pressures of society [1061], he was credited for having said, "life is a journey, not a destination." Enjoy your journey, and pay attention to the little things in life that will determine your destination. The ancient Chinese philosopher and writer Lao Tzu said, "a journey of a thousand miles must begin with a single step." Do the difficult things while they are comfortable and do the great things while they are small [1062].

Diana liked these ideas. We need to start looking into the random details. Dan was more into "planned randomness." His idea was to make use of randomness. The "random little things" concept was only a small part of it.

So, we need to look differently at small, random details. We also need to reflect on the details. But we should not ignore the big picture. So, from time to time, climb a few miles above ground and look at yourself and the world around us.

Investors are told to pay attention to detail: Review every element and every piece of information about every company before a purchase. Does this routine improve their decisions? There are so many theories, books, and lectures that tell us about the best way to invest. If there are so many of them, it only means that there is no ideal one. "Look at the last 10 years of financial statements. Look at gross profit margins, profit after tax, and cash from operations, look at shareholder's funds, these should be ideally increasing, displaying the characteristics of a franchise. Finally look at the return on equity, the higher it is, the better the compounding of wealth for shareholders. Highly capital efficient businesses give an organic accretion of capital which does not require the owner to infuse funds into the business time and again" [1063]. Technical analysis is the art of drawing a crooked line from an unproven assumption to a foregone conclusion.

How about random investing? Jonathan Keats asks in Wired, "Why investing at random is as effective as hiring a financial adviser?"[1063]. There are anecdotes aplenty of creatures beating the stock market with arrows or a toy mouse. The physicist Alessandro Pluchino said, "Maybe the success of these random investment 'strategies' wasn't so random after all."

Pluchino teamed up with Alessio Biondo, an economist who worked with him at the University of Catania in Italy, to study the hypothesis that investing blindly is a better strategy than hiring a financial adviser. Are random trading strategies more successful than technical ones?[1064] They explored whether randomness plays a role in success in financial markets, based on the finding that noise is beneficial in many physical systems and complex socio-economic systems. They evaluated some of the most common trading strategies for predicting the dynamics of financial markets for different international stock exchange indexes, and compared them to the performance of a completely random strategy. They obtained15 years of data from four of the world's biggest stock exchanges and pitted four top trading algorithms against one that was programmed to trade at random. The random algorithm did at least as well as the others. It also experienced a lot less day-to-day volatility. [1064, 1065]

This means that widespread adoption of a random approach for financial transactions would result in a more stable market with lower volatility. Random strategies may reduce herding behavior over the whole market. If agents knew that financial transactions do not necessarily carry an information role, bandwagon effects could probably fade[1065]. This means that "for the individual trader, a purely random strategy represents a costless alternative to expensive professional financial consulting, being at the same time also much less risky if compared to the other trading strategies"[1065]. But this does not mean that you should fire your advisors or start using a mouse to select stocks. It is only food for thought. The study also claims that the data obtained at a micro-level could have many implications for real markets at the macro-level, where other important phenomena, like herding, asymmetric information, and rational bubbles, occur[1065].

How about intervention by central banks?[1065] If policymakers interfere by randomly buying and selling financial assets, agents will suffer less on account of asymmetric or insider information, due to the consciousness of a "fog of uncertainty" created by the random investments. From a systemic point of view, herding behavior would decrease and eventual bubbles would burst while they were still small and less dangerous. The entire financial system would be less prone to the speculative behavior of "credible traders," "gurus," or so-called experts[1066, 1067]. Policies based on random strategies are associated with a reduction in serious financial extreme events such as bubbles and crashes. Both the micro- and macro-benefits of random investments in financial markets have been demonstrated. [1068] Most investors see patterns of random fluctuations or computer glitches and then pile on. This herding instinct amplifies mistakes[1064]. But true randomness has no pattern.

Even if we are skeptical about these studies, and tend to think that we can only make safe investments by studying every detail about the companies we invest in, it's worth looking at a whole new field where randomness can be of benefit.

A teacher, a doctor, and an investment banker die and find themselves at the gates of heaven.

God asks the teacher to tell him one reason why he should be let in. The teacher says, "I taught small children how to read and write." God is happy with this answer and welcomes him with open arms.

God then asks the doctor the same question, to which the doctor says "I have saved many people's lives and cured many people of deadly diseases." God welcomes him to heaven too.

God then turns to the investment banker. The man tells God that he was an investment banker, and that he helped banks package their subprime mortgages into highly marketable CDOs. "Welcome to heaven, my son," says God, "but you have to leave in two days."

Dan was thinking, "If randomness can lead to better revenues than standard techniques, then randomness may indeed represent the highest level of order. This is easy to quantify when we talk about money. But what about other aspects of our lives? Can true randomness be planned?"

# CHAPTER 60

Randomness and selection: How were
Maria Callas and Arturo Toscanini chosen?

Several researchers seem to agree with the notion that we can use physics to understand everyday life events. Dan was one of those.

Physicists are collaborating with economists and social scientists in order to get a more quantitative understanding of social science mechanisms[1069-1071]. In the social sciences, simple schematic models and computer simulations based on statistical physics have been used to understand the unexpected collective behaviors of large groups of individuals. These methods have revealed new features that are independent of individual psychological attributes. These are very often counterintuitive and difficult to predict based on common sense alone [1072].

Diana was warming up the idea that randomness could be used to improve efficiency. The only thing she did not get was how randomness could be planned. She was telling Dan about the debate surrounding random selection methods in corporations. In relation to this, Biondo and Pluchino have used mathematical models to argue that corporate promotions and legislative appointments should be made at random[1064]. Promotion strategies are fundamental to a hierarchical organization, and these strategies are constantly in development. Take a look at the Google example [1073].

In management theory, Laurence J. Peter formulated what came to be known as the Peter Principle, in 1969, that a candidate is selected for a position based on their current performance rather than for abilities relevant to the intended role. Thus, employees are promoted only as long as they perform adequately, and "managers rise to the level of their incompetence" [1074]. However, this meritocratic method can negatively affect the efficiency of a pyramidal organization. This has led many organizations to look for alternative promotion strategies.

Still, random selection seems totally illogical.

The effects of the Peter Principle have been studied within a general context in which different promotion strategies were investigated to maximize global efficiency in a given hierarchical system [1074, 1075]. The gains in efficiency due to both the organizational topology (modular or pyramidal) and the introduction of a variable percentage of random promotions after a meritocratic transient were evaluated. The efficiency of an organization was found to significantly increase when a random strategy of promotion was adopted as opposed to a simple meritocratic promotion of the best members.

In 2001, two researchers at the Dallas School of Management, Texas, published a study on management in real companies through computer simulations and found that the promotion of the best performers actually degrades overall organizational performance when compared to just promoting a random member of the group [1076]. Further studies showed that the random strategy could be used as an alternative to the meritocratic one [1072]. The increase in efficiency triggered by random promotions may be the result of the synergistic effect of several promotion events under the Peter hypothesis. One does not need a completely random strategy to obtain an increase in efficiency. Random selection for promotion of only 50% of agents is enough to obtain a consistent increment in efficiency. The random strategy improves the efficiency of the system consistently, and has been shown to have very persistent robustness.

A frequent objection to the adoption of a random promotion strategy, by a company or a public administration, concerns the possible adverse psychological feedback of employees who are denied an expected promotion. Why should we work hard if the promotion is going to be random?

In a massive company, it is likely that employees ignore the promotion strategies of their managers. So, their promotion strategies probably have minimal influence on their work. However, it is necessary to distinguish promotions from rewards and incentives for any good work that is done.

The most exceptional employees expect a prize for their work, and such a reward may be essential for making sure their competence is not lowered. These rewards do not necessarily have to overlap with a promotion [1072]. Receiving an increase in salary, more responsibility or more freedom in their schedule could be a much more appreciated reward for excellent performance. If someone is the best candidate for a particular role, it is much better to let them continue with the role than to risk changing it, a change that, if the Peter hypothesis holds, exposes the company to the risk of a decrease in efficiency [1072].

Why are random promotions better? The simple reason is that it circumvents the Peter effect by favoring the emergence of hidden skills among less competent employees, which otherwise might have had a very low probability of being appreciated. A random strategy seems to be a straightforward and exciting way to increase the efficiency of any real organization for which the Peter hypothesis of uncorrelated competence transmission holds true [1072]. There are other analogies in nature that favor this strategy, including natural selection. During evolution, natural selection proceeds through random mutations and not through something that is akin to top-down meritocratic promotions [1072]. If a random mutation results in a significant advantage for some species, it is maintained and reinforced, and never changed or removed on purpose.

The significant turning point in well-known opera singer Maria Callas's career occurred in 1949 in Venice, at the Teatro la Fenice. Margherita Carosio, who was engaged to sing Elvira in I Puritani in the same theatre, fell ill. Callas was selected, by chance and all of a sudden, to substitute for the main singer, in a role that she had never expected [1077]. Similarly, the famous conductor Arturo Toscanini debuted at the age of 19 years just by chance when he substituted for the official conductor, who had abandoned the orchestra in which Toscanini was a musician, during a tour in South America. While presenting Aida in Rio de Janeiro on June 25, Leopoldo Miguez, a locally hired conductor, had reached the peak of a two-month escalating conflict with the performers on account of his poor command of the work. The singers went on strike as a result, and the manager was forced to look for a substitute conductor. Toscanini was persuaded by the musicians to take up the baton at 9:15 PM, and he led the two-and-a-half-hour opera entirely from memory. The public was taken by surprise. The result was astounding acclaim. Thus began his career as a conductor [1078]. There are many similar stories about successful people who had been only randomly selected for their roles.

This concept has also been extended to politics: Improving democracy by random selection [1079]. It is argued that elections are subject to manipulation by money and other powerful forces, and because legislative elections give power to a few powerful groups, they are believed to be a less democratic system than selection by lot from amongst the population [1080]. Whether we like politicians or not, can we improve democracy by randomness?

Late one night, a mugger wearing a ski mask jumped into the path of a well-dressed man and stuck a gun in his ribs. "Give me your money," he demanded. Indignant, the affluent man replied, "You can't do this—I'm a U.S. Congressman!" "In that case," replied the robber, "Give me MY money!"

A recent study used a model of a parliament with two parties or two political coalitions to show that the introduction of a variable percentage of randomly selected independent legislators can increase the global efficiency of a legislature, in terms of both number of laws passed and common social welfare [1079]. The researchers claimed to have discovered what they call an "efficiency golden rule," which allows the fixing of an optimal number of legislators to be selected at random after the regular election has established the relative proportion of the two parties or coalitions.

The logic behind the sortition process lies in the idea that "power corrupts" [1080]. In governance, there is a history of sortation used to select a random sample of officials from a larger pool of candidates [1081]. We read about it almost every day around the globe. For that reason, when the time came to choose individuals to be assigned to empowering positions, the ancient Athenians resorted to choosing by lot. In ancient Athens, sortition was the traditional and primary method for appointing political officials, and it was considered as a principal characteristic of true democracy[1082]. Sortition was considered to be a way of achieving full fairness. Aristotle relates equality and democracy: "Democracy arose from the idea that those who are equal in any respect are equal absolutely. All are alike free. Therefore, they claim that all are free absolutely...The next is when the Democrats, on the grounds that they are all equal, claim equal participation in everything." Athenian democracy was characterized as being run by the "many" or the ordinary people, who were allotted to committees which ran the government. Allocation of public offices by lot is considered a democratic process [1080]. The Athenians believed sortition, but not elections, to be democratic, and they used complex procedures with purpose-built allotment machines, or kleroteria, to avoid the corrupt practices used by oligarchs to buy their way into office [4] [1083].

Both Aristotle and Herodotus, one of the earliest writers on democracy, described selection by lot as a test of democracy: "The rule of the people has the fairest name of all, equality, and does none of the things that a monarch does. The lot determines offices, power is held accountable, and deliberation is conducted in public" [1080, 1084]. In Athens, citizens self-selected themselves into the available pool of eligible candidates, and then lotteries were drawn from the kleroteria machines. The magistracies assigned by lot generally had to serve a one-year term. A citizen could not hold magistracy more than once in his lifetime, but could hold other magistracies[1085].

In several cities in northern Italy during the 12th and 13th centuries and in Venice until the late 18th century, people chosen randomly swore an oath that they were not acting under bribes, and then they elected members of the council[1086]. The lot system was used in Venice only to select members of committees that nominated candidates for the Great Council. Thus, a combination of the election and lot system was used in this multi-stage process [1080]. By reducing intrigue and power moves within the Great Council, the lot system maintained cohesiveness, contributing to stability[1087]. In Florence, starting in 1328, nominations and voting together was used to create a pool of candidates from different sectors of the city. These men had their names deposited in a sack, and lots were drawn to determine who would get the magistracy positions. Florence utilized a combination of lots and scrutiny by the people, as set forth by the ordinances of 1328[1088]. Some parts of Switzerland also used random selection methods during the years 1640 to 1837 in order to fight corruption [1089].

Randomness provides power, fairness, and prevents corruption. Sortition is inherently egalitarian in that it ensures all citizens have an equal chance of entering office irrespective of any biases in society[1090]. That is, ordinary citizens do not have to compete against more powerful or influential adversaries to gain an administrative position. The selection procedure does not favor those who have pre-existing advantages or connections, as happens with election by preference [1086]. The Greeks also realized that sortition broke up factions, diluted power, and gave positions to such a large number of disparate people that they would all keep an eye on each other, making collusion reasonably rare. Power did not necessarily go to those who wanted it and had schemed for it[1082].

With sortition, there is a diversity of perspectives and heuristics that helps individuals create different solutions for the same problems [1080, 1091]. Cognitive diversity, which comes with random selection of people, is more important to generating fruitful ideas than the average ability level of a group. This "diversity trumps ability theorem" is essential to understanding why sortition is a viable democratic option [1092]. A random selection of persons of average intelligence will result in better performance than a collection of the best individual problem solvers [1093].

Random selection can overcome biases in race, religion, sex, degree of education, and many additional factors apparent in most legislative assemblies. Further, greater perceived fairness can be added by using stratified sampling. In one such instance where this strategy was used, the Citizens' Assembly on Electoral Reform in British Columbia sampled one woman and one man from each electoral district and also ensured representation for First Nations members [1080].

A common argument against "pure" sortition is that it does not discriminate among those selected and does not take into account the particular skills or experiences that might be needed to efficiently discharge the duties of particular offices. In other words, with sortition, there is no guarantee that the person selected has the skills required to do the job. To solve this issue, the group from which the lots are drawn should be composed entirely of persons with the required skills. The Athenians did not fill the roles of military commander by sortition for this reason [1080]. Selecting someone to fly an airplane cannot be through random selection from people at a restaurant or airport. Another drawback is the statistical possibility that sortition may bring to power an individual or group that does not represent the views of the population from which they were drawn [1080].

Elected representatives typically rely on political parties in order to gain and retain office. They are often more loyal to the party than to the nation, and are likely to vote in such a way as to support the party position than the general conscience. On the contrary, representatives appointed by sortition do not owe anything to anyone for their position. Perhaps for this reason, today, sortition is used to select prospective jurors in legal systems and is sometimes used in forming citizen groups with political advisory power[1094] [1080]. Law court juries are also formed through sortition in some countries, such as the United States and United Kingdom [1080]. While some think that this random selection method is not ideal, in some countries, people think it leads to more justice.

Sortition is also used in military conscription, in awarding US green cards, and in placing students in public schools, in a California nursing college, and in schools of medicine in the Netherlands[1095]. MASS LBP, a Canadian company, is using Citizens' Reference Panels for addressing a range of policy issues for public sector clients [1096]. The Reference Panels use public lotteries, a modern form of sortition, to randomly select citizen-representatives from the general public. Danish Consensus conferences also use sortition to give ordinary citizens a chance to make their voices heard in debates on public policy. The selection of citizens is not entirely random but aims to be representative [1097]. The Samaritan Ministries health plan uses a panel of 13 randomly selected members to resolve disputes, which sometimes leads to policy changes[1098]. In other sectors, many commercial companies use random people for determining the taste of their food products, colors of clothes, and other product specification. The power of randomness under this condition is essential for increasing sales [1099].

The statistical possibility that sortition may put into power an individual that does not represent the values of the population from which he was selected may apply to juries. It is less of a problem when evaluating larger groups where the probability of, for example, an oppressive majority, is statistically insignificant [1080]. However, the modern processes of jury selection and the right to object to and exclude jurors that is given to both the plaintiff and defense lessen the possibility of a jury not being representative of the community, or being prejudicial towards one side or the other. Today, juries in most jurisdictions are not ultimately chosen through pure sortition alone [1080].

In an elected system, the representatives are to a degree self-selecting for their enthusiasm for the job. Sortition represents a system that is not based on the enthusiasm of the representatives[1088]. However, individuals who are chosen at random have no particular enthusiasm for their role and therefore may not make the right advocates for a constituency[1100]. Sortition does not offer a mechanism by which the population expresses satisfaction or dissatisfaction with individual members of the allotted body. There is no re-election, and no feedback or accountability mechanism for the performance of officials. But this could be solved by putting the necessary processes in place for feedback, accountability or re-election, as required.

Can random selection of political representatives really improve the efficiency of a parliament? [1072] This idea has regained some strength recently with popular juries, who believe that such methods should be used to monitor the work of politicians, as witnessed with Ségoléne Royal in France and with the Barnett and Carty proposal for a radical reform of the House of Lords by random election [1101].

Diana was falling in love with randomness. Dan was now moving more and more into learning how to "organize" randomness.

# CHAPTER 61
## Can randomness create good noise?

Dan was sitting alone and reading about how to deal with noise. The issue of random noise disrupting true good randomness was bothering him. Dan was telling Diana how people tend to perceive noise as a bad thing. But can noise be of benefit?

Air traffic controller: "Flight 1234, for noise abatement, turn right 45 degrees."

Airline pilot: "But Center, we are at 35,000 feet. How much noise can we make up here?"

Air traffic controller: "Sam, have you ever heard the noise a 747 makes when it hits a 737?"

There are many examples in physics where noise has a positive influence. There are models in which it has been shown that noise enhances stability in an unstable physical system [1102]. Dan was reading about a model in which the average escape time from a periodically driven system is measured under a stable regime and under an unstable regime in a noisy environment. In the unstable regime, the average escape time has a maximum value for a limited value of the noise intensity. One can compare the scaling properties of the average escape time and the variance of escape times with the predictions obtained for a system in a marginal state. In simple words, it means creating order out of noise.

A similar example is present in physical chemistry. A useful but counterintuitive trick to obtaining highly ordered protein crystals is to "seed" particles on disordered porous surfaces. Microporous materials are useful as seed substrates for protein crystallization where the aim is to make only a few crystals. While the vast majority of pores are ineffective, it doesn't matter as long as a few work well [1103]. If this principle is applied to life, it implies that a great multitude of random substrates or highly diverse environments could lead to at least one successful event. The evolution of life may be a case in point.

Other examples in physics come from studies on the nucleation of a new thermodynamic phase in pores. Nucleation often proceeds via two steps: nucleation of pore filling and nucleation out of the pore. The rates at which these two steps proceed have opposing dependencies on pore size, and there is one pore size at which the nucleation rate of the new phase is maximal [1104]. This means that by using a random system, with opposing courses, a new protein can be made.

Randomness induces much noise. But out of this noise, something good may come after all. Dan was wondering if this principle could be applied to other aspects of our lives. Every minute and every second of our lives, there are so many random noisy events happening around us or to us. It often feels like there is too much noise. Some of this is "good noise," and it can probably be channeled to our benefit.

Excitation transfer through interacting systems plays a role in many areas of physics, chemistry, and biology. The uncontrollable interaction of the transmission network with a noisy environment can deteriorate its transport capacity, especially in the case of a quantum mechanical system. Noise, such as dephasing, counter-intuitively, may actually aid transport through a dissipative network by opening up additional pathways for excitation transfer [1105]. It may also enhance the efficiency of transmitting classical and quantum information, encoded in quantum systems, through communication networks. Thus, for a large family of quantum channels, the transmission rates for quantum and classical information could be enhanced by introducing dephasing noise in the complex network dynamics [1106]. The interplay of quantum mechanical features with the unavoidable environmental noise may lead to optimal system performance. This could mean that noise, or too much noise, might sometimes open a new path for us that will help us move forward.

Noise-associated processes inhibit destructive interference and exploitation of line-broadening effects. These effects may explain the efficiency of excitation energy transfer from the light-harvesting chlorosomes to the bacterial reaction center in photosynthetic complexes[1105]. So, if noise is useful in physics and physical chemistry, why can we not use it in our everyday lives? The first step is to stop looking at noise as a negative entity. Instead, we should enjoy standing in long lines, missing our train. We need to see what good can come of these random and "noisy" events. Perhaps the person standing next to us in line is our next friend or investor. Perhaps they can give us some good advice?

For Dan, it was much more than just a change in attitude. Similar to the models in physics, he was thinking of how to model noise in real life.

There are many examples from physics to the social sciences of stochastic thermal fluctuations actually helping positive movements. The Parrondo paradox is an example wherein noise has a constructive role: Here, a combination of losing strategies becomes a winning one [1107] . Counter to conventional intuition, it is possible to mix two losing games into a winning combination [1108]. Juan Parrondo discovered the paradox in 1996, through his analysis of the Brownian ratchet (described in Chapter 55) [1109].

Imagine two kinds of probability-dependent games: A and B. Assume that the result of these games is based on coin tosses. Each of them, when played separately and repeatedly, results in the player losing. The paradox appears when A and B are played together randomly or in periodic sequences: A combination of two losing games results in a winning game! [1110]. While the counterintuitive result is impressive, the model can very well be thought of as a discretized version of Brownian flashing ratchets which are employed to understand the noise-induced order[1107, 1111].

Let's assume that in Game A, we lose $1 every time we play. In Game B, we count how much money we have left. If it is an even number, we win $3. Otherwise, we lose $5. Say we begin with $100 in our pocket. If we start playing Game A exclusively, we will naturally lose all our money in 100 rounds. Similarly, if we decide to play Game B exclusively, we will also lose all our money in 100 rounds. However, consider playing the games alternatively, starting with Game B, followed by A, then by B, and so on

(BABABA…). We will steadily earn a total of $2 every two games. Even though each game is a losing proposition if played alone, because the results of Game B are affected by Game A, the sequence in which the games are played can affect how often Game B earns us money [1107]. That is, if the two losing games are played in some alternating sequence, for example, two games of A followed by two games of B (AABBAABB…), the combination of both games is, paradoxically, a winning game.

One way to explain this paradox is that it is possible to win as long as there is at least one state in which the outcome is positive. As the distribution of outcomes of Game B depends on the player's capital, the two games cannot be independent. Therefore, a player is more likely to enter states in which Game B has a positive outcome, so that the losses from Game A can be overcome [1107]. The paradox thus resolves itself. The individual games result in losses only under a distribution that differs from that which is actually encountered when playing the compound game [1107, 1112]. Parrondo's paradox does not seem that paradoxical if we think about it as a combination of three simple games: two of which have losing probabilities and one of which has a high probability of winning. In such a situation, the probability of creating a winning strategy with three such games is neither counterintuitive nor paradoxical[1111, 1113]. Problems in evolutionary biology and ecology have also been modeled and explained based on this paradox [1114, 1115].

Dan thought that if random events can be turned into wins, we just need to know how to play it right. What is the right sequence of playing to get a winning order in our disordered lives? Is it possible to model it?

# CHAPTER 62

## Moving from stagnation to success: can we use randomness to overcome our plateaus?

For Dan, the goal was simple: He wanted to improve efficiency. Things were more complicated for Diana, as she was not sure that her aim in life, or everyone else's aim, is to improve their capabilities. "Do we not just want to be happy?" she asked.

If we look at athletes, they need to attain a certain level of performance or efficiency to reach the Olympics or to play in the top leagues. But does this mean that most of them are satisfied with their achievements? They know that while they practice, all their competitors in countries all over the world are trying to reach better numbers. Running faster, jumping higher. No one wants to reach a plateau. A plateau means staying where you are and never lifting the bar again. It means not getting better. For top athletes, a plateau means losing the game. Losing a gold medal.

Even if we are not top athletes, do we or should we still wish to become better, or even the best, at what we do? And even if we do not want to be the best, maybe we want to make the most out of ourselves. And even if we are not interested in making the most out of our abilities, do we want to sit on a plateau? Isn't it boring to be stuck in one place?

Most people invest a lot of their time in trying to improve themselves, or at least, this is what they believe they do. Is not learning all about that? We all invest in learning throughout our lives. We all want to make some progress and not be left behind. Even if it is only for ourselves. We want to show ourselves that we are getting better and feel better, whether it is in our professional lives, our hobbies, or any other field in our life.

If we practice, we get better. If we practice more, we may get even better. If we invest in learning, we know more. We are better than before. The problem is that for many fields, additional practice adds a delta of improvement, but at some point, more and more practice may still leave us where we are. We reach a plateau. The delta is minimal. We practice more, but we do not get much better. Why?

The plateau effect is a force of nature that lessens the effectiveness of once-effective measures over time [1116]. We reach a point where we feel there is no improvement or even a decline in our performance [1117]. We fail to be as effective as we were in the past. Continuous training or learning suddenly does not result in much improvement. Others pass us by.

In the book *The Plateau Effect*, Bob Sullivan and Hugh Thompson talk about this powerful law of nature that affects everyone [1118]. They try to teach us to recognize plateaus and break through stagnancy in many aspects of our lives, including diet, exercise, work, and even relationships. Athletes, scientists, therapists, companies, husbands, wives, children, musicians—we all need to break through the plateaus. In their words, the aim is "to turn off the forces that cause people to 'get used to' things, and turn on human potential and happiness in ways that seemed impossible."

According to the law of diminishing returns, in all productive processes, adding more amounts of one factor, while keeping the others constant, will at some point yield lower incremental per-unit returns [1119]. In economics, diminishing returns is defined as the decrease in the marginal incremental output of a production process, as the amount of a single factor of production is incrementally increased while the amounts of all other factors of production stay constant [1120]. This concept is important in production theory [1121]. It should be noted that this law does not imply that total production decreases, a condition known as negative returns, which is common nonetheless. For example, if we consider the assembly of a car on a factory floor, at some point, adding more workers will cause problems, as workers will get in each other's way or have to wait for access to a part of the car. As a result, producing one more unit of output per unit of time will eventually cost more due to the inputs being used less efficiently[1122, 1123].

There are many other examples of the plateau effect [1116]. It appears in learning, when students experience a declining benefit of their studying efforts. In elementary school students, a plateau effect in reading level is observed during the upper elementary years[1124]. In acclimation, this effect enables a process by which organisms adjust to changes in its environment. Our nose becomes acclimated to a particular smell. We may want to view it as a defense mechanism to distraction from the stimulus. Another example is drug tolerance, which occurs when our reaction to a drug is progressively reduced. This can lead to a need for higher dosages of the drug. But many over-the-counter medications have a maximum possible effect, regardless of their dose[1125, 1126], so we take larger amounts of the drug without achieving a considerably better effect. In the context of software testing techniques, too, Boris Bazor mentions that every method used to find bugs leaves a residue of bugs against which those methods become incompetent. This can lead to "superbugs," indicating that traditional methods have gradually lost their efficacy [1127].

In fitness, a phenomenon known as the exercise plateau effect occurs when the body no longer responds to a particular stimulus because it becomes accustomed to it. This effect can be one of the most frustrating, yet inevitable consequences of regular workout programs [1128]. Plateau effects can derail any progress we hope to make in our fitness program and eventually lead to reversibility. Reversibility is when improvements from training begin to deteriorate, and fitness levels decrease. In order to overcome the fitness plateau effect, we need to change our workout, including the periods of rest, change the volume of exercises, or increase/decrease the weights used in strength exercises[1129, 1130]. We can also apply more significant demands on our body. This is the principle of overload. The point at which the muscles are overloaded and exercise is demanding enough to have an effect on the body is known as "threshold training." To overcome the lull of the exercise plateau, one must always aim for threshold training. Variety is another critical factor in fighting exercise plateaus. "If we habitually run on the treadmill every morning, try running on an incline. Better yet, try a new machine" [1128]. There is a linear relationship between fitness and intensity levels. We need to increase or change the resistance and stride pace continuously.

"Sometimes it only takes a small change to shock our body. Something as subtle as switching the order of exercises can do the trick. If we regularly start with push-ups, followed by squats, and then make our way to seated row, try mixing the order and do squats first, seated row, and then push-ups. When our body becomes accustomed to a specific sequence of exercises, it knows what to expect and when to expect it. Our job is to stop that from happening. When we deviate from the regular routine, our body is forced to work and adapt."[1129, 1130]

For Dan, this meant adding some randomness to our exercise routines and lives in order to achieve better results and overcome the plateaus.

Achievements in sports and in learning are easy to quantify. How about other areas in our life such as relationships? If shaking the order of muscle training can overcome a plateau, can this be used for all the other plateaus we hit?

In the book *Moonwalking with Einstein* by Joshua Foer, three stages that lead to the plateau effect are described. The theory of the three stages that was proposed by Fitts and Posner is thought to be based on the theory of K. Anders Ericcson [1131] [1116]. The first stage of the plateau effect is the cognitive stage. In this stage, we intellectualize the task and discover new strategies for accomplishing it more proficiently. The second stage is the associative stage, in which we concentrate less, make fewer major errors, and generally become more efficient. The last stage is the autonomous stage, which is characterized by the plateau effect: "We figure that we've gotten as good as we need to get at the task and we're basically running on autopilot." [1132, 1133].

Ericcson described several factors which affect the level of achievement. The first is an extensive experience of activities in a domain which is necessary to reach very high levels of performances. Extensive experience does not always lead to expert levels of achievement [1134]. When individuals are introduced to a professional domain after completion of their basic training and formal education, they often work as trainees and are supervised by more experienced professionals. After many months of experience, they typically attain an acceptable level of proficiency, and with more extended experience, often after several years of experience, they are able to work as independent professionals. This is true for many types of activities. Most professionals manage to reach such a stable, average level of performance, which they maintain for the rest of their careers, despite it being ordinary, somewhat dull and unimaginative. In contrast, some continue to improve themselves and eventually reach the highest levels of professional mastery [1134].

Some of us top artists, athletes, scientists, writers, cooks, can break the plateau ceiling.

Ericsson said, "our civilization has always recognized exceptional individuals, whose performance in sports, the arts, and science is vastly superior to that of the rest of the population" [1135].

How can we get from stagnation to success?

There are many methods for overcoming plateaus in our lives. Sullivan and Thompson describe in their book the forces that generate plateaus, the principles by which the plateaus can be destroyed, and the actions that can be taken to achieve peak behavior [1118]. "Anything we want to do better we can accomplish faster by understanding the plateau effect." Common causes of plateaus are immunity, the greedy algorithms, lousy timing, flow issues, distorted data, distraction, slow failures, and perfectionism. Overcoming some of these will break the plateau ceiling [1116].

One such plateau-breaking method is deliberate practice, which refers to a particular type of practice that is purposeful and systematic. While regular practice might include mindless repetition, deliberate practice requires focused attention. It is conducted with the specific goal of improving performance [1136]. Can we achieve anything with enough practice? If this was true, there would be no candidates for the gold medal, as all of us would be able to run 100 meters in less than 9 seconds. The theory of deliberate practice does not imply that we can fashion ourselves into anything with enough focused practice. We have a remarkable ability to develop our skills, but there are limits to how far an individual can go [1136]. We all have our boundaries, which are determined by our genes, our environment, epigenetics, and many other factors. James Clear says in his blog that "while genes influence performance, they do not determine performance. Do not confuse destiny with opportunity. Genes provide opportunity. They do not determine our destiny" [1136]. He explains this with the example of card games. We have a better opportunity if we are dealt a better hand, but we also need to play the hand well if we want to win. The concept is that deliberate practice can help us maximize our potential. "It turns potential into reality."

Can it get us above the plateau?

In a blog about deliberate practice, Janie Kliever describes the six steps of deliberate practice[1137]. The first is to get motivated. If we want to push past the hard phases of skill growth, which involves frustration, failures, and periods of slow progress, we must be motivated. Ericsson described competition and determination as being associated with motivation. If it is something that we care about and are willing to devote considerable time and effort to, our motivation levels tend to be higher.

The second step it setting specific and realistic goals. We need to keep the prize in sight. Vague aspirations such as "getting better" will not do it. Deliberate practice relies on small, achievable, well-defined steps that help us work our way towards meaningful improvement. These steps should take into account our current knowledge and skill level and push those boundaries one small step at a time. Goal setting is not about making a New Year's resolution and hoping we'll stick to it. It involves planning, identifying areas for improvement, and creating a specific plan for building on top of our current abilities[1137].

Dan was bothered with this step. Will this bring us to a new plateau? Where is the randomness? What about anti-planning?

The third step is to break out of the comfort zone. In his book *Peak: Secrets from the New Science of Expertise*, Ericsson wrote, "if we never push ourselves beyond our comfort zone, we will never improve"[1138]. Improvement means constantly challenging our current abilities. Simply repeating skills, we already know how to do will get us stuck. But many of us who keep practicing to reach a better goal, find ourselves stuck at a plateau.

So, what did we do wrong? We get ourselves to train or learn approaches that do not enhance our skill level or improve performance. Ericsson emphasizes that when it comes to skill development, breaking out of our comfort zone isn't about "trying harder," but about "trying differently." Some interpret deliberate practice as setting targets that teeter on the edge of what we are and are not capable of doing. Then, if we cannot move forward with one technique, try another and keep experimenting until we break through the barrier that's blocking our improvement[1137].

It was becoming clear to Dan that this is the step where randomness can play a role.

Can randomness be one of these methods? Does it mean that if we sometimes do not "follow the rules," we can get better? He was thinking of a classroom where every student does not follow the systematic learning method. A factory where several workers decide not to be bored...It may quickly become a messy world.

Step four is about consistency. Deliberate practice calls for regularity. Ericsson and his colleagues share the finding that top performers maintain a similar practice regimen of brief and intense, daily or semi-weekly solo practice sessions [1135]. An accumulated amount of regular, focused practice had a direct impact on musicians' level of performance. The continued effort is frustrating and uncomfortable at times. But pushing through these tight spots is claimed to lead to improvement.

For Dan, organized randomness, pre-planned randomness, or an algorithm for generating randomness was the answer.

Step five of deliberate practice is about feedback. According to Ericsson, "without feedback, either from ourselves or from outside observers, we cannot figure out what we need to improve on or how close we are to achieving our goals."[1137].Feedback is important for identifying areas for improvement and getting a realistic view of our progress.

The final step is recovery time. Because deliberate practice requires our full attention and maximal mental and/or physical effort, it can only be sustained for a short period of time. A high level of normal intense concentration makes recovery time important.

In a New York Times story, Ericsson was quoted as saying, "a lot of people believe there are some inherent limits they were born with. But there is surprisingly little hard evidence that anyone could attain any kind of exceptional performance without spending a lot of time perfecting it." This is not to say that all people have equal potential. Michael Jordan, even if he hadn't spent countless hours in the gym, would still have been a better basketball player than most of us. But without those hours in the gym, he would never have become the player he was [1139]. But even Mr. Jordan reached a plateau. He got better with hard practice; his plateau was better than that of most of us. But it was still a plateau.

Could Mr. Jordan or Bob Fisher have become better if they had used random practice techniques? Could they have broken their high-level plateaus?

Diana surprised him again. She came up with an empowering quote. In the book *The Guide to Computer Simulations and Games* by Becker and Parker, John Locke is quoted as saying, "that which is static and repetitive is boring. That which is dynamic and random is confusion. In between lies art." The same book also quotes Gottfried Leibniz: "But when a rule is extremely complex, that which conforms to it passes with random"[1140].

# CHAPTER 63
## My randomness

Dan was looking at how randomness and chaos could be channeled in a more committed way. More connections in our brain. More hard work. More ambition. He felt that REAL randomness could be found at a higher level.

In their bestselling book *Made to Stick: Why Some Ideas Survive, and Others Die* [1141], Chip Heath and Dan Heath describe how the laws of physics are the same in every frame of reference. In fact, their claim is that Einstein argued that things do not happen in an unexpected way, and that it can be surprising how organized they are. Most of us tend to think differently about his theory of relativity.

Dan knew that small things that occur randomly lead to dramatic changes in history. Randomness affects our history, our day, every moment in our life, and every part of our world. Randomness is part of our life. We need to make the most out of it by looking at random events as random opportunities, and then turning them into real opportunities that can result in the good changes we are looking for. At the same time, we need to recognize the random events which can be harmful and handle them properly. But also, random events which may seem detrimental could turn out to be opportunities.

Dan knew what had to be done. He was not sure how to go about doing it though. He wanted to apply this concept of randomness as possible opportunity to every field in life. He wanted to find a way to "algorithmize the brain" using randomness, to find a way to create randomness or transform existing randomness into powerful randomness that can have a positive effect on life.

During the Second World War, a scientist calculated that to minimize attacks, it would be enough to randomize 70% of the patrols. He was able to save many lives just by randomizing some of the patrol times.

Diana pointed out to Dan that many authors have dealt with the topic of randomness in their books. For example, in *Dear Mr. M* [1142], Herman Koch says that while it is true that randomness can only occur in a place with some kind of order, the reality is somewhat more complicated. Miguel de Unamuno wrote in his book *Mist: A Tragicomic Novel* [1143] that "there is logic in the chess game, and yet, how vague and random it is in the end. Perhaps logic is something random, something coincidental...An accidental revelation? What revelation is not accidental? What is the logic of revelations? The same logic that exists in the succession of characters rising from cigar smoke. The randomness! ... The submissive, routine, modest life is a pendulum ode that springs from a thousand every day trivialities. Everyday! What need is there for God or the world or anything else to exist? Why was there anything at all? Do not you think that the idea of necessity is nothing more than the supernatural form of the randomness of our mind? ... We set ourselves a path with our own feet as we walk without direction. Some believe that they follow a star; I believe I'm following a double star, Twin Star. And that star is nothing but the reflection of the path that leads to heaven, the reflection of the randomness."

"Is not he implying the same thing: a high level of randomness?" Dan asked Diana. He continued, "My algorithm will be a universal one. Randomness is the highest level of order. Randomness is a necessity. We should be able to make it work for us. We can benefit from it." In his book *The Undoing Project: A Friendship That Changed Our Minds* [1144], Michael Lewis describes the work of Nobel Prize winning psychologists Daniel Kahneman and Amos Tversky, who wrote a series of breathtakingly original papers that laid the groundwork for the field of behavioral economics. They had the idea of writing a book for the general public that would deal with the different ways in which the human mind copes with uncertainty. Tversky had a clear perception of how people mistakenly perceived randomness. They do not understand that random sequences only seem to have patterns. They identify in these patterns a meaning that does not actually exist. Lewis describes Tversky's lecture "Historical interpretation: judgment under conditions of uncertainty." In his talk, he showed that throughout our personal and professional lives, we often encounter situations that confuse us at first sight. In no way can we understand why Mr. A behaved in a certain way, and neither can we understand why the experiment yielded such and such results. But usually, it does not take long before we find an explanation, a hypothesis or an interpretation that makes them understandable, bright or natural. People readily recognize patterns and trends even in random data [1144]. He claimed that, too often, we cannot predict what will happen, but in retrospect, we explain what happened with high confidence. It is a fake "ability" to explain what cannot be predicted, even in the absence of any additional information. We like to think that the world is less uncertain than it actually is. If we can explain tomorrow what we could not predict today, with no other information aside from knowing the actual result, it means that the outcome must have been decided in advance, and that we should have been able to predict too often that what we cannot. Our skill in inventing scenarios, explanations and interpretations or our ability to assess their reasonableness, or to look at them critically, is fundamentally flawed. After we have developed a hypothesis or a particular interpretation, we greatly overestimate the hypothesis and find it very difficult to look at things from any other point of view [1144].

Kahneman and Tversky came to the conclusion that when people make predictions and judgments under conditions of uncertainty, they do not seem to calculate the odds or follow the statistical prediction theory. They rely on a limited number of heuristics, which sometimes yield reasonable judgments and sometimes lead to severe and systematic errors. The more the situation requires judgment, the more complex it is. In many cases of complex and realistic problems, people tend to build scenarios. The stories that we invent, rooted in our memory, actually substitute judgments of probability. The production of a convincing scenario is likely to limit future thinking, as Kahneman wrote in his book *Thinking fast and slow* [1145].

There is evidence that after an uncertain situation is perceived or interpreted in a certain way, it is challenging to see it any other way. But the stories people tell themselves are influenced by the availability of the material used to build them. Images of the future have been shaped by experiences of the past. But what people remember from the past is likely to disrupt their judgment of the future. We often decide that an outcome is extraordinarily unreasonable or even impossible because we cannot imagine any event that could bring about its occurrence. On more than one occasion, the flaw lies in our imagination.

"Random" randomness seems to be missing from the real random sequences. If you randomly divide twenty marbles among five children, the probability that each of them will get precisely four marbles is higher than the probability that the marbles will be unequally divided. But still, students have insisted that the unequal distribution is more reasonable because equal distribution seems too systematic to be the result of a random process [1144]. "Provoking randomness deliberately is a means to keep our thinking fresh, to avoid slipping into routine thinking. However, you have to admit, to do that is leaving our comfort zone." [304] The comfort zone is a state within which a person operates in an anxiety-neutral condition, delivering a steady level of performance. In most cases, there is no sense of risk. A comfort zone means operating within boundaries. Such boundaries create an unfounded sense of security. Being outside our comfort zone does not mean being uncomfortable. It does not mean something rough or painful. It does not mean paying the price for a "more creative life, more interesting life, and more productive life." On the contrary, what we believe to be our comfort zone is indeed not comfortable at all. It may seem so, but when we look deeper, we know it is not. The "uncomfortable zone" is where we want to be, as it is much more comfortable, pleasant, and enjoyable. Yes, it is the REAL comfort zone. And, yes, it is indeed more interesting, more creative, more fun, and much closer to the upper limit of our capabilities.

Highly successful people routinely step outside their comfort zones. They experiment with new and different behaviors and then experience the new and different responses that occur within their environment. Some of the most potent inventions were not deliberately designed. They were a result of an accident, a random event or a failed experiment. Highly successful transformers were prepared for unusual results and used randomness as a tool for progress. "Provoking randomness and building it into our daily routine as a thinking strategy could provide us with powerful insights" [304].

"I will design an algorithm to provoke randomness," thought Dan.

This book is about randomness. It was not meant to be a textbook. You can always go back to some of the Wikipedia sites and references mentioned. It is not a book of recipes or a self-help manual. There is no appendix with a list of steps. You will need to find the right way to apply some of these concepts to your own working life, personal life, companies, or nations that you care about. The personal range for randomness is a concept which by definition is personalized. Moreover, the range may be different for you today than in say, two months from now. It keeps on changing, as do we all.

***

# THE END OF THE BEGINNING

It was a beautiful Sunday morning on Long Island. Sunny and not too warm. Dan's plan was to sit on the balcony with a glass of red wine.

Last evening, he was watching the news when his phone rang.

Edna and Jeremy were on the other end.

"Guess what?" they asked in unison.

Dan was surprised. What would make them call him on a Saturday evening?

"We are at the airport and flying over for an unexpected visit. We booked a motel not far from your house. We want to meet you for lunch."

Dan was surprised but happy to hear from them.

"But guess what?" both of them asked again.

"Have you not surprised me enough?"

"Aren't you asking why?"

"Okay friends, why?"

"We have an idea we want to pursue. Both of us quit our jobs last week. And when we asked ourselves who should be our partner, we could not think of anyone better than you."

"Ok," Dan was laughing, "Let's have a business lunch."

Jeremy got serious. "Dan, it is all about randomness."

Dan paused for a second. He had never believed in coincidences. He was hesitant about telling Jeremy that as of last week, he had seen the light too. He had had an idea on how to move things ahead with his randomness research. In fact, he had been thinking of making another trip to Arizona to discuss it with Jeremy and Edna. "Here they come to me."

"I also have a surprise for you," Dan said, "But I will only tell you over lunch."

"Give me a hint." Edna was laughing.

"It is about randomness."

While making coffee, his phone rang. 8 AM on a Sunday morning? Who can it be? It was David. Something must have happened.

"Dad?" David was very calm.

"Yes David, is everything all right?"

"Did I wake you up?"

"No, I am expecting friends for lunch."

"Dad, you know, I have been thinking about this cliff idea and randomness for some time now. I believe I have an idea. I wanted to discuss it with you. Can I come over?"

Dan sat down.

"Sure David, come over for lunch. This is going to be a big random lunch."

"Dad, you need to understand, I am thinking of leaving my job to explore it. I need your help. I want to partner with you."

This was a surprise. David had never seemed to Dan like someone who was willing to take risks.

"David, you only live once. Do it, and I will help you as much as I can. Let me warn you that I also have an idea about that."

Dan was coming out of the shower when the phone rang again. This time, he was not surprised. He had been expecting this phone call for some time now.

Diana was on the line.

"I know this is strange," she said, "But I have been keeping a secret from you. I am totally into this randomness. I have some ideas. I am with you on that."

Dan had felt it during their dinner two days ago. He had been sharing some of his ideas with Diana, and asking her to join the venture. "I am a book reviewer, not a physicist," she answered. "What do I know about these things?"

"Some of the most significant ideas about the world have emerged from literature and not from the lab," he replied.

Diana knew that he was right.

"Diana, please meet me for lunch. You are about to meet some interesting random people."

While hanging up, he knew that he had to invite one more person.

"Olivia?"

"Yes, Dad."

"Are you sleeping?"

"Yes, Dad. The baby kept us up all night."

"Come over for lunch today. We are moving forward with the randomness venture."

Olivia had called him last weekend to tell him she had decided to explore some new ideas about randomness and aging. Her company had let her go, as they had decided that the idea was too risky for them. They wanted to continue in a steadier direction with their significant data analysis.

"So, we have added five people, with five more sparks about randomness."

"If these sparks are synergistic with mine, this can become a big thing."

At the age of 70, Dan did not feel young again, but he felt much smarter and capable of moving forward.

He had written down a very well organized plan on a piece of paper.

*If we want to use randomness for getting better and improving our efficiency, we should start by thinking on the second law of thermodynamics. We will then use quantum indeterminacy; as real randomness can only be achieved by quantum measurement. We will build on top of this the chaos theory. Slightly changing initial conditions will result in significant (exponential) change in the outcome. We will use deep machine learning and develop an insightful database from randomness. We can then help people create personalized-tailored randomness that will help them become better at what they want to do, better at life.*

**Disclosures:**

- The author is the founder of Oberon Sciences, a company involved in the development of random-based algorithms.

- Permission to reproduce and modify text on Wikipedia is granted to anyone anywhere by the authors of individual articles as long as such reproduction and modification complies with licensing terms. To re-distribute text on Wikipedia in any form, provide credit to the authors either by including a) a hyperlink (where possible) or URL to the page or pages you are re-using, b) a hyperlink (where possible) or URL to an alternative, stable online copy which is freely accessible, which conforms with the license, and which provides credit to the authors in a manner equivalent to the credit given on this website, or c) a list of all authors.

- Text from external sources may attach additional attribution requirements to work, which should be indicated on an article's face or on its talk page. The text of Wikipedia is copyrighted (automatically, under the Berne Convention) by Wikipedia editors and contributors and is formally licensed to the public under one or several liberal licenses. Most of Wikipedia's text and many of its images are co-licensed under the Creative Commons Attribution-ShareAlike 3.0 Unported License (CC BY-SA) and the GNU Free Documentation License (GFDL) (unversioned, with no invariant sections, front-cover texts, or back-cover texts). Wikipedia content can be copied, modified, and redistributed if and only if the copied version is made available on the same terms to others and acknowledgment of the authors of the Wikipedia article used is included (a link back to the article is generally thought to satisfy the attribution requirement; see below for more details). Copied Wikipedia content will, therefore, remain free under an appropriate license and can continue to be used by anyone subject to certain restrictions, most of which aim to ensure that freedom. This principle is known as copyleft in contrast to standard copyright licenses.

- Permission is granted to copy, distribute and/or modify Wikipedia's text under the terms of the Creative Commons Attribution-ShareAlike 3.0 Unported License and, unless otherwise noted, the GNU Free Documentation License. Unversioned, with no invariant sections, front-cover texts, or back-cover texts.

- A copy of the Creative Commons Attribution-ShareAlike 3.0 Unported License is included in the section entitled "Wikipedia:Text of Creative Commons Attribution-ShareAlike 3.0 Unported License" A copy of the GNU Free Documentation License is included in the section entitled "GNU Free Documentation License." Content on Wikipedia is covered by disclaimers. The English text of the CC BY-SA and GFDL licenses is the only legally binding restriction between authors and users of Wikipedia content. What follows is our interpretation of CC BY-SA and GFDL, as it pertains to the rights and obligations of users and contributors.

# REFERENCES AND NOTES

1. https://www.youtube.com/watch?v=6dwsrXh9wfA: May 13 2018.
2. https://en.wikipedia.org/wiki/IPod_Shuffle: May 13 2018.
3. https://www.youtube.com/watch?v=TE4EEwQAfxo: May 13 2018.
4. http://lowendmac.com/2015/ipod-and-itunes-shuffle-is-not-random/: Daniel Knight - 2015.05.19 viewed May 13 2018.
5. https://www.random.org/randomness/: Introduction to Randomness and Random Numbers by Dr Mads Haahr. viewed May 13 2018.
6. https://medium.economist.com/why-people-get-happier-as-they-get-older-b5e412e471ed The Economist Dec 23: Ret: May 15 2018.
7. Marshall Goldsmith MR: Triggers: Creating Behavior That Lasts--Becoming the Person You Want to Be. Crown Bussiness 2015.
8. https://en.oxforddictionaries.com/definition/randomness: viewed May 13 2018.
9. https://en.wikipedia.org/wiki/Randomness: Viewed May 13 2018.
10. Johnston SI: Religions of the Ancient World: A Guide. Harvard University Press Reference Library 2004.
11. Chance Lo: The Logic of Chance: An Essay on the Foundations and Province of the Theory of Probability, with Especial Reference to Its Logical Bearings and Its Application to Moral and Social Science.
12. H.A. David AWFE: Annotated Readings in the History of Statistics. Springer Science & Business Media 2001, ISBN 0-387-98844-0 page 115:p. 173–190.
13. DELBRÜCK M: A Physicist Looks at Biology; Address Delivered at the Thousandth Meeting of the Academy. California Institute of Technology, Pasadena, California (http://faculty.washington.edu/lynnhank/Dehlbruck.htmlRet: May 2018).
14. Hoffmann PM: How molecular motors extract order from chaos (a key issues review). Rep Prog Phys 2016, 79(3):032601.
15. Lopes R, Imanaliev A, Aspect A, Cheneau M, Boiron D, Westbrook CI: Atomic Hong-Ou-Mandel experiment. Nature 2015, 520(7545):66-68.
16. Acin A, Masanes L: Certified randomness in quantum physics. Nature 2016, 540(7632):213-219.
17. Pironio S, Acin A, Massar S, de la Giroday AB, Matsukevich DN, Maunz P, Olmschenk S, Hayes D, Luo L, Manning TA et al: Random numbers certified by Bell's theorem. Nature 2010, 464(7291):1021-1024.
18. Frank A: Uncertain for a century: quantum mechanics and the dilemma of interpretation. Ann N Y Acad Sci 2015, 1361:69-73.
19. Le Bellac M: The role of probabilities in physics. Prog Biophys Mol Biol 2012, 110(1):97-105.
20. https://www.amazon.com/Q-QUANTUM-Encyclopedia-Particle-Physics/dp/0684863154 Q for Quantum JG.
21. https://en.wikipedia.org/wiki/Hidden_variable_theory. October 2018
22. The Born-Einstein letters: correspondence between Albert Einstein and Max and Hedwig Born from 1916–1955 wcbMBMp, (Private letter from Einstein to Max Born,

3 March 1947.

23. Born PltM: Private letter to Max Born. Albert Einstein Archives reel 8, item 180 4 December 1926.
24. https://en.wikipedia.org/wiki/Randomness. October 2018
25. https://en.wikipedia.org/wiki/Cleromancy. October 2018
26. Lynch M, Ackerman MS, Gout JF, Long H, Sung W, Thomas WK, Foster PL: Genetic drift, selection and the evolution of the mutation rate. Nat Rev Genet 2016, 17(11):704-714.
27. Caporale LH, Doyle J: In Darwinian evolution, feedback from natural selection leads to biased mutations. Ann N Y Acad Sci 2013, 1305:18-28.
28. Longo GM, Maël Extended criticality, phase spaces and enablement in biology. Chaos, Solitons & Fractals Emergent Critical Brain Dynamics 2013, 55: 64-79.
29. Griffiths AJF MJ, Suzuki DT, et al.: Genes, the environment, and the organism.An Introduction to Genetic Analysis. 7th edition. New York: W. H. Freeman;. 2000.
30. https://www.webmd.com/skin-problems-and-treatments/guide/moles-freckles-skin-tags#1. October 2018
31. Breathnach AS: A long-term hypopigmentary effect of thorium-X on freckled skin. Br J Dermatol 1982, 106(1):19-25.
32. Kolmogorov A: "On Tables of Random Numbers". . Sankhyā Ser A 25: 369-375 1963.
33. https://en.wikipedia.org/wiki/Kolmogorov_complexity. October 2018
34. Complexity. YWRa: PhD Thesis, 1996, http://webpages.uncc.edu/yonwang/papers/thesis.pdf.
35. Gaspard P CI: Chaos and fractals in dynamical models of transport and reaction. . Philos Trans A Math Phys Eng Sci 2002, 360(1792):303-315.
36. Meiggs R: https://www.britannica.com/biography/Cleisthenes-of-Athens#ref5504. October 2018
37. Thomas M. Cover JAT: Kolmogorov complexity. Chapter 7. Elements of Information Theory; . John Wiley & Sons, Inc Print ISBN 0-471-06259-6 Online ISBN 0-471-20061-1 1991.
38. http://gaming.nv.gov/. October 2018
39. Anthony Cabot and Robert C. Hannum: Gambling regulation and mathematics: A marriage of necessity. The John Marshall Law Review 2002, 35(3):333-358.
40. https://plato.stanford.edu/entries/chance-randomness/ October 2018
41. Borel É, 1909, 'Les Probabilités Dénombrables et Leurs Applications Arithmétiques',Rendiconti del Circolo Matematico di Palermo, 27: 247–71.
42. http://www.telegraph.co.uk/news/2017/05/22/pick-lottery-numbers-win/. October 2018
43. http://www.bbc.com/news/world-us-canada-34883294. October 2018
44. http://www.nba.com/news/draft/nba-draft-lottery-what-will-happen-2016/. October 2018
45. https://www.smartplay.com/. October 2018
46. https://en.wikipedia.org/wiki/Monte_Carlo_method. October 2018
47. http://www.palisade.com/risk/monte_carlo_simulation.asp. October 2018
48. https://en.wikipedia.org/wiki/Stochastic_process. October 2018
49. Siegmund DO: Probability theory, MATHEMATICS. Britanica, https://www.britannica.com/science/probability-theory; October 2018

50. Tabak J: Probability and Statistics: The Science of Uncertainty. Infobase Publishing pp 24-26 ISBN 978-0-8160-6873-9 2014.

51. Bellhouse D: Decoding Cardano's Liber de Ludo Aleae. Historia Mathematica 32 (2): 180-202 doi:101016/jhm200404001 ISSN 0315-0860 2005.

52. Maistrov LE: Probability Theory: A Historical Sketch. . Elsevier Science p 56 ISBN 978-1-4832-1863-2 2014.

53. Brush SG: Foundations of statistical mechanics 1845?1915. Archive for History of Exact Sciences 4 (3): 150-151 doi:101007/BF00412958 ISSN 0003-9519 1967.

54. Brush SG: The development of the kinetic theory of gases IV. Maxwell. Annals of Science 14 (4): 243-255 doi:101080/00033795800200147 ISSN 0003-3790 1958.

55. Bingham N: Studies in the history of probability and statistics XLVI. Measure into probability: from Lebesgue to Kolmogorov. Biometrika 87 (1): 145-156 doi:101093/biomet/871145 ISSN 0006-3444 2000.

56. Williams LCGRD: Diffusions, Markov Processes, and Martingales. Volume 1, Foundations Cambridge University Press p 1 ISBN 978-1-107-71749-7 2000.

57. Processes ItS: Introduction to Stochastic Processes - University of Kent. https://wwwkentacuk/smsas/personal/lb209/files/notes1pdf:p1-13. October 2018

58. Doob JL: Stochastipoic processes. . Wiley p 46 and 47 1990.

59. https://en.wikipedia.org/wiki/Index_set. October 2018

60. Weisstein EIS: Wolfram MathWorld. Wolfram Research. . Retrieved 30 December 2013.

61. Florescu I: Probability and Stochastic Processes. John Wiley & Sons pp 294 and 295 ISBN 978-1-118-59320-2 2014.

62. Brémaud P: Fourier Analysis and Stochastic Processes. Springer p 120 ISBN 978-3-319-09590-5 2014.

63. https://en.wikipedia.org/wiki/Random_variable. October 2018

64. https://en.wikipedia.org/wiki/Probability_distribution#Continuous_probability_distribution. October 2018

65. Lamperti J: Stochastic processes: a survey of the mathematical theory. . Springer-Verlag pp 1- 2 ISBN 978-3-540-90275-1 1977.

66. Taylor SKHE: A First Course in Stochastic Processes. Academic Press p 26 ISBN 978-0-08-057041-9 2012.

67. Ibe OC: Elements of Random Walk and Diffusion Processes. John Wiley & Sons p 11 ISBN 978-1-118-61793-9 2013.

68. Tsitsiklis DPBJN: Introduction to Probability. . Athena Scientific p 273 ISBN 978-1-886529-40-3 2002.

69. Klebaner FC: Introduction to Stochastic Calculus with Applications. Imperial College Press p 56 ISBN 978-1-86094-555-7 2005.

70. https://en.wikipedia.org/wiki/Bernoulli_process. October 2018

71. Klenke A: Probability Theory. Springer-Verlag ISBN 978-1-84800-047-6 2006.

72. Limic GFLV: Random Walk: A Modern Introduction. . Cambridge University Press p 1 ISBN 978-1-139-48876-1 2010.

73. Shreve SE: Stochastic Calculus for Finance II: Continuous Time Models. . Springer p 114 2008, ISBN 978-0-387-40101-0.

74. SHEPHERD DIWALC: POISSON POINT PROCESS MODELS SOLVE THE "PSEUDO-ABSENCE PROBLEM" FOR PRESENCE-ONLY DATA IN ECOLOGY. The

Annals of Applied Statistics 2010, Vol. 4, No. 3, 1383–1402.

75. Rozanov YA: Markov Random Fields. . Springer Science & Business Media p 58 ISBN 978-1-4613-8190-7 2012.

76. Kroese RYRDP: Simulation and the Monte Carlo Method. . John Wiley & Sons p 225 ISBN 978-1-118-21052-9 2011.

77. Papoulis ACiP: Brownian Movement and Markoff Processes. Random Variables, and Stochastic Processes, 2nd ed New York: McGraw-Hill 1984.:515-553,.

78. Williams D: Probability with Martingales. Cambridge University Press ISBN 978-0-521-40605-5 1991:pp. 93 and 94. .

79. Applebaum D: Lévy processes: From probability to finance and quantum groups. Notices of the AMS 51 (11): 1337 2004.

80. Applebaum D: Lévy Processes and Stochastic Calculus. Cambridge University Press p 69 ISBN 978-0-521-83263-2 2004.

81. http://www.commongroundgroup.net/2012/05/28/evolution-science-and-religion-16-randomness-and-the-building-blocks-of-nature/. October 2018

82. https://en.wikipedia.org/wiki/Pseudorandomness. October 2018

83. https://www.rand.org/pubs/monograph_reports/MR1418/index2.html: A MILLION Random Digits WITH 100,000 Normal Deviates. The RAND Corporation ISBN-13: 978-0833030474; ISBN-10: 0833030477.

84. https://en.wikipedia.org/wiki/Derrick_Henry_Lehmer. October 2018

85. https://www.americanscientist.org/article/the-quest-for-randomness. October 2018

86. https://en.wikipedia.org/wiki/Does_God_Play_Dice%3F. October 2018

87. Martin-Löf P: The definition of random sequences. Information and Control 1966, 9 (6): 602-619. .

88. Solomonoff R: A Formal Theory of Inductive Inference Part I". Information and Control 1964, 7 (1): 1-22. .

89. https://en.wikipedia.org/wiki/Berry_paradox. October 2018

90. Smith P, 1998, Explaining Chaos. Cambridge: Cambridge University Press.

91. Liddell HGS, Robert; Jones, Henry Stuart; McKenzie, Roderick (1984). A Greek-English Lexicon. Oxford University Press.

92. Menezes AJvO, P. C.; Vanstone, S. A. Handbook of Applied Cryptography. ISBN 0-8493-8523-7. Archived from the original on 7 March 2005.

93. https://en.wikipedia.org/wiki/Cryptography.

94. Farnsworth JRBaDL: What Is Benford's Law? Teaching Statistics Volume 31, Number 1, Spring 2009, https://onlinelibrary.wiley.com/doi/pdf/10.1111/j.1467-9639.2009.00347.x.

95. https://en.wikipedia.org/wiki/Benford%27s_law. October 2018

96. Hill ABaTP: An Introduction to Benford's Law. Princeton University Press; ISBN 9780691163062 2015.

97. Paul H. Kvam BV, Nonparametric Statistics with Applications to Science and Engineering, p. 158.

98. Steven W. Smith. "The Scientist and Engineer's Guide to Digital Signal Processing c, Explaining Benford's Law". .

99. Fewster RM: A simple explanation of Benford's Law. The American Statistician 2009, 63 (1): 26-32. doi:10.1198/tast.2009.0005.

100. Hill TP: A Statistical Derivation of the Significant-Digit Law. Statistical Science 1995,

10: 354-363. doi:10.1214/ss/1177009869

101. Varian H: Benford's Law Letters to the Editor. The American Statistician 26 (3) 1972.

102. Erdös FBt: Radio Lab. Episode 2009-10-09 2009-09-30 2009.

103. Roukema BF: A first-digit anomaly in the 2009 Iranian presidential election. Journal of Applied Statistics 2013, https://arxiv.org/pdf/0906.2789.pdf.

104. Johnson G: Playing the Odds. The New York Times 8 June 2008.

105. http://www.probability.ca/jeff/writing/montysimple.html. October 2018

106. The Drunkard's Walk: How Randomness Rules Our Lives Paperback – May 5 bLM.

107. Futuyma DJ, 2005, Evolution. Cumberland, MA: Sinauer.

108. Suppes P, 1984, Probabilistic Metaphysics, Oxford: Blackwell.

109. Hájek A, 2007, 'The Reference Class Problem is Your Problem Too', Synthese, 156: 563–85.

110. Biased Random Walks Yossi Azar AZB, Anna R. Karlin, Nathan Linial, Steven Phillips; http://www.cs.huji.ac.il/~nati/PAPERS/bias_rw.pdf.

111. D. Lichtenstein NLaMS, "Some extremal problems arising from discrete control processes," Combinatorica, 9 (1989), pp. 269–287.

112. https://en.wikipedia.org/wiki/Biased_random_walk_on_a_graph. October 2018

113. Kakajan Komurov MAW PTR: Use of Data-Biased Random Walks on Graphs for the Retrieval of Context-Specific Networks from Genomic Data. PLoS Comput Biol 6: e1000889 2010.

114. Da-Cheng Nie Z-KZ QD, Chongjing Sun,Yan Fu: Information Filtering via Biased Random Walk on Coupled Social Network. The Scientific World Journal 2014.

115. http://www.flandershealth.us/microbiology/a-biased-random-walk.html. October 2018

116. Carnap R, 1945, 'The Two Concepts of Probability', Philosophy and Phenomenological Research, 5: 513–32.

117. Schaffer J, 'Deterministic Chance?' British Journal for the Philosophy of Science, 58: 113–40.

118. Mellor DH, 2000, 'Possibility, Chance and Necessity', Australasian Journal of Philosophy, 78: 16–27.

119. Lewis D, 1980, 'A Subjectivist's Guide to Objective Chance', in his Philosophical Papers, volume 2, Oxford: Oxford University Press, 1986, pp. 83–132.

120. Albert DZ, 2000, Time and Chance, Cambridge, MA: Harvard University Press.

121. Bell JS, 1964, 'On the Einstein-Podolsky-Rosen paradox', Physics, 1: 195–200.

122. Shimony A, 2009, 'Bells' Theorem', in The Stanford Encyclopedia of Philosophy (Summer 2009 edition), Edward N. Zalta (ed.), URL =<=<https://plato.stanford.edu/archives/sum2009/entries/bell-theorem/>>.

123. Wallace D, 2007, 'Quantum Probability from Subjective Likelihood: Improving on Deutsch's Proof of the Probability Rule'. Studies in History and Philosophy of Modern Physics, 38: 311–32.

124. Loewer B, 2001, 'Determinism and Chance', Studies in History and Philosophy of Modern Physics, 32: 609–20.

125. Earman J, 1986, A Primer on Determinism, Dordrecht: D. Reidel.

126. RAND Corporation, A Million Random Digits with 100,000 Normal Deviates, New York: Free Press.

127. Kahneman DaAT, 1972, 'Subjective Probability: A judgment of representativeness',

Cognitive Psychology, 3: 430–54.

128. Bar-Hillel MaWAW, 1991, 'The Perception of Randomness', Advances in Applied Mathematics, 12: 428–54.

129. Hahn UaPAW, 2009, 'Perceptions of Randomness: Why Three Heads Are Better Than Four', Psychological Review, 116: 454–61.

130. Ville J, 1939, Étude Critique de la Notion Collectif, Paris: Gauthier-Villars.

131. Laplace P-S, 1826, Philosophical Essay on Probabilities, New York: Dover, 1951.

132. Dasgupta A, 2011, 'Mathematical Foundations of Randomness', in Prasanta Bandyopadhyay and Malcolm Forster (eds.), Philosophy of Statistics (Handbook of the Philosophy of Science: Volume 7), Amsterdam: Elsevier, pp. 641–710.

133. Gaifman Haim and Marc Snir, 'Probabilities Over Rich Languages, Testing and Randomness', Journal of Symbolic Logic, 47: 495–548.

134. Eagle Antony, 'Probability and Randomness', In The Oxford Handbook of Probability and Philosophy, Alan Hájek and Christopher Hitchcock (eds.), Oxford: Oxford University Press, pp. 440–59.

135. Martin-Löf P, 1966, 'The Definition of a Random Sequence', Information and Control, 9: 602–619.

136. Champernowne DG, 1933, 'The Construction of Decimals Normal in the Scale of Ten', Journal of the London Mathematical Society, 8: 254–60.

137. von Mises R, Probability, Statistics and Truth. New York: Dover.

138. Church A, 1940, 'On the Concept of a Random Sequence', Bulletin of the American Mathematical Society, 46: 130–135.

139. Downey RaDRH, 2010, Algorithmic Randomness and Complexity, Berlin: Springer.

140. Porter CP, 2016, 'On Analogues of the Church-Turing Thesis in Algorithmic Randomness', The Review of Symbolic Logic, 9 (3): 456–79.

141. https://iuuk.mff.cuni.cz/~koucky/vyuka/ZS2013/kolmcomp.pdf. Ret: December 2018.

142. Kolmogorov AN, and V. A. Uspensky, 1988, 'Algorithms and Randomness'. SIAM Theory of Probability and Applications, 32: 389–412.

143. Chaitin G, 1966, 'On the Length of Programs for Computing Finite Binary Sequences', Journal of the Association for Computing Machinery, 13: 547–69.

144. Li MaPMBV, 2008, An Introduction to Kolmogorov Complexity and Its Applications, Berlin and New York: Springer Verlag, 3rd edition.

145. Schnorr CP, 1971, 'A unified approach to the definition of random sequences', Theory of Computing Systems, 5: 246–58.

146. Downey RaEG, 2004, 'Schnorr randomness', Journal of Symbolic Logic, 69: 533–54.

147. Jeffrey RC, 1977, 'Mises Redux', in Basic Problems in Methodology and Linguistics, Robert E. Butts and Jaakko Hintikka (eds.), Dordrecht: D. Reidel, pp. 213–222.

148. https://www.scientificamerican.com/article/how-randomness-rules-our-world/. October 2018

149. http://neurosciencenews.com/predictability-action-randomness-6703/. October 2018

150. Masayoshi Murakami HS, Yonatan Loewenstein, and Zachary F. Mainen in Neuron. Published online May 17 2017 doi:10.1016/j.neuron.2017.04.040.

151. http://blogs.plos.org/blog/2016/09/17/as-simple-as-random-can-be-by-jasmine-reggiani/. October 2018

152. http://forum2016.fens.org/PublishingImages/contact-press/press-releases/Abbott%20

pr%20release.pdf. October 2018

153. Caron SJ, Ruta V, Abbott LF, Axel R: Random convergence of olfactory inputs in the Drosophila mushroom body. Nature 2013, 497(7447):113-117.

154. Aso Y, Hattori D, Yu Y, Johnston RM, Iyer NA, Ngo TT, Dionne H, Abbott LF, Axel R, Tanimoto H et al: The neuronal architecture of the mushroom body provides a logic for associative learning. eLife 2014, 3:e04577.

155. https://www.merriam-webster.com/dictionary/diversity. October 2018

156. Kenneth M Heilman M, Stephen E. Nadeau, MD, and David Q. Beversdorf, MD. "Creative Innovation: Possible Brain Mechanisms" Neurocase (2003) Archived 2009-03-19 at the Wayback Machine.

157. https://en.wikipedia.org/wiki/Creativity_techniques. October 2018

158. Flaherty AW: Frontotemporal and dopaminergic control of idea generation and creative drive. J Comp Neurol 2005, 493(1):147-153.

159. Mayseless NE, Ayelet; Shamay-Tsoory, Simone G (2015). "Generating original ideas: The neural underpinning of originality". NeuroImage. 116: 232–9. .

160. Vandervert L: Research on innovation at the beginning of the 21st century: What do we know about it? . Chapter in LV Shavinina (Ed), The International Handbook of Innovation (pp 1101-1111) Elsevier Science 2003.

161. Miller MB, Handy TC, Cutler J, Inati S, Wolford GL: Brain activations associated with shifts in response criterion on a recognition test. Can J Exp Psychol 2001, 55(2):162-173.

162. Vandervert L: The Origin of Mathematics and Number Sense in the Cerebellum: with Implications for Finger Counting and Dyscalculia. Cerebellum Ataxias 2017, 4:12.

163. Vandervert L: The prominent role of the cerebellum in the learning, origin and advancement of culture. Cerebellum Ataxias 2016, 3:10.

164. Imamizu H, Kawato M: Neural correlates of predictive and postdictive switching mechanisms for internal models. The Journal of neuroscience : the official journal of the Society for Neuroscience 2008, 28(42):10751-10765.

165. Imamizu H, Kawato M: Brain mechanisms for predictive control by switching internal models: implications for higher-order cognitive functions. Psychol Res 2009, 73(4):527-544.

166. Imamizu H, Kawato M: Cerebellar internal models: implications for the dexterous use of tools. Cerebellum 2012, 11(2):325-335.

167. Vandervert L: How music training enhances working memory: a cerebrocerebellar blending mechanism that can lead equally to scientific discovery and therapeutic efficacy in neurological disorders. Cerebellum Ataxias 2015, 2:11.

168. Koziol LF, Budding D, Andreasen N, D'Arrigo S, Bulgheroni S, Imamizu H, Ito M, Manto M, Marvel C, Parker K et al: Consensus paper: the cerebellum's role in movement and cognition. Cerebellum 2014, 13(1):151-177.

169. Brown JeaOVeaWmc, and creativity"". Creat. Res. J. 19: 25–29. doi:10.1080/10400410709336875.

170. Cai D. J.; Mednick S. A.; Harrison E. M.; Kanady J. C.; Mednick S. C. (2009). "REM ni, improves creativity by priming associative networks". Proc Natl Acad Sci U S A. 106 (25): 10130–10134. doi:10.1073/pnas.0900271106. PMC 2700890 . PMID 19506253.

171. Isen AM, Daubman KA, Nowicki GP: Positive affect facilitates creative problem solving. J Pers Soc Psychol 1987, 52(6):1122-1131.

172. Fredrickson BL, Joiner T: Positive emotions trigger upward spirals toward emotional well-being. Psychol Sci 2002, 13(2):172-175.

173. Schmidhuber JFToC, Fun, and Intrinsic Motivation (1990–2010)". IEEE Transactions on Autonomous Mental Development. 2 (3): 230–247. doi:10.1109/tamd.2010.2056368.

174. Schmidhuber J: PowerPlay: Training an Increasingly General Problem Solver by Continually Searching for the Simplest Still Unsolvable Problem. Front Psychol 2013, 4:313.

175. Schmidhuber J: Discovering Neural Nets with Low Kolmogorov Complexity and High Generalization Capability. Neural Netw 1997, 10(5):857-873.

176. Schmidhuber J, A Formal Theory of Creativity to Model the Creation of Art. In McCormack, Jon and M. d'Inverno (eds), Computers and Creativity, Springer 2012.

177. Srivastava RK, Steunebrink BR, Schmidhuber J: First experiments with POWERPLAY. Neural Netw 2013, 41:130-136.

178. https://machinelearningmastery.com/what-is-deep-learning/. October 2018

179. Bengio Y: Deep Learning of Representations for Unsupervised and Transfer Learning Proceedings of ICML Workshop on Unsupervised and Transfer Learning 2012, PMLR 27:17-36.

180. LeCun Y, Bengio Y, Hinton G: Deep learning. Nature 2015, 521(7553):436-444.

181. Ian Goodfellow YBaAC: Deep Learning. . Cambridge, MA, USA: The MIT Press ISBN: 978-0262035613 2016.

182. https://en.wikipedia.org/wiki/Deep_learning. October 2018

183. Control IIFoA: Deep Learning vs. Wise Learning: A Critical and Challenging Overview Peter P. Groumpos. IFAC-Papers OnLine 49-29; 180-189 ScienceDirect 2016.

184. Ghasemi FM, AR.; Fassihi, A.; Perez-Sanchez, H. (2017). "Deep Neural Network in Biological Activity Prediction using Deep Belief Network". Applied Soft Computing.

185. Krizhevsky AS, Ilya; Hinton, Geoffry (2012). "ImageNet Classification with Deep Convolutional Neural Networks" (PDF). NIPS 2012: Neural Information Processing Systems, Lake Tahoe, Nevada.

186. Conventional neural networks http://cs231n.github.io/neural-networks-1/ December 2018

187. Marcus GN, 2012). "Is "Deep Learning" a Revolution in Artificial Intelligence?". The New Yorker. Retrieved 2017-06-14.

188. Schmidhuber J: Deep learning in neural networks: an overview. Neural Netw 2015, 61:85-117.

189. Schmidhuber J, Gers F, Eck D: Learning nonregular languages: a comparison of simple recurrent networks and LSTM. Neural Comput 2002, 14(9):2039-2041.

190. Rushton JP: Race, brain size, and intelligence: a reply to Cernovsky. Psychol Rep 1990, 66(2):659-666.

191. Batey MF, A. F.; Safiullina, X. (2010). "Intelligence, General Knowledge and Personality as Predictors of Creativity". Learning and Individual Differences. 20: 532–535. doi:10.1016/j.lindif.2010.04.008.

192. Touched with Fire: Manic-Depressive Illness and the Artistic Temperament Paperback – October 18 KRJ.

193. Kyaga SL, P.; Boman, M.; Hultman, C.; Långström, N.; Landén, M. (2011). "Creativity and mental disorder: Family study of 300 000 people with severe mental disorder". The

British Journal of Psychiatry. 199 (5): 373–379. .

194. Jeff DeGraff KAL: Creativity at Work: Developing the Right Practices to Make Innovation Happen. ISBN: 978-0-787-95725-4 Willey.

195. Mark Batey a AFb, Xeniya Safiullina: Intelligence, general knowledge and personality as predictors of creativity Learning and Individual Differences 2010, 20:532-535.

196. Mark Batey a AFb, Xeniya Safiullina: Intelligence, general knowledge and personality as predictors of creativity Learning and Individual Differences 2010, 20:532-535.

197. Robert J. Sternberg KS: Cognitive Psychology; Cengage Learning. 2016. October 2018

198. Fang BGM: Pay, Intrinsic Motivation, Extrinsic Motivation, Performance, and Creativity in the Workplace: Revisiting Long-held Beliefs Annual Review of Organizational Psychology and Organizational Behavior 2015, Volume 2 http://www.annualreviews.org/journal/orgpsych.

199. Zhou J, Shin SJ, Brass DJ, Choi J, Zhang ZX: Social networks, personal values, and creativity: evidence for curvilinear and interaction effects. J Appl Psychol 2009, 94(6):1544-1552.

200. Zhang LF, Sternberg RJ, Fan J: Revisiting the concept of 'style match'. Br J Educ Psychol 2013, 83(Pt 2):225-237.

201. Gardner H: The relationship between early giftedness and later achievement. Ciba Found Symp 1993, 178:175-182; discussion 182-176.

202. Sternberg RJ: Creativity as a decision. Am Psychol 2002, 57(5):376.

203. Sternberg RJ: What is the common thread of creativity? Its dialectical relation to intelligence and wisdom. Am Psychol 2001, 56(4):360-362.

204. Aad G, Abbott B, Abdallah J, Abdel Khalek S, Abdelalim AA, Abdesselam A, Abdinov O, Abi B, Abolins M, AbouZeid OS et al: Search for gluinos in events with two same-sign leptons, jets, and missing transverse momentum with the ATLAS detector in pp collisions at sqrt[s]=7 TeV. Physical review letters 2012, 108(24):241802.

205. Oppezzo MS, Daniel L. "Give your ideas some legs: The positive effect of walking on creative thinking". Journal of Experimental Psychology: Learning, Memory, and Cognition. 40 (4): 1142–1152. doi:10.1037/a0036577.

206. Aad G, Abbott B, Abdallah J, Abdelalim AA, Abdesselam A, Abdinov O, Abi B, Abolins M, Abouzeid OS, Abramowicz H et al: Search for a light Higgs boson decaying to long-lived weakly interacting particles in proton-proton collisions at sqrt[s] = 7 TeV with the ATLAS detector. Physical review letters 2012, 108(25):251801.

207. https://www.koozai.com/blog/content-marketing-seo/eight-awesome-creative-thinking-techniques-plus-tools/. October 2018

208. creativity-innovation.eu: Creativity techniques. http://wwwcreativity-innovationeu/creativity-techniques/ 2017. October 2018

209. Benjamin Baird JS, Michael D. Mrazek , Julia W. Y. Kam , Michael S. Franklin , and Jonathan W. Schooler: Distraction was shown in many studies to increase creativity. Psychological Science 23(10) 1117-1122; Chaos and Complexity Theory for Management: Nonlinear Dynamics; Santo Banerjee 2012.

210. Baird BS, Jonathan; Mrazek, Michael D.; Kam, Julia W. Y.; Franklin, Michael S.; Schooler, Jonathan W. (1 October 2012). "Inspired by Distraction: Mind Wandering Facilitates Creative Incubation". Psychological Science. 23 (10): 1117–1122. doi:10.1177/0956797612446024. ISSN 0956-7976.

211. Hoffer, https://www.harpercollins.com/9780060505912/the-true-believer. November

2018

212. https://en.wikipedia.org/wiki/Eric_Hoffer. November 2018

213. http://thinkergy.com/let-randomness-kick-start-your-creativity-part-1/. November 2018

214. http://thinkergy.com/let-randomness-kick-start-your-creativity-part-2/. November 2018

215. https://books.google.co.il/books?id=mN9V7XLVw64C&pg=PT14&lpg=PT14&d-q=The+world+is+governed+by+chance.+Randomness+stalks+us+every+-day+of+our+lives&source=bl&ots=MkGUwdnf_O&sig=D9vOlWVwDgV8uBt1PC6x_9Q3oaM&hl=en&sa=X&ved=0ahUKEwjP0O7R7ePXAhWLCewKHexUD6QQ6A-EIMDAC#v=onepage&q=The%20world%20is%20governed%20by%20chance.%20Randomness%20stalks%20us%20every%20day%20of%20our%20lives&f=false. November 2018

216. Williamson T, 2007, 'How Probable is an Infinite Sequence of Heads?' Analysis, 67: 173–80.

217. Venn J, 1876, The Logic of Chance, London: Macmillan and Co., 2nd edition.

218. Salmon WC, 1977, 'Objectively Homogeneous Reference Classes', Synthese, 36: 399–414.

219. Reichenbach H, 1949, The Theory of Probability, Berkeley: University of California Press.

220. Gillies D, 2000, 'Varieties of Propensity', British Journal for the Philosophy of Science, 51: 807–35.

221. Glynn L, 2010, 'Deterministic Chance', British Journal for the Philosophy of Science, 61: 51–80.

222. Ekeland I, 1988, Mathematics and the Unexpected, Chicago: University of Chicago Press.

223. Sklar L, 1993, Physics and Chance, Cambridge: Cambridge University Press.

224. Norton JD, 2003, 'Causation as Folk Science', Philosophers' Imprint, 3(4), .

225. Eagle A, 2005, 'Randomness is Unpredictability', British Journal for the Philosophy of Science, 56: 749–90.

226. Kyburg J, Henry E., 1974, The Logical Foundations of Statistical Inference, Dordrecht: D. Reidel.

227. Frigg R, 2004, 'In What Sense is the Kolmogorov-Sinai Entropy a Measure for Chaotic Behaviour?—Bridging the Gap Between Dynamical Systems Theory and Communication Theory', British Journal for the Philosophy of Science, 55: 411–34.

228. Clark P, 1987, 'Determinism and Probability in Physics', Proceedings of the Aristotelian Society, Supplementary Volume, 61: 185–210.

229. Hoefer C, 2007, 'The Third Way on Objective Probability: A Sceptic's Guide to Objective Chance', Mind, 116: 549–96.

230. Sober E, 2010, 'Evolutionary Theory and the Reality of Macro Probabilities'. in Probability in Science, Ellery Eells and James H. Fetzer (eds.), Dordrecht: Springer, 133–61.

231. Weiner MaNB, 2006, 'How Causal Probabilities Might Fit Into Our Objectively Indeterministic World', Synthese 149(1): 1–36.

232. Black R, 1998, 'Chance, Credence, and the Principal Principle', British Journal for the Philosophy of Science, 49(3): 371-85.

233. Humphreys PW, 1978, 'Is "Physical Randomness" Just Indeterminism in Disguise?', in

PSA 1978, volume 2, Peter D. Asquith and Ian Hacking (eds.), Chicago: University of Chicago Press, pp. 98–113.

234. Williams JRG, 2008, 'Chances, Counterfactuals, and Similarity', Philosophy and Phenomenological Research, 77: 385–420.

235. Hellman G, 1978, 'Randomness and Reality', in PSA 1978, volume 2, Peter D. Asquith and Ian Hacking (eds.), Chicago: University of Chicago Press, pp. 79–97.

236. Bishop RC, 2003, 'On Separating Predictability and Determinism', Erkenntnis, 58: 169–88.

237. Schurz G, 1995, 'Kinds of Unpredictability in Deterministic Systems', in Law and Prediction in the Light of Chaos Research, P. Weingartner and G. Schurz (eds.), Berlin: Springer, pp. 123–41.

238. Werndl C, 2009, 'What Are the New Implications of Chaos for Unpredictability?' British Journal for the Philosophy of Science, 60: 195–220.

239. https://www.goodreads.com/book/show/49168.Four_Letters_of_Love. November 2018 November 2018

240. http://labs.blogs.com/its_alive_in_the_lab/2013/01/heraclitus-a-whack-on-the-side-of-the-head-by-roger-van-oech.html.

241. http://www.iep.utm.edu/locke/. November 2018

242. https://books.google.co.il/books?id=UoCq4FeTeHkC&pg=PA103&lpg=PA103&d-q=That+which+is+static+and+repetitive+is+boring.+That+which+is+dy-namic+and+random+is+confusing.+In+between+lies+art,%E2%80%9D&-source=bl&ots=tQtTMW8762&sig=SEGBpXAQoIChIpA6oqwkaQyTVL-w&hl=en&sa=X&ved=0ahUKEwiR8YS0vuXXAhXH5qQKHdgQCT04ChDoAQgn-MAE#v=onepage&q=That%20which%20is%20static%20and%20repetitive%20is%20boring.%20That%20which%20is%20dynamic%20and%20random%20is%20confus-ing.%20In%20between%20lies%20art%2C%E2%80%9D&f=false. November 2018

243. Mel Rhodes: An Analysis of Creativity. in Phi Delta Kappan 1961 V, No. 7, p. 306–307.

244. Sternberg, eds. Cognitive Psychology. Learning. p. 468. ISBN 978-0-495-50629-4.

245. https://ais.ku.edu.tr/course/20319/Sutton_2001.pdf ; Harvard Business Review Harvard Business Review Sep 2001, p. 161. Ret: December 2018

246. https://www.iep.utm.edu/greekphi/ Ret: December 2018

247. Albert RSR, M. A. (1999). ":A History of Research on Creativity". In Sternberg, R. J. Handbook of Creativity. Cambridge University Press. p. 5.

248. Niu WS, Robert J. (2006). "The Philosophical Roots of Western and Eastern Conceptions of Creativity". Journal of Theoretical and Philosophical Psychology. 26: 18–38. doi:10.1037/h0091265 & Michel Weber, "Creativity, Efficacy and Vision: Ethics and Psychology in an Open Universe," in Michel Weber and Pierfrancesco Basile (eds.), Subjectivity, Process, and Rationality, Frankfurt/Lancaster, ontos verlag, Process Thought XIV, 2006, pp. 263-281.

249. Humanism: https://en.wikipedia.org/wiki/Humanism. Rert: May 2018.

250. "Leonardo da Vinci | Italian artist e, and scientist". Encyclopædia Britannica. Retrieved 2015-11-23.

251. Dacey J: Concepts of Creativity: A history. In Mark A Runco; Steven R Pritzer Encyclopedia of Creativity, Vol 1 1999, Elsevier. ISBN 0-12-227076-2.

252. Whitehead AN: Process and reality : an essay in cosmology. Gifford Lectures delivered in the University of Edinburgh during the session 1927-28 (Corrected ed) 1978, New

York: Free Press. ISBN 0-02-934580-4.

253. Wallas G: Art of Thought. 1926.

254. Kaufman JCB, Ronald A. (2009). "Beyond Big and Little: The Four C Model of Creativity". Review of General Psychology. 13 (1): 1–12. doi:10.1037/a0013688.

255. Trends in neuroscience: Randomness and creativity; Volume 24 I, p694, 1 December 2001.

256. Nat Neurosci. 2000 Aug;3(8):827-30. The influence of urgency on decision time. Reddi BA CR.

257. Smith SM: Incubation. In M A Runco; S R Pritzker Encyclopedia of Creativity Volume I (2nd ed) 2011, Academic Press. ISBN 978-0-12-375039-6.:653-657.

258. Ward TCIN, L. Encyclopaedia of Cognition. New York: Macmillan.

259. Ward TBWsoaniISMS, T. B. Ward & R. A. & Finke (Eds.) The creative cognition approach, 157–178, London: MIT Press.

260. Anderson JR: Cognitive psychology and its implications. Worth Publishers ISBN 0-7167-1686-0 2000.

261. Gilhooly KJ: Incubation and Intuition in Creative Problem Solving. Front Psychol ; 7: 1076 2016.

262. Weisberg RW: Creativity: Beyond the myth of genius. Freeman ISBN 0-7167-2119-8 1993.

263. Helie S.; Sun R. (2010). "Incubation i, and creative problem solving: A unified theory and a connectionist model". Psychological Review. 117: 994–1024. doi:10.1037/a0019532. PMID 20658861.

264. Koestler A: The Act of Creation. . London: Pan Books ISBN 0-330-73116-5 1964.

265. Gabora LS, A. (2011). Creative interference and states of potentiality in analogy problem solving. Proceedings of the Annual Meeting of the Cognitive Science Society. July 20–23, 2011, Boston MA.

266. Roese NJO, J. M. (1995). What Might Have Been: The Social Psychology of Counterfactual Thinking. Mahwah, New Jersey: Erlbaum.

267. http://www.creativitypost.com/psychology/you_are_sooo_random_randomness_creativity_research1. November 2018

268. Robinson, North Dakota State University. Psychology of Aesthetics C, and the Arts © 2010 American Psychological Association, 2010 V, No. 3, 136–143.

269. Vartanian, Creativity, and the Arts, 3, 57-59.

270. Kozbelt AB, Ronald A.; Runco, Mark A. (2010). "Theories of Creativity". In James C. Kaufman; Robert J. Sternberg. The Cambridge Handbook of Creativity. Cambridge University Press. ISBN 978-0-521-73025-9.

271. Craft A: Creativity in Schools: Tensions and Dilemmas. Abingdon: Routledge 2005.

272. Kim KH: Can We Trust Creativity Tests? Lawrence Erlbaum Associates 2006.

273. Thyer BAP, Monica G. (2015-05-15). Science and Pseudoscience in Social Work Practice. Springer Publishing Company. pp. 56–57, 165–167. .

274. Forster EA, & Dunbar, K. N. (2009). Creativity evaluation through latent semantic analysis. In Proceedings of the 31st Annual meeting of the Cognitive Science Society (pp. 602–607).

275. Beketayev KR, M. A. (2016). "Scoring Divergent Thinking Tests by Computer With a Semantics-Based Algorithm". Europe's Journal of Psychology. 12 (2): 210–220. doi:10.5964/ejop.v12i2.1127.

276. Sternberg RJL, T. I. (1999). "The Concept of Creativity: Prospects and Paradigms". In Sternberg, R. J. Handbook of Creativity. Cambridge University Press. ISBN 0-521-57285-1.

277. Feist GJ: A meta-analysis of the impact of personality on scientific and artistic creativity. Personality and Social Psychological Review 2: 290-309 doi:101207/s15327957pspr0204_5 1998.

278. Guilford JP: The nature of human intelligence. New York: McGraw-Hill 1967.

279. Hayes JRCpicIJAG, R. R. Ronning, & C. R. Reynolds (Eds.), Handbook of creativity (pp. 135–145). New York: Plenum.

280. Sternberg RJ: Successful Intelligence. NewYork: Simon & Schuster 1996.

281. Sternberg RJ, Kaufman, J. C., & Grigorenko, E. L. (2008). Applied intelligence. Cambridge: Cambridge University Press.

282. Gardner H: Creating minds. New York: Basic Books 1993.

283. Silvia PJB, R. E.; Nusbaum, E. C. (2013). "Verbal fluency and creativity: General and specific contributions of broad retrieval ability (Gr) factors to divergent thinking". Intelligence. 41: 328–340. doi:10.1016/j.intell.2013.05.004.

284. Kaufman JC, Kaufman, S.B., & Plucker, J.A. (2013). Contemporary theories of intelligence. In J. Reisberg (Ed.), The Oxford Handbook of Cognitive Psychology (pp. 811-822). New York, NY: Oxford University Press.

285. Amabile TM: Social psychology of creativity: A consensual assessment technique. Journal of Personality and Social Psychology 43: 997-1013 doi:101037/0022-3514435997 1982.

286. Baer JK, J. C. (2005). "Bridging generality and specificity: The Amusement Park Theoretical (APT) Model of creativity". Roeper Review. 27: 158–163. doi:10.1080/02783190509554310.

287. Renzulli JS: What makes giftedness? Reexamining a definition. Phi Delta Kappan 60: 180-261 1978.

288. Naglieri JAK, J. C. (2001). "Understanding intelligence, giftedness, and creativity using PASS theory". Roeper Review. 23: 151–156. .

289. Torrance EP: Guiding creative talent. Englewood Cliffs, NJ: Prentice-Hall 1962.

290. Wai JL, D.; Benbow, C. P. (2005). "Creativity and occupational accomplishments among intellectually precocious youths: An age 13 to age 33 longitudinal study". Journal of Educational Psychology. 97: 484–492. doi:10.1037/0022-0663.97.3.484.

291. Barron F: Creative person and creative process. . New York: Holt, Rinehart & Winston 1969.

292. Perkins DN: The mind's best work. Cambridge, MA: Harvard University Press 1981.

293. Getzels JW, & Jackson, P. W.: Creativity and intelligence: Explorations with gifted students. New York: Wiley 1962.

294. https://www.webpagefx.com/blog/web-design/using-random-input-technique-kick-start-creativity/. November 2018

295. https://tinkerlab.com/8-ideas-kick-start-creativity-new-year/. November 2018

296. De Bono E: Serious creativity: using the power of lateral thinking to create new ideas. HarperBusiness; ISBN 9780887305665 1992:p. 145. .

297. Evans J: A Review and Synthesis of OR/MS and Creative Problem Solving. J of Msmt So, Vol 17, No 6, pp 499-524, 1989, https://ac.els-cdn.com/0305048389900558/1-s2.0-0305048389900558-main.pdf?_tid=9d2ff0b0-7754-42b3-aa3f-060789a7dedd&acd-

nat=1526386885_43d8a9246a6b7aeeb57d230c74abbf06. November 2018

298. https://en.wikipedia.org/wiki/Lateral_thinking. November 2018

299. Ibsen H: An Enemy of the People. World Library 2004

300. de Bono E: Six Thinking Hats: An Essential Approach to Business Management. . Little, Brown, & Company ISBN 0-316-17791-1 1985.

301. http://www.debonogroup.com/serious_creativity.php. November 2018

302. Daily Rituals: How Artists Work Hardcover – April 23, (Editor) bMC, reviews oosc.

303. https://digital-photography-school.com/adding-randomness-to-your-photos/. November 2018

304. https://thinkibility.com/2013/03/14/provoke-randomness-as-a-thinking-strategy/. November 2018

305. https://www.amazon.com/Michael-Michalko/e/B001JRWY3E. November 2018

306. https://globalizationicas.com/creative-lounge/leonardo-da-vinci-the-first-creative-genius/. November 2018

307. http://www.bl.uk/onlinegallery/features/leonardo/insights.html. November 2018

308. http://www.tate.org.uk/context-comment/articles/deliberate-accident-art. November 2018

309. http://yorkfestivalofideas.com/2014/talks/randomness/. November 2018

310. Creative Thinkering: Putting Your Imagination to Work Paperback – September 6 bMM.

311. Hua ZY, J.; Coulibaly, S.; Zhang, B. (2006). "Integration TRIZ with problem-solving tools: a literature review from 1995 to 2006". International Journal of Business Innovation and Research. 1 (1-2): 111–128. Retrieved 2 October 2010.

312. Sheng ILSK-S, T. (2010). "Eco-Efficient Product Design Using theory of Inventive Problem Solving (TRIZ) Principles" (PDF). American Journal of Applied Sciences. 7 (6): 852–858. Retrieved 30 September 2010.

313. https://en.wikipedia.org/wiki/TRIZ. November 2018

314. Altshuller GSS, R. B. (1956). "О Психологии изобретательского творчества (On the psychology of inventive creation)". Вопросы Психологии (The Psychological Issues) (in Russian) (6): 37–39. Retrieved 4 October 2010.

315. Alshuller, A. Gordon and Breach Science Publishers Inc. https://searchworks.stanford.edu/view/1223823; ret: December 2018.

316. http://www.triz-journal.com/whatistriz.htm. November 2018

317. https://news.efinancialcareers.com/us-en/230786/top-undergraduate-majors-investment-banking-jobs-wall-street. November 2018

318. https://triz-journal.com/ariz-algorithm-inventive-problem-solving/. November 2018

319. https://triz-journal.com/su-field-analysis/. November 2018

320. http://www.legalbusiness.co.uk/index.php/lb-blog-view/2727-the-overall-benefits-are-potentially-enormous-bucks-county-council-granted-abs-licence-with-emergency-services-group]. November 2018

321. https://www.forbes.com/sites/haydnshaughnessy/2013/03/07/why-is-samsung-such-an-innovative-company/2/#69bf72087f96. November 2018

322. https://www.triz.co.uk/who/case-studies/mars-chocolate-packaging-case-study. November 2018

323. www.etria.eu E November 2018.

324. https://www.amazon.com/creative-Writers-Kit-Judy-Reeves/dp/B008VXV0Q6. No-

vember 2018

325. John Sweller Cognitive Bases of Human Creativity. Educational Psychology Review 2009 V, Issue 1, pp 11–19
326. Sweller J, & Sweller, S. (2006). Natural information processing systems. Evolutionary Psychology, 4, 434–458.
327. Clark RC, Nguyen, F., & Sweller, J. (2006). Efficiency in learning: Evidence-based guidelines to manage cognitive load. San Francisco: Pfeiffer.
328. Chen J MB, Furano AV (April 2014). "Repair of naturally occurring mismatches can induce mutations in flanking DNA". eLife. 3: e02001. doi:10.7554/elife.02001. PMC 3999860.
329. https://en.wikipedia.org/wiki/Mutation. November 2018
330. https://evolution.berkeley.edu/evolibrary/article/mutations_07. November 2018
331. Peterson L, & Peterson, M. J. (1959). Short-term retention of individual verbal items. Journal of Experimental Psychology, 58, 193–198.
332. Ericsson KA, & Kintsch, W. (1995). Long-term working memory. Psychological Review, 102, 211–245.
333. Schmidhuber J: Formal Theory of Creativity, Fun, and Intrinsic Motivation. IEEE Transactions on Autonomous Mental Development 2010, 2(3): 230-247.
334. Gladwell M: Outliers: The Story of Success Little, Brown and Company 2008.
335. https://en.wikipedia.org/wiki/Outliers_(book). November 2018
336. http://www.businessinsider.com/new-study-destroys-malcolm-gladwells-10000-rule-2014-7. November 2018
337. Deliberate Practice and Performance in Music G, Sports, Education, and Professions A Meta-Analysis Brooke N. Macnamara, David Z. Hambrick, Frederick L. Oswald , Psychological Science Vol 25 I, 2014.
338. Johansson F: The Click Moment: Seizing Opportunity in an Unpredictable World https://wwwamazoncom/Click-Moment-Seizing-Opportunity-Unpredictable/dp/1591844932 2012.
339. Meadow A, Parnes, S., & Reese, H. (1959). Influence of brainstorming instruction and problem sequence on a creative problem solving test. The Journal of Applied Psychology, 43, 413–416. .
340. https://en.wikipedia.org/wiki/Brainstorming. November 2018
341. Osborn AF: Applied imagination: Principles and procedures of creative problem solving New York, NY: Charles Scribner's Sons 1963.
342. Bouchard TJ, & Hare, M. (1970). Size, performance and potential in brainstorming groups. The Journal of Applied Psychology, 54, 51–55. .
343. Dillon PC, Graham, W. K., & Aidells, A. L. (1972). Brainstorming on a "hot" problem: Effects of training and practice on individual and group performance. The Journal of Applied Psychology, 56, 487–490. .
344. Osborn AF: Brainstorming and beyond. https://wwwgooglecoil/search?ei=WhtXW-aZDYPOgQa937joAQ&q=Osborn+%E2%80%9Ccreative+efficacy%E2%80%9D+of+brainstorming+&oq=Osborn+%E2%80%9Ccreative+efficacy%E2%80%9D+of+brainstorming+&gs_l=psy-ab-31041214584015609000000000001164psy-ab0000bZWzpeie5cc 2012. November 2018
345. Toubia OIG, Creativity, and Incentives" (PDF). Marketing Science. Retrieved 28 April 2011.

346. Is Electronic Brainstorming the Most Effective Approach? . In: Barki, Pinsonneault / BRAINSTORMING AND IDEA QUALITY, http://citeseerx.ist.psu.edu/viewdoc/ download?doi=10.1.1.827.2345&rep=rep1&type=pdf.

347. Furnham A, & Yazdanpanahi, T. (1995). Personality differences and group versus individual brainstorming. Personality and Individual Differences, 19, 73-80.

348. Furnham A: The brainstorming myth. Bussiness strategy Review 2000, 11:4:21-28(https://pdfs.semanticscholar.org/a2f4/5b4a13c822f1710338670693bc-d233aef987.pdf).

349. Hassan Ait-Haddou GC, Pascale ZaratÉ: Prediction of Ideas Number During a Brainstorming Session. Group Decision and Negotiation, INFORMS, 2014,, vol. 23 (n° 2), pp. 271-298.(https://hal.archives-ouvertes.fr/hal-01119518/document).

350. Kohn NS, Steven M. (2011). "Collaborative fixation: Effects of others' ideas on brainstorming". Applied Cognitive Psychology. 25 (3): 359–371. .

351. Upmanyu VV, Bhardwaj S, Singh S: Word-association emotional indicators: associations with anxiety, psychoticism, neuroticism, extraversion, and creativity. J Soc Psychol 1996, 136(4):521-529.

352. Sity Rahmy Maulidya RUH, and Endah Retnowat: Can goal-free problems facilitating students' flexible thinking? AIP Conference Proceedings 1868, 050001; doi: 101063/14995128 2017, https://aip.scitation.org/doi/pdf/10.1063/1.4995128.

353. https://www.mindtools.com/brainstm.html. November 2018

354. http://www.free-management-ebooks.com/news/paired-comparison-analysis/. November 2018

355. de Bono, Brown, & Company. ISBN 0-316-17791-1 (hardback) and 0316178314 (paperback).

356. Edward De Bono 1971. Lateral Thinking for Management: A Handbook Of Creativity. American Management Association NY.

357. Six Thinking Hats; Official training materials DTS. http://www.dtssydney.com/ blog/6_thinking_hats:_praise_and_criticism; Ret: December 2018

358. Morrison J: Spanx on Steroids: How Speedo Created the New Record-Breaking Swimsuit. smithsoniancom 2012, https://www.smithsonianmag.com/science-nature/spanx-on-steroids-how-speedo-created-the-new-record-breaking-swimsuit-9662/#3S6QcKBDBYkfiefs.99; https://www.smithsonianmag.com/science-nature/ spanx-on-steroids-how-speedo-created-the-new-record-breaking-swimsuit-9662/?c=y&story=fullstor. November 2018

359. Gladwell M: Blink: The Power of Thinking Without Thinking. Back Bay Books 2005.

360. https://en.wikipedia.org/wiki/Blink:_The_Power_of_Thinking_Without_Thinking. November 2018

361. Think!: Why Crucial Decisions Can't Be Made in the Blink of an Eye Paperback – October 24, (Author) bMRL.

362. Charlie Rose Show broadcast February 28, 2012. Ret: December 2018.

363. Isenman L: Understanding Unconscious Intelligence and Intuition: "Blink" and Beyond. Perspectives in Biology and Medicine 2013, 56 (1):148-166.

364. https://en.wikipedia.org/wiki/Borda_count; Ret: December 2018.

365. https://geneticfractals.wordpress.com/2017/04/12/randomness-as-the-origin-of-creativity/. November 2018

366. Goldberger AL, Rigney DR, West BJ: Chaos and fractals in human physiology. Sci Am

1990, 262(2):42-49.

367. Goldberger AL: Non-linear dynamics for clinicians: chaos theory, fractals, and complexity at the bedside. Lancet 1996, 347(9011):1312-1314.

368. https://fractalfoundation.org/resources/what-are-fractals/ Ret: December 2018.

369. http://www.chopra.com/articles/5-ways-to-improve-creativity-through-meditation#sm.0001ldlwy97medd6v1d23unj27aqz. November 2018

370. http://www.pasteurbrewing.com/louis-pasteur-chance-favors-the-prepared-mind/ Ret: December 2018

371. http://www.lindau-nobel.org/chance-favors-the-prepared-mind/. November 2018

372. A. G. OgstonAustralian Biochemical Society Annual Lecture August 1970 hwnonpmlslp.

373. Aatish Bhatia E: What does randomness look like? . http://wwwempiricalzealcom/2012/12/21/what-does-randomness-look-like/. November 2018

374. Pinker S: The Better Angels of Our Nature: Why Violence Has Declined Publisher: Viking 2012.

375. https://en.wikipedia.org/wiki/The_Better_Angels_of_Our_Nature.

376. Glowworms in the Waitomo Caves. https://wwwgreatsightsconz/glowworms-in-the-waitomo-caves/. November 2018

377. Bhatia A: What does randomness look like. wired 2012, https://www.wired.com/2012/12/what-does-randomness-look-like/What does randomness look like. . November 2018

378. A. Q: Sur l'homme et le development de ses faculties, ou Essai de physique sociale. 1835, Vol 2. Paris.

379. http://journals.lww.com/epidem/Fulltext/2012/09000/Adolphe_Quetelet___Statistician_and_More.18.aspx. November 2018

380. Space and time variations in crime-recording practices within a large municipal police agency. International Journal of Police Science and Management 2014, Vol. 16 No. 3, pp. 171-183

381. Quetelet A: Tales of Statisticians. https://wwwumassedu/wsp/resources/tales/quetelethtml.

382. https://www.umass.edu/wsp/resources/tales/poisson.html. November 2018

383. Aldous D: On Chance and Unpredictability: lectures on the links between mathematical probability and the real world. UC Berkeley Statistics 2015, https://www.stat.berkeley.edu/~aldous/Real-World/book_april_2015.pdf.

384. https://hbr.org/1998/03/bringing-discipline-to-project-management. November 2018

385. http://csc.ucdavis.edu/~chaos/courses/ncaso/Readings/Chaos_SciAm1986/Chaos_SciAm1986.html.

386. https://en.wikipedia.org/wiki/Chaos_theory. November 2018

387. https://dictionary.cambridge.org/dictionary/english/chaos. November 2018

388. Chaos. From Theory to Applications. New York, London: Plenum Press 1992. , Volume 133, Issue 1:pp. 114-115.

389. Kyriazis M: Practical applications of chaos theory to the modulation of human ageing: nature prefers chaos to regularity. Biogerontology 2003 -.

390. Mackey LGMC: From Clocks to Chaos The Rhythms of Life. https://pressprincetonedu/titles/4308html 1988

391. Skinner JE: Low-dimensional chaos in biological systems. Biotechnology (N Y) 1994,

12(6):596-600.

392. https://www.amazon.com/Explaining-Chaos-Peter-Smith-1998-11-13/dp/B01FJ-1D64G. November 2018

393. Goldberger AL, Amaral LA, Hausdorff JM, Ivanov P, Peng CK, Stanley HE: Fractal dynamics in physiology: alterations with disease and aging. Proc Natl Acad Sci U S A 2002, 99 Suppl 1:2466-2472.

394. https://www.igi-global.com/book/chaos-complexity-theory-management/68194. November 2018

395. Danforth CM: Chaos in an Atmosphere Hanging on a Wall. Mathematics of Planet Earth 2013.

396. Stinnett B: The Butterfly Effect: Why Small Acts Can Have Big Effects. http://wwwgordontrainingcom/leadership/the-butterfly-effect-why-small-acts-can-have-big-effects/ 2011.

397. Boeing G: Visual Analysis of Nonlinear Dynamical Systems: Chaos, Fractals, Self-Similarity and the Limits of Prediction. Systems Research and Behavioral Science 2016, 4 (4): 37. doi:10.3390/systems4040037.

398. Lorenz EN: Deterministic non-periodic flow. Journal of the Atmospheric Sciences 1963, 20 (2): 130-141. Bibcode:1963JAtS...20..130L.

399. Gleick J: Chaos: Making a New Science. London: Cardinal p 17 1987.

400. Kellert SH: In the Wake of Chaos: Unpredictable Order in Dynamical Systems. University of Chicago Press 1993, ISBN 0-226-42976-8.:p. 32.

401. Werndl C: What are the New Implications of Chaos for Unpredictability. The British Journal for the Philosophy of Science 2009, 60 (1): 195-220.

402. Chan S: Complex Adaptive Systems. ESD83 Research Seminar in Engineering Systems 2001, http://web.mit.edu/esd.83/www/notebook/Complex%20Adaptive%20Systems.pdf.

403. Strogatz S: The Emerging Science of Spontaneous Order. Hyperion, New York, 2003: pages 189-190.

404. Chaos: Making a New Science Paperback – August 26, https://www.amazon.com/Chaos-Making-Science-James-Gleick/dp/0143113453 November 2018.

405. Poincaré JH: The three-body problem and the equations of dynamics : Poincaré's foundational work on dynamical systems theory. Cham, Switzerland: Springer International Publishing ISBN 9783319528984 2017.

406. Hadamard J: Les surfaces à courbures opposées et leurs lignes géodesiques. Journal de Mathématiques Pures et Appliquées 1898, 4: 27-73.

407. Ueda A: World Scientific Series on Nonlinear Science Series A; The Chaos Avant-Garde; Memories of the Early Days of Chaos Theory. ISBN: 978-981-238-647-2 2001, Chapters 3 and 4.

408. Talk T: Benoit Mandelbrot: Fractals and the art of roughness. . tedcom 2010, https://www.ted.com/talks/benoit_mandelbrot_fractals_the_art_of_roughness.

409. Mandelbrot B: The variation of certain speculative prices. Journal of Business 1963, 36 (4): 394-419.

410. B. BJMM: A new model for error clustering in telephone circuits. IBM Journal of Research and Developmen 1963, 7: 224-236.

411. Mandelbrot BBH, Richard L. : The (Mis)behavior of Markets: A Fractal View of Risk, Ruin, and Reward. New York: Basic Books 2004:p. 201.

412. Mandelbrot B: How Long Is the Coast of Britain? Statistical Self-Similarity and Fractional Dimension. Science 1967, 156(3775: 636-8).

413. https://blogs.scientificamerican.com/roots-of-unity/a-few-of-my-favorite-spaces-the-menger-sponge/.

414. https://io9.gizmodo.com/5827482/the-menger-sponge-literally-straddles-the-line-between-different-dimensions. November 2018

415. Allouche J-PS, Jeffrey (2003). Automatic Sequences: Theory, Applications, Generalizations. Cambridge University Press. pp. 405–406.

416. Mandelbrot B: The Fractal Geometry of Nature. New York: Macmillan 1982.

417. Huberman BA: A Model for Dysfunctions in Smooth Pursuit Eye Movement. Annals of the New York Academy of Sciences 1987, 504 Perspectives in Biological Dynamics and Theoretical Medicine: 260-273. Bibcode:1987NYASA.504..260H.

418. Buldyrev SVG, A.L.; Havlin, S.; Peng, C.K.; Stanley, H.E. (1994). "Fractals in Biology and Medicine: From DNA to the Heartbeat". In Bunde, Armin; Havlin, Shlomo. Fractals in Science. Springer. pp. 49–89. .

419. Bak PT, Chao; Wiesenfeld, Kurt; Tang; Wiesenfeld (27 July 1987). "Self-organized criticality: An explanation of the 1/f noise". Physical Review Letters. 59 (4): 381–4. Bibcode:1987PhRvL..59..381B. doi:10.1103/PhysRevLett.59.381.

420. https://en.wikipedia.org/wiki/Self-organized_criticality. November 2018

421. Hasselblatt BAK: A First Course in Dynamics: With a Panorama of Recent Developments. Cambridge University Press ISBN 978-0-521-40605-5 2003.

422. Ovchinnikov IVS, R. N.; Wang, K. L. (2016). "Topological supersymmetry breaking: Definition and stochastic generalization of chaos and the limit of applicability of statistics". Modern Physics Letters B. 30: .

423. Watts RG: Global Warming and the Future of the Earth. . Morgan & Claypool 2007:p. 17.

424. Devaney RL: An Introduction to Chaotic Dynamical Systems (2nd ed.). Westview Press 2003.

425. Strogatz S: Sync: The Emerging Science of Spontaneous Order,. Hyperion 2003.

426. Hubler AF, G.; Phelps, K. (2007). "Managing chaos: Thinking out of the box". Complexity. Bibcode:2007Cmplx..12c..10H.

427. Akhavan AS, A.; Akhshani, A. (2017-10-01). "Cryptanalysis of an image encryption algorithm based on DNA encoding". Optics & Laser Technology. 95: 94–99. .

428. Behnia SA, A.; Mahmodi, H.; Akhavan, A. (2008-01-01). "A novel algorithm for image encryption based on mixture of chaotic maps". Chaos, Solitons & Fractals. 35 (2): 408–419. .

429. Wang XZ, Jianfeng An improved key agreement protocol based on chaos. Commun Nonlinear Sci Numer Simul 2012, 15 (12): 4052-4057. .

430. Babaei M: A novel text and image encryption method based on chaos theory and DNA computing. Natural Computing an International Journal 2013, 12 (1): 101-107. .

431. Nehmzow UKW: Quantitative description of robot-environment interaction using chaos theory. Robotics and Autonomous Systems 2005, 53(3-4): 177-193.

432. Goswami AT, Benoit; Espiau, Bernard (1998). "A Study of the Passive Gait of a Compass-Like Biped Robot: Symmetry and Chaos". The International Journal of Robotics Research. 17 (12): 1282–1301. .

433. Eduardo LR-H, Alfonso (2012). "Chaos in discrete structured population models".

SIAM Journal on Applied Dynamical Systems. 11 (4): 1200–1214.

434. Lai D: Comparison study of AR models on the Canadian lynx data: a close look at BDS statistic. Computational Statistics \& Data Analysis 1996, 22 (4): 409-423.

435. Bozóki Z: Chaos theory and power spectrum analysis in computerized cardiotocography. European Journal of Obstetrics & Gynecology and Reproductive Biology 1997, 71 (2): 163-168.

436. Qu Z, Weiss JN: Mechanisms of ventricular arrhythmias: from molecular fluctuations to electrical turbulence. Annu Rev Physiol 2015, 77:29-55.

437. Sivakumar B: Chaos theory in hydrology: important issues and interpretations. Journal of Hydrology 2000, 227 (1-4): 1-20. .

438. Prediction of gas solubility in polymers by back propagation artificial neural network based on self-adaptive particle swarm optimization algorithm and chaos theory. Fluid Phase Equilibria 2013, 356: 11-17.

439. Morbidelli A: Chaotic diffusion in celestial mechanics. Regular & Chaotic Dynamics 2001, 6 (4): 339-353. .

440. Pryor: Probabilities and Possibilities: The Strategic Counseling Implications of the Chaos Theory of Careers. The Career Development Quarterly 2008, 56: 309-318.

441. Juárez F: Applying the theory of chaos and a complex model of health to establish relations among financial indicators. Procedia Computer Science 2011, 3: 982-986.

442. Brooks C: Chaos in foreign exchange markets: a sceptical view. Computational Economics 1998, 11: 265-281. ISSN 1572-9974.

443. Wang JQS: Short-term traffic speed forecasting hybrid model based on Chaos-Wavelet Analysis-Support Vector Machine theory. Transportation Research Part C: Emerging Technologies 2013, 27: 219-232. .

444. Dal Forno AM, Ugo (2013). "Nonlinear dynamics in work groups with Bion's basic assumptions". Nonlinear Dynamics, Psychology, and Life Sciences. 17 (2): 295–315. .

445. Pasternack GB.Watershed Hydrology G, and Ecohydraulics: Chaos in Hydrology. http://pasternack.ucdavis.edu/research/projects/waterfalls/ ret: December 2018

446. Pasternack GB: Does the river run wild? Assessing chaos in hydrological systems Advances in Water Resources 1999, 23 (3): 253-260. .

447. Rides for Amusement Parks C, and Fairs – Made in the USA https://en.wikipedia.org/wiki/Tilt-A-Whirl. November 2018

448. https://en.wikipedia.org/wiki/Atwood_machine. November 2018

449. https://en.wikipedia.org/wiki/Swinging_Atwood%27s_machine. November 2018

450. Tufillaro NBA, Tyler A.; Griffiths, David J. (1984). "Swinging Atwood's Machine". American Journal of Physics. 52 (10): 895–903. Bibcode:1984AmJPh..52..895.

451. Julyan H. E. Cartwright MF, & Oreste Piro: An Introduction to Chaotic Advection Published in "Mixing: Chaos and Turbulence", Eds H Chate,´ E Villermaux, & J M Chomez, Kluwer, 1999, https://pdfs.semanticscholar.org/9fd0/502089ad7f-52de7f8382e328db676cfe2d2b.pdf:pp. 307-342,.

452. Sediment Transport A Geophysical Phenomenon. Springer Science & Business Media 2006, file:///C:/Users/owner/Downloads/2006-GyrHoyer-SedimentTransport-Springer.pdf.

453. Ergodic Problems in Classical Mechanics. . New York: Benjamin 1967. https://www.amazon.com/Problems-Classical-Mechanics-Mathematical-monograph/dp/B0006B-V20K. Ret: December 2018

454. https://en.wikipedia.org/wiki/Arnold%27s_cat_map. November 2018
455. Brancazio PJ: Trajectory of a fly ball. The Physics Teacher 1985, 23 (1): 20.
456. Rössler OE, "An Equation for Continuous Chaos", Physics Letters, 57A (5): 397–398,.
457. Peitgen H-OJ, Hartmut; Saupe, Dietmar (2004), "12.3 The Rössler Attractor", Chaos and Fractals: New Frontiers of Science, Springer, pp. 636–646.
458. https://en.wikipedia.org/wiki/R%C3%B6ssler_attractor. November 2018
459. http://order.ph.utexas.edu/standardmap/. November 2018
460. https://en.wikipedia.org/wiki/List_of_chaotic_maps. November 2018
461. https://en.wikipedia.org/wiki/Horseshoe_map. November 2018
462. Ruelle D: What is a strange attractor? Notices of the American Mathematical Society 2006, 53 (7): 764-765.
463. https://en.wikipedia.org/wiki/Standard_map. November 2018
464. Chirikov BV: A universal instability of many-dimensional oscillator systems. Phys Rep 1979, v.52. p.263(Elsvier, Amsterdam).
465. http://order.ph.utexas.edu/standardmap/introduction.html. November 2018
466. Chaos synchronization in Chua's circuit LOC, Berkeley : Electronics Research Laboratory, College of Engineering, University of California, [1992], .
467. Chua's Circuit Implementations: Yesterday TaT, L. Fortuna, M. Frasca, M.G. Xibilia, World Scientific Series on Nonlinear Science, Series A - Vol. 65, 2009.
468. https://en.wikipedia.org/wiki/Chua%27s_circuit. November 2018
469. https://en.wikipedia.org/wiki/Coupled_map_lattice. November 2018
470. Kaneko K: Overview of Coupled Map Lattices. Chaos 1992, 2, Num3: 279.
471. Chazottes J-R, and Bastien Fernandez. Dynamics of Coupled Map Lattices and of Related Spatially Extended Systems. Springer, 2004. pgs 1–4.
472. Xu JW, Xioa Fan. : Cascading failures in scale-free coupled map lattices. IEEE International Symposium on Circuits and Systems 2005, ISCAS Volume 4, 3395-3398.
473. R. Badii, A. Politi 1997, Complexity : hierarchical structures and scaling in physics. https://trove.nla.gov.au/work/14072211?q&versionId=46590826. Ret: December 2018
474. https://en.wikipedia.org/wiki/Double_pendulum. November 2018
475. Levien RBT, S. M. (1993). "Double Pendulum: An experiment in chaos". American Journal of Physics. 61 (11): 1038.
476. https://www.myphysicslab.com/pendulum/double-pendulum-en.html. November 2018
477. https://en.wikipedia.org/wiki/Dynamical_billiards. November 2018
478. Burago DF, S.; Kononenko, A. (1 January 1998). "Uniform Estimates on the Number of Collisions in Semi-Dispersing Billiards". Annals of Mathematics. 147 (3): 695–708.
479. https://en.wikipedia.org/wiki/Chaotic_scattering. November 2018
480. https://en.wikipedia.org/wiki/Cliodynamics. November 2018
481. Turchin P: Arise 'cliodynamics'. Nature 2008, 454(7200):34-35.
482. Turchin. P: A. Historical Dynamics: Why States Rise and Fall. Princeton, NJ: Princeton University Press 2003.
483. Spinney L: Human cycles: History as Science. Nature; 2012.
484. Seabright P: Historical Dynamics: Why States Rise and Fall. Peter Turchin Princeton, NJ: Princeton University Press 2004.
485. Spinney L: The database that is rewriting history to predict the future. New Scientist 2016.

486. Koyama M: Warfare and the Evolution of Social Complexity: A Multilevel-Selection Approach. Structure and Dynamics 2016, 4(3(1)):1-37.

487. Goldstone J. 1991.Revolution and Rebellion in the Early Modern World. Berkeley.

488. Dzogang FL-W, Thomas; Team, FindMyPast Newspaper; Cristianini, Nello (2016-11-08). "Discovering Periodic Patterns in Historical News". PLOS ONE. 11 (11): e0165736.

489. Joseph A. Tainter, The Collapse of Complex Societies. https://www.amazon.com/Collapse-Complex-Societies-Studies-Archaeology-ebook/dp/B001AOZ3PM/ref=s-r_1_1?ie=UTF8&qid=1544880231&sr=8-1&keywords=joseph+tainter. ISBN-13: 978-0521340922

490. Turchin. BP: Historical Dynamics: Why States Rise and Fall. Princeton, NJ: Princeton University Press, 2003.

491. https://en.wikipedia.org/wiki/Economic_bubble. November 2018

492. https://www.forbes.com/sites/tomkonrad/2011/08/30/chaos-theory-financial-markets-and-global-weirding/#2ed55d616f2f. November 2018

493. Galbraith JK: A Short History of Financial Euphoria: Financial Genius is Before the Fall. Penguin Bussiness 1990.

494. http://www.economist.com/node/6877092. December 2018

495. https://en.wikipedia.org/wiki/John_Kenneth_Galbraith. December 2018

496. https://en.wikipedia.org/wiki/Attractor. December 2018

497. Grebogi C, Edward Ott, and James A. Yorke. "Chaos, Strange Attractors, and Fractal Basin Boundaries in Nonlinear Dynamics." Science 238, no. 4827 (1987): 632–638.

498. https://en.wikipedia.org/wiki/Chaotic_bubble. December 2018

499. P. Smereka BB, and S. Banerjee. "Regular and Chaotic Bubble Oscillations in Periodically Driven Pressure Fields." Physics of Fluids November 1987, 30(11), pp. 3342–3350.

500. Werner Lauterborn. "Numerical Investigation of Nonlinear Oscillations of Gas Bubbles in Liquids." Journal of the Acoustical Society of America 1976, pp. 283–293.

501. Richard H. Day and Weihong Huang. "Bulls B, and Market Sheep." Journal of Economic Behavior and Organization December 1990, 14(3), pp. 299–329.

502. Paul De Grauwe HD, and Mark Embrechts. Exchange Rate Theory: Chaotic Models of Foreign Exchange Rate Markets. Oxford: Blackwell, 1993.

503. Krugman PMB, Blower of Bubbles?". New York Times. Retrieved 10 May 2013.

504. http://press.uchicago.edu/ucp/books/book/chicago/T/bo5414939.html. December 2018

505. Dale R: The First Crash: Lessons from the South Sea Bubble. . London: Princeton University Press 2004:p. 40.

506. Smith VLS, Gerry L.; Williams, Arlington W. (1988). "Bubbles, Crashes, and Endogenous Expectations in Experimental Spot Asset Markets". Econometrica. 56 (5): 1119–1151. .

507. Lei VN, Charles N.; Plott, Charles R. (2001). "Nonspeculative Bubbles in Experimental Asset Markets: Lack of Common Knowledge of Rationality Vs. Actual Irrationality". Econometrica. 69 (4): 831. .

508. Brooks CK, Apostolos (2005). "A three-regime model of speculative behaviour: modelling the evolution of the S&P 500 composite index". The Economic Journal. 115 (505): 767–797.

509. Robert E. Wright FAL, Serious Look at America's Economic Ills (Buffalo, N.Y.: Prometheus, 2010), 51–52.

510. Zhi-Qiang Jiang W-XZ, Didier Sornette, Ryan Woodard, Ken Bastiaensen, Peter Cauwels: Bubble Diagnosis and Prediction of the 2005-2007 and 2008-2009 Chinese stock market bubbles. Journal of Economic Behavior & Organization 2010, 74 (3), 149-162 ).

511. Garber PM: Famous First Bubbles. The Journal of Economic Perspectives 1990, 4 (2): 35-54.

512. Froot KAO, Maurice (1991). "Intrinsic Bubbles: The Case of Stock Prices". American Economic Review. 81: 1189–1214.

513. Topol R: Bubbles and Volatility of Stock Prices: Effect of Mimetic Contagion. The Economic Journal 1991, 101 (407): 786-800.

514. Buchanan M: Why economic theory is out of whack. New Scientist Archived from the original on 19 December 2008 2008.

515. Leonhardt D: Part of the Problem: Stocks Are Expensive NYTimescom 25 August 2015.

516. https://www.investopedia.com/terms/g/greaterfooltheory.asp. December 2018

517. https://en.wikipedia.org/wiki/Greater_fool_theory. December 2018

518. Levine SSZ, Edward J. (27 June 2007). "The Institutional Nature of Price Bubbles".

519. Teeter PS, Jorgen (2017). "Cracking the enigma of asset bubbles with narratives". Strategic Organization. 15 (1): 91–99. .

520. Harmon D LM, de Aguiar MAM, Chinellato DD, Braha D, Epstein IR, et al. (2015). "Anticipating Economic Market Crises Using Measures of Collective Panic." PLoS ONE 10(7): e0131871.

521. Blodget H: Why Wall Street Always Blows It. https://wwwtheatlanticcom/magazine/archive/2008/12/why-wall-street-always-blows-it/307147/ 2008.

522. Porter DS, V. L. (1994). "Stock market bubbles in the laboratory". Applied Mathematical Finance. 1 (2): 111–128.

523. Caginalp GE, G. B. (1990). "A kinetic thermodynamics approach to the psychology of fluctuations in financial markets". Applied Mathematics Letters. 4 (4): 17–19. .

524. Sharp LF, Priesmeyer HR: Tutorial: chaos theory--a primer for health care. Qual Manag Health Care 1995, 3(4):71-86.

525. Butz M: Practical applications from chaos theory to the psychotherapeutic process, a basic consideration of dynamics. Psychol Rep 1993, 73(2):543-554.

526. Galatzer-Levy RM: The edge of chaos: A nonlinear view of psychoanalytic technique Int J Psychoanal 2016, 97:409-427.

527. LeBlanc VR, McConnell MM, Monteiro SD: Predictable chaos: a review of the effects of emotions on attention, memory and decision making. Adv Health Sci Educ Theory Pract 2015, 20(1):265-282.

528. https://en.wikipedia.org/wiki/Matryoshka_doll. December 2018

529. Ambros VS, 2004). "The functions of animal microRNAs". Nature. 431 (7006): 350–5.

530. RNAs M: Extracellular/Circulating MicroRNAs: Release Mechanisms, Functions and Challenges. Achievements in the Life Sciences 10: 175-186.

531. Taki FA, Pan X, Zhang B: Revisiting Chaos Theorem to Understand the Nature of miRNAs in Response to Drugs of Abuse. Journal of cellular physiology 2015, 230(12):2857-2868.

532. Springer NM, Lisch D, Li Q: Creating Order from Chaos: Epigenome Dynamics in Plants with Complex Genomes. The Plant cell 2016, 28(2):314-325.

533. Nicolini P, Ciulla MM, De Asmundis C, Magrini F, Brugada P: The prognostic value of heart rate variability in the elderly, changing the perspective: from sympathovagal balance to chaos theory. Pacing Clin Electrophysiol 2012, 35(5):622-638.

534. Derry PS, Derry GN: Menstruation, perimenopause, and chaos theory. Perspectives in biology and medicine 2012, 55(1):26-42.

535. http://www.ei-resource.org/illness-information/environmental-illnesses/gulf-war-syndrome/. December 2018

536. Martinez-Lavin M, Infante O, Lerma C: Hypothesis: the chaos and complexity theory may help our understanding of fibromyalgia and similar maladies. Semin Arthritis Rheum 2008, 37(4):260-264.

537. https://en.wikipedia.org/wiki/Complexity_theory_and_organizations. December 2018

538. Burnes B: Complexity theories and organizational change. International Journal of Management Reviews 2005, 7 (2): 73-90.

539. "Ten Principles of Complexity & Enabling Infrastructures" Professor Eve Mitleton-Kelly DCRP, London School of Economics. Archived from the original on 29 December 2009.

540. Grobman GM: Complexity Theory: a new way to look at organizational change. Public Administration Quarterly 2005, 29 (3).

541. Kieren Diment PY, Karin Garrety, . Complex Adaptive Systems as a Model for Evaluating Organisational : Change Caused by the Introduction of Health Information Systems. Health Informatics Research Lab, Faculty of Informatics, University of Wollongong, School of Management, University of Wollongong, NSW.

542. Terra L, João Luiz: Symbiotic Dynamic: The Strategic Problem from the Perspective of Complexity. Systems Research and Behavioral Science 2016, 33 (2): 235.

543. "Insights from Complexity Theory: Understanding Organisations better". by Assoc. Prof. Amit Gupta Sc-SA, IIM Bangalore. Retrieved 1 June2012.

544. http://www.labs.hp.com/research/idl/papers/ranking/ranking.html. December 2018

545. Anderson P: Complexity theory and organization science. Organization Science 1999, 10 (3): 216-232.

546. Saynisch MBfotpmAate, self-organizational principles and the complexity theory—results of the research program". Project Management Journal. 41 (2): 21–37. .

547. Agile Project Management: Essentials from the Project Management Journal https://books.google.co.il/books?id=xhWSN0jEMHYC&pg=RA2-PT1&lpg=RA2-PT1&dq=culture+of+trust%22+that+%22welcomes+outsiders eni, +and+promotes+cooperation&source=bl&ots=G2SVsam5lK&sig=Uhx-ALjP60nmGEzOlppxACsyRMqc&hl=en&sa=X&ved=0ahUKEwiMlIKn3Y3YAhX-SAewKHRebAlkQ6AEIJTAA#v=onepage&q=culture%20of%20trust%22%20that%20%22welcomes%20outsiders%2C%20embraces%20new%20ideas%2C%20and%20promotes%20cooperation&f=false. December 2018

548. Rob Goffee GJ: What Holds the Modern Company Together? Harvard Bussiness Review 1996, November-December.

549. Lewin RP, T. & Regine, B. (1998). "Complexity theory and the organization: Beyond the metaphor". Complexity. 3 (4): 36–40.

550. Systems, Century., https://www.ncbi.nlm.nih.gov/books/NBK222267/. December 2018

551. Conflict, Llopis G, https://www.forbes.com/sites/glennllopis/2014/11/28/4-ways-leaders-effectively-manage-employee-conflict/3/#40cf3b026c6e. December 2018

552. Tension in Teams Jim Kling HBR, https://hbr.org/2009/01/tension-in-teams.html.

553. Klepper MG, Michael (1996), The Wealthy 100: From Benjamin Franklin to Bill Gates—A Ranking of the Richest Americans, Past and Present, Secaucus, New Jersey: Carol Publishing Group, p. xiii,.

554. https://en.wikipedia.org/wiki/Edge_of_chaos. December 2018

555. Upadhyay RK: Dynamics of an ecological model living on the edge of chaos. Applied Mathematics and Computation 2009, 210 (2): 455-464.

556. Lewin bR, https://www.amazon.com/Complexity-Life-at-Edge-Chaos/dp/0226476553. December 2018

557. https://plato.stanford.edu/entries/cellular-automata/. December 2018

558. http://math.hws.edu/xJava/CA/EdgeOfChaos.html. December 2018

559. https://www.britannica.com/biography/Christopher-Langton. December 2018

560. Christopher G. Langton. "Computation at the edge of chaos". Physica D, 1990.

561. http://complexitylabs.io/edge-of-chaos/Complexity Labs EoC, " in Complexity Labs, August 24, 2016, http://complexitylabs.io/edge-of-chaos/. December 2018

562. Complexity and Organization: Readings and Conversations. Robert Macintosh, Donald Maclean, Ralph Stacey, Douglas Griffin. https://www.amazon.com/Complexity-Organization-Conversations-Robert-Macintosh/dp/0415352401.

563. Complexity Labs EoC, " in Complexity Labs, August 24, 2016, http://complexitylabs.io/edge-of-chaos/. December 2018

564. Abel DL: The capabilities of chaos and complexity. Int J Mol Sci 2009, 10(1):247-291.

565. Pauwelyn, How It Emerged and How It Can Be Reformed". ICSIDReview. 29 (2): 372.

566. chaos Eo: Biologists Find New Rules for Life at the Edge of Chaos. WIRED 2014, https://www.wired.com/2014/05/criticality-in-biology/. December 2018

567. Beggs JM: The criticality hypothesis: how local cortical networks might optimize information processing. Philos Trans A Math Phys Eng Sci 2008, 366(1864):329-343.

568. https://www.amazon.com/COMPLEXITY-EMERGING-SCIENCE-ORDER-CHAOS/dp/0671872346. December 2018

569. http://www.referenceforbusiness.com/management/Bun-Comp/Complexity-Theory.html. December 2018

570. https://www.investopedia.com/terms/j/joseph-schumpeter.asp. December 2018

571. https://www.wired.com/2002/03/schumpeter/. December 2018

572. https://economics.mit.edu/files/1785. December 2018

573. Cori J. Bussolari and Judith A. Goodell. Chaos Theory as a Model for Life Transitions Counseling: Nonlinear Dynamics and Life's Changes. https://www.counseling.org/docs/david-kaplan's-files/bussolari-c-goodell-j-.pdf Ret: December 2018

574. https://books.google.co.il/books?id=oywqCwAAQBAJ&pg=PA4&lpg=PA4&dq=Robert+Bilder+edge+of+chaos&source=bl&ots=ncxn8d1-ap&sig=BEMIo06BtEbaCXMzYPCgXfKqrk4&hl=en&sa=X&ved=0ahUKEwi7ianXvZDYAhXEC-wKHZC-4BR04ChDoAQgkMAA#v=onepage&q=Robert%20Bilder%20edge%20of%20chaos&f=false. December 2018

575. http://www.ideafestival.com/blog/2413.

576. Scaruffi P: Human Societies Are Systems at the Edge of Chaos. https://wwwscaruffi-com/phi/syn27html December 2018

577. Haigh CA: Using simplified Chaos Theory to manage nursing services. Journal of nursing management 2008, 16(3):298-304.

578. Cashin A, Waters C: The undervalued role of over-regulation in autism: Chaos Theory as a metaphor and beyond. J Child Adolesc Psychiatr Nurs 2006, 19(4):224-230.

579. Kernick D: Migraine--new perspectives from chaos theory. Cephalalgia 2005, 25(8):561-566.

580. Panidis DK, Rousso DH, Kourtis AI, Papathanasiou KV: Could the theory of chaos contribute to the interpretation of pathogenesis of polycystic ovary syndrome? Clin Exp Obstet Gynecol 2003, 30(4):187-189.

581. Kyriazis M: Practical applications of chaos theory to the modulation of human ageing: nature prefers chaos to regularity. Biogerontology 2003, 4(2):75-90.

582. Dokoumetzidis A, Iliadis A, Macheras P: Nonlinear dynamics and chaos theory: concepts and applications relevant to pharmacodynamics. Pharm Res 2001, 18(4):415-426.

583. http://www.ynharari.com/book/sapiens/. December 2018

584. https://danielmiessler.com/blog/first-second-order-chaos/. December 2018

585. http://granddaddyssecrets.com/chaos-creates-a-dancing-star/. December 2018

586. Strogatz S: Nonlinear dynamics and Chaos. Westview Press 1994.

587. http://www.zo.utexas.edu/courses/THOC/Adaptation.html. December 2018

588. Kauffman SA: The Origins of Order Self-Organization and Selection in Evolution. New York: Oxford University Press 1993.

589. Pierre De, al.: A theory for adaptation and competition applied to logistic map dynamics. Physica A 1994, D. 75: 343-360.

590. Langton CA: Computation at the edge of chaos. Physica A 1990, D. 42.

591. https://www.americangeosciences.org/education/k5geosource/content/fossils/how-are-living-things-adapted-to-their-environments. December 2018

592. http://www.zo.utexas.edu/courses/THOC/Model.html. December 2018

593. Takayoshi Ubuka GEB, and Kazuyoshi Tsutsui: Neuroendocrine regulation of gonadotropin secretion in seasonally breeding birds. Front Neurosci 2013, 7: 38.

594. Mitchell MH, P.; Crutchfield: Revisiting the edge of chaos: Evolving cellular automata to perform computations. Complex Systems 1993, 7 (2): 89-130.

595. Melby Pe, al. (2000). "Adaptation to the edge of chaos in the self-adjusting logistic map". Phys.Rev.Let. doi:10.1103/PhysRevLett.84.5991.

596. Bayam Me, al. (2006). "Conserved quantities and adaptation to the edge of chaos". Physical Review E. 73.

597. Wotherspoon Te, al.: Adaptation to the edge of chaos with random-wavelet feedback. J Phys Chem 2009.

598. Deragon J: Managing On The Edge Of Chaos. Relationship Economy. http://www.relationship-economy.com/2012/08/managing-on-the-edge-of-chaos/ Ret: December 2018

599. Goldberger AL RD, Mietus J, Antman EM, Greenwald S. Nonlinear dynamics in sudden cardiac death syndrome: heartrate oscillations and bifurcations. Experientia 1988; 44: 983-87. .

600. Peng CK, Havlin S, Stanley HE, Goldberger AL: Quantification of scaling exponents and crossover phenomena in nonstationary heartbeat time series. Chaos 1995, 5(1):82-87.

601. Szeto H CP, Decena JA, ChengY,Wu D L, Dwyer G.: Fractal properties of fetal breathing dynamics. Am J Physiol 1992, 263: R141-47.

602. Marsh DJ OJ, Cowley AW.: 1/f fluctuations in arterial pressure and regulation of renal blood flow in dogs.. Am J Physiol ; 1990, 258: F1394-400.

603. Hausdorff JM PC-K, Ladin Z, Wei JY, Goldberger AL. Is walking a random walk? Evidence for long-range correlations in the stride interval of human gait. J Appl Physiol 1995; 78: 349-58. .

604. Reimann HA. Periodic diseases. Philadelphia: FA Davis SJ, Carpeggiani C, Landesman CE, Fulton KW. The correlation-dimension of the heartbeat is reduced by myocardial ischemia in conscious pigs. Circ Res 1991; 68: 966-76. .

605. Skinner JE CC, Landesman CE, Fulton KW. The correlation-dimension of the heartbeat is reduced by myocardial ischemia in conscious pigs. Circ Res 1991; 68: 966-76. .

606. http://www.visitcyprus.com/index.php/en/news/195-kyriazis-the-museum-the-man-and-the-medicine. December 2018

607. Turcotte DL, Rundle JB: Self-organized complexity in the physical, biological, and social sciences. Proc Natl Acad Sci U S A 2002, 99 Suppl 1:2463-2465.

608. Carlson JM, Doyle J: Complexity and robustness. Proc Natl Acad Sci U S A 2002, 99 Suppl 1:2538-2545.

609. Mackey JK, Alexieva-Jackson B, Fetters DV, Edwards SM, McBride JP, Cole RL, Trapp WG: Bone and gallium scan findings in malignant fibrous histiocytoma. Case report with radiographic and pathologic correlation. Clin Nucl Med 1987, 12(1):17-21.

610. Belair J, Glass L, An Der Heiden U, Milton J: Dynamical disease: Identification, temporal aspects and treatment strategies of human illness. Chaos 1995, 5(1):1-7.

611. Frauenfelder H: Proteins: paradigms of complexity. Proc Natl Acad Sci U S A 2002, 99 Suppl 1:2479-2480.

612. Hopfield JJ, Brody CD: What is a moment? Transient synchrony as a collective mechanism for spatiotemporal integration. Proc Natl Acad Sci U S A 2001, 98(3):1282-1287.

613. Lewis M, Rees DC: Fractal surfaces of proteins. Science 1985, 230(4730):1163-1165.

614. Freeman KA, Tallarida RJ: A quantitative study of dopamine control in the rat striatum. J Pharmacol Exp Ther 1994, 268(2):629-638.

615. Wagner CD, Stauss HM, Persson PB, Kregel KC: Correlation integral of blood pressure as a marker for exercise intensities. Am J Physiol 1998, 275(5 Pt 2):R1661-1666.

616. Wise PM, Krajnak KM, Kashon ML: Menopause: the aging of multiple pacemakers. Science 1996, 273(5271):67-70.

617. Elger CE, Widman G, Andrzejak R, Arnold J, David P, Lehnertz K: Nonlinear EEG analysis and its potential role in epileptology. Epilepsia 2000, 41 Suppl 3:S34-38.

618. Sarbadhikari SN, Chakrabarty K: Chaos in the brain: a short review alluding to epilepsy, depression, exercise and lateralization. Med Eng Phys 2001, 23(7):445-455.

619. Fitch RB, Montgomery RD, Milton JL, Garrett PD, Kincaid SA, Wright JC, Terry GC: The intercondylar fossa of the normal canine stifle an anatomic and radiographic study. Vet Surg 1995, 24(2):148-155.

620. Edelstein-Keshet L, Israel A, Lansdorp P: Modelling perspectives on aging: can mathematics help us stay young? J Theor Biol 2001, 213(4):509-525.

621. Warhaft Z: Turbulence in nature and in the laboratory. Proc Natl Acad Sci U S A 2002, 99 Suppl 1:2481-2486.

622. Ghil M, Robertson AW: "Waves" vs. "particles" in the atmosphere's phase space: a

pathway to long-range forecasting? Proc Natl Acad Sci U S A 2002, 99 Suppl 1:2493-2500.

623. Smith LA: What might we learn from climate forecasts? Proc Natl Acad Sci U S A 2002, 99 Suppl 1:2487-2492.

624. Sornette D: Predictability of catastrophic events: material rupture, earthquakes, turbulence, financial crashes, and human birth. Proc Natl Acad Sci U S A 2002, 99 Suppl 1:2522-2529.

625. Sammis CG, Sornette D: Positive feedback, memory, and the predictability of earthquakes. Proc Natl Acad Sci U S A 2002, 99 Suppl 1:2501-2508.

626. Rundle JB, Tiampo KF, Klein W, Sa Martins JS: Self-organization in leaky threshold systems: the influence of near-mean field dynamics and its implications for earthquakes, neurobiology, and forecasting. Proc Natl Acad Sci U S A 2002, 99 Suppl 1:2514-2521.

627. Stanley HE, Amaral LA, Buldyrev SV, Gopikrishnan P, Plerou V, Salinger MA: Self-organized complexity in economics and finance. Proc Natl Acad Sci U S A 2002, 99 Suppl 1:2561-2565.

628. Newman ME, Watts DJ, Strogatz SH: Random graph models of social networks. Proc Natl Acad Sci U S A 2002, 99 Suppl 1:2566-2572.

629. Willinger W, Govindan R, Jamin S, Paxson V, Shenker S: Scaling phenomena in the Internet: critically examining criticality. Proc Natl Acad Sci U S A 2002, 99 Suppl 1:2573-2580.

630. Ramakrishnan A, Sadana A: A mathematical analysis using fractals for binding interactions of nuclear estrogen receptors occurring on biosensor surfaces. Anal Biochem 2002, 303(1):78-92.

631. Kyriazis M: Applications of chaos theory to the molecular biology of aging. Exp Gerontol 1991, 26(6):569-572.

632. Soloviev MV. On possible role of chaotic behavior of the gene regulation system in aging. Advances in gerontology. Uspekhi gerontologii 2001, 8:27-33.

633. Lipsitz LA, Goldberger AL: Loss of 'complexity' and aging. Potential applications of fractals and chaos theory to senescence. JAMA 1992, 267(13):1806-1809.

634. Guarini G: [New horizons in medicine. The application of "fuzzy logic" in clinical and experimental medicine]. Recenti Prog Med 1994, 85(6):335-339.

635. Guarini G: [New horizons in medicine. Aging and the laws of modern physics]. Recenti Prog Med 1994, 85(1):32-36.

636. Toussaint O, Schneider ED: The thermodynamics and evolution of complexity in biological systems. Comp Biochem Physiol A Mol Integr Physiol 1998, 120(1):3-9.

637. Busciglio J, Andersen JK, Schipper HM, Gilad GM, McCarty R, Marzatico F, Toussaint O: Stress, aging, and neurodegenerative disorders. Molecular mechanisms. Ann N Y Acad Sci 1998, 851:429-443.

638. Lipsitz LA: Dynamics of stability: the physiologic basis of functional health and frailty. J Gerontol A Biol Sci Med Sci 2002, 57(3):B115-125.

639. Lipsitz LA: Age-related changes in the "complexity" of cardiovascular dynamics: A potential marker of vulnerability to disease. Chaos 1995, 5(1):102-109.

640. Collins JJ, De Luca CJ, Burrows A, Lipsitz LA: Age-related changes in open-loop and closed-loop postural control mechanisms. Exp Brain Res 1995, 104(3):480-492.

641. Huikuri HV, Makikallio TH, Airaksinen KE, Seppanen T, Puukka P, Raiha IJ, Sou-

rander LB: Power-law relationship of heart rate variability as a predictor of mortality in the elderly. Circulation 1998, 97(20):2031-2036.

642.  Schierwagen AK: Growth, structure and dynamics of real neurons: model studies and experimental results. Biomed Biochim Acta 1990, 49(8-9):709-722.

643.  Skinner JE, Molnar M, Vybiral T, Mitra M: Application of chaos theory to biology and medicine. Integr Physiol Behav Sci 1992, 27(1):39-53.

644.  Molnar M, Skinner JE: Low-dimensional chaos in event-related brain potentials. Int J Neurosci 1992, 66(3-4):263-276.

645.  Kaplan DT, Furman MI, Pincus SM, Ryan SM, Lipsitz LA, Goldberger AL: Aging and the complexity of cardiovascular dynamics. Biophys J 1991, 59(4):945-949.

646.  Edwards R, Beuter A, Glass L: Parkinsonian tremor and simplification in network dynamics. Bull Math Biol 1999, 61(1):157-177.

647.  Peng CK, Mietus JE, Liu Y, Lee C, Hausdorff JM, Stanley HE, Goldberger AL, Lipsitz LA: Quantifying fractal dynamics of human respiration: age and gender effects. Ann Biomed Eng 2002, 30(5):683-692.

648.  Hausdorff JM, Purdon PL, Peng CK, Ladin Z, Wei JY, Goldberger AL: Fractal dynamics of human gait: stability of long-range correlations in stride interval fluctuations. J Appl Physiol (1985) 1996, 80(5):1448-1457.

649.  https://www.khanacademy.org/science/biology/dna-as-the-genetic-material/dna-replication/a/telomeres-telomerase . Ret: December 2018

650.  Goyns MH: Genes, telomeres and mammalian ageing. Mech Ageing Dev 2002, 123(7):791-799.

651.  Vaillancourt DE, Newell KM: Changing complexity in human behavior and physiology through aging and disease. Neurobiol Aging 2002, 23(1):1-11.

652.  Kirkwood TB: Changing complexity in aging: a metric not an hypothesis. Neurobiol Aging 2002, 23(1):21-22.

653.  Thaler DS: Design for an aging brain. Neurobiol Aging 2002, 23(1):13-15.

654.  de Grey AD, Baynes JW, Berd D, Heward CB, Pawelec G, Stock G: Is human aging still mysterious enough to be left only to scientists? Bioessays 2002, 24(7):667-676.

655.  de Grey AD, Gavrilov L, Olshansky SJ, Coles LS, Cutler RG, Fossel M, Harman SM: Antiaging technology and pseudoscience. Science 2002, 296(5568):656.

656.  Yarosh DB: Why is DNA damage signaling so complicated? Chaos and molecular signaling. Environ Mol Mutagen 2001, 38(2-3):132-134.

657.  Rubelj I, Vondracek Z: Stochastic mechanism of cellular aging--abrupt telomere shortening as a model for stochastic nature of cellular aging. J Theor Biol 1999, 197(4):425-438.

658.  Bessell EM, Punt J, Firth J, Hope T, Holland I, Lowe J: Primary non-Hodgkin's lymphoma of the central nervous system: phase II study of chemotherapy (BVAM) prior to radiotherapy. Clin Oncol (R Coll Radiol) 1991, 3(4):193-198.

659.  Faure P, Korn H: Is there chaos in the brain? I. Concepts of nonlinear dynamics and methods of investigation. C R Acad Sci III 2001, 324(9):773-793.

660.  Sayad Kocahan and Zumrut Doğan. Mechanisms of Alzheimer's Disease Pathogenesis and Prevention: The Brain, Neural Pathology, N-methyl-D-aspartate Receptors, Tau Protein and Other Risk Factors. Clin Psychopharmacol Neurosci. 2017 Feb; 15(1): 1-8.

661.  Topp B, Promislow K, deVries G, Miura RM, Finegood DT: A model of beta-cell mass,

insulin, and glucose kinetics: pathways to diabetes. J Theor Biol 2000, 206(4):605-619.

662.  Goldberger AL: Heartbeats, hormones, and health: is variability the spice of life? Am J Respir Crit Care Med 2001, 163(6):1289-1290.

663.  Weng G, Bhalla US, Iyengar R: Complexity in biological signaling systems. Science 1999, 284(5411):92-96.

664.  Ruedi Stoop,Norbert Stoop,and Leonid Bunimovich. Complexity of Dynamics as Variability of Predictability. Journal of Statistical Physics, Vol. 114, Nos. 3/4, February 2004. https://pdfs.semanticscholar.org/df1c/8b308356865a9f08c14afa095864f38fb3ec. pdf Ret: December 2018

665.  Levy G: Predicting effective drug concentrations for individual patients. Determinants of pharmacodynamic variability. Clin Pharmacokinet 1998, 34(4):323-333.

666.  Macheras P, Argyrakis P: Gastrointestinal drug absorption: is it time to consider heterogeneity as well as homogeneity? Pharm Res 1997, 14(7):842-847.

667.  Valsami G, Dokoumetzidis A, Macheras P: Modeling of supersaturated dissolution data. Int J Pharm 1999, 181(2):153-157.

668.  Chakraborty A, Blum RA, Cutler DL, Jusko WJ: Pharmacoimmunodynamic interactions of interleukin-10 and prednisone in healthy volunteers. Clin Pharmacol Ther 1999, 65(3):304-318.

669.  Midha KK, Rawson MJ, Hubbard JW: Prescribability and switchability of highly variable drugs and drug products. J Control Release 1999, 62(1-2):33-40.

670.  Tallarida RJ: Further characterization of a control model for ligand-receptor interaction: phase plane geometry, stability, and oscillation. Ann Biomed Eng 1990, 18(6):671-684.

671.  Karagueuzian HS, Kogan BY, Khan SS, Denton TA, Karplus WJ, Mandel WJ, Diamond GA: Induction of cellular chaos during quinidine toxicity. Predictive power of nonlinear dynamic analysis for drug-induced proarrhythmia--a hypothesis. J Electrocardiol 1992, 24 Suppl:91-96.

672.  Lifshitz M, Gavrilov V, Gorodischer R: Off-label and unlicensed use of antidotes in paediatric patients. Eur J Clin Pharmacol 2001, 56(11):839-841.

673.  Tsonis bAA, https://www.amazon.com/Chaos-Theory-Applications-Tsonis/dp/0306441713. December 2018

674.  Zamuner S, Gomeni R, Bye A: Estimate the time varying brain receptor occupancy in PET imaging experiments using non-linear fixed and mixed effect modeling approach. Nucl Med Biol 2002, 29(1):115-123.

675.  Hipkiss AR: On the "struggle between chemistry and biology during aging"--implications for DNA repair, apoptosis and proteolysis, and a novel route of intervention. Biogerontology 2001, 2(3):173-178.

676.  Hipkiss AR: On the anti-aging activities of aminoguanidine and N-t-butylhydroxylamine. Mech Ageing Dev 2001, 122(2):169-171.

677.  Zhang Y, Herman B: Apoptosis and successful aging. Mech Ageing Dev 2002, 123(6):563-565.

678.  Zhang Y, Herman B: Ageing and apoptosis. Mech Ageing Dev 2002, 123(4):245-260.

679.  https://en.wikipedia.org/wiki/History_of_the_hippie_movement. December 2018

680.  https://www.mucusfreelife.com/ehret-library/overview/gordon-kennedy/hippie-roots-the-perennial-subculture/ December 2018

681.  Semsei I: On the nature of aging. Mech Ageing Dev 2000, 117(1-3):93-108.

682. Alves da Costa C, Paitel E, Mattson MP, Amson R, Telerman A, Ancolio K, Checler F: Wild-type and mutated presenilins 2 trigger p53-dependent apoptosis and down-regulate presenilin 1 expression in HEK293 human cells and in murine neurons. Proc Natl Acad Sci U S A 2002, 99(6):4043-4048.

683. Day L, Fildes B, Gordon I, Fitzharris M, Flamer H, Lord S: Randomised factorial trial of falls prevention among older people living in their own homes. BMJ 2002, 325(7356):128.

684. Inouye SK, Bogardus ST, Jr., Charpentier PA, Leo-Summers L, Acampora D, Holford TR, Cooney LM, Jr.: A multicomponent intervention to prevent delirium in hospitalized older patients. N Engl J Med 1999, 340(9):669-676.

685. Ninan PT, Rush AJ, Crits-Christoph P, Kornstein SG, Manber R, Thase ME, Trivedi MH, Rothbaum BO, Zajecka J, Borian FE et al: Symptomatic and syndromal anxiety in chronic forms of major depression: effect of nefazodone, cognitive behavioral analysis system of psychotherapy, and their combination. J Clin Psychiatry 2002, 63(5):434-441.

686. Kveiborg M, Rattan SI, Clark BF, Eriksen EF, Kassem M: Treatment with 1,25-dihydroxyvitamin D3 reduces impairment of human osteoblast functions during cellular aging in culture. Journal of cellular physiology 2001, 186(2):298-306.

687. Ji LL, Leeuwenburgh C, Leichtweis S, Gore M, Fiebig R, Hollander J, Bejma J: Oxidative stress and aging. Role of exercise and its influences on antioxidant systems. Ann N Y Acad Sci 1998, 854:102-117.

688. Tulppo MP, Hughson RL, Makikallio TH, Airaksinen KE, Seppanen T, Huikuri HV: Effects of exercise and passive head-up tilt on fractal and complexity properties of heart rate dynamics. Am J Physiol Heart Circ Physiol 2001, 280(3):H1081-1087.

689. Iversen PO, Nicolaysen G: High correlation of fractals for regional blood flows among resting and exercising skeletal muscles. Am J Physiol 1995, 269(1 Pt 2):H7-13.

690. Heath M, Roy EA: The expression of manual asymmetries following extensive training of the nondominant hand: a kinematic perspective. Brain Cogn 2000, 43(1-3):252-257.

691. Lewen GD, Bialek W, de Ruyter van Steveninck RR: Neural coding of naturalistic motion stimuli. Network 2001, 12(3):317-329.

692. Gonzalez-Lima F, Ferchmin PA, Eterovic VA, Gonzalez-Lima EM: Metabolic activation of the brain of young rats after exposure to environmental complexity. Developmental psychobiology 1994, 27(6):343-351.

693. The Effect of Music on Cognitive Performance: Insight From Neurobiological and Animal Studies January 2006. Behavioral and Cognitive Neuroscience Reviews 4(4):235-61

694. Watt WC, Sakano H, Lee ZY, Reusch JE, Trinh K, Storm DR: Odorant stimulation enhances survival of olfactory sensory neurons via MAPK and CREB. Neuron 2004, 41(6):955-967.

695. Valero J, Espana J, Parra-Damas A, Martin E, Rodriguez-Alvarez J, Saura CA: Short-term environmental enrichment rescues adult neurogenesis and memory deficits in APP(Sw,Ind) transgenic mice. PLoS One 2011, 6(2):e16832.

696. Rizzi S, Bianchi P, Guidi S, Ciani E, Bartesaghi R: Impact of environmental enrichment on neurogenesis in the dentate gyrus during the early postnatal period. Brain Res 2011, 1415:23-33.

697. Paperin GG, D.; Sadedin, S. : Dual-phase evolution in complex adaptive systems. J R

Soc Interface 2011, 8, 609-629.

698.    Gershenson C, Prokopenko M: Complex networks. Artificial life 2011, 17(4):259-261.

699.    Gershenson C: The sigma profile: A formal tool to study organization and its evolution at multiple scales. Complexity 2011, 16, 37-44.

700.    Dhamala M, Pagnoni G, Wiesenfeld K, Berns GS: Measurements of brain activity complexity for varying mental loads. Phys Rev E Stat Nonlin Soft Matter Phys 2002, 65(4 Pt 1):041917.

701.    Fratiglioni L, Launer LJ, Andersen K, Breteler MM, Copeland JR, Dartigues JF, Lobo A, Martinez-Lage J, Soininen H, Hofman A: Incidence of dementia and major subtypes in Europe: A collaborative study of population-based cohorts. Neurologic Diseases in the Elderly Research Group. Neurology 2000, 54(11 Suppl 5):S10-15.

702.    Mueller PS, Plevak DJ, Rummans TA: Religious involvement, spirituality, and medicine: implications for clinical practice. Mayo Clinic proceedings 2001, 76(12):1225-1235.

703.    http://www.squarewheels.com/jokes/computerjokes.html.

704.    Kyriazis M: Technological integration and hyperconnectiv December 2018ity: Tools for promoting extreme human lifespans. Complexity 2015, Volume20, Issue6(http://onlinelibrary.wiley.com/doi/10.1002/cplx.21626/abstract.):Pages 15-24.

705.    Collier J: Entropy in evolution. Biol Philos 1986, 1, 5-24.

706.    Dix A: The brain and the web-Intelligent interactions from the desktop to the world. Keynote at IHC 2006; Natal, Brazil, 2006 2006

707.    Adami C, Ofria C, Collier TC: Evolution of biological complexity. Proc Natl Acad Sci U S A 2000, 97(9):4463-4468.

708.    Frieden BR, Gatenby RA: Information dynamics in living systems: prokaryotes, eukaryotes, and cancer. PLoS One 2011, 6(7):e22085.

709.    Kyriazis M: Reversal of informational entropy and the acquisition of germ-like immortality by somatic cells. Curr Aging Sci 2014, 7(1):9-16.

710.    Kyriazis M: Biological ageing and clinical consequences of modern technology. Biogerontology 2017, 18(4):711-715.

711.    http://www.elon.edu/e-web/imagining/surveys/2018_survey/Digital_Life_and_Well-Being_Anecdotes.xhtml . December 2018

712.    http://www.everydayhealth.com/heart-health/havinga- DEHahaosYik, heart-attack-or-stroke-your-iphone-knows-6152.aspx.

713.    Rowland NC BJ, Chang E December 2018F (2013) Neurosurgery and the dawning age of brain–machine interfaces. Surg Neurol Int 4(Suppl 1):S11–S14. .

714.    O'Doherty JE, Lebedev MA, Ifft PJ, Zhuang KZ, Shokur S, Bleuler H, Nicolelis MA: Active tactile exploration using a brain-machine-brain interface. Nature 2011, 479(7372):228-231.

715.    Li G, Zhang D: Brain-Computer Interface Controlled Cyborg: Establishing a Functional Information Transfer Pathway from Human Brain to Cockroach Brain. PLoS One 2016, 11(3):e0150667.

716.    Kyriazis. M: Reversal of informational entropy and the acquisition of germ-like immortality by somatic cells. Curr Aging Sci 2014, 7(1), 9-16.

717.    Rattan SI: Aging is not a disease: implications for intervention. Aging Dis 2014, 5(3):196-202.

718.    Kyriazis M. A 'war of trade-offs' between the soma and the germ line. In challenging

ageing: the anti-senescence effects of hormesis ee, and information exposure 2016. Bentham Science Publishers.

719. Raefsky SM, Mattson MP: Adaptive responses of neuronal mitochondria to bioenergetic challenges: Roles in neuroplasticity and disease resistance. Free Radic Biol Med 2017, 102:203-216.

720. Xu L, Scheenen WJ, Roubos EW, Kozicz T: Peptidergic Edinger-Westphal neurons and the energy-dependent stress response. Gen Comp Endocrinol 2012, 177(3):296-304.

721. Levi-Ferber M, Salzberg Y, Safra M, Haviv-Chesner A, Bulow HE, Henis-Korenblit S: It's all in your mind: determining germ cell fate by neuronal IRE-1 in C. elegans. PLoS Genet 2014, 10(10):e1004747.

722. Mason PH, Maleszka R, Dominguez DJ: Another stage of development: Biological degeneracy and the study of bodily ageing. Mech Ageing Dev 2017, 163:46-51.

723. https://www.brainhq.com/brain-resources/brain-plasticity/what-is-brain-plasticity. December 2018

724. https://en.wikipedia.org/wiki/Neuroplasticity. December 2018

725. Characterizing brain cortical plasticity and network dynamics across the age-span in health and disease with TMS-EEG and TMS-fMRI. Brain Topography 2011, 24: 302-315.

726. Ganguly K PM: Activity-dependent neural plasticity from bench to bedside. Neuron 2013, 80 (3): 729-741.

727. Kolb B, Harker A, Gibb R: Principles of plasticity in the developing brain. Dev Med Child Neurol 2017, 59(12):1218-1223.

728. Fernandes J, Arida RM, Gomez-Pinilla F: Physical exercise as an epigenetic modulator of brain plasticity and cognition. Neurosci Biobehav Rev 2017, 80:443-456.

729. Kowianski P, Lietzau G, Czuba E, Waskow M, Steliga A, Morys J: BDNF: A Key Factor with Multipotent Impact on Brain Signaling and Synaptic Plasticity. Cell Mol Neurobiol 2017.

730. Tay TL, Savage JC, Hui CW, Bisht K, Tremblay ME: Microglia across the lifespan: from origin to function in brain development, plasticity and cognition. J Physiol 2017, 595(6):1929-1945.

731. Ho NTT, Kutzner A, Heese K: Brain plasticity, cognitive functions and neural stem cells: a pivotal role for the brain-specific neural master gene. Biol Chem 2017, 399(1):55-61.

732. Horton JC, Fahle M, Mulder T, Trauzettel-Klosinski S: Adaptation, perceptual learning, and plasticity of brain functions. Graefes Arch Clin Exp Ophthalmol 2017, 255(3):435-447.

733. Ismail FY, Fatemi A, Johnston MV: Cerebral plasticity: Windows of opportunity in the developing brain. Eur J Paediatr Neurol 2017, 21(1):23-48.

734. Merzenich MMN, R.J.; Stryker, M.P.; Cynader, M.S.; Schoppmann, A.; Zook, J.M. (1984). "Somatosensory Cortical Map Changes Following Digit Amputation in Adult Monkeys". Journal of Comparative Neurology. 224 (4): 591–605.

735. Luo Y, Anderson TA: Phantom Limb Pain: A Review. Int Anesthesiol Clin 2016, 54(2):121-139.

736. Phillips C: Lifestyle Modulators of Neuroplasticity: How Physical Activity, Mental Engagement, and Diet Promote Cognitive Health during Aging. Neural Plast 2017, 2017:3589271.

737. Pin-Barre C, Constans A, Brisswalter J, Pellegrino C, Laurin J: Effects of High- Versus Moderate-Intensity Training on Neuroplasticity and Functional Recovery After Focal Ischemia. Stroke 2017, 48(10):2855-2864.

738. Eckberg DL, Diedrich A, Cooke WH, Biaggioni I, Buckey JC, Jr., Pawelczyk JA, Ertl AC, Cox JF, Kuusela TA, Tahvanainen KU et al: Respiratory modulation of human autonomic function: long-term neuroplasticity in space. J Physiol 2016, 594(19):5629-5646.

739. Massie CL, Kantak SS, Narayanan P, Wittenberg GF: Timing of motor cortical stimulation during planar robotic training differentially impacts neuroplasticity in older adults. Clin Neurophysiol 2015, 126(5):1024-1032.

740. Fertonani A, Pirulli C, Miniussi C: Random noise stimulation improves neuroplasticity in perceptual learning. J Neurosci 2011, 31(43):15416-15423.

741. Young J. A. TMT: Neuroplasticity and its Applications for Rehabilitation. American Journal of Therapeutics 2011, 18 (1): 70-80.

742. Simons DJ BW, Charness N, Gathercole SE, Chabris CF, Hambrick DZ, Stine-Morrow EA (2016). "Do "Brain-Training" Programs Work?" (PDF). Psychological Science in the Public Interest. 17 (3): 103–186. .

743. Davidson RJ, Lutz A: Buddha's Brain: Neuroplasticity and Meditation. IEEE Signal Process Mag 2008, 25(1):176-174.

744. Davidson R: Meditation and neuroplasticity: training your brain. Interview by Bonnie J. Horrigan. Explore (NY) 2005, 1(5):380-388.

745. Vestergaard-Poulsen PvB, Martijn; Skewes, Joshua; Bjarkam, Carsten R; Stubberup, Michael; Bertelsen, Jes; Roepstorff, Andreas (28 January 2009). Long-term meditation is associated with increased gray matter density in the brain stem. NeuroReport. 20 (2): 170–174. .

746. Szuhany KL BM, Otto MW (October 2014). A meta-analytic review of the effects of exercise on brain-derived neurotrophic factor. J Psychiatr Res. 60C: 56–64.

747. Carvalho A RI, Parimon T, Cusack BJ (2014). Physical activity and cognitive function in individuals over 60 years of age: a systematic review. Clin Interv Aging. 9: 661–682. .

748. Buckley J CJ, Kramer AF, McAuley E, Mullen SP (2014). Cognitive control in the self-regulation of physical activity and sedentary behavior. Front Hum Neurosci. 8: 747.

749. Carnes BA, Olshansky SJ, Hayflick L: Can human biology allow most of us to become centenarians? J Gerontol A Biol Sci Med Sci 2013, 68(2):136-142.

750. Kyriazis M: Third phase science: defining a novel model of research into human ageing. Front Biosci (Landmark Ed) 2017, 22:982-990.

751. Kyriazis M: Apostolides: The Fallacy of the Longevity Elixir: Negligible Senescence May be Achieved, but Not by Using Something Physical. Curr Aging Sci 2015, 8(3), 227-34.

752. KC Bausch: The Theory and Practice of Third Phase Science SSaDTSS, 129-145 (2014)

753. Hall, Maher, Latimer, Ferreira: The Influence of the Therapist Patient Relationship on Treatment Outcome in Physical Rehabilitation. Phys Ther, 90, 1099-1110 (2010).

754. C Gershenson NF: Complexity and information: Measuring emergence, selforganization, and homeostasis at multiple scales. . Complexity 2012, 18(2), 29-44.

755. G de Zeeuw: Three phases of science: A methodological exploration. Working paper nr. 7 of the Centre for Systems and Information Sciences UoH, ISBN 1 86050 025. (1996)

756. EA Necka SC, JT   Cacioppo: Social   Neuroscience of the Twenty-First Century. The University of Chicago, Chicago, IL, USA (2015)

757. Cacioppo JT, Berntson GG: Social psychological contributions to the decade of the brain. Doctrine of multilevel analysis. Am Psychol 1992, 47(8):1019-1028.

758. Vezina P, Pierre PJ, Lorrain DS. The effect of previous exposure to amphetamine on drug-induced locomotion and self-administration of a low dose of the drug. Psychopharmacology (Berl). 1999 Nov;147(2):125-34.

759. Cole SW: Social regulation of human gene expression: mechanisms and implications for public health. Am J Public Health 2013, 103 Suppl 1:S84-92.

760. Kyriazis M: The impracticality of biomedical rejuvenation therapies: translational and pharmacological barriers. Rejuvenation Res 2014, 17(4):390-396.

761. Ogino S, Nishihara R, VanderWeele TJ, Wang M, Nishi A, Lochhead P, Qian ZR, Zhang X, Wu K, Nan H et al. The Role of Molecular Pathological Epidemiology in the Study of Neoplastic and Non-neoplastic Diseases in the Era of Precision Medicine. Epidemiology 2016, 27(4):602-611.

762. Nishi A, Milner DA, Jr., Giovannucci EL, Nishihara R, Tan AS, Kawachi I, Ogino S: Integration of molecular pathology, epidemiology and social science for global precision medicine. Expert Rev Mol Diagn 2016, 16(1):11-23.

763. Chudek M, Henrich J: Culture-gene coevolution, norm-psychology and the emergence of human prosociality. Trends in cognitive sciences 2011, 15(5):218-226.

764. M Kyriazis: Technological integration and hyper-connectivity: Tools for promoting extreme human lifespans. Complexity 20 -.

765. Kyriazis M: Clinical Effects of a 'Human-Computer' Interaction. SSRN 2016, https://papers.ssrn.com/sol3/papers.cfm?abstract_id=2798529. December 2018

766. Limerick H, Coyle D, Moore JW: The experience of agency in human-computer interactions: a review. Front Hum Neurosci 2014, 8:643.

767. Seifert L, Komar J, Araujo D, Davids K: Neurobiological degeneracy: A key property for functional adaptations of perception and action to constraints. Neurosci Biobehav Rev 2016, 69:159-165.

768. Estepp JR, Christensen JC: Electrode replacement does not affect classification accuracy in dual-session use of a passive brain-computer interface for assessing cognitive workload. Front Neurosci 2015, 9:54.

769. The Innovators: How a Group of Hackers GaGCtDR, Isaacson bW, https://www.amazon.com/Innovators-Hackers-Geniuses-Created-Revolution/dp/1476708703. December 2018

770. https://en.wikipedia.org/wiki/Quantum_indeterminacy. December 2018

771. A. Einstein BP, and N. Rosen, Can quantum-mechanical description of physical reality be considered complete? Phys. Rev. 47 777 (1935). .

772. Jaeger G: Quantum randomness and unpredictability. Philosophical Transactions of the Royal Society of London 2016, A doi/10.1002/prop.201600053; Online=http://onlinelibrary.wiley.com/doi/10.1002/prop.201600053/epdf. December 2018

773. S Kochen and E P Specker Tpohviqm, Journal of Mathematics and Mechanics 17 (1967), 59–87.

774. Cole SW: Social regulation of human gene expression: mechanisms and implications for public health. Am J Public Health 2013, 103 Suppl 1:S84-92.

775. Alain Aspect PG, and Gérard Roger, Experimental realization of Einstein-Podolsky-Rosen-Bohm gedankenexperiment: A new violation of Bell's inequalities, Physical Review Letters 49 (1982), no. 2, 91–94.

776. Tomasz Paterek JK, Robert Prevedel, Peter Klimek, Markus Aspelmeyer, Anton Zeilinger, and Caslav Brukner, "Logical independence and quantum randomness", New Journal of Physics 12 (2010), no. 013019, 1367–2630.

777. Process Q: Technology review: First Evidence That Quantum Processes Generate Truly Random Numbers. MIT Technological Review 2010, https://www.technologyreview.com/s/418445/first-evidence-that-quantum-processes-generate-truly-random-numbers/MIT . December 2018

778. Calude CS, Calude E, Svozil K: The complexity of proving chaoticity and the Church-Turing thesis. Chaos 2010, 20(3):037103.

779. C. S. Calude MJD, Monica Dumitrescu, K. Svozil. Experimental evidence of quantum randomness incomputability, Physical Review A 82, 022102 (2010), 1—8.

780. How Random Is Quantum Randomness? An Experimental Approach; Cristian S. Calude MJD, Monica Dumitrescu, Karl Svozil; https://arxiv.org/pdf/0912.4379.pdf.

781. Rukhin Aea: A Statistical Test Suite for Random and Pseudorandom Number Generators for Cryptographic Applications. National Institute of Standards and Technology: NIST Special Publication 2010, http://csrc.nist.gov/groups/ST/toolkit/rng/index.html 800-822.

782. Markowsky G: The sad history of random bits. J Cyber Secur Mobil 2014, 3, 1-24.

783. Bell JS: On the Einstein Podolsky Rosen paradox. Physics 1964, 1, 195-200.

784. Barrett J, Hardy, L. & Kent, A. No signaling and quantum key distribution. Phys. Rev. Lett. 95, 010503 (2005). A quantum key distribution protocol is described that is secure against non-signalling eavesdroppers on the basis of Bell inequality violations. .

785. Masanes L, Acín, A. & Gisin, N. : General properties of nonsignaling theories. Phys Rev Lett 2006, A 73, 012112.

786. Pironio Sea: Random numbers certified by Bell's theorem. Nature 2010, 464, 1021-1024.

787. Hall MJW: Complementary contributions of indeterminism and signalling to quantum correlations. Phys Rev 2010, A 82, 062117.

788. Colbeck RK, A. Private randomness expansion with untrusted devices. J. Phys. A 44, 095305 (2011). .

789. Vazirani UVV, T. Certifiable quantum dice. Phil. Trans. R. Soc. Lond. A 370, 3432–3448 (2012). .

790. Chung KM, Shi, Y. & Wu, X. Physical randomness extractors: generating random numbers with minimal assumptions. Preprint at http://arxiv.org/ abs/1402.4797 (2015). .

791. Arnon-Friedman R, Renner, R. & Vidick, T. Simple and tight device independent security proofs. Preprint at http://arxiv.org/abs/1607.01797 (2016).

792. Colbeck RR, R. No extension of quantum theory can have improved predictive power. Nat. Commun. 2, 411 (2011). .

793. Gallego Rea: Full randomness from arbitrarily deterministic events. Nat Commun 2013, 4, 2654.

794. Brandão FGSL: Robust device-independent randomness amplification with few devices. Nat Commun 2016, 7, 11345.

795. Hofmann J: Heralded entanglement between widely separated atoms. . Science 2012, 337, 72-75.

796. Acín A, Gisin, N. & Masanes, L.: From Bell's theorem to secure quantum key distribution. Phys Rev Lett 2006, 97, 120405.

797. Masanes L: Universally-composable privacy amplification from causality constraints. Phys Rev Lett 2009, 102, 140501.

798. Masanes L, Renner, R., Christandl, M., Winter, A. & Barrett, J. Full security of key distribution from no-signaling constraints. IEEE Trans. Inf. Theory 60, 4973–4986 (2014). .

799. Reichardt B, Unger, F. & Vazirani, U.: Classical command of quantum systems. Nature 2013, 496, 456-460.

800. Pearle P: Hidden-variable example based upon data rejection. Phys Rev Lett 1970, D 2, 1418-1425.

801. Acín A, Cavalcanti, D., Passaro, E., Pironio, S. & Skrzypczyk, P. Necessary detection efficiencies for secure quantum key distribution and bound randomness. Phys. Rev. A 93, 012319 (2016). .

802. Giustina MeaBvwep, free of the fairsampling assumption. Nature 497, 227–230 (2013).
.

803. Hensen Bea: Loophole-free Bell inequality violation using electron spins separated by 1.3 kilometres. Nature 2015, 526, 682-686.

804. Kent A: Causal quantum theory and the collapse locality loophole. Phys Rev Lett 2005, A 72, 012107.

805. Scheidl Tea: Violation of local realism with freedom of choice. Proc Natl Acad Sci USA 2010, 107, 19708-19713.

806. Pironio S: Random 'choices' and the locality loophole. http://arxiv org/abs/151000248 2015.

807. Pawłowski MB, N. Semi-device-independent security of one-way quantum key distribution. Phys. Rev. A 84, 010302(R) (2011). .

808. Gallego R, Brunner, N., Hadley, C. & Acín: A. Device-independent tests of classical and quantum dimensions. Phys Rev Lett 2010, 105, 230501.

809. Tommaso Lunghi, Jonatan Bohr Brask, Charles Ci Wen Lim, Quentin Lavigne, Joseph Bowles, Anthony Martin, Hugo Zbinden, and Nicolas Brunner. Self-Testing Quantum Random Number Generator. Phys. Rev. Lett. 114, 150501, April 2015

810. Wiseman HM, Jones, S. J. & Doherty, A. C. Steering, entanglement, nonlocality, and the EPR paradox. Phys. Rev. Lett. 98, 140402 (2007). .

811. Branciard C, Cavalcanti, E. G., Walborn, S. P., Scarani, V. & Wiseman, H. M. One-sided device-independent quantum key distribution: security, feasibility, and the connection with steering. Phys. Rev. A 85, 010301(R) (2012).

812. Dhara C, de la Torre, G. & Acín, A. Can observed randomness be certified to be fully intrinsic? Phys. Rev. Lett. 112, 100402 (2014). .

813. de la Torre G, Hoban, M. J., Dhara, C., Prettico, G. & Acín, A. Maximally nonlocal theories cannot be maximally random. Phys. Rev. Lett. 114, 160502 (2015). .

814. https://www.random.org/randomness/. & Introduction to Randomness and Random Numbers Mads Haahr. https://cran.r-project.org/web/packages/random/vignettes/

random-essay.pdf. December 2018

815.  https://www.scientificamerican.com/article/quantum-random-numbers/. December 2018

816.  https://en.wikipedia.org/wiki/Dada. December 2018

817.  Paul N. Humble. "Anti-Art and the Concept of Art". In: "A companion to art theory". Editors: Paul Smith and Carolyn Wilde W-B, 2002, p. 250.

818.  Dawn Adès EHZ, 1914–18, MoMA, Grove Art Online, Oxford University Press, 2009.

819.  Schneede UM, George Grosz, His life and work, New York: Universe Books.

820.  Brenneman K: Chance in Art. https://wwwdartmouthedu/~chance/course/student_projects/Kristin/Kristinhtml. December 2018

821.  https://www.moma.org/interactives/exhibitions/1998/pollock/website100/txt_possibilities_drip.html. December 2018

822.  http://faculty.georgetown.edu/irvinem/visualarts/Pollock-ArtStatements-1943-1947.pdf. December 2018

823.  http://www.tate.org.uk/context-comment/articles/jackson-pollock-man-myth. December 2018

824.  Rohn ML: Visual Dynamics in Jackson Pollock's Abstractions  Studies in the Fine Arts : Art Theory, No 14: Publisher: Umi Research Pr ISBN-13: 978-0835717908; ISBN-10: 0835717909.

825.  https://www.goodreads.com/book/show/500612.Dada December 2018.

826.  https://en.wikipedia.org/wiki/Marcel_Duchamp. December 2018

827.  https://www.moma.org/collection/works/78990. December 2018

828.  https://en.wikipedia.org/wiki/Jean_Arp. December 2018

829.  http://www.theartstory.org/artist-arp-hans.htm. December 2018

830.  http://www.mdc.edu/wolfson/academic/artsletters/art_philosophy/humanities/dada2/Dada.htm. December 2018

831.  http://digicult.it/digimag/issue-015/c-stem-generative-art-forms/. December 2018

832.  https://en.wikipedia.org/wiki/Paul_Klee. December 2018

833.  http://ing.univaq.it/continenza/Corso%20di%20Disegno%20dell'Architettura%202/TESTI%20D'AUTORE/Paul-klee-Pedagogical-Sketchbook.pdf. December 2018

834.  Consciousness T, Literature and the Arts 2013 edited by Daniel Meyer-Dinkgräfe; http://www.cambridgescholars.com/consciousness-theatre-literature-and-the-arts-2013-10.

835.  Stochastic: https://en.oxforddictionaries.com/definition/Stochastic. Ret: May 2018.

836.  Michael Eckersley, Randomness, Rules and Compositional Structure in Design, Vol. 23, No. 1 (1990), pp. 75-80, https://www.jstor.org/stable/1578469?seq=1#page_scan_tab_contents, Ret: December 2018

837.  Design Methodology and Relationships with Science Editors: de Vries MJ, Cross, Nigel, Grant, D.P. ;http://www.springer.com/gp/book/9780792321910. Ret: May 2018.

838.  Brian G. Marsden Fred Lawrence Whipple (1906–2004) https://www.jstor.org/stable/10.1086/497156?seq=1#metadata_info_tab_contents; Ret: December 2018

839.  Fred L. Whipple; Stochastic Painting, Vol. 1, No. 1 Jan., 1968), pp. 81-83 https://www.jstor.org/stable/1571909?seq=1#page_scan_tab_contents . & https://muse.jhu.edu/article/596733 Ret: May 2018.

840.  https://en.wikipedia.org/wiki/Fred_Lawrence_Whipple Ret: December 2018

841. https://en.wikipedia.org/wiki/Stephen_Jay_Gould. Ret: May 2018.

842. https://www.amazon.com/Triumph-Tragedy-Mudville-Lifelong-Baseball/dp/0393325571. Ret: May 2018.

843. http://www.nybooks.com/articles/1988/08/18/the-streak-of-streaks/. Ret: May 2018.

844. M. Treisman and A. Faulkner. Generation of Random Sequences by Human Subjects: Cognitive Operations or Psychological Process? Journal of Experimental Psychology, 1987. .

845. W.A.Wagenaar: Generationof Random Sequences byHuman Subjects:A Critical Surveyof Literature. Psychological Bulletin 1972, 77(1):65-72.

846. D. Fudenberg and J. Tirole. Game Theory. MIT Press. https://mitpress.mit.edu/books/game-theory Ret: December 2018

847. G. Brown MC, J. Salmeron, and K. Wood. Defending Critical Infrastructure. In Interfaces, volume 36, pages 530 – 544, 2006. .

848. J. Pita MJ, C. Western, C. Portway, M. Tambe, F. Ord´o˜nez, S. Kraus, and P. Parachuri. Deployed ARMOR protection: The application of a game-theoretic model for security at the Los Angeles International Airport. In AAMAS-08 (Industry Track), 2008. .

849. https://en.wikipedia.org/wiki/Stackelberg_competition. Ret: May 2018

850. H. von Stackelberg. Marktform und Gleichgewicht. Springer V, 1934.

851. Scalable Randomized Patrolling for Securing Rapid Transit Networks. PradeepVarakantham H, ZhiYuan; https://pdfs.semanticscholar.org/3821/8eecd51b9efc2f5aecf-384976109da370b69.pdf. Ref: December 2018

852. K. wei Lye and J. M. Wing. Game Strategies in Network Security. International Journal of Information Security, 2005. .

853. T. Sandler and D. G. A. M. Terrorism and Game Theory. Simulation and Gaming, 2003.

854. Jain M: Software Assistants for Randomized Patrol Planning for The LAX Airport Police and The Federal Air Marshals Service. https://pubsonlineinformsorg/doi/abs/101287/inte11000505?journalCode=inte; Ret: May 2018.

855. P. Paruchuri MT, F. Ordonez, and S. Kraus.: Security in Multiagent Systems by Policy Randomization. AAMAS 2006.

856. R. Larson. A Hypercube Queueing Modeling for Facility Location and Redistricting in Urban Emergency Services. In Journal of Computers and Operations Research v, pages 67–95, 1974. .

857. L. M. Wein. Homeland Security: From Mathematical Models to Policy Implementation. In Operations Research. OPERATIONS RESEARCH Vol. 57, No. 4, July–August 2009, pp. 801–811; https://pdfs.semanticscholar.org/25ed/9b1e18a617fdafab-45f50e36104bb8155b16.pdf; Ret: December 2018

858. R. Avenhaus BvS, and S. Zamir. Inspection Games. In R. J. Aumann and S. Hart, editors, Handbook of Game Theory, volume 3, chapter 51, pages 1947–1987. North-Holland, Amsterdam, 2002.

859. Lau HC, and Gunawan, A. 2012. The patrol scheduling problem. In Practice and Theory of Automated Timetabling. Practice and Theory of Automated Timetabling (PATAT 2012), 29-31 August 2012, Son, Norwayhttps://pdfs.semanticscholar.org/160d/d042e00dced2d8e04805f93ddbbbebbfedb2.pdf. Ret: December 2018

860. Tsai JR, S.; Kiekintveld, C.; Ordonez, F.; and Tambe, M. 2009. Iris - a tool for strategic

security allocation in transportation networks. In AAMAS.

861. Big Data SaBS, and National Security; Fred S. Roberts, CCICADA Center, Rutgers University, Piscataway, NJ ; http://sites.nationalacademies.org/cs/groups/dbassesite/documents/webpage/dbasse_179907.pdf. Ret: May 2018

862. Brafman RI, Roberts, F.S., and Tsoukias, A. (Eds.), Algorithmic Decision Theory, Proc. Second Intl. Conf. ADT; 2011, Lecture Notes in Computer Science book series (LNCS, volume 6992), Springer, 2011.

863. Stroud PD, Saeger, K.J., "Enumeration of increasing Boolean expressions and alternative digraph; implementations for diagnostic applications," in H. Chu, J. Ferrer, T. Nguyen, and Y. Yu (eds), Proceedings Volume IV, Computer, Communication and Control Technologies: I, International Institute of Informatics and Systematics, Orlando, FL, 2003, 328-333.

864. Kantor P, Boros, E., "Deceptive detection methods for effective security with inadequate budgets: The testing power," Risk Analysis, 30 (2010), 663-673.

865. Roberts FS, "Computer science and decision theory," Annals of Operations Research, 163 (2008), 209-253.

866. An B, et al., "PROTECT – A deployed game theoretic system for strategic security allocation for the United States Coast Guard," AI Magazine, 4 (2012) 96-110.

867. Linial N, "Game-theoretic aspects of computing," in R.J. Aumann and S. Hart (eds.), Handbook of Game Theory with Economic Applications, II, chapter 38, (1994), 1340-1395.

868. Myerson R, Game Theory, Harvard University Press, Cambridge, MA, 1991.

869. Camerer CF, Ho, T.H., and Chong, K., "Models of thinking, learning and teaching in games," American Econ. Review Papers and Proceedings, 93 (2003), 192-195.

870. Harstad RM, "Dominant strategy adoption, efficiency, and bidder's experience with pricing rules," Experimental Economics, 3 (1990), 261-280.

871. Costa Gomes M, Crawford, V. Broseta, B., "Experimental studies of strategic sophistication and cognition in normal-form games," Econometrica, 69 (2001), 1193-1235.

872. Barrett S, "Eradication versus control: The economics of global infectious disease policies," Bull. World Health Organ., 82 (2004), 683-688.

873. Shepherd LOV: Suicide terrorism: Modeling group dynamics and individual behavior. JI Victoroff (ed), Tangled Roots: Social and Psychological Factors in the Genesis of Terrorism 2006:pp. 410-430.

874. Wang H, Hovy, E., Dredze, M., "The Hurricane Sandy Twitter corpus," Proceedings AAAI Workshop: WWW and Pubic Health Intelligence, 2015. .

875. McKenzie E, Roberts, F., Modeling Social Responses to Bioterrorism Involving Infectious Agents, Report, DIMACS Center, Rutgers University, July 2003.

876. CCICADA Center BPiA-tSfSaEVRG, CCICADA Center, Rutgers University, July 2013, available at https://www.safetyact.gov/externalRes/refdoc/CCICADA%20BPATS. pdf. & https://www.science.gov/topicpages/s/stadium+kritischer+ischaemie.html & https://worldwidescience.org/topicpages/r/rice-eccles+olympic+stadium.html Ret: May 2018

877. Multi-Robot Adversarial Patrolling: Facing Coordinated Attacks; Efrat Sless Noa Agmon Sarit Kraus; Alessio Lomuscio PS, Ana Bazzan, and Michael Huhns (eds.), Proceedings of the 13th International Conference on Autonomous Agents and Multiagent Systems (AAMAS 2014), May 5-9, 2014, Paris, France. Copyright c 2014, International

Foundation for Autonomous Agents and Multiagent Systems (www.ifaamas.org). .

878. Basilico NG, and F. Amigoni. Leader-follower strategies for robotic patrolling in environments with arbitrary topologies. In Proceeding of the Eighth International Conference on Autonomous Agents and Multiagent Systems (AAMAS), pages 57–64, 2009.

879. Y. Vorobeychik BA, and M. Tambe. : Adversarial patrolling games. In Proceeding of the Eleventh International Conference on Autonomous Agents and Multiagent Systems (AAMAS), 2012:pages 1307-1308.

880. Z. Yin AXJ, M. P. Johnson, C. Kiekintveld, K. Leyton-Brown, T. Sandholm, M. Tambe, and J. P. Sullivan. : TRUSTS: Scheduling randomized patrols for fare inspection in transit systems. AI Magazine 2012, 33(4):59-72.

881. Y. Elmaliach AS, and G. Kaminka. : A realistic model of frequency-based multi-robot polyline patrolling. In Proceeding of the Seventh International Conference on Autonomous Agents and Multiagent Systems (AAMAS) 2008: pages 63-70.

882. N. Agmon GK, and S. Kraus. Multi-robot adversarial patrolling: facing a full-knowledge opponent. Journal of Artificial Intelligence Research, 42(1):887–916, 2011. .

883. https://en.wikipedia.org/wiki/Fooled_by_Randomness. Ret: May 2018

884. https://www.amazon.com/Fooled-Randomness-Hidden-Markets-Incerto/dp/0812975219. Ret: May 2018

885. Sizemore C: Nassim Taleb's 'Antifragile' Celebrates Randomness In People, Markets. Forbescom 2013.

886. Useem J: The Smartest Books We Know. Fortune 2005.

887. https://jamesclear.com/book-summaries/fooled-by-randomness. December 2018

888. https://fourminutebooks.com/fooled-by-randomness-summary/. December 2018

888A. James A. Coffman. On the meaning of chance in biology. Biosemiotics. 2014 Dec 1; 7(3): 377–388.

889. https://www.amazon.com/Social-Animal-Sources-Character-Achievement/dp/0812979370. December 2018

890. Hsu M, Bhatt M, Adolphs R, Tranel D, Camerer CF: Neural systems responding to degrees of uncertainty in human decision-making. *Science* 2005, 310(5754):1680-1683.

891. https://www.forbes.com/2006/02/11/neuroeconomics-MRI-economics-cx_mh_money06_0214neuroeconomics.html#612daed35380. & http://www.ircs.upenn.edu/pinkel/lectures/camerer/index.shtml. Ret: December 2018

892. Knutson B, Westdorp A, Kaiser E, Hommer D: FMRI visualization of brain activity during a monetary incentive delay task. *Neuroimage* 2000, 12(1):20-27.

893. Knutson B, Adams CM, Fong GW, Hommer D: Anticipation of increasing monetary reward selectively recruits nucleus accumbens. *J Neurosci* 2001, 21(16):RC159.

894. Kuhnen CM, Knutson B: The neural basis of financial risk taking. *Neuron* 2005, 47(5):763-770.

895. Samanez-Larkin GR, Knutson B: Decision making in the ageing brain: changes in affective and motivational circuits. *Nat Rev Neurosci* 2015, 16(5):278-289.

896. Wu H, Miller KJ, Blumenfeld Z, Williams NR, Ravikumar VK, Lee KE, Kakusa B, Sacchet MD, Wintermark M, Christoffel DJ *et al*: Closing the loop on impulsivity via nucleus accumbens delta-band activity in mice and man. *Proc Natl Acad Sci U S A* 2018, 115(1):192-197.

897. Hare TA, Camerer CF, Rangel A: Self-control in decision-making involves modulation

of the vmPFC valuation system. *Science* 2009, 324(5927):646-648.

898. https://en.wikipedia.org/wiki/Metis_(mythology). December 2018

899. Brown NO: The Birth of Athena. *Transactions and Proceedings of the American Philological Association* 1952, 83:pp. 130-143.

900. http://www.mpi.nl/news/news-archive/beliefs-colour-sentence-comprehension-within-milliseconds.

901. https://en.wikipedia.org/wiki/Joshua_Greene_(psychologist). December 2018

902. Greene JD: Moral Tribes: Emotion, Reason, and the Gap Between Us and Them. *New York: Penguin Press ISBN 9781101638675* 2013.

903. Greene JDS, R Brian; Nystrom, Leigh E; Darley, John M; Cohen, Jonathan D (2001). "An fMRI investigation of emotional engagement in moral judgment". Science. 293 (5537): 2105–2108.

904. Greene JDM, Sylvia A; Lowenberg, Kelly; Nystrom, Leigh E; Cohen, Jonathan D (2008). "Cognitive load selectively interferes with utilitarian moral judgment". Cognition. 107 (3): 1144–1154.

905. Greene JDN, Leigh E; Engell, Andrew D; Darley, John M; Cohen, Jonathan D (2004). "The neural bases of cognitive conflict and control in moral judgment". Neuron. 44 (2): 389–400.

906. https://harvardmagazine.com/2012/01/the-biology-of-right-and-wrong. December 2018

907. http://www.just-one-liners.com/topic/decisions/. December 2018

908. Keats J, Cambridge Edition. Houghton, Mifflin and Company. p. 277. https://www.worldcat.org/title/complete-poetical-works-and-letters-of-john-keats/oclc/276921

909. https://en.wikipedia.org/wiki/Negative_capability. December 2018

910. https://en.wikipedia.org/wiki/Random_number_generation. December 2018

911. http://www.wisdom.weizmann.ac.il/~naor/PAPERS/games_for_extracting_randomness.pdf. December 2018

912. http://users.encs.concordia.ca/~kharma/COEN691A/OldWebSites/Website2/proposal.pdf. December 2018

913. RN: Random Number God. *http://tvtropesorg/pmwiki/pmwikiphp/Main/RandomNumberGod* Ret: May 2018.

914. RNG: Random number generators. *https://webmstedu/~taylorpat/Courses_files/IntroProgramming/Content/10_Random_number_generationpdf* Ret: July 2018, Comp Sci 1570 Introduction to C++(Missouri ST).

915. MÁRTON, SĂCĂREA, CREȚ: Generation and testing of randome number for cryptographic applications. *PROCEEDINGS OF THE ROMANIAN ACADEMY, Series A,* Ret: July 2018, Volume 13, Number 4/2012, pp. 368–377 https://pdfs.semanticscholar.org/c4a4/97ad7cd33b9a75c0d2cec0b8cebbf84e2784.pdf. Ret: May 2018

916. http://www.robertnz.net/true_rng.html Ret: December 2018

917. Li PW, Yun-Cai; Zhang, Jian-Zhong (2010-09-13). "All-optical fast random number generator". Optics Express. 18 (19): 20360–20369. .

918. Wang AL, Pu; Zhang, Jianguo; Zhang, Jianzhong; Li, Lei; Wang, Yuncai (2013-08-26). "4.5 Gbps high-speed real-time physical random bit generator". Optics Express. 21 (17): 20452–20462. .

919. www.random.org. December 2018.

920. https://www.nag.co.uk/numeric/cl/nagdoc_cl23/html/frontmatter/manconts.html.

December 2018

921. https://wikivisually.com/wiki/Random_number_generation. December 2018

922. Massar S: Quantum information: Bad randomness comes good. *NATURE PHYSICS* 2012, VOL 8 p: 447.

923. Santha MV, U. V. Proc. 25th IEEE Symp.Found. Comput. Sci. (FOCS-84) 434–440 (1984).

924. Born Z: Born. *Phys Rep* 1926, 37, 863-867.

925. Vazirani UV, T. Preprint at http://arxiv.org/ abs/1111.6054 (2011). .

926. Barrett JG, N. Phys. Rev. Lett. 106, 100406 (2011). .

927. https://www.design-reuse.com/articles/27050/true-randomness-in-cryptography.html. December 2018

928. https://www.isoc.org/isoc/conferences/ndss/10/pdf/15.pdf; December 2018.

929. https://rist.tech.cornell.edu/papers/ndss10x.pdf. December 2018

930. https://www.kb.cert.org/vuls/id/925211 V December 2018

931. Leo Dorrendorf ZG, and Benny Pinkas. Cryptanalysis of the windows random number generator. In CCS 2007. ACM, 2007.

932. Zvi Gutterman and Dahlia Malkhi. Hold your sessions: An attack on java session-id generation. In CT-RSA 2005. Springer.

933. Robert Woolley MM, Maxim Dounin, and Ruslan Ermilov. arc4random predictable sequence vulnerability. http://security.freebsd.org/advisories/ FreeBSD-SA-08:11. arc4random.asc, 2008. .

934. Murray MRV: An implementation of the Yarrow PRNG for FreeBSD. *Proceeding BSDC'02 Proceedings of the BSD Conference* 2002: Pages 6-6.

935. Zvi Gutterman BP aTR: Analysis of the linux random number generator. *In Symposium on Security and Privacy* 2006., IEEE, 2006.

936. Eastlake D, Schiller, J. and Crocker, S. RFC 4086. RFC Editor. http://www.ietf.org/rfc/ rfc4086.txt. Ret: December 2018

937. Rukhin A, et al. NIST Special Publication 800-22rev1a: A Statistical Test Suite for Random and Pseudorandom Number Generators. Computer Security Resource Center. http://csrc.nist.gov/groups/ST/toolkit/rng/documents/SP800-22rev1a.pdf . Ret: May 2018

938. http://csrc.nist.gov/publications/PubsSPs.html December 2018.

939. http://csrc.nist.gov/publications/PubsDrafts.html December 2018.

940. http://webstore.ansi.org/RecordDetail.aspx?sku=ANSI+X9.82-1%3A2006 December 2018.

941. Killmann WaS, W. Dr. A Proposal For: Functionality classes and evaluation methodology for true (physical) random number generators. https://www.bsi.bund.de/ SharedDocs/Downloads/DE/BSI/Zertifizierung/Interpretationen/trngk31e_pdf.pdf. December 2018

942. http://www.iso.org/iso/catalogue_detail.htm?csnumber=30816 December 2018.

943. http://www.authentec.com. December 2018

944. https://simple.wikipedia.org/wiki/Entropy. December 2018

945. https://www.vocabulary.com/dictionary/entropy. December 2018

946. https://en.wikipedia.org/wiki/Entropy. December 2018

947. Carnot S: Sadi Carnot and the Second Law of Thermodynamics. *RESONANCE I November 2001* Ret: May 2018, https://www.ias.ac.in/article/fulltext/reso/006/11/0042-

0048.

948. Clausius, and on the Laws which can be deduced from it for the Theory of Heat. Pog-gendorff's Annalen der Physick, LXXIX (Dover Reprint).

949. law S: Second law of thermodynamics. *https://wwwthermalfluidscentralorg/encyclope-dia/indexphp/Second_law_of_thermodynamics* & *https://www.britannica.com/science/Boltzmann-constant* Ret: May 2018.

950. https://en.wikipedia.org/wiki/Introduction_to_entropy.Ret: May 2018

951. Callen HB: Thermodynamics and an Introduction to Thermostatistics. *(2nd ed) New York: John Wiley & Sons ISBN 0-471-86256-8* 1985.

952. de Rosnay J: The Macroscope - a New World View. *Harper & Row, Publishers ISBN 0-06-011029-5* 1979.

953. Sethna JPSme: order parameters, and complexity. *Oxford: Oxford University Press*, p. 78. .

954. Sandler SIC, biochemical, and engineering thermodynamics(4th ed.). New York: John Wiley & Sons. p. 91. .

955. Entropy: Entropy and the Second Law of Thermodynamics: Disorder and the Un-availability of Energy. *Lumen Physics* Ret: July 2018, https://courses.lumenlearning.com/physics/chapter/15-6-entropy-and-the-second-law-of-thermodynamics-disor-der-and-the-unavailability-of-energy/. Ret: July 2018

956. work L: Irreversibility, Entropy Changes, and ``Lost Work''. *http://webmitedu/16uni-fied/www/FALL/thermodynamics/notes/node48html* Ret: July 2018.

957. https://www.fs.blog/2017/03/scientific-concepts-know/. Ret: July 2018

958. Angrist S, Loren G. (1967). Order and Chaos – Laws of Energy and Entropy (pg. 215). New York: Basic Books.

959. http://www.eoht.info/page/Thermodynamics+humor. Ret: July 2018

960. https://chem.libretexts.org/Core/Physical_and_Theoretical_Chemistry/Thermody-namics/The_Four_Laws_of_Thermodynamics/Second_Law_of_Thermodynamics. Ret: July 2018

961. Daintith J: Entropy. *Oxford Dictionary of Physics* 2005, Oxford University Press. ISBN 0-19-280628-9.

962. Martyushev LMS, V. D. (2014). "The restrictions of the maximum entropy production principle". Physica A: Statistical Mechanics and its Applications. 410: 17–21.

963. Onsager L: Reciprocal Relations in Irreversible Processes. *Phys Rev Lett* 1931, 37: 405.
.

964. Belkin Ae a: Self-assembled wiggling nano-structures and the principle of maximum entropy production. *Scientific reports* 2015, 5.

965. Balian RE, a Protean concept". In Dalibard, Jean. Poincaré Seminar 2003: Bose-Ein-stein condensation – entropy. Basel: Birkhäuser. pp. 119–144. .

966. I. Klotz RR, Chemical Thermodynamics - Basic Concepts and Methods, 7th ed., Wiley (2008), p. 125.

967. https://physics.stackexchange.com/questions/10577/entropy-and-how-it-applies-to-everyday-activities-like-eating-food. Ret: July 2018

968. https://en.wikipedia.org/wiki/Entropy_and_life & Natalie Wolchover, A New Physics Theory of Life, Quanta Magazine on January 28, 2014

https://www.scientificamerican.com/article/a-new-physics-theory-of-life/ Ret: November 2018

969. Adams H: A Letter to American Teachers of History *https://www3ndedu/~powers/ ame20231/adams1910pdf* Originally published 1910.

970. McCulloch RS: Treatise on the mechanical theory of heat and its applications to the steam-engine. *New York: D Van Nostrand* 1876.

971. Schrödinger E: What is Life - the Physical Aspect of the Living Cell. . *Cambridge University Press ISBN 0-521-42708-8* 1944.

972. https://en.wikipedia.org/wiki/Entropy_and_life & https://www.britannica.com/biography/Erwin-Schrodinger Ret: December 2018

973. https://www.britannica.com/science/Schrodingers-cat Ret: December 2018 & Schneider EDS, Dorion (2005). Into the Cool: Energy Flow Thermodynamics and Life. Chicago, United States: The University of Chicago Press. .

974. Lovelock J: GAIA - A New Look at Life on Earth. *Oxford University Press ISBN 0-19-286218-9* 1979.

975. https://en.wikipedia.org/wiki/Gibbs_free_energy. Ret: July 2018

976. Philosophy SEo: Hermann von Helmholtz. *https://platostanfordedu/entries/hermann-helmholtz/* Ret: March 2018, Stanford Encyclopedia of Philosophy.

977. J. W. Gibbs AMoGRotTPoSbMoS, Transactions of the Connecticut Academy of Arts and Sciences 2, Dec. 1873, pp. 382–404.

978. J.W. Gibbs AMoGRotTPoSbMoS, " Transactions of the Connecticut Academy of Arts and Sciences 2, Dec. 1873, pp. 382-404

979. Moroz A: The Common Extremalities in Biology and Physics. *Elsevier ISBN 978-0-12-385187-1* 2012.

980. Perrot P: A to Z of Thermodynamics. *https://globaloupcom/academic/product/a-to-z-of-thermodynamics-9780198565529?cc=il&lang=en&*, Oxford university press.

981. https://www.khanacademy.org/science/chemistry/thermodynamics-chemistry/gibbs-free-energy/a/gibbs-free-energy-and-spontaneity Ret: November 1981

982. Higgs PG, & Pudritz, R. E. (2009). "A thermodynamic basis for prebiotic amino acid synthesis and the nature of the first genetic code"

983. Peterson J, Understanding the Thermodynamics of Biological Order, The American Biology Teacher, 74, Number 1, January 2012, pp. 22–24.

984. Lehninger: Albert L. Lehninger. *https://enwikipediaorg/wiki/Albert_L_Lehninger* Ret: July 2018.

985. Avery J: Information Theory and Evolution *Publisher: World Scientific* 2003.

986. Kaila VRA, A. (8 November 2008). "Natural selection for least action". Proceedings of the Royal Society A. 464 (2099): 3055–3070. .

987. Manipulation G: Methods and Mechanisms for Genetic Manipulation of Plants, Animals, and Microorganisms. *In: Safety of Genetically Engineered Foods Approaches to Assessing Unintended Health Effects. National Research Council (US) Committee on Identifying and Assessing Unintended Effects of Genetically Engineered Foods on Human Health* 2004., Washington (DC): National Academies Press (US); ISBN-10: 0-309-09209-4ISBN-10: 0-309-53194-2.

988. Ben-Naim A: Entropy and the Second Law: Interpretation and Misss-Interpretations *World Scientific*, ISBN-13: 978-9814374897; ISBN-10: 981437489X.

989. Licker MD: McGraw-Hill concise encyclopedia of chemistry. *New York: McGraw-Hill Professional ISBN 978-0-07-143953-4* 2004.

990. Statistical Mechanics Entropy OP, and Complexity. James P. Sethna; http://pages. physics.cornell.edu/~sethna/StatMech/EntropyOrderParametersComplexity.pdf.

991. Jaynes ET, "The Gibbs Paradox," In Maximum Entropy and Bayesian Methods; Smith, C. R; Erickson, G. J; Neudorfer, P. O., Eds; Kluwer Academic: Dordrecht, 1992, pp. 1–22.

992. Lambet FL: A modern view of entropy. *Chemistry* 2006, Vol. 15, Iss. 1.

993. https://jamesclear.com/entropy. Ret: July 2018

994. Simon DAMJD: Molecular thermodynamics. *Sausalito (California)* : University Science *Books* 1999.

995. Haynie D T: Biological Thermodynamics. . *Cambridge University Press* 2001.

996. Eddington S: The nature of physical world. *Cambridge University Press* 1948.

997. entropy Tlo: https://www.goodreads.com/quotes/947685-the-law-that-entropy-always-increases-holds-i-think-the. Ret: July 2018

998. http://web.mit.edu/keenansymposium/overview/background/. Ret: July 2018

999. Hoffmann PM: Life's Ratchet: How Molecular Machines Extract Order from Chaos *ISBN-13: 978-0465022533; ISBN-10: 0465022537.*

1000. von Ballmoos C WA, Dimroth P. : Essentials for ATP synthesis by F1F0 ATP synthases. *Annu Rev Biochem* 2009, 78:649-72. (doi: 10.1146/annurev.biochem.78.081307.104803.).

1001. MO. M: Forced thermal ratchets. *Phys Rev Lett* 1993, 71(10):1477-1481.

1002. A. V. Hill SRS: The heat of shortening and the dynamic constants of muscle. *Proceeding Royal Society* Published 10 October 1938., Volume 126, issue 843 136-195.

1003. AF. H: Muscle structure and theories of contraction. *Prog Biophys Biophys Chem* 1957, 7:255-318.

1004. N J Córdova BE, and G F Oster: Dynamics of single-motor molecules: the thermal ratchet model. *PNAS* 1992, 89 (1) 339-343.

1005. Smoluchowski M: Experimentally Demonstrable Molecular Phenomena, Which Contradict Standard Thermodynamics" ("Experimentell nachweisbare der ublichen Thermodynamik widersprechende Molekularphanomene. *Phys Z* 1912, 13:1069-80(http://www.eoht.info/page/Marian+Smoluchowski).

1006. Jarzynski ZLDMC: Engineering Maxwell's demon. *Physics Today* 2014, 67, 8, 60.

1007. Ratchet B: Feynman's "Brownian Ratchet". *This Month in Physics History: May 11, 1962* 2013, Volume 22, Number 5(https://www.aps.org/publications/apsnews/201305/physicshistory.cfm).

1008. https://en.wikipedia.org/wiki/Richard_Feynman Ret: July 2018

1009. Lectures TF: The Feynman Lectures on Physics; Vol. I. *American Journal of Physics* 1965, 33, 750 (https://aapt.scitation.org/doi/10.1119/1.1972241).

1010. Jarzynski C: Nonequilibrium Equality for Free Energy Differences. *Phys Rev Lett* 1997, 78, 2690-3.

1011. Smoluchowski M 1912 Experimentell nachweisbare düTwMPZ.

1012. Bier RDAaM: Fluctuation driven ratchets: Molecular motors. *Phys Rev Lett*, 72, 1766 -1994.

1013. Lee S H LK, Polin M and Grier D G 2005 Observation of flux reversal in a symmetric optical thermal ratchet Phys. Rev. Lett. 94 110601.

1014. Magnasco MO: Molecular combustion motors. *Phys Rev Lett* 1994, 72, 2656 -9.

1015. C S Peskin GMO, and G F Oster: Cellular motions and thermal fluctuations: the Brownian ratchet. . *Biophys J* 1993, Jul; 65(1): 316-324.

1016. Busch AE, Herzer T, Wagner CA, Schmidt F, Raber G, Waldegger S, Lang F: Positive regulation by chloride channel blockers of IsK channels expressed in Xenopus oocytes. *Mol Pharmacol* 1994, 46(4):750-753.

1017. Sagawa T: Review of Maxwell's Demon. *Thermodynamics of Information Processing in Small Systems* 2013, Chapter 2 (Springer Theses, DOI: 10.1007/978-4-431-54168-4_2).

1018. Charles L. Asbury ANF, Steven M. Block: Kinesin Moves by an Asymmetric Hand-Over-Hand Mechanism. *Science* 2003, Vol. 302, (Issue 5653, ):pp. 2130-2134.

1019. Svoboda K, Schmidt CF, Schnapp BJ, Block SM: Direct observation of kinesin stepping by optical trapping interferometry. *Nature* 1993, 365(6448):721-727.

1020. Yildiz A, Tomishige M, Vale RD, Selvin PR: Kinesin walks hand-over-hand. *Science* 2004, 303(5658):676-678.

1021. Asbury CL, Fehr AN, Block SM: Kinesin moves by an asymmetric hand-over-hand mechanism. *Science* 2003, 302(5653):2130-2134.

1022. Mateos S: AC-driven Brownian motors: A Fokker-Planck treatment. *Am J Phys* 2009, 77 7, (http://www.physik.uni-augsburg.de/theo1/hanggi/Papers/534.pdf ).

1023. Phillips RaQ, Stephen R.: The Biological Frontier of Physics. *Physics Today* 2006, 59 (5). pp. 38-43.(ISSN 0031-9228).

1024. Hammond KJVJW: Traffic control: regulation of kinesin motors. *Nature Reviews Molecular Cell Biology* 2009, volume10, pages765-777.

1025. Knight AE MJ: Coupling ATP hydrolysis to mechanical work. *Nat Cell Biol* 1999, 1(4):E87-9.

1026. Sakamoto T, Webb MR, Forgacs E, White HD, Sellers JR: Direct observation of the mechanochemical coupling in myosin Va during processive movement. *Nature* 2008, 455(7209):128-132.

1027. LA. A: Molecular motors: not quite like clockwork. *Cell Mol Life Sci* 2008, 65(4):509-15.

1028. Mark J. Schnitzer KVSMB: Force production by single kinesin motors. *Nature Cell Biology* 2000, volume2, pages718-723

1029. Adio S BM, Hartel M, Leier S, Geeves M A and Woehlke G 2006 Kinetic and mechanistic basis of the nonprocessive kinesin-3 motor NcKin3 J. Biol. Chem. 281 37782–93.

1030. Sowa Y1 BR: Bacterial flagellar motor. *Q Rev Biophys* 2008, 41(2):103-32.

1031. Glynn IM: Annual review prize lecture. 'All hands to the sodium pump'. *J Physiol* 1993, 462: 1-30.

1032. Cramer P1 BD, Kornberg RD. : Structural basis of transcription: RNA polymerase II at 2.8 angstrom resolution. *Science* 2001, 8;292(5523):1863-76.

1033. V. R: Ribosome structure and the mechanism of translation. *Cell* 2002 22;108(4):557-72.

1034. Endow SA: Microtubule motors in spindle and chromosome motility. *Eur J Biochem* 1999, 262, 12-18.

1035. Jahn R SR: SNAREs--engines for membrane fusion. *Nat Rev Mol Cell Biol* 2006 ;7(9):631-43.

1036. RA. C: The kinetic mechanism of kinesin. *Trends Biochem Sci* 2004, 29(6):301-9.

1037. Gilbert SP G-LS, Rayment I.: Kinesin-2 motors: Kinetics and biophysics. *J Biol Chem* 2018, 23;293(12):4510-4518.

1038. Mallik R GS: Molecular motors: strategies to get along. *Curr Biol* 2004, 14(22):R971-82.

1039. LS. G: Kinesin molecular motors: transport pathways, receptors, and humandisease. *Proc Natl Acad Sci U S A* 2001, 98(13):6999-7003.
1040. Houtgraaf JH VJ, van der Giessen WJ.: A concise review of DNA damage checkpoints and repair in mammaliancells. *Cardiovasc Revasc Med* 2006, 7(3):165-72.
1041. Coskun A BM, Astumian R D, Stoddart J F and Grzybowski B A 2012 Great expectations: can artificial molecular machines deliver on their promise? Chem. Soc. Rev. 41 19–30.
1042. KE. D: Molecular engineering: An approach to the development of general capabilities for molecularmanipulation. *Proc Natl Acad Sci U S A* 1981, 78(9):5275-8.
1043. H H: Engineering applications of biomolecular motors. *Annu Rev Biomed Eng* 2011, 15;13:429-50. .
1044. https://www.postmodernnaturalism.com/blog/2017/4/10/the-second-law-of-thermo-dynamics-and-human-meaning. Ret: July 2018
1045. https://en.wikipedia.org/wiki/Yvon_Chouinard. Ret: July 2018
1046. https://en.wikipedia.org/wiki/Cesar_A._Hidalgo. Ret: July 2018
1047. https://jcdverha.home.xs4all.nl/scijokes/9_6.html. Ret: July 2018
1048. https://scholar.google.com/citations?user=Ohhyr84AAAAJ&hl=en. Ret: July 2018
1049. http://sourcesofinsight.com/concrete-abstract-random-and-sequential/. Ret: July 2018
1050. http://www.skilledatlife.com/why-planning-our-lives-is-important/. Ret: July 2018
1051. distortion R: https://en.wikipedia.org/wiki/Reality_distortion_field. Ret: May 2018.
1052. Field AHRD: The Original Macintosh: Anecdotes about the development of Apple's original Macintosh, and the people who made it (122 stories). *http://wwwfolk-loreorg/StoryViewpy?project=Macintosh&story=Reality_Distortion_Fieldtxt&sortOrder=Sort+by+Date* February 1981, Ret: May 2018.
1053. https://en.wikipedia.org/wiki/Andy_Hertzfeld. Ret: July 2018
1054. https://en.wikipedia.org/wiki/Reality_distortion_field. Ret: July 2018
1055. Dudrow A: Notes from the Epicenter: Exploring the Reality Distortion Field. *Ceative Pro* 200, https://creativepro.com/notes-epicenter-exploring-reality-distortion-field/.
1056. Isaacson W: The Real Leadership Lessons of Steve Jobs. *Harvard Bussiness Review* APRIL 2012, https://hbr.org/2012/04/the-real-leadership-lessons-of-steve-jobs.
1057. Ferriss T: How It Works: Clinton's "Reality Distortion Field" Charisma. *https://tim-blog/2010/11/21/bill-clinton-reality-distortion-field/* 2010.
1058. Hart B: Trump's Reality Distortion Field Could Be a Huge Asset for Democrats This Fall. *New Yorker* 2018, http://nymag.com/daily/intelligencer/2018/04/trumps-reality-distortion-field-could-help-tank-republicans.html.
1059. Waters R: Elon Musk, billionaire tech idealist and space entrepreneur. *Financial Times* 2016, https://www.ft.com/content/8ca82034-86d0-11e6-bcfc-debbef66f80e. Ret: July 2018
1060. https://www.elitedaily.com/life/life-really-little-things/658655. Ret: July 2018
1061. https://en.wikipedia.org/wiki/Ralph_Waldo_Emerson. Ret: July 2018
1062. https://www.huffingtonpost.com/rajan-thapaliya/life-is-a-journey-not-a-d_1_b_14001718.html. Ret: july 2018
1063. https://www.quora.com/What-should-I-pay-attention-to-when-investing-in-stocks.& https://www.wired.com/2013/08/ap-biondi/ Ret: July 2018
1064. Alessio Emanuele Biondo AP, Andrea Rapisarda, Dirk Helbing: Are Random Trading Strategies More Successful than Technical Ones? . *PLOS ONE* 2013, Vol-

ume 8, 7, e68344. http://journals.plos.org/plosone/article/file?id=10.1371/journal. pone.0068344&type=printable.

1065. Helbing DaK, Alan: Rethinking Economics Using Complexity Theory. *Real-world economics review* 2013, issue no. 64. https://ssrn.com/abstract=2292370or http://dx. doi.org/10.2139/ssrn.2292370 Ret: July 2018 & http://www2.econ.iastate.edu/tesfatsi/ RethinkingEconomicsUsingComplexityTheory.DHelbingAKirman2013.pdf). Ret: July 2018

1066. A.E. Biondo APAR: Micro and macro benefits of random investments in financial markets. *Journal Contemporary Physics* 2014, Volume 55, - Issue 4: 318-334

1067. Tedeschi G IG GM: Herding effects in order driven markets: The rise and fall of gurus. *Journal of Economic Behavior & Organization* 2012, 81: 82-96.

1068. In praise of soft science. *Nature* 2005, 435(7045):1003.

1069. Buchanan M: Nexus: Small Worlds and the Groundbreaking Theory of Networks. *ISBN-13: 978-0393324426; ISBN-10: 0393324427* 2002.

1070. Hedstrom P: The Oxford Handbook of Analytical Sociology. *Oxford University Press ISBN 0-19-286218-9* 2009.

1071. Alessandro Pluchinoa AR, Cesare Garofalo Efficient promotion strategies in hierarchical organizations. *Physica A* 2011, A 390: 3496-3511.

1072. Physica A 390 (2011) 3496–3511 Efficient promotion strategies in hierarchical organizations Alessandro Pluchinoa, Andrea Rapisarda , Cesare Garofalo

1073. https://www.amazon.com/How-Google-Works-Eric-Schmidt-ebook/dp/B00HU-U13Y0. Ret: July 2018

1074. Peter LJH, Raymond (1969). The Peter Principle: Why Things Always Go Wrong. New York: William Morrow and Company. p. 8.

1075. A. Pluchino AR, C. Garofalo, The Peter Principle revisited: a computational study, Physica A 389 (467) (2010).

1076. S.E. Phelan ZL, Promotion systems and organizational performance: a contingency model, Comput. Org. Theory 7 (2001) 207.

1077. https://en.wikipedia.org/wiki/Maria_Callas. Ret: July 2018

1078. https://en.wikipedia.org/wiki/Arturo_Toscanini. Ret: July 2018

1079. A. Pluchino CG, A. Rapisarda, S. Spagano and M. Caserta, (2011) arXiv:1103.1224v2 Physica A 390 (2011) 3944 Accidental politicians: how randomly selected legislators can improve Parliament efficiency.

1080. https://en.wikipedia.org/wiki/Sortition. Ret: July 2018

1081. Landemore HJ, 2010). "Deliberation, Representation, and the Epistemic Function of Parliamentary Assemblies: a Burkean Argument in Favor of Descriptive Representation" (PDF). International Conference on "Democracy as Idea and Practice," University of Oslo. Retrieved November 2, 2015.

1082. Headlam JW: Election by Lot at Athens. *p 12* 1891.

1083. The Athenian Democracy in the Age of Demosthenes MHH, ISBN 1-85399-585-1.

1084. Herodotus: The Histories. *3806*, http://www.perseus.tufts.edu/hopper/text?doc=Perseus%3Atext%3A1999.01.0126%3Abook%3D3%3Achapter%3D80%3Asection%3D6. Ret: July 2018

1085. Hansen MH: Election by Lot at Athens. . *Cambridge: Cambridge University Press* 1981.

1086. Dowlen O: The Political Potential of Sortition: A study of the random selection of citizens for public office. *Imprint Academic* 2008.

1087. Rousseau: On the Social Contract. *New York: St Martin's Press* 1762:p. 112.

1088. Manin B: The Principles of Representative Government. *Cambridge: Cambridge University Press* 1997, ISBN 0-521-45891-9.

1089. Carson LM, Brian (1999). Random Selection in Politics. Praeger. p. 33.

1090. Gil Delannoi (Editor) ODE: Sortition: Theory and Practice (Sortition and Public Policy) ISBN-13: 978-1845401993; ISBN-10: 1845401999.

1091. Landemore H: Deliberation, cognitive diversity, and democratic inclusiveness: an epistemic argument for the random selection of representatives. *Synthese* 2013, Volume 190, Issue 7, pp 1209–1231.

1092. Dreifus CJ, 2008). "New York Times". In Professor's Model, Diversity= Productivity. https://www.nytimes.com/2008/01/08/science/08conv.html Ret: December 2018

1093. Page (2007). How the power of diversity creates better groups f, schools, and societies. Princeton University Press.

1094. Fishkin J: When the People Speak: Deliberative Democracy & Public Consultation. . *Oxford: Oxford University Press* 2009, ISBN 978-0199604432.

1095. Boyle C: Lotteries for education : origins, experiences, lessons. *https://booksgooglecoil/ books/about/Lotteries_for_Educationhtml?id=dFk2QwAACAAJ&redir_esc=y*, ISBN: 9781845402105; ISBN: 1845402103

1096. https://www.masslbp.com/profile/. Ret: July 2018

1097. http://www.loka.org/trackingconsensus.html. Ret: July 2018

1098. Leonard K: Christians Find Their Own Way to Replace Obamacare. *US News & World Report* 2016.

1099. http://www.mmrstrategy.com/wp-content/uploads/2015/02/Concept-and-Product-Testing-5-25-121.pdf. Ret: July 2018

1100. Bouricius TG: Democracy Through Multi-Body Sortition: Athenian Lessons for the Modern Day. *Journal of Public Deliberation* 2013, Vol. 9 : Iss. 1 , Article 11. (https:// www.publicdeliberation.net/jpd/vol9/iss1/art11).

1101. A. Barnett PC, The Athenian Option Radical Reform for the House of Lords, Demos, 1998. .

1102. R. Mantegna BS, Noise enhanced stability in an unstable system, Phys. Rev. Lett. 76 (1996) 563. .

1103. Frenkel D: Physical chemistry: seeds of phase change. *Nature* 2006, 443(7112):641.

1104. A.J. Page RPS, Heterogeneous nucleation in and out of pores, Phys. Rev. Lett. 97 (2006)

1105. F. Caruso AWC, A. Datta, S.F. Huelga, M.B. Plenio, Highly efficient energy excitation transfer in light-harvesting complexes: the fundamental role of noise-assisted transport, J. Chem. Phys. 131 (2009) 105106.

1106. F. Caruso SFH, M.B. Plenio, Noise-enhanced classical and quantum capacities in communication networks, Phys. Rev. Lett. 105 (2010)

1107. https://en.wikipedia.org/wiki/Parrondo%27s_paradox. Ret: July 2018

1108. https://www.cut-the-knot.org/ctk/Parrondo.shtml. Ret: July 2018

1109. Shu J-JW, Q.-W. (2014). "Beyond Parrondo's paradox". Scientific Reports. 4(4244): 1–9.

1110. https://arxiv.org/ftp/arxiv/papers/1602/1602.04783.pdf. Ret: July 2018

1111. Harmer GPA, D. (1999). "Losing strategies can win by Parrondo's paradox". Nature. 402: 864.

1112. Thomas K. Philips and Andrew B. Feldman PsPinP, Social Science Research Network

(SSRN) Working Papers, August 2004.

1113. G. P. Harmer DA, P. G. Taylor, and J. M. R. Parrondo, in Proc. 2nd Int. Conf. Unsolved Problems of Noise and Fluctuations, D. Abbott, and L. B. Kish, eds., American Institute of Physics, 2000.

1114. Cheong KHT, Zong Xuan; Xie, Neng-gang; Jones, Michael C. (2016-10-14). A Paradoxical Evolutionary Mechanism in Stochastically Switching Environments. Scientific Reports. 6: 34889. .

1115. Tan Z, Kang Hao (2017-01-13). Nomadic-colonial life strategies enable paradoxical survival and growth despite habitat destruction. eLife. 6: e21673. .

1116. https://en.wikipedia.org/wiki/Plateau_effect. Ret: July 2018

1117. Honeybourne J, Michael Hill & Helen Moors (2000). Physical Education and Sport for AS-level. Nelson Thornes. p. 112. .

1118. https://www.amazon.com/Plateau-Effect-Getting-Stuck-Success/dp/0525952802.

1119. Samuelson PAN, William D. (2001). Microeconomics (17th ed.). McGraw-Hill. p. 110. .

1120. https://en.wikipedia.org/wiki/Diminishing_returns. Ret: July 2018

1121. Case KEF, Ray C. (1999). Principles of Economics (5th ed.). Prentice-Hall.

1122. Productivity M: Law Of Diminishing Marginal Productivity. *https://wwwinvestopedia-com/terms/l/law-diminishing-marginal-productivityasp* Ret: May 2018.

1123. https://en.wikipedia.org/wiki/Diminishing_returns. Ret: May 2018.

1124. Hattie J: Visible Learning: A Synthesis of Over 800 Meta-Analyses Relating to Achievement. . *Routledge* 2008, ISBN 0-415-47617-8.:p. 141.

1125. https://en.wikipedia.org/wiki/Drug_tolerance. Ret: May 2018.

1126. Hanson G PVAF: Drugs and Society. *Jones and Bartlett* 2009, http://www.jblearning.com/catalog/9781284110876/:p. 130.

1127. https://www.cs.cmu.edu/~luluo/Courses/17939Report.pdf Ret: July 2018.

1128. Overcoming the Exercise Plateau Effect by Kamila Fontanilla PFT, Seattle Athletic Club Northgate; https://sacng.com/blog/2010/10/overcoming-the-exercise-plateau-effect/. Ret: July 2018

1129. Lawrenson L, Poole JG, Kim J, Brown C, Patel P, Richardson RS: Vascular and metabolic response to isolated small muscle mass exercise: effect of age. *Am J Physiol Heart Circ Physiol* 2003, 285(3):H1023-1031.

1130. Ben Ounis O, Elloumi M, Amri M, Zbidi A, Tabka Z, Lac G: Impact of diet, exercise end diet combined with exercise programs on plasma lipoprotein and adiponectin levels in obese girls. *Journal of sports science & medicine* 2008, 7(4):437-445.

1131. The Role of Deliberate Practice in the Acquisition of Expert Performance KAE, Ralf Th. Krampe, and Clemens Tesch-Romer; Psychological Review 1993, Vol. 100. No. 3, 363-406.

1132. Deliberate Practice and Acquisition of Expert Performance: A General Overview. K. Anders Ericsson  2008; Academic emergency medicine. volume 15 IP.

1133. https://blog.supplysideliberal.com/post/51204513930/joshua-foer-on-deliberate-practic Ret: July 20181134.; http://citeseerx.ist.psu.edu/viewdoc/download?-doi=10.1.1.459.3750&rep=rep1&type=pdf Ret: July 2018.

1135. The role of deliberate practice in the acquisition of expert performance (1993); K. Anders Ericsson RTK, Clemens Tesch-romer; Psychological Review; Vol. 100. No. 3, 363-406.

1136. https://jamesclear.com/deliberate-practice-theory. Ret: July 2018
1137. Kliever J: Get Better at Anything: 6 Steps of Deliberate Practice. *https://mediumcom/ the-crossover-cast/get-better-at-anything-6-steps-of-deliberate-practice-19830bfc9460* 2017, Ret: May 2018.
1138. Anders Ericsson RP: Secrets from the New Science of Expertise. *https://wwwamazon-com/Peak-Secrets-New-Science-Expertise-ebook* 2016. Ret: July 2018
1139. http://www.nytimes.com/2006/05/07/magazine/07wwln_freak.html. Ret: July 2018
1140. K. Becker (Author) JRP: The Guide to Computer Simulations and Games 1st Edition. *https://wwwamazoncom/Guide-Computer-Simulations-Games/dp/1118009231* 2012, ISBN-13: 978-1118009239; ISBN-10: 1118009231.
1141. https://www.amazon.com/Made-Stick-Ideas-Survive-Others/dp/1400064287. Ret: July 2018
1142. https://www.goodreads.com/book/show/28186095-dear-mr-m. Ret: July 2018
1143. https://www.amazon.com/Mist-Tragicomic-Novel-Miguel-Unamuno/dp/0252068947/ ref=sr_1_7?s=books&ie=UTF8&qid=1522471301&sr=1-7&keywords=Mi-guel+de+Unamuno. Ret: July 2018
1144. https://www.amazon.com/Undoing-Project-Friendship-Changed-Minds/ dp/0393354776/ref=la_B000APZ33E_1_1?s=books&ie=UT-F8&qid=1522474766&sr=1-1. Ret: July 2018
1145. Daniel Kahneman. Thinking, Fast and Slow. Farrar, Straus and Giroux. ISBN: 9780141033570, https://www.amazon.com/Thinking-Fast-Slow-Daniel-Kahneman/ dp/0374533555